'[Brian McLaren] actually believes that Jesu̲ ┊┊┊ the world. This book is no exception – he you realise just how serious he is about doin̲ Helpful, timely, and really, really inspiring.'

— Rob Bell, author of *Love Wins*

'An extraordinary book: a thought-provoking introduction to one of the biggest challenges confronting the church in our globalised world, and a profoundly biblical and brave beginning to a Christ-centred cultural revolution.'

— Rev. Steve Chalke MBE, founder of
Oasis Global and Stop The Traffik

'Brian has resisted the temptation to create an all-you-can-eat buffet of religions, where you can pick and choose what you want. Instead, he curiously explores what it looks like to be unashamedly Christian and still be nice to people who aren't. As one who wants the world to know the love of Jesus, I am deeply troubled that one of the major obstacles to Christ is Christians . . . and I am deeply grateful for thinkers like Brian who are helping us discover a Christianity that looks like Jesus again.'

— Shane Claiborne, activist and author
of *The Irresistible Revolution*

'Brian McLaren is a genius in provoking – in a constructive way. You won't see relations among religions in the same way after you read this book.'

— Miroslav Volf, Professor of Theology, Yale University

'I think Brian McLaren is a spiritual genius! Not only does he have the courage to say what must and can be said, but he says it with a deep knowledge of both Scriptures and Tradition, and then says it very well besides – in ways that both the ordinary layperson and the scholar can respect and understand. You can't get any better than that, which is why I call him a genius!'

— Richard Rohr, OFM, Center for Action and Contemplation

'In its relationship to those who believe differently, Christian formation all too often takes shape with hostile reaction, or collapses into some washed-out common denominator. Brian helps us recover, and explore a vital and exciting alternative – of how learning from "others" of all persuasions is possible and intrinsic to vibrant Christian identity.'

— Jason Clark, Deep Church

'This is a major work in every sense of the word – so major, in fact, that it would be impossible to exaggerate either its importance or its worth to the current conversation about religion and religions. Mapping the space between Christian exclusivitism and inert universalism, McLaren brilliantly reclaims the ancient Christian imperative to abandon the accommodations of static religion and pursue instead the principles of Kingdom-living.'

– Phyllis Tickle, author of *Emergence Christianity*

'Genuine dialogue with difference has often been avoided by the Christian community because of a fear that it will undermine, weaken or erode the faith. Here McLaren shows us that far from being something that is acidic to Christian identity, such engagement is part of its deepest expression.'

– Peter Rollins, author of *Insurrection*

'Brian McLaren is a master of pointing us to the right question, and he has done it again by asking *Why Did Jesus, Moses, the Buddha and Mohammed Cross the Road?* This is a dangerous question. Dangerous in that it will not leave you alone once you invite it in . . . Brian reminds us that this question is not new, but that it is ours. I, for one, am grateful to Brian for the introduction to this immensely important book and question.'

– Doug Pagitt, pastor and author

'Brian McLaren is the most creative Christian theologian and spiritual teacher writing and preaching today in the US, yet his universal message is as relevant to people of all faiths and none. A champion of love, joy, peace, patience, kindness, goodness, gentleness – and rooting these in the biblical texts – McLaren helps heal CRIS – Conflicted Religious Identity Syndrome. As a Jewish theologian, I welcome this important contribution to showing the path through which all religions can become an emancipatory force for human liberation.'

– Rabbi Michael Lerner, Editor, *Tikkun*,
Chair of the Interfaith Network of Spiritual Progressives

'Surely there is no problem more important – and more vexing – to people of various faiths than how we can all get along in this pluralistic, postmodern world. In Brian McLaren's capable and gentle hands, these questions are answered, and a new way forward is offered. This is a book for Christians (and others) who want to maintain their religious distinctiveness but develop loving compassion for their neighbours of other religions.'

– Tony Jones, author of *The New Christians*

WHY DID JESUS, MOSES, THE BUDDHA AND MOHAMMED CROSS THE ROAD?

Christian Identity in a Multi-Faith World

BRIAN D. MCLAREN

HODDER &
STOUGHTON

First published in Great Britain in 2012 by Hodder & Stoughton
An Hachette UK company

This paperback edition first published in 2013

1

A CIP catalogue record for this title is available from the British Library

ISBN 978 1 444 70368 9
eBook ISBN 978 1 444 70369 6

Typeset in Sabon by Hewer Text UK Ltd, Edinburgh
Printed and bound by CPI Group (UK) Ltd, Croydon, CR0 4YY

Hodder & Stoughton policy is to use papers that are natural, renewable and recyclable products and made from wood grown in sustainable forests. The logging and manufacturing processes are expected to conform to the environmental regulations of the country of origin.

Hodder & Stoughton Ltd
338 Euston Road
London NW1 3BH

www.hodderfaith.com

Contents

FOUR: The Missional Challenge

CHAPTER 1

The Scene of a Thousand Jokes

Laughter is one of the ways we cope with the discrepancies of our lives. There is a dream we all have for this world, and then there is, well, this world. There are expectations we have of our religions, and then there are our religions ... Our capacity to love God, ourselves, people, and all of life grows with our capacity to laugh. We are ridiculous, and not to laugh at our religions, our worldviews, and our philosophies (that is, ourselves), would be a false witness ... This ability to laugh in the midst of our imperfections in the presence of God is what we call grace.

Samir Selmanovic[1]

Why did Jesus, Moses, the Buddha and Mohammed cross the road?[2]

The question, of course, recalls an old riddle about a chicken. The riddle goes back at least to 1847 when it appeared in a New York magazine. By the 1890s, the joke was so well known that it was generating riffs and variations on the theme.[3]

The original riddle exemplifies 'anti-humour' – a joke that is funny because it isn't funny. Anti-humour works by setting up a convention that leads us to expect a joke, and then reversing that expectation in a humorous way.[4] In the nearly countless 'Chicken-Joke 2.0' riffs and variations being hatched around the world, jokesters build humour upon the anti-humour, like this:

Why did the chicken cross the road?

GRANDPA: In my day we didn't ask why the chicken crossed the road. Somebody told us the chicken crossed the road to get to the other side, and that was good enough for us.

ALBERT EINSTEIN: Did the chicken really cross the road, or did the road move beneath the chicken?

SIR ISAAC NEWTON: Chickens at rest tend to stay at rest. Chickens in motion tend to cross the road.

A NUN: It was a habit.

HAMLET: That is not the question.

DONNE: It crosseth for thee.

COLONEL SANDERS: Did I miss one?

So, why is it funny to ask about Jesus, Moses, the Buddha and Mohammed crossing the road? Before looking for a punch line, just for fun try to imagine the scene: four of history's greatest religious leaders . . . not fighting, not arguing, not damning and condemning one another, not launching crusades or jihads, but walking together, moving together, leading together. Doesn't that already reverse some of our expectations? And doesn't that reversal expose our unspoken expectation – that different religions are inherently and unchangeably incompatible, disharmonious, fractious and hostile towards one another?

The image of the four men crossing a road also surprises and interests us because it puts the four in a similar situation, in a common predicament. Whatever the answer will be, it will be the same for all of them, perhaps even rendering them companions rather than competitors. That possibility makes claims on all of us who follow them.

If you're a Christian like me, of whatever sort – Catholic, Protestant or Eastern Orthodox; conservative, liberal or moderate; traditional or whatever – if you love Jesus, if you know and have confidence in him as Lord, Saviour, Son of God, Son of Man, God incarnate, Word made flesh and more, let me ask you to seriously consider this: *how do you think Jesus would treat Moses, Mohammed and Siddhartha Gautama (the Buddha) if they took a walk across a road together?*

Would Jesus push Moses aside and demand to cross first, claiming that his ancestor's failed religion had been forever superseded by his own? Would he trade insults with Mohammed, claiming his crusaders could whip Mohammed's jihadists any day of the week, demanding that Mohammed cross behind, not beside him? Would Jesus demand the Buddha kneel at his feet and demonstrate submission before letting him cross? Or would he walk with them and, once on the other side, welcome each to a table of fellowship, not demanding any special status or privileges, maybe even taking the role of a servant – hanging up their coats, getting them something to eat and drink, making sure each felt welcome, safe and at home?

If his three counterparts reached out their hands in friendship, it's pretty hard to imagine that 'the friend of sinners' would cross his arms or turn his back, refusing to reciprocate.[5] It's much more likely he would embrace them with open arms and without hesitation, proving himself over time to be the best friend they ever had. It's pretty hard to imagine Jesus cursing or 'smiting' them, but entirely natural to imagine him blessing them and 'doing unto others' as he would want them to do for him. I have no doubt that Jesus would actually practise the neighbourliness he preached rather than following our example of religious supremacy, hostility, fear, isolation, misinformation, exclusion or demonisation.

After all, according to the four Gospels, Jesus had extraordinary insight into human character. He saw value where others saw only flaws. He saw the love of a sinful woman who anointed his feet with tears at a banquet, the spiritual thirst of an oft-married woman at a well in Samaria, the big seed of hope in a little chap named Zacchaeus, the undeniable faith of a Syrophoenician mother, the flinty strength of loudmouth Peter and the deep and spunky wisdom of Mary of Bethany. With that track record in mind, we can only imagine what he would see in Mohammed, Moses or the Buddha, not to mention Confucius, Lao Tsu, Nanak or Wovoka.[6]

It seems ridiculous to imagine that he would be insecure among them, considering them his rivals, or that he would find it necessary to extract from them explicit agreement on fundamental doctrines before condescending to cross a road with them. It's unthinkable, if one of them came to confer with him by night like Nicodemus, or in broad daylight like the rich young ruler, that he would intimidate them, threaten them, call down fire upon them, patronise them or humiliate them. Maybe his followers would pull out a sword and slash off their ears, or herd them and their followers into ghettoes, concentration camps or reservations where their influence could be limited. But never Jesus. Never.

And if you know anything about Mohammed, Moses and the Buddha, how do you think they would approach Jesus, and one another, if they encountered one another along the road? Is it a joke to think they would respect one another and be drawn towards one another as friends, allies, collaborators? Isn't it more ridiculous to imagine any other outcome? I can't help but think of recent scenes of Archbishop Desmond Tutu and the Dalai Lama, a Christian and a Buddhist, almost giddy in their friendship and mutual regard.

So why might Jesus, Moses, the Buddha and Mohammed cross the road?[7] Imagine if the answer were, 'To go to a bar.' That answer wouldn't be funny, and many, in fact, would find it offensive.[8] But wouldn't that open the way for another joke that would begin, 'Jesus, Moses, the Buddha and Mohammed walk into a bar . . .'

Walking into a bar, of course, is the scene of even more jokes than crossing a road. So we might expect a chuckle as Mohammed orders a Wahabi cocktail – a mixed drink of warm milk, sugar, and hot tea (since alcohol is officially forbidden to Muslims, and the Wahabis are known for their strictness on such matters). We might expect a smile as the Buddha makes a sage comment about the mindful breaking of the Fifth Precept, after which he orders a mojito, then makes a toast 'to moderation in all things, including following the Fifth Precept'.[9] And perhaps there would be outright laughter if Moses were to part his margarita and Jesus were to order water and then, with a wink, turn it into a fine Stellenbosch pinotage.

Like the road waiting to be crossed, the bar is quintessential comedic space, indeed. It is also prime secular space, a place for the imbibing of spirits rather than Spirit. It's the place of profanity, not sacredness; levity, not liturgy; and relaxation, not reverence, right? What could the pub possibly have in common with the narthex?[10]

The scarily brilliant Romantic poet and visionary William Blake dared to say what many of us have perhaps thought but kept to ourselves: 'A good local pub has much in common with a church, except that a pub is warmer, and there's more conversation.'[11] Blake had a keen eye for irony. He knew how easily congregations can become cold, hostile places where we Christians intoxicate ourselves on unholy spirits. He knew how, drunk on dogmatism, we can say and do shockingly profane and unholy things. So for Blake the church can become profane and the bar can become sacred, as he portrayed in his poem 'The Little Vagabond'. A precocious and innocent child speaks to his mother:

> Dear mother, dear mother, the Church is cold,
> But the Ale-house is healthy and pleasant and warm;
> Besides I can tell where I am used well,
> Such usage in Heaven will never do well.

> But if at the Church they would give us some ale,
> And a pleasant fire our souls to regale,
> We'd sing and we'd pray all the livelong day,
> Nor ever once wish from the Church to stray.

> Then the Parson might preach, and drink, and sing,
> And we'd be as happy as birds in the spring;
> And modest Dame Lurch, who is always at church,
> Would not have bandy children, nor fasting, nor birch.

And God, like a father, rejoicing to see
His children as pleasant and happy as He,
Would have no more quarrel with the Devil or the barrel,
But kiss him, and give him both drink and apparel.

Blake, of course, was neither the only nor the first visionary with an eye for irony. Jesus himself spoke pithily and often about religious absurdity. He surely elicited some laughs when he portrayed religious leaders as straining at gnats and swallowing camels, whitewashing tombs, scrubbing only the outside of a filthy bowl, and so on. His whole ministry was a kind of guerrilla theatre, playing – can we say devilishly? – on irony, overturning figuratively as well as literally the money-laden tables of the religious elite.

If the Temple has been turned into a den of robbers – a joke, in other words – where then can the Spirit be found? Jesus dramatises the answer. The Spirit, driven from the Temple, shows up in one surprising place after another . . . in the treetops like the wind, on the sandy banks of the muddy River Jordan, on a hillside in the presence of the birds of the air and the flowers of the field, among wine bibbers and sinners, by a crime scene on the Jericho road, among rowdy children and a boisterous crowd, in a stranger on the road to Emmaus, in the last, the least and the lost.[12]

Given the bizarre and hostile state of our religious communities too often these days, isn't a bar the perfect place for the Spirit to convene a scandalous parliament of the world's religious leaders? Don't we need some 'secular' social space where diverse people of faith can encounter one another with some level of privacy and anonymity? Isn't the real scandal not that our religious leaders might be imagined talking as friends together in a bar, but rather that their followers are found speaking against one another as enemies, day after day in situation after situation?

Questions like these have always mattered. But in the years since 9/11, more and more of us are realising just how much they matter. So to imagine Jesus, Moses, the Buddha and Mohammed taking a walk across a road or even getting together as friends for a meal and conversation doesn't have to introduce a joke: it could introduce one of the most important conversations possible in today's world.

And all over the world, this is the conversation Christians want and need to have. In Cape Town and Bujumbura, in Bethlehem and Amsterdam, in Mombasa and Santo Domingo, in Santiago and Kuala Lumpur, in San Francisco and Phnom Penh, I've heard deeply earnest and highly committed Christians raise questions about what it means to be Christian in a multi-faith world. I knew that I should write on the subject, but what approach should I take? I could take an educational approach – informing Christians about other religions, overturning misconceptions and showing what Christians do and don't have in common with people of other faiths. I could take an apologetic or evangelistic approach – showing what is special and unique about Christianity, encouraging people to become or remain Christians – without insulting or misrepresenting other religions. I could take an approach of moral outrage, venting righteous fury about religious violence and bigotry. I could follow a deconstructive approach, grappling with the problematic philosophical assumptions that commonly lead to violence and bigotry. But in the end I felt I should take a different tack – a practical, pastoral and constructive one, focusing on how to develop a healthy, sane and faithful Christian identity in a multi-faith world like ours.[13]

Simply put, we Christians already know how to do two things very well. First, some of us know how to have a strong Christian identity that responds negatively towards other religions. The stronger our Christian commitment, the stronger our aversion or opposition to other religions. The stronger our Christian commitment, the more we emphasise our differences with other faiths and the more we frame those differences in terms of good/evil, right/wrong and better/worse. We may be friendly to individuals of other religions, but our friendship always has a pretext: we want them to switch sides and be won over to our better way. We love them (or say that we do) *in spite of* their religious identity, hoping that they will see the light and abandon it to find shelter under the tent of our own.[14]

Alternatively, others of us know how to have a more positive, accepting response to other religions. We never proselytise. We always show respect for other religions and their adherents. We always minimise differences and maximise commonalities. But we typically achieve coexistence by weakening our Christian identity. We make it matter less that *they* are Muslim or Hindu by making it matter less that *we* are Christian. We might even say that we love them in spite of *our own* religious identity.

For reasons that will become clear in the pages ahead, I'm convinced that neither of these responses is good enough for today's world. So I will explore the possibility of a third option, a Christian identity that is both strong and kind. By *strong* I mean vigorous, vital, durable, motivating, faithful, attractive and defining – an authentic Christian identity that matters.[15] By *kind* I mean something far more robust than mere tolerance, political correctness or coexistence: I mean benevolent, hospitable, accepting, interested and loving, so that the stronger our Christian faith, the more goodwill we will feel and show towards those of other faiths, seeking to understand and appreciate their religion from their point of view.[16] My pursuit, not just in this book but in my life, is a Christian identity that moves me towards people of other faiths in wholehearted love, not in spite of their non-Christian identity and not in spite of my own Christian identity, but *because of* my identity as a follower of God in the way of Jesus.

As in all of my books, I'm writing for a general audience of thoughtful Christians, especially Christian leaders, rather than a specialised audience of scholars.[17] Even though I've been somewhat restrained in quoting and footnoting scholarship in these pages, I hope it will be clear that I myself am an avid reader of relevant scholarship.[18] With over two decades of my life invested as a pastor in a local congregation, and another decade invested in writing for and speaking with Christian leaders, I'm drawn to bring good scholarship to bear on the grass-roots struggles faced by pastors and laypeople day to day in our multi-faith world.

I'm especially mindful of two other audiences as I write. First, I'm conscious of a new generation of young Christians – high school and college students, young adults coming of age and emerging leaders grappling with the formation of their identities. I hope they will find in these pages a way of staying and being wholeheartedly Christian without hostility, and I hope they will pioneer ways of raising future generations of children and youth in that path as well. And I also think of the young non-religious or post-religious adults I meet almost every week, not practising any religion, but deeply interested in finding a way to be human that is informed by the best of our religious traditions – including the hard lessons learned by the failures of those religious traditions.

Although I find the integrated vision presented in these pages to be both persuasive, coherent and beautiful, I expect some readers to find the book baffling because it proposes not minor changes within the existing paradigm of Christian identity, and not even major changes, but rather a different paradigm altogether. (It is terribly difficult to understand a different paradigm from the outside.) I expect some readers to say, 'I'm with you in certain chapters, not so much in others.' Rather than being disappointed in less than complete agreement or understanding, I'll be grateful for even small steps we can take together in challenging dangerous features of the status quo and opening up better possibilities for the future. Where you can't follow some of my proposals, I plead only that you pursue – in your own way, according to the lines of reasoning and imagination that seem best to you – the benevolence, the kindness and the love without which all our words are noise and we ourselves are nothing. We are increasingly faced with a choice, I believe, not between kindness and hostility, but between kindness and non-existence.[19]

That is the choice we must make, the road we must cross.

CHAPTER 2

Conflicted Religious Identity Syndrome

Give people a common enemy, and you will give them a common identity. Deprive them of an enemy and you will deprive them of the crutch by which they know who they are.

James Alison[1]

What does it mean to be a Christian in a multi-faith world?[2] Does Christian fidelity require us to stand against Islam, Hinduism, Buddhism, Sikhism, Judaism and other religions as rivals, impostors or enemies? Does Christian charity require us to believe that all religions are the same, that religious affiliation is an accident of birth or matter of taste, or that it doesn't really matter what you believe, as long as you're sincere? Is it OK to create a kind of religious salad, tossing together elements from many different faiths and adding some ideological dressing for flavour? Is it possible to be both faithful to Christian faith and charitable to other faiths?

I've struggled with these questions since I was a teenager.[3] Even at this moment, I feel two opposing realities churning within me. On the one hand, I feel the pull of Jesus' words 'Blessed are the peacemakers', or Paul's words about the gospel being a message of reconciliation, or James's assertion that God's wisdom is first pure and then peaceable.[4] But on the other hand, I keep noticing how my religion has, over its first two thousand years of existence, spent too little energy making peace and too much erecting and perfecting walls of separation, suspicion and hostility. In the Bible I read about love, love, love, but in various Christian subcultures in which I've participated, I keep encountering fear, superiority and hostility. In a wild array of forms, the message comes to me from the centres of religious power: I can't belong to our *us* unless I am against our *them*.

I've found that a lot of old-fashioned nastiness can lurk within that old-time religion. And new-fangled religion is sometimes worse.

Over the decades, I suppose I have in some ways grown more realistic and perhaps resigned, more willing to accept the Christian tradition for what it is, hostilities, hypocrisies and all. I've tempered my youthful idealism, you might say. At the same time, I've tried to avoid the bitter, cynical, sullen or whiny reactivity that one often encounters in the religiously disillusioned. I've resisted, sometimes not very successfully, the urge to accuse or vilify the easy target of a corrupt majority and I've fought the related urge to idealise a superior, elite minority. But even so, I haven't been able to reconcile myself to the status quo in the Christian community to which I belong – a status quo that too often pits Christian faith against every other faith in a cosmic death-match.

There is something real and good in my faith – a call to love God and neighbours – that I can't abandon without feeling a pang of betrayal. There is also something wrong in my faith – a vague hostility towards the cherished religions of my non-Christian neighbours – that I can't tacitly support without feeling an equal and opposite pang of betrayal.[5] To accept and love God, must I betray my neighbour of another religion? To accept and love my neighbour, must I betray the God of my religion? The stronger this internal conflict grows, the more certain is my sense of calling to imagine and strive for something better. Hence this book.

You may share this conflicted identity to some degree. An internal unrest about your Christian identity may have factored in your decision to open this book. You are seeking a way of being Christian that makes you more hospitable, not more hostile ... more loving, not more judgemental ... more like Christ and less (I'm sad to have to say this) like many Christians you have met. More and more of us are seeking treatment for what we might call Conflicted Religious Identity Syndrome (CRIS).

Novelist Anne Rice went public about her case of CRIS a few years ago when she officially 'quit Christianity'. I blogged about Anne's struggle a few days after her announcement:

> Anne was raised Catholic, left the faith at 18, described herself as an atheist for most of her adult life, returned to Catholicism in her fifties, and then last week announced – via Facebook – that she is no longer a Christian.
>
> She has concluded that she will never truly belong to the 'quarrelsome, hostile, disputatious, and deservedly infamous group' known as Christians unless she becomes 'anti-gay ... anti-feminist ... anti-artificial birth control ... anti-Democrat ... anti-secular humanism ... anti-science ... anti-life'.

That cost of membership simply isn't worth it. So she's opting out.

Tell that much of the story, and you have the sort of thing the news media love to report – another celebrity break-up, if you will. But this time, the celebrity is divorcing God.

But that's not the whole story. Really, it's not the story at all. Anne explains that, 'My faith in Christ is central to my life.' She is still 'an optimistic believer in a universe created and sustained by a loving God'. 'But,' she says, 'following Christ does not mean following His followers. Christ is infinitely more important than Christianity and always will be, no matter what Christianity is, has been or might become.'

And so, she concludes, 'In the name of Christ . . . I quit Christianity and being Christian.'

Her brief announcement raises lots of fascinating questions. For example, when a person quits Christianity in the name of Christ, what do you call that person? If Christianity means 'following Christ's followers', what do you call someone who wants to skip the middlemen?[6]

You can sense some of my own identity struggle in my reflections on Anne's.

Many of us haven't gone as far as quitting Christianity, but we too show signs of CRIS when we compulsively add adjectives in front of the noun *Christian*, as in, 'I'm a/an _____ Christian.' We might fill the blank with a single, simple adjective like 'progressive' or 'emergent' or (I like this one for its ironic boldness) 'bad'.[7] Or we might fill it with a string of highly nuanced adjectives: 'non-religious-right-mainstream Evangelical' or 'missional post-institutional post-colonial mainline

Protestant' or 'Red-letter **Social-**Justice' or 'Big-Tent Barthian-Reformed' or 'Vatican II **Progres**sive Catholic' or 'generously orthodox Quaker-Anabaptist **Contem**plative-Activist' or whatever. Proof positive of my CRIS diagnosis came when I subtitled my book *Generous Orthodoxy* (Zondervan, 2004) in this memory-defying way:

> Why I am a missional, evangelical, post/protestant, liberal/conservative, mystical/poetic, biblical, charismatic/contemplative, fundamentalist/calvinist, anabaptist/anglican, methodist, catholic, green, incarnational, depressed-yet-hopeful, emergent, unfinished Christian.

The noun *Christian* alone either says too much for us or not enough, so it must be either dropped (as Anne Rice did) or modified (as many of us do). Bring in the adjectives.[8]

So what happens when an Evangelical/Pentecostal pastor in Florida burns a Quran? Or when a famous Christian televangelist describes the tragic Haitian earthquake as God's punishment for Haitian sins? Or when a bizarre Baptist sect sends still more protesters to yet another military funeral holding up the same old 'God hates fags' signs? Or when a hyper-Calvinist radio preacher predicts the world will end on 21 May 2011, and then on 22 May offers a fallback date in October, which passes uneventfully as well? Or when some officials in the Catholic Church secretly protect paedophile priests while refusing to consider ordaining married men or even celibate women?[9]

You feel symptoms of CRIS twitching on your face, rumbling in your gut, and aching in your lower back. You think, *Give me some adjectives, quick, so I won't be identified with 'that kind' of Christian*. Or maybe you think, like Anne Rice, *I'll keep loving and following Christ, but if being identified as a Christian requires me to be hostile towards others, it's about time for me to turn in my ID card as a member of the Christian religion.*

Of course, CRIS isn't just a Christian problem. Islamic terrorists shout 'God is great!' as they blow up soldiers and civilians without distinction. As they maim, torture and murder their fellow human beings, their shouts reveal an absolute certainty, without a shred of Dylan-esque irony, that God is on their side. Their confident violence sends the majority of Muslims to their verbal medicine cabinets, seeking their own palliative adjectives to modify their affiliation – *moderate, progressive, peace-loving* and so on – so they can distinguish themselves from 'that kind' of Muslim. And the same could be said for Jews, Hindus, Buddhists and atheists, too. For example, if you're simultaneously Jewish and deeply committed to human rights for Palestinians, how do you deal with CRIS?[10] If you're an atheist, yet you respect the valid role of religion in society, how do you self-differentiate from more militant atheists? What is it about our faith (and even non-faith) traditions that we are so uneasy about?

Whether we realise it or not, most of us who suffer from CRIS are trying to distance ourselves from *religious hostility*. By *hostility* I mean opposition, the sense that the other is the enemy.[11] Hostility makes one unwilling to be a host (the two words are historically related). The other must be turned away, kept at a distance as an unwanted outsider, not welcomed in hospitality as a guest or friend.[12] Hostility is an attitude of exclusion, not embrace; of repugnance, not respect; of suspicion, not extending the benefit of the doubt; of conflict, not conviviality.[13]

Those of us with CRIS don't want to be held hostage (another related word) to a religion that is hostile towards science and learning, hostile towards honest questions and new ways of thinking, and above all, hostile towards other human beings – especially those of other religions (or other versions of our own religion). Something deep in our conscience tells us that hostility is part of the problem to be overcome in the world, not the means by which problems will be overcome. Hostility is a symptom of the disease, not part of the cure.

Consider the wise words of Catholic theologian James Alison with which this chapter began. When religions develop an oppositional identity – *we oppose, therefore we are*, or *we know who we are because we know whom we oppose* – their strong identity comes at a high cost, first to others and eventually to themselves. No wonder so many of us are running to the adjective cabinet seeking relief, while others of us are taking out a pair of scissors to cut up our religious ID cards.

Yes, something good still shines from the heart of our religions – a saving drive towards peace, goodness, self-control, integrity, charity, beauty, duty. And something shadowy struggles to overcome that luminosity – a hostile drive, dangerous, resilient and deeply ingrained, a black hole in our identity that needs an enemy to help us know who we are and how good we are.[14] How do we disassociate from the hostility without abandoning the identity? How do we remain loyal to what is good and real in our faith without giving tacit support to what is wrong and dangerous? How do we, as Christians, faithfully affirm the uniqueness and universality of Christ without turning that belief into an insult or a weapon?

There lies our – my – conflicted identity in a nutshell.

As soon as you crack open this nut, additional questions begin spilling out: How do you oppose hostility without becoming hostile against its promoters? How do you oppose division without dividing from dividers? How do you oppose exclusion without excluding excluders? How do you oppose rage without raging against the ragers? How do you distinguish yourself from those who need enemies to know who they are – without rendering them the enemy by whom you know who you are?

Looking back, much of my writing has been literary self-therapy for my own chronic case of CRIS. Even in my blog post about Anne Rice's decision to disaffiliate from Christian identity once and for all, I made my own confession:

> I reached a conclusion very close to Anne's in my book *A New Kind of Christianity*: 'I do not believe in Christianity the way I believe in Jesus. I am a Christian who does not believe in Christianity as I used to, but who believes in Christ with all my heart, more than ever.'[15]
>
> So I do not condemn or criticize Anne in any way. I'm glad she has followed her conscience and articulated the reasons for doing so. That's good for her, and it may be good for the church, too. Sometimes, powerful people only listen when they see enough people voting with their feet.
>
> I haven't taken that step myself, though I think about it quite often. (As recently as last week when I heard about the pastor planning to burn Qurans on September 11. Sheesh.)
>
> I hang in there for several reasons. First, if I want to be affiliated with any group of human beings, sooner or later I will be associated with bigotry, intolerance, violence, stupidity, and pride. In fact, even if I stand alone, distancing myself from every

other group, I know that within me there are the seeds of all these things. So there's no escaping the human condition.

Second, if I were to leave to join some new religion that claims to have – at last! – perfected the way of being pristine and genuine through and through, we all know where that's going to lead. There's one thing worse than a failed old religion: a naïve and arrogant new one. In that light, maybe only religions that have acknowledged and learned from their failures have much to offer.

Third, I've decided that if I'm going to have solidarity with one failed religion, I might as well have solidarity with them all. So rather than surrendering my identity as a Christian, I've redefined it so it doesn't mean that I feel superior to anybody. Instead, it means that as a failed member of a failed religion, I'm in solidarity with all other failed members of failed religions . . . and with people who have dropped out of failed religions as well.

Perhaps it's this truly catholic (small-c) solidarity in failure that really counts most, for Catholics, Protestants, and everybody else. Those who leave religion and those who stay can work to expand that gracious space of solidarity, which, I think, is what Jesus called 'the kingdom of God'.

This is a book about finding and inhabiting that gracious space and welcoming others into it. Writing it has been part of my ongoing therapy for CRIS, and reading it will, I hope, be part of yours. I have real hope that a great turning is underway, a profound emergence and reformulation, a worldwide spiritual awakening, a healing of our conflicted identities.[16] This healing won't come easy. It will require some profound rethinking – repentance, in the sturdiest and best sense of the word. It will, as every important breakthrough does, engender push-back and critique, which will call for humble, thoughtful and patient response. (Ironically, there are few actions better guaranteed to engender conflict than proposing love and understanding for those identified as outsiders and enemies.) And along with repentance and humble, thoughtful patience, it will demand an appropriate urgency.

At a party recently, I was introduced to a fellow who asked what I do for a living. I replied, 'Well, I used to be a college English teacher, and then I spent twenty-four years as a pastor. Now I'm an author and speaker, and I guess a sort of activist too.'

'What do you write and speak and activate about?' he asked.

'Among other things, these days I try to convince religious people to stop hating and killing each other and to work for the common good instead,' I replied.

He nodded, paused for a moment, and replied, 'I'm not religious myself. On most days I'm an atheist. But I've always wondered why more religious people don't get off their [hindquarters] and work harder for peace than their counterparts do for violence. So . . . good luck with your work. It's about time. Even though I'm pretty much agnostic, I just have to say, "God bless you."'

'Thanks,' I said. 'I take that to heart.' After we both moved on to other conversations, I kept thinking about his impromptu blessing. Doesn't God seem more plausible, more real, more present, in the presence of peacemakers? And in the presence of hostile religious people, doesn't God seem less and less credible?[17]

I've written this book primarily for my fellow Christians, but I'm sure that peaceable Muslims, Jews, Hindus, Buddhists and others will find much to stimulate their own creative engagement with their own epidemics of CRIS. If my proposals about Christian identity are in any way legitimate, they will be easy to translate into other contexts.

ONE

THE CRISIS OF CHRISTIAN IDENTITY

I can't know if God exists, but I do know the word *God* is operating in the world, running around doing all kinds of work, good and bad, and I think, as a theologian, I have a responsibility to think critically about the kinds of gods we make and worship and to try to come up with versions of god that might make the world a more just and life-giving place for everyone.

Sarah Sentilles[1]

CHAPTER 3

How a Muslim Boy Converted Me

Given the geo-political state of our world today, given the role that religions are playing in that world and the role that they are called to play, given the looming necessity of turning the impending clash of civilizations into a dialogue of civilizations, the religious communities that populate our planet have reached a point in their history in which they must lay aside or radically reinterpret their traditional and various ways of claiming that 'My God is bigger than your God.' The religions can no longer continue to make the kinds of claims of superiority that most of them have made in the past . . . The religious communities of the world can and must form a 'community of communities' – a community in which each tradition will preserve its identity and at the same time deepen and broaden that identity through learning from, appealing to, and working with other communities.

Paul Knitter[1]

Just before our wedding day, Grace and I signed a rental agreement on an apartment. It was going to be cleaned and painted while we were away on our honeymoon. My brother Peter kindly offered to move in some furniture for us while we were gone so we could go directly from the airport to our new apartment when we returned.

As brothers often do at times like this, Peter decided a practical joke was in order. After hauling in the furniture, he blew up what seemed like a few million balloons and filled the apartment's only bathroom with them. When I say filled, I mean that the room was jammed with balloons floor to almost-ceiling. (It must have been a challenge to squeeze the last few dozen in there.)

Imagine us returning to the airport about midnight, catching a taxi to an apartment we had never been inside before, and finding the key under a welcome mat – right where Peter had left it for us. Bleary-eyed and excited about spending our first night in our own place, we wandered around with a mix of excitement and exhaustion, seeing what our shabby-chic assemblage of hand-me-down furniture looked like in our new residence. But when we tried to open the bathroom door, it . . . wouldn't . . . open!

Once we diagnosed the problem, the question became how to treat it. We felt a predictable sense of urgency in doing so, having just completed a long plane ride. Popping several hundred balloons after midnight would surely elicit 911 calls from our new neighbours, and not make the ideal first impression: 'They're setting off fireworks down there in Apartment 101!' Or 'Wow, that new marriage doesn't seem to be going too well. Gunshots already!'

So we gingerly reached in and began pulling out balloons, one at a time, careful not to pop any but driven by our intensifying biological need to use the toilet. After fifteen or twenty minutes, the bathroom was more or less empty, but an ankle-deep flood of balloons had spread through our apartment, covering the floor of our living room, dining room and kitchen like a motley tide. 'I'll deal with it in the morning,' I told Grace, trying to sound like a competent, problem-solving husband.

The next morning, as Grace slept in, I stepped out on our front stoop to survey our new neighbourhood. There I bumped into a boy of about eight, rushing into the apartment building like a bat into a cave. He struck me as friendly and energetic, maybe precocious, maybe even brash. 'You're the new guy,' he said, eyeing me for a moment. 'Gotta go!' I heard his sneakers slapping the stairs up to the second floor.

I sat down on the stoop to ponder what I was going to do with a couple million – more or less – balloons. A few minutes later, the boy returned and plopped down on the step next to me, still breathless but talkative. He was Aatif, eight years old, from Iran, living in the apartment directly above ours.

If life were a cartoon, about three minutes into our conversation, one of those little light bulbs would have appeared above my head with a little *ta-ting!* sound. 'Hey Aatif, do you like balloons?' 'Sure. You got some?' 'Come with me,' I replied.

We went inside and I opened our door and he peered in. His eyes widened and he flashed me a huge smile. 'I can help you, Brian. I can help you with these.' But instead of grabbing even one, he raced out the door. As I listened to the sound of his sneakers slapping down the sidewalk outside, I was a little puzzled, but Aatif seemed like a young man who knew what he was doing.

A few minutes later, the door opened – no knock: I learned that Aatif never knocked. In came a stream of kids, seven, eight, nine, ten, eleven. Each of them took as many balloons as he or she could hold, the little ones two, the bigger ones three or four. A few minutes later, they came back for a second load, and after a few loads, all the balloons were gone.

That day earned us a heroic reputation with the neighbourhood kids and a slightly less stellar reputation with their parents who had to endure the random bangs of balloons popping for days to come. My friendship with Aatif also began that day. I'd have to say that Aatif was my first Muslim friend.

Soon we got to know his mom, Liza (Anglicised from a Farsi name). We never succeeded in getting Aatif to knock. I think we became his second family, which meant a lot to both him and his mom, for reasons that gradually became clear.

Aatif's dad was a graduate student at the university where I was also studying and teaching. He had come to the United States a year before his family to get things ready for their arrival and to get acclimatised to his studies in a foreign language. A few months after their arrival, Liza realised that her husband had grown close – very close – with an American student. Soon he moved in with her, leaving Liza and Aatif stuck in America with no husband, no father, no work and no English.

We and our balloons moved in about a year after the break-up. In that time, Aatif had gone to school and mastered English as only kids can. Liza got a job at a McDonald's, and her English had improved from non-existent to broken but functional. Over the next few years, our friendship deepened, and Liza expressed that friendship in a most delicious way: Iranian dishes delivered to our door. We once hosted a party for her Iranian friends. It turned out Americans, back in those days after the Iranian Revolution and the hostage situation, weren't very welcoming to

Iranians, so word spread that Liza knew some Americans who liked Iranians.

My brain was filled with the same ignorant stereotypes about Islam and Muslims that many Americans share today. Liza and Aatif re-educated me. They helped me know Muslims as my neighbours, my friends, human beings who struggled with the same mice and cockroaches that Grace and I did in that grimy little apartment building.

Since then, I've been blessed with many more Muslim friends in my life. Each has brought a gift to me, but none greater than Aatif. By becoming my first Muslim friend, he forever shattered my preconceptions and false assumptions. Through him, 'the other' became my neighbour.[2]

The standard approach to Muslims from my conservative Evangelical upbringing was clear: be nice to them when necessary in order to convert them to Christianity; otherwise, see them as spiritual competitors and potential enemies. In effect, this approach tended to dehumanise the other, turning others into 'evangelistic targets' (an ugly phrase if ever there was one), rivals and threats. Aatif had no interest in being converted, and as a child he was neither rival nor threat. His jubilant, exuberant, invincible humanity overwhelmed any move to dehumanise him, and so he began converting me – not from my Christianity to his Islam, but from an old kind of oppositional Christian identity to a new kind. As a naturally bold and precocious child who never learned to knock before entering, he was determined to be part of my life – in all his charming, irreducible humanity – unless I locked the door.

I'm glad I didn't.

I lost touch with Aatif and Liza. But their friendship left its mark on me. Since they became friends in my neighbourhood, guests at my table, and part of my life, *Muslim* could never again be a faceless label for me. And my own Christian identity could no longer be a locked door that kept them at a distance.

As a committed Christian, I have always struggled with locked doors – doors by which we on the inside lock out 'the others' – Jews, Muslims, Mormons, liberals, doubters, agnostics, gay folks, whomever. The more we insiders succeed in shutting others out, the more I tend to feel locked in, caged, trapped.

So over the years, like many of my fellow Christians, I have increasingly found myself trapped between a strong Christian identity that is hostile towards outsiders and a weak Christian identity that is benign (or harmless) towards outsiders. The stronger my Christian identity grows, the stronger my opposition grows towards non-Christian religions and the more hostile I appear to their faithful adherents. But if I try to reduce that hostility by weakening my Christian identity, I have less and less reason for staying Christian. Meanwhile, if my friends of other faiths have a strong religious identity, my suppressed Christian identity may pressure them to similarly inhibit their own, leaving both of us uncomfortable.

Why can't there be a third option? Couldn't the kind of friendship I enjoyed with Aatif and Liza be – not unusual and exceptional, but normal and normative? Shouldn't it be possible to have a strong Christian identity that is strongly benevolent towards people of other faiths, accepting them not *in spite of* the religion they love, but *with* the religion they love? Could my love and respect for them as human beings lead me to a loving and respectful encounter with their religion as well?

In order to explore that kind of identity, we'll have to deal with a host of questions. Why has the Christian faith been so irreconcilable to other faiths? Why is deep commitment to Christian faith so deeply linked with aversion to all other faiths? When Christians claim that Jesus is the only way, what do they mean, and does that mean that other religions must be opposed as frauds, mistakes, delusions or distractions? Can one whole-heartedly love and trust Jesus as Lord and Saviour without hating – or at least opposing – the Buddha, Mohammed, Lao Tzu or Confucius? Must sincere commitment to the Bible make Christians antagonistic towards the Quran, the Baghavad Gita, the Analects of Confucius, the coyote myths of the Plains Indians or the Tao Te Ching? Does sincere faith in the uniqueness and universality of Jesus Christ require one to see other faiths as false, dangerous or even demonic?

We'll address these questions in due time. But we can't answer them without seeking to understand what lies behind them, what they assume and why these questions remain so provocative in many circles. I hope you'll find the journey from questions to answers to be as fascinating, rewarding and enlightening as I have.

CHAPTER 4

How a Book in the 1970s Anticipated the Story Line of the Early Twenty-First Century

> Why is it that the choice among churches always seems to be the choice between intelligence on ice and ignorance on fire?
>
> as quoted by Diana Butler Bass[1]

Many of us have felt unable to accept either of the two typical responses of Christian faith to other faiths. On the one hand, we can't in good conscience maintain a position of hostility towards or superiority over the religious commitments of our Jewish, Muslim, Hindu, Buddhist and other friends. On the other hand, we don't feel right or faithful in watering down or suppressing our own deep commitment to Christ, the Bible and the rich inheritance we have received in the Christian community. We hope, we dream, we pray that another option will come into view – one that doesn't pit us against others in hostility, and one that allows us to remain true to our own deepest Christian convictions.

We aren't the first people to seek this third option. Back in 1972, Dean Kelley rocked the religious world with *Why*

Conservative Churches Are Growing.[2] He spoke the then-shocking truth that 'Mainline' Protestantism, which had historically been the main form of Christianity in the United States, was fast becoming 'old line' as it declined in numbers.[3] It was losing ground to a 'new line' of conservative churches characterised by *seriousness* and *strictness*. These churches were *serious* about the meaning they offered and *strict* in regards to wholehearted conformity to their norms of belief and behaviour. This seriousness and strictness, Kelley asserted, made them *socially strong*, and this social strength made them grow – as their adherents enthusiastically recruited others.

In contrast, old-line churches were increasingly ecumenical – respectful of and open to dialogue with other faith communities and the meaning they offered. They were about making friends, not converts. Old-line churches valued individual freedom over group conformity when it came to issues of purpose, belief and behaviour.[4]

To old-liners, ecumenism, respect, dialogue, individualism, non-conformity and freedom were precious qualities. But in terms of creating growth or even sustainability for the future, Kelley claimed they were counterproductive at least, and potentially even suicidal.[5] Because these qualities discouraged energetic proselytising and might even tempt adherents to stop adhering so strongly, Kelley described old-line churches with unflattering terms like *lukewarmness* and *leniency*. Kelley portrayed the contrast between old-line lukewarmness/leniency and new-line strictness/seriousness as a paradox:

> Though the paradox can be reduced, it cannot be eliminated without being unfair to one pole or the other. There is about any

serious meaning venture a certain irreducible fierceness, asperity, insistence, exclusiveness, rigor – a fanaticism that brushes everything else aside. Yet that very single-mindedness renders it objectionable to those who value balance, brotherhood, respect for individual diversity, mutual forbearance and self-restraint, civic peace, pluralism – and dialogue – as much as, or more than, they value any single formulation of meaning or any one meaning-system (including their own). (page 164)

Those who haven't actually read the book might conclude that Kelley was himself a conservative apologist. But he made it clear that his sympathies lay with the declining 'liberal' churches. Kelley saw, as many of us have since, that the same intensity that produced strength and growth in strict and serious churches also produced problems, and those problems were real. Strict, serious and growing groups are characterised by dogmatism, judgemental moralism, obsession with cultic purity, fanaticism and unwillingness to listen (except to find weaknesses to exploit in rebuttal). They

... are not 'reasonable', they are not 'tolerant', they are not ecumenical, they are not 'relevant'.[6] Quite the contrary! They often refuse to recognize the validity of other churches' teachings, ordinations, sacraments. They observe unusual rituals ... they [persist] in irrational behavior ... They try to impose uniformity of belief and practice among members by censorship, heresy trials, and the like. (pages 25–26)

So for Kelley, however attractive the dynamism of growing groups may be, 'living in close proximity to such movements, trying to get along with their members, can be strenuous, if not intensely irritating' (page 78). One can almost guess what his next-door neighbours were like.

In light of this paradox – that irritating and obnoxious faith communities tend to grow, and that compassionate and neighbourly faith communities tend to decline – it's no wonder Kelley entitles Chapter 6 of his book, 'Why Not a Strong Ecumenical Religion?' Interestingly, no clear answer comes in that chapter. Almost a hundred pages later, he describes the pain of Christian church leaders who are committed 'to the ultimate meaning embodied in the Christian faith' on the one hand, and yet are equally committed on the other hand to 'freedom, justice, beauty, (empirical) truth, and respect for others – including those who are deeply devoted to non-Christian ultimate meanings, or to none at all.' And at this point the question raised back in Chapter 6 resurfaces:

> But why must there be any conflict? Are not freedom, justice, respect for others essential parts of the Christian faith? Ideally they should be, if rightly understood. One can conceive of a high-demand religious movement devoted to justice, freedom, beauty, respect for others, and so on, which could effectively explain life to [humankind] without fanaticism, absolutism, intolerance, or judgmental moralism. That is what – ideally – Christianity ought to be. (page 165)

Sadly, Kelley cannot see that kind of Christianity anywhere on the horizon, as his next sentence indicates: 'Yet where is such a phenomenon to be found?' It's not that he says such a strong-and-benevolent faith is inconceivable or impossible; it's just that he has not yet found it actual or visible.

As the twenty-first century unfolds, the need for this ideal-but-as-yet-uncommon Christianity becomes more acute.[7] That's where people like you and me come in. It remains for us to explore and embody the possibility that Kelley opened in his book – the possibility of a Christian faith that combines certain key elements of conservative 'new line' Christianity (strength, commitment, intensity of meaning) with other elements of liberal 'old line' Christianity (ecumenism, reasonableness, a peaceable attitude). Perhaps such a strong-benevolent faith will never be 'main line', but it can certainly be a lifeline in these conflicted and challenging times.

From his vantage point in the 1970s, Kelley couldn't have predicted 9/11 in the US or 7/7 in the UK. He couldn't have anticipated the ways that Christian, Muslim and Jewish fundamentalism would move from the religion pages to the front pages of our newspapers. He couldn't foresee that a generation later, the new-line groups of his day would have lost their lustre so that their statistics would show similar patterns of plateau and decline.[8]

But by naming a trend that was emerging in his day, he sensitised a generation of Christian leaders to an issue they and their children would not be able to avoid: what it means to have a strong Christian identity in a world torn by religious hostility.

CHAPTER 5

How a Mentor Shocked Me – and Gently Nudged Me towards Higher Ground

Human beings never do evil so completely and so joyously as when they do it from a religious motivation.

Blaise Pascal[1]

Good mentors sometimes unsettle you. It's part of their job. One of mine got me squirming one Sunday morning when I was driving him from his hotel to a church service where he was about to speak. It was about four months after 11 September 2001, and I was sharing with him my discomfort with the anti-Muslim sentiment that was rising among our fellow Evangelicals. He commented, '*Remember, Brian: in a pluralistic world, a religion is judged by the benefits it brings to its non-members.*'

His words jolted me because I assumed, as most people probably do, that religions survive and thrive by promising benefits to their members – and conversely, by either withholding benefits from non-members or threatening them with punishment in this life or the next. The idea of a religion bringing benefits to non-members sounded crazy to me. I was too taken aback even to ask him to explain what he meant, much less argue. So after a few seconds of uncomfortable silence, I guess we moved on to another topic. But his seemingly offhand comment stuck with me like the hook of a popular song. I couldn't get it out of my head.

I now suspect he knew how unsettling and curious his statement would appear to me. He knew that I might not be ready for it yet. But rather than spare me the discomfort, he simply let the statement fall like a seed into disturbed soil, waiting to germinate in its own time.

I lived, as many people do, on a line between liberal and conservative forms of Christian faith. On the conservative side (B), there was a strong identity characterised by strong hostility towards non-Christians. On the liberal side (A), there was a benign attitude towards non-Christians – what we might call tolerance, with (to a conservative mind, anyway) a correspondingly weak identity. In between, there was a more moderate zone, (C), characterised by moderated tolerance, moderated hostility and moderately strong identity:

Fig. 1

A: Weak/Benign	C. Moderately Strong/Moderately Benign	B: Strong/Hostile

In my twenties and thirties, I had been moving slowly from the right side of the diagram towards the middle – in my terms at the time, from conservative Fundamentalist to Mainstream Evangelical. But my mentor was talking about something that I couldn't locate in my frame of reference. He wasn't pointing farther to the left on the line, but rather towards a third alternative (D) I hadn't even imagined, a space above the line entirely, where a strong, generous, benevolent Christian identity was possible.

Fig. 2

D. Strong/Benevolent

A: Weak/Benign

C. Moderately
Strong/Moderately Benign

B: Strong/Hostile

What Dean Kelley pointed towards back in 1974, my mentor was pointing towards over twenty-five years later: a new kind of Christian identity, common ground on higher ground 'above the line', characterised by strong benevolence, generosity and hospitality towards others, not hostility on the one hand and not mere 'niceness' or 'tolerance' on the other.[2]

This little diagram helps me be more understanding and less judgemental about my fellow Christians. It helps me remember that Christians settle on the right side not because they want hostility but because they want a strong faith identity. Christians cluster on the left side not because they want weakness but because they don't want hostility. And Christians in the middle want to manifest not mediocrity, but as much strength and as much tolerance as possible, avoiding the extremes on both sides. That understanding is essential. If we judge, shame and reject those on line, whether on the left or right or somewhere in between, if we paint them as the enemy and develop an identity in opposition to or hostile towards them, we lock them in a defensive posture. And we lock ourselves into mirroring the very behaviour we condemn.

I'm convinced that the only viable response to religious hostility is love, empathy, compassion, understanding – not more hostility. (What could be more pathetic than a hostile fight against hostility?) And so I must have the empathy to understand that some readers have already been deeply offended by the diagnosis I'm offering. *We are not hostile*, I can imagine them saying. *That term is inherently judgemental. We are faithful, and if you judge our faithfulness as hostility, that's your problem, not ours.*

I am sensitive to this response in large part because I can imagine that I might have made it myself twenty years ago. Few hostile people would ever see hostility lurking in their hearts: they would see love – love for God as they understand God, love for their religion, love for their community, their ancestors, their history, their future. And this is part of the power of religion – not that it inspires hate, but rather that it inspires loves so powerful that they can be expressed without conscious intention through hateful actions. Here's how Georgetown University's Ariel Glucklich has expressed it:

> The biggest myth about religion and violence, I believe, is that religion teaches hatred . . . I think the violence comes from a kind of love or desire for love for one's own group and a willingness to do whatever it takes to obtain it.[3]

Glucklich's words can help us see why many faithful Christians see our plea for them to become less hostile as a temptation to love God, their religion, their community, their ancestors, their history and their future less. Before they'll listen to our case for a new kind of strong-benevolent Christian identity, they must be convinced it is the path to more love and fidelity, more strength and meaning, not less. But even then, embracing a new Christian identity will not be easy for them. People from strong-hostile backgrounds like mine know how costly it will be to depart from their home turf on the conventional liberal-moderate-conservative line. They know they will face a sense of betrayal from their closest religious friends, even their own family members, those they most trust and love.

That's why identity formation – and reformation – takes time and can't be forced or pushed. It involves many dangers, toils and snares – threats and setbacks, wrong turns and recoveries. Even under the best of conditions, there are limits to the speed by which a religious identity can come of age and face the challenges before it. Perhaps that's why a book like this can be important: it can provide privacy, time and space for people to consider the unsettling and dangerous proposal of an identity change. Like my gentle mentor who casually dropped his comment about a religion providing benefits to its non-adherents and then left me to ponder what he had said on my own, a book makes no demands. It remains easy to put down and easy to ignore. That very gentleness can be its greatest power. It is hard to defend against something that is not aggressive.

CHAPTER 6

How Your Friends Can Be More Dangerous Than Your Enemies (And How You Can Be More Dangerous Than Both)

The causes of religious violence are like bad breath: you need other people to make you aware of it.

Paul Knitter[1]

If you dare depart from traditional identity categories – whether in the strong/hostile zone, in the weak/benign zone, or in the moderate zone in between – you will be seen with suspicion by your former colleagues in that zone. They will see you as abandoning them personally, betraying your heritage and its ideals, violating the 'us-ness' by which you once were identified with them. In response, they may threaten you, hoping that fear will make you stay, not realising that it is more likely to drive you farther away.

I recently saw this dynamic playing out in a fascinating online conversation of which I was part – a conversation that included Christians, Muslims and Jews. The conversation was launched by an Evangelical Christian friend who has devoted his life to building bridges between people of different faiths. He would post an observation or question that would get us talking, first with him and then with each other. When conversation died down, he would post another prompt. In one of these interchanges, a Christian participant told how he had recently been harshly criticised by a friend for asserting that Christians and Muslims pray to the same God. I posted this in response:

All of us are poised between two dangers. The obvious one is 'The Other'. The subtle one is 'Us'. If we defend ourselves against the Other, if we attack the Other, we gain credibility with 'Us'. We show that we are loyal, supportive, believers, members of Us, and we are generously rewarded and affirmed. We gain a lot by attacking the Other – in religious circles as well as political ones.

Ironically, Us can be an equally great threat to each of us as individuals as does the Other, probably greater. Us might withdraw its approval of me. It might label me disloyal, unsupportive, unbeliever, unorthodox, liberal, anathema, etc. To be rebuked, marginalized, or excluded by Us is an even greater threat than to be attacked by the Other.

I don't think we Christians often realize the great degree to which we live in fear of Us. This is true whether we're Evangelical, Catholic, Mainline Protestant, Orthodox, Pentecostal, or whatever. (Each religion has its various Us groups, and then there are the Us groups of academia, politics, ethnicity, etc.)

Our fear becomes all the more acute when we venture to do what many of us in this dialogue are doing: we are daring to defend and humanize the Other. We are showing – however feebly and adolescently – a grain of neighborliness and solidarity with the Other. At that moment, we become vulnerable as never before to attacks by Us, i.e. our fellow Christians. In my experience, it takes much more courage to stand up to or apart from Us than it does to stand either against or with the Other . . .

Sometimes, when I've tried to insert myself between Us and Other, I managed to get shot at by both sides. It's hazardous work. As they say, being a bridge means you'll get walked on from both sides . . . I offer this simply because I think we in this discussion need to face the great power that Us holds over each of us. In attempting to avoid the punishment or suspicion of Us, even as we try to communicate to our fellow Christians on behalf of our Muslim friends, we can unintentionally play to dangerous, powerful Christian prejudices and unintentionally reinforce them.

This is the perilous situation, I think we would agree, into which Jesus went, as did Paul and Peter and St Francis and Dr King and Desmond Tutu and many others in our tradition and outside of it. Crucifixion happens, not at the hands of the Other, but Us. It is not easy risking that, even when we are trying to build solidarity with the Other.

So, even as I seek to build relationships with my Muslim friends (or whomever), I confess that I am held hostage to fear of what Us will say. To give myself to the Other without reserve or concern for what Us will say . . . that is a level of love I do not think I often attain. But it is something to which I aspire because of the example and teaching of Jesus, and because my heart/the Spirit tells me it is right or at least my calling.

By the way, I wouldn't be surprised if this tension with Us helps explain why [famous novelist] Anne Rice famously quit Christianity recently . . . Perhaps Anne felt that remaining a member in good standing of the Us of Christianity made it impossible for her to show Christ-like solidarity with the Other, whether the other is gay, liberal, Muslim, etc.

One last tangent – I suspect this is what Paul was trying to say in 2 Corinthians (and elsewhere, i.e. 1 Cor. 9 or Gal. 3). To be 'in Christ' is to be in solidarity with all people – and all creation. That solidarity contrasts starkly with the realities of being 'in Christianity' or any other 'Us' religion. I think that's what your [critic] was getting at when he said 'as if man were outside of God'. To be in God or in Christ would mean – or should mean – to be in a one-anotherness that transcends and in some way includes all the smaller 'us' and 'other' groups. Again, forgive me for all the ways in which I have misspoken, and feel free to disagree.

Several participants – Christians, Muslim, Jewish – contacted me in private, apart from the group, and responded positively, saying that yes, their greatest opposition came not from 'Them' but 'Us'. For example, a Muslim man who lives in the Middle East responded with great passion:

> We don't know each other, yet I want to tell you how courageous and admirable your approach is and I can understand how difficult one's life can become just because of 'Us's' intolerance. But believe me, how much intolerant and extremist your 'Us' could be, ours are ten times more extremist and more intolerant with the difference that you can survive the intolerance from your 'Us' while we cannot survive the ones coming from our 'Us-es'.

He went on to explain how a famous Saudi anthropologist had recently called for the sword to be removed from the Saudi flag, where it sits below the words *La-Ilah-Illa-Allah* (There is no God but God). The sword, the anthropologist suggested, presents an unflattering view of Islam, seeming to combine the essential creed of Islam with a threat of violence, as if God needs a sword to enforce God's will. In response, the anthropologist was threatened with death. 'I am not talking about stuff that happened centuries ago. This was months ago,' he said:

> Islam is an Identity Religion and you probably know that there are several Islamic particular identities all in conflict one with each other. When I speak with a Muslim, telling him that I too am a Muslim means nothing to him. I could have been Atheist or Christian or Jew, it would have made more sense. But if I add that I am a Sunni Muslim then it starts to make sense – a good sense if he too is a Sunni and a bad one if he is a Shiite and of course vice-versa.

Another Muslim participant wrote to me privately that he tried to distinguish between hostile religious institutions and the spirit of faith:

> I know many people started to consider themselves outsiders to their religious institutions while they stay committed to the spirit and the faith. They see themselves as victims of the very institutions supposedly meant to help them become better followers and ambassadors of their faith. This is true for every religious establishment without any exception. That was the real cause behind the establishment of Sufi orders as rejection to the heavily politicized Islamic establishment at that time. Sufi orders were themselves later rejected by many when they started to see them

falling into the same trap of heavy politicization. Hope this will help a little bit in drawing a clear differentiating line between Christ and the Christian institutions in the same way we, Muslims, are trying desperately to differentiate between the spirit of Islam and its establishment . . . There is nothing that hurts any religion today more than its own establishment. Established and well funded religious institutions are becoming their own enemies. There is no better way to say it than: 'We find the enemy and it is us.'[2] Salaam.

A Jewish participant spoke up as well, reflecting on his own experience as an advocate for human rights for Palestinians who suffer under the Israeli occupation:

'Us' is the biggest threat to the Jewish community today as we try to deal with the horror of what our national homeland project has brought us to. There is a civil war going on within the Jewish community – brother/sister against brother/sister. There are very clear rules on what you cannot feel and say about Israel. They are based on a profound denial of the pain of our history (yes – denial, although that may seem strange to say, given the focus, even preoccupation with the Nazi Holocaust, and indeed all of Jewish history for the past 2,000 years.) But here's the evidence for that fundamental denial: the projection of our fear and pain onto the Palestinians. The behavior that says: we are only safe if we take what is yours. The behavior that says: the violence is in you, not us. That says: the danger is out there, not in here. And in order to maintain the denial, avoid the fear, disown the violence, the rules are enforced. The rules are two: (1) Jewish 'sensitivities' trump all other values: 'don't say that, it makes us feel insecure'. 'Don't say that, it could be perceived as anti-Semitism.' (2) Don't touch the Zionist ideology. Nibble around the edges, talk about Palestinian rights, but don't touch the thing itself: the Land is ours. Those of us who break the rules pay that price.

I was especially fascinated when he added this:

> [This] is why the story of the gospels is so critically relevant for us now. The critical conversation happening in the first century when the church was being born was among Jews, not between Jews and Gentiles. Jesus, as a Jew, came as a reformer, as one challenging who 'Us' had become. So that's why we need Jesus today. I mean we Jews need Jesus. Not to become Christians, but to become better Jews.[3]

My Muslim and Jewish friends, like many of my Christian friends, are converging on a similar conclusion: all our religious identities need reform. We need to become better Muslims, better Jews and better Christians. (And we all agree that Jesus has a lot to offer to all of us in this predicament.) But doing so will demand a high cost from us. It will subject us to criticism and maybe even threats and worse – from our religious fellows.

Even so, the single greatest obstacle to rethinking Christian identity won't be imposed from the outside by other people, whether 'us' or 'them'. The single greatest obstacle will arise inside each of us. Your greatest obstacle will be in you and mine will be in me. In the end, it's not the threats of others that cause me to shrink back, but rather my own fear. It's not the difficulty of rethinking long-held beliefs that will discourage me, but my stubborn refusal to accept that difficulty. It's not the danger of being criticised or rejected that will cause me to abandon identity reform, but my self-protective reflex to avoid the danger. If enough of us count these internal costs and accept them – beginning with the fear, refusal and self-protective reflexes within each of us, a strong-benevolent Christian identity can and will emerge.

But there's always an easy way out, an escape clause – the temptation to stop thinking, to suppress our questions and concerns, to submit to intimidation, to 'go along' and 'get along', to resign ourselves to hostility – maybe a nice, respectable, moderate hostility. And of course, there's a cost to that escape route, too.

So there are costs either way, costs we all must count, some of them agonising.

Many parents of gay children feel this agony (these days, anyway – it may be different in the future). I think of a friend of mine who came from the same background of Christian fundamentalism I hail from. When his son came out, he had no support to help him accept the possibility that his son could be both gay and good. With deep ambivalence, he stood with his tradition and condemned his son. The cost – alienation from his son – was high, but it grew unspeakably higher when his son internalised the rejection and condemnation of his community and took his own life. Or I think of another friend, the mother of a gay son, also from my heritage. She came to me in secret to talk, knowing that one of my sons had come out around the same time as hers. Through tears she said, 'I feel like I'm being forced to choose between my father and my son. If I affirm my son, I'm rejecting everything my father stood for. If I stand with my father, I'm rejecting my son.'

In religion as in parenthood, uncritical loyalty to our ancestors may implicate us in an injustice against our descendants: imprisoning them in the errors of our ancestors. Yes, there are costs either way.

CHAPTER 7

How an Atheist Made – and Missed – an Essential Point about Religion

In fact, it may well be that, for all our talk of a postenlighten-
ment new world order, most wars in our time are still, at root,
fueled by pathological religious passions, however vehemently
denied at the official levels ... Despotic theology ... leads
directly to despotic theocracy. Tyrannical Gods breed tyrannical
humans. And vice versa.

Richard Kearney[1]

Do you hear statements like these as often as I do?

'Religions, especially monotheistic ones, are inherently
violent.'

'Most wars are caused by religion.'

'Imagine a world with no religions. Wouldn't it be a more
peaceable place?'

Whether you consider them to be clichés, truisms, exaggera-
tions, myths or blasphemies depends on your assumptions and
experience. Many people agree with outspoken atheist Sam

Harris who, before specifying about a dozen centres of conflict in today's world, makes this generalisation:

> Incompatible religious doctrines have balkanized our world into separate moral communities, and these divisions have become a continuous source of bloodshed. Indeed, religion is as much a living spring of violence today as it has been at any time in the past . . . Religion has been the explicit cause of literally millions of deaths in recent decades.[2]

Then he asks why religion has been so fruitful in terms of violence rather than peace, and answers his question simply and confidently:

> There is no other sphere of discourse in which human beings so fully articulate their differences from one another, or cast these differences in terms of everlasting rewards and punishments. Religion is the one endeavor in which us–them thinking achieves a transcendent significance. If you really believe that calling God by the right name can spell the difference between eternal happiness and eternal suffering, then it becomes quite reasonable to treat heretics and unbelievers rather badly. The stakes of our religious differences are immeasurably higher than those born of mere tribalism, racism, or politics.

Obviously, I agree with Sam Harris that religion plays a big and ugly role in creating and sustaining hostility in our world.[3] But I think he's mistaken when he locates the tensions between religions only in their differences.[4] Yes, religious differences can indeed lead to division, and division to hostility, and hostility to violence, and so there is indeed a danger to religious differences.[5] But achieving and sustaining sameness can lead us into other cycles of violence no less vicious. Secular totalitarian regimes, for example, typically attempt to produce their version of peace through the suppression of difference and the promotion of sameness. The results have been horrifying.[6]

Treating difference-based religious violence with peace through secular sameness may be like treating stage-four pancreatic cancer with stage-four colon cancer. When secularists see no hope for peace apart from the eradication of religion from the earth, they open up possible atheistic scenarios that could easily become as scary as the theocratic scenarios of their counterparts.[7]

That's why, as someone who agrees with Sam Harris about the danger of religious violence, I propose a diagnosis quite different from his. *The tensions between our conflicted religions arise not from our differences, but from one thing we all hold in common: an oppositional religious identity that derives strength from hostility.*

When religions – including Christianity – grow strong by incorporating hostility to otherness into their identity, they become more like one another. In light of that similarity, their differences seem increasingly trivial. Like rival twins, they are joined in the conflicted unity of a hostile identity, differing in content but mirroring one another in attitude and behaviour.[8] As a result, they begin to appear as different manifestations of the same religion – the religion of us-them hostility – rather than as different religions. As Jack Nelson-Pallmeyer says: 'If religion and faith are about ultimate allegiance, then it can be said that violence is the world's principal religion.'[9]

Now by *identity* I mean an array of characteristics that make an individual recognisable as a member or an affiliate of a group, or that make one group recognisable and distinct from others. Those characteristics might include matters of dress, hairstyle, bodily marking or mutilation, or skin colour.[10] They might include matters of diet, schedule, ritual or language. They might include matters of belief, attitude, affection or opposition. Whatever the markers, these indicators help us transcend personal selfishness in what Jonathan Haidt calls *groupishness*, and groupishness has survival value that grows from a group's ability to circle around a sacred centre.

Despite what you might have learned in Economics 101, people aren't always selfish. In politics, they're more often groupish. When people feel that a group they value – be it racial, religious, regional or ideological – is under attack, they rally to its defence, even at some cost to themselves. We evolved to be tribal, and politics is a competition among coalitions of tribes.

The key to understanding tribal behaviour is not money, it's sacredness. The great trick that humans developed at some point in the last few hundred thousand years is the ability to circle around a tree, rock, ancestor, flag, book or god, and then treat that thing as sacred. People who worship the same idol can trust one another, work as a team and prevail over less cohesive groups. So if you want to understand politics, and especially our divisive culture wars, you must follow the sacredness.[11]

Social psychoanalyst Vamik Volkan theorises that groupishness produces a potentially dangerous side effect: an attitude of superiority about 'us' and a corresponding tendency to dehumanise 'them':

> . . . at the outset of human history, each human group developed
> a distinct sense of identity, wearing skins and feathers like armor
> to protect it from other groups who wore different kinds of skins
> and feathers. [Erik] Erikson hypothesized that each group
> became convinced that it was the sole possessor of the true
> human identity. Thus each group became a pseudospecies, adopt-
> ing an attitude of superiority over other groups.[12]

With Erikson, Volkan describes how children enter the world as
'generalists', devoid of the concepts or categories of nationality,
ethnicity and religion. Gradually, influential adults induct children into the various large-group identities that frame adult
lives: they are male or female, Americans or Australians, Hutu
or Twa, Republicans or Democrats, Christians or agnostics, rich
or poor, high-caste or low-caste, and so on. In imagery parallel
to Haidt's description of a tribe circling around a sacred centre,
Volkan adapts Peter Berger's image of a 'sacred canopy', comparing large-group identities to big tents under which children
grow.[13] In the shelter of these big tents of ethnic, national, tribal
and religious identity, children develop their individual identities, expressed for example in their chosen styles of dress or hair
or speech. They normally take the larger identity for granted
until it is threatened or becomes a problem for them in some
way.[14] A problematised group identity may then plunge them
into a crisis of personal identity – because *who I am* is bound up
in the struggle of *who we are*. Volkan explains:

> In our routine lives we are more concerned with subgroups under
> the tent: families or professional organizations, for example.
> Our relationship with our large-group identity, in ordinary times,

is like breathing. While we breathe constantly, we do not usually notice it unless our ability to breathe is threatened, such as if we are caught in a smoke-filled house on fire. When the large-group identity is threatened, people under the metaphorical tent become like the people who are caught in a smoke-filled room. They become constantly aware of their large-group identities and become preoccupied with its [sic] protection and maintenance, even if this preoccupation leads to destructive acts.[15]

So my evolving personal sense of *who I am* is normally strengthened and supported by a stable groupish sense of *who we are*. But when *who we are* is threatened or destabilised in some way, my *who I am* is also threatened, and not just mine, but also the *who I am* of all my neighbours. Unified and energised by a perceived threat, and driven by survival instincts from our unconscious, evolutionary past, our fight/flight mechanisms activate, preparing us – if we cannot flee – for hostility.

The individual body prepares for a fight by pumping adrenaline into the system. The heart beats faster, respiration accelerates, muscles tense and warm, pain centres prepare for an onslaught, reactions are heightened. The religious, social or political body similarly prepares by pumping a kind of social adrenaline into society. This social adrenaline must prepare us for conflict, conflict that each society must normally inhibit in order to keep the peace. The group must, in other words, prepare to break the rules by which it normally functions. We in the group must, to a degree, suspend our normal pursuits – business, agriculture, art, sport and recreation in civil society, and worship, teaching, fellowship and prayer in religious communities. We must divert a portion of our attention and energy to hostility, and we must focus that hostility on a target – real or imagined, legitimate or manufactured, among *them* (as a classic enemy) or among *us* (as an internal scapegoat).

Once the target of hostility is identified, our threatened group identity begins to energise itself by emphasising our goodness and the target's evil, our innocence and the target's guilt, our uniqueness or chosen-ness and the target's banality, our desire for peace and the target's desire for violence, and so on. Thus we are given permission to see ourselves as good, as innocent victims, as lovers of peace who are authorised to use violence in order to restore peace. And we are given permission to see the enemy as irrational, evil, demonic, even subhuman. Recalling the words of James Alison we considered earlier, we are simultaneously defining ourselves and uniting ourselves through our shared hostility.[16]

The identified enemy may pose an actual threat. For example, the Al Qaeda network may actually plot the murder of Christians (perhaps more as Westerners than as Christians per se, a worthwhile distinction to keep in mind). And some Christian extremists really do believe that Muslims must either be converted, contained and marginalised or eradicated.

But the identified enemy may also simply be an innocent bystander, chosen to fill the role of a scapegoat upon whom the group's anxieties may be focused and around whose removal (by expulsion or killing) the group may be unified. One thinks, for example, of women identified as witches during the outbreaks of witch-hunting in Christian history, or the peculiar obsession among some Christians in America and Africa with the 'the gay agenda'. Sometimes, the enemy may not even exist except in the imaginations of the anxious, as is often the case with conspiracy theories.

When we increasingly understand who we are in relation to an enemy – whether that enemy is legitimate, innocent or imaginary – we develop an increasingly hostile identity. Such an identity teaches us to see *sameness as safety* and *otherness as danger*. It is characterised by duality: us and them, right and wrong, good and evil, light and darkness. It promotes a mentality of us *versus* them, us *apart from* them, us *instead of* them, us *without* them, us *over* them, us *using* them, us *in spite of* them, us *oppressed by* them, or us *occupying* them, but never us *for* them or us *with* them.

It teaches us to see the long-term existence and well-being of *them* or *the other* as unacceptable, perhaps as an offence or threat to us and our religion, and perhaps even as an offence to God. It requires us to believe that the world would be a better place without *them* in it as *them*, and it only allows us to accept the other by converting them to be part of *us*, so they are no longer *other*. Ultimately, a hostile or oppositional identity values *us* as inherently more human, more holy, more acceptable, more pure or more worthy than *them*. After all, if *they* were good, they would ask to be admitted under *our* sacred canopy and they would join us in circling around *our* sacred centre.

So I'm convinced, with Sam Harris and many others, that religion does indeed play a critical role in human conflict. But I'm certain the problem is less simple and more interesting than our typical discussions of the subject might suggest. Our root problem is neither religious *difference* nor religious *identity*, nor even *strong* religious identity. Our root problem is the *hostility* that we often employ to make and keep our identities strong

– whether those identities are political, economic, philosophical, scientific or religious.

It is not merely our differences that divide us, then, but a profound similarity – the oppositional way in which we build strong identities. It's an easy shortcut that takes us places we never intended to go.

CHAPTER 8

How (Not) to Create a Strong-Benevolent Christian Identity

It's difficult to get a man to understand something when his salary depends upon his not understanding it.

Upton Sinclair

Let's imagine we are so brokenhearted by the fruits of hostility in our Christian history that we decide to water down, dilute, de-emphasise and otherwise weaken Christian identity altogether so there will be less hostility in the future. What might happen?

With a loss of strong Christian identity, we could for a while draw on the bank account of Christian legacy, the accumulated personal and social capital created when Christian identity was strong. But over time, if we make more withdrawals than deposits, the benefits of that legacy will shrink. If no strong-and-benevolent religious identity replaces our strong-and-hostile Christian identity, the majority of us would in all likelihood be left with consumerism as our dominant cultural ethos.[1] We would then embark on a massive cultural experiment: can humanity live by bread (and circuses, and gadgets) alone? Can a healthy, sustainable identity – personal and social – be built under the big tent of corporate media and corporate politics by whose godlike provision we enjoy our daily bread? Can our lives consist in the abundance of products we buy, the standard of living we seek, the economic policies we consider orthodox and the debt load we carry?

If we in the so-called *developed world* embark on this experiment (might we have done so already without realising it?), we will find consumerism to be the strongest but most subtle identity of all. We will discover that consumerism comes equipped with its own set of hostilities and consequences, many of which will prove every bit as catastrophic as those of the old Christian hostility.[2] And here's the kicker: in such a consumerist system, a weak and benign form of Christianity or any other religion would be cherished and rewarded. It would provide the perfect chaplaincy or priesthood to support and enhance the established consumerist enterprise, giving it an air of legitimacy and even sacredness, and never playing the role of prophet to confront the status quo and challenge its legitimacy.[3]

Let's play out the scenario a little bit farther. A consumerist society, without a higher framing story or sacred vision to resource it, would probably produce decreasing levels of personal responsibility, self-restraint, community-mindedness, reconciliation, or concern for equity, fidelity, loyalty and personal morality. Losses in those areas would probably lead to corresponding losses in personal and social well-being that may in turn lead to rising levels of addiction, competition, divorce, crime, social conflict, violence, accelerated exploitation of others and of the environment, and so on.

What will be left to hold individuals, families, communities and nations together when our legacy of Christian virtues breaks down like decaying, unmaintained social infrastructure and when consumerism runs its bitter course?

Many of us would probably feel a poignant nostalgia for the good old days when Christian identity was strong. A whole range of new strong identities would then form to fill the vacuum. Some of us might affiliate with a reinvigorated ideology like capitalism, communism, libertarianism or Ayn Randian objectivism. Some might gravitate towards a revived ethnic or class identity – white supremacy, black power or the proletariat. Some might join strong secular political parties or nativist movements, and others would choose (or be chosen by) a strong non-religious power structure like a gang or mafia. Some of us might move towards strong and violent revolutionary movements – whether religious (like Al Qaeda) or non-religious (like Pol Pot's Khmer Rouge). And many of us, no doubt, would seek to revive old forms of oppositional, hostile Christianity, seeking a neo-Christendom complete with neo-Crusades, neo-witch hunts and so on.

When we engage in this kind of imaginative exercise, a sobering realisation begins to set in. In our attempts to exorcise the strong and hostile religious identities that are so familiar to us, we may be possessed by the demons of other identities that are equally strong and perhaps even more hostile.[4] The old truism echoes back to us once again: the only good antidote to bad religion is not no religion, but good religion, or, slightly altered, the antidote to strong-hostile religion is not weak-benign religion, but strong-benevolent religion.

So, if both strong-hostile and weak-benign Christian identities produce undesirable unintended consequences, we have to imagine ways both can be redeemed and transformed into what we need. This thought experiment involving a ten-item test might help us in that re-imagination process:

Respond to each item using this 0–5 scale:

0 = absolutely untrue

1 = strongly disagree

2 = disagree

3 = somewhat agree

4 = agree

5 = strongly agree

1. *Validity*: My Christian faith is highly significant to me because it adds true meaning and value to my life.

2. *Intentionality*: For me, Christian faith is not merely an unchosen inheritance, a social custom, a matter of convenience or the path of least resistance; it is an intentional commitment that I uphold and practise by conscious choice.

3. *Durability*: I plan to remain at least as committed to my Christian faith as I am now, over the course of my lifetime, through both hard times and easy times, and I hope to pass vital Christian faith on to my children and grandchildren.

4. *Intensity*: My Christian faith is so central to my life that it requires of me sacrifices and commitments that are sometimes costly and even painful.

5. *Purity/Consistency*: I conform to the beliefs, behaviours, habits, examples, prohibitions, ideas and values that are consistent with my Christian faith, and I resist or reject their opposites as inconsistent with my Christian faith.

6. *History*: I consider myself to be part of the history and traditions of my faith community; Christian history is in some real sense my history.

7. *Responsibility*: I feel responsible for the health and well-being of the Christian community, now and in the future.

8. *Missionality*: I invest my time, energy, money and abilities to participate in the Christian mission as I understand it.

9. *Loyalty*: I feel a special sense of loyalty to my fellow Christians because we are connected to one another through our shared faith and mission.

10. *Hostility*: I see other faiths as wrong, false or evil, and I maintain a posture of opposition to all faiths but the Christian faith.

Now imagine that a score of zero to twenty-five would indicate a weak Christian identity, a score of twenty-six to thirty-nine would indicate a moderate Christian identity, and a score of forty to fifty would indicate a strong Christian identity. How would you score on this test? Would you consider these results an accurate assessment of the strength of your Christian identity?

If your score was low or moderate, would you say that an aversion to hostility (Item 10) has led to an overall weakening of your Christian identity? If your score was high, how do you feel about the tenth item? Is it essential to the list? Must you as a Christian maintain hostility to other faiths if you are going to hold a strong Christian identity? Could you imagine the tenth item being replaced with this alternative indicator?

10. *Solidarity*: My understanding of Jesus and his message leads me to see each faith, including my own, as having its own

history, value, strengths and weaknesses. I seek to affirm and celebrate all that is good in each faith, and I build intentional relationships of mutual sharing and respectful collaboration with people of all faiths, so all our faiths can keep growing and contributing to God's will being done on earth as in heaven.

If hostility could be replaced by solidarity, would any of the previous nine items need to be changed?[5] How might the substitution strengthen them? What obstacles stand in the way of this kind of substitution? What kind of re-engineering of the first nine items would a substitution of the tenth require? For example, if we replaced hostility with solidarity, how would we need to rethink the validity or history of our faith, or how would our understanding of mission and loyalty change? Do these kinds of changes seem sensible and modest to you, or radical and revolutionary?

Clearly, if the Christian faith of 2117 or 2517 is going to be less hostile and more peaceable than the Christian faith of 1517 or 2017, profound change at all levels will be required of us.

We might wish for our paid clergy to provide bold leadership in this change process. But we must be realistic about the ways in which 'the religious-industrial complex' profits by maintaining the status quo of strong-oppositional identity on the one hand and weak-benign identity on the other. Every religious professional can imagine a scenario of fear playing out like this: *If we boldly step out and preach against Christian hostility, we will be seen as betrayers of strong identity. Religious gatekeepers on websites and in magazines will single us out as liberal, relativist and weak.[6] As a result, our vital statistics will plummet*

– meaning losses of bums in seats and dollars in budgets. Our churches, denominations, agencies, seminaries, mission agencies and pensions will suffer. And shortly thereafter, we will be unemployed.[7]

Just as we might wish that more clergy were willing to take that risk, our clergy might wish that more of the rest of us were willing to step forward in a grassroots movement of RSR (religious social responsibility) to complement CSR (corporate social responsibility). Just as we need corporations to convert from dirty fossil fuels to clean, sustainable energy, we need the religion industry to be converted from its reliance on the toxic energy of oppositional identity and hostility. We need to research, develop and deploy the renewable and renewing fuel source of divine-human kindness and benevolence. Through advocacy, education and conversation – and perhaps the religious equivalents of boycotts, carrot mobs and buycotts – we will need to gently but firmly pressure our religious institutions to stop polluting our environment with toxic beliefs and rhetoric that raise our global social temperature and push us ever closer to conflict and collapse.[8] We need our religious institutions to do what we need all our institutions to do: put long-term benefit (or *the common good*) over short-term profit (for *us* and not *them*). We need to imagine Jesus' own voice asking, 'What shall it profit you to have a big, fat, rich, powerful religion when the bullets are flying and the nuclear bombs are falling and the world is being destroyed because of your religious hostility?'

As this kind of grass-roots movement gains momentum, more and more courageous and creative Christian leaders will emerge to communicate and embed this new strong-benevolent identity in sermons, books, liturgies, prayers, hymns, curricula for adults and kids and mission plans. Over time, as others 'taste and see' how good this new identity is in practice, it will spread and become increasingly normative. The ultimate result won't simply be a change in Christian identity: it will be a new direction in human history.

But before we consider that new direction in the future, we need to look back at our past, because the past walks with us in the present in more ways than we know.

CHAPTER 9

How a Liberal Arts Education Ruined My Opinion of Christopher Columbus

There is a word, an Igbo word, that I think about whenever I think about the power structures of the world, and it is *nkali*. It's a noun that loosely translates to 'to be greater than another.' Like our economic and political worlds, stories too are defined by the principle of *nkali*. How they are told, who tells them, when they're told, how many stories are told, are really dependent on power.

Power is the ability not just to tell the story of another person, but to make it the definitive story of that person. The Palestinian poet Mourid Barghouti writes that if you want to dispossess a people, the simplest way to do it is to tell their story, and to start with, 'secondly'. Start the story with the arrows of the Native Americans, and not with the arrival of the British, and you have an entirely different story. Start the story with the failure of the African state, and not with the colonial creation of the African state, and you have an entirely different story.

Chimamanda Adichie[1]

Why do we Christians have an oppositional or hostile identity today? In large part, the answer lies in our history. And our history hides more complexity than many of us realise. Yes, we are rooted in Jesus and the apostles, as we'd expect, and yes, Jesus and the apostles were rooted in Judaism. But Christians today also have deep historical roots in the Roman Empire, and so to understand our hostility, we must come to terms with our Roman imperial history.

Now by *history*, I don't simply mean the objective record of *what we did and what happened to us*. Rather, our history is *how we understand and interpret what we did and how we understand and interpret what happened to us*. The differences and tensions between *what happened* and *how we interpret and understand what happened* are highly nuanced and highly interesting.

I began to grapple with these differences and tensions, as many people do, in my teenage years, especially when I went to university. The 'liberal' in 'liberal arts education', I came to understand, had to do with being liberated or freed from one unchallenged viewpoint, one single, unquestioned story, one authorised and conventional interpretation of our past. When I was exposed to the insights of people from across many centuries in my own culture, and even more, when I was exposed to the insights from varied historical contexts from many diverse cultures, I began to experience that liberation. But it wasn't all pleasant. Liberation of this sort can be rather disillusioning and depressing, at least in the short run. Take my view of the man who 'discovered' America, Christopher Columbus.

I had grown up in one of the most highly rated public school systems in the United States. There I learned the standard, state-of-the-art 1960s version of American history. I knew without any doubt, as did my classmates, that my history classes taught me objective fact, not propaganda. Of course in other countries, especially Communist countries, teachers taught their children distorted, sanitised and false histories. But here in the United States, I knew we were free and we learned the truth, the whole truth and nothing but the truth. So in my primary and secondary education, like most kids, I read my history textbooks, watched a few films (older readers will remember *filmstrips*, the archaic precursor to the slideshow and video), listened to lectures, took notes and usually passed my tests with flying colours, thinking I 'knew American history', which included knowing about Christopher Columbus.

Early on I learned, as all American schoolkids do, that Columbus sailed the ocean blue in 1492. Because of his courageous voyage into the unknown, he was a hero, a brave explorer, a model worthy of a public holiday every September. Yes, I learned that he mistakenly thought he had arrived in India when he had actually made landfall in what we call the Dominican Republic, part of the island of Hispaniola. (My Native American friends like to say that their ancestors discovered Columbus in 1492.) But apart from that one small and highly forgivable error, Columbus remained for us a heroic figure.

It wasn't until my college years that I learned the darker sides of the Christopher Columbus story, starting with his brutal treatment of the native people of Hispaniola, the Taino. As Thom Hartmann explains in *The Last Hours of Ancient Sunlight*, part of the 'booty' of Columbus's second voyage in 1495 were sixteen hundred male and female Taino slaves to be exported to Spain.[2] He wrote to the Spanish king and queen, 'It is possible, with the name of the Holy Trinity, to sell all the slaves which it is possible to sell . . . Here there are so many of these slaves . . . although they are living things they are as good as gold.'[3]

The Spaniards who remained in Hispaniola were encouraged to take Taino slaves 'in the amount desired'. Columbus himself gave a teenage girl to one of his crew, Miguel Cuneo, for his personal 'use'. Cuneo wrote that she 'resisted with all her strength' when he attempted to have sex with her, so he 'thrashed her mercilessly and raped her'. Being given a Taino woman to rape was, in fact, a popular 'company perk' for Columbus's men. Columbus himself wrote to a friend, 'There are plenty of dealers who go about looking for girls; those from nine to ten [years old] are now in demand.'

If the Taino people resisted Spanish exploitation (and if they survived smallpox and other diseases the Spanish brought with them), they would be maimed, attacked with dogs, 'skewered on poles from anus to mouth' or shot. No wonder many committed suicide, as a more sympathetic Spaniard wrote in 1517. It is hard to read his account without tears:

> As a result of the sufferings and hard labor they endured, the Indians choose and have chosen suicide. Occasionally a hundred have committed mass suicide. The women, exhausted by labor, have shunned conception and childbirth . . . Many, when pregnant, have taken something to abort and have aborted. Others after delivery have killed their children with their own hands, so as not to leave them in such oppressive slavery.[4]

Of the estimated 300,000 Taino alive when Columbus 'discovered' them in 1492, about 12,000 remained in 1516, fewer than

200 in 1546, and zero in 1555. What our history calls 'the discovery of America', Taino history might call 'the arrival of the Christian genociders', if, that is, any Taino survived to tell an alternate history. None did.

I never learned the story of the Taino in my secondary education. But I did learn a cute (and misleading) tale about the pilgrims inviting Squanto over for a hospitable Thanksgiving dinner. I never learned about the early colonists' common practice of comparing the Native Peoples of New England to the Canaanites in the Bible, thus rendering them a legitimate target for displacement and genocide.[5] But I did learn an inspiring (and distorted) story of a romance between John Smith and Pocahontas.[6] I never learned about the US government's staggering record of slaughter, land theft and broken treaties with the Native Americans from the Atlantic to the Pacific, nor did I learn about the boarding schools and their abuse of Native American children. But I did learn about the Indian Wars, always told from the perspective of the good white people who, on their intrepid journey west, were constantly being harassed and attacked by those brutal, ignorant, rebellious and duplicitous savages.

I imagine that Canadian, Mexican and Filipino children (and more recently, no doubt, Panamanian, Haitian, Iraqi and Afghan children) learn in their history classes about US invasions of their countries. But according to my secondary education in the 1960s, the United States never invaded anybody.[7] We may have come in to help when needed, but our intentions were always purely humanitarian. After all, we were and are 'one nation, under God, indivisible, with liberty and justice for all'.

If these were simply isolated incidents, a few gaps or slips in an otherwise excellent history education, they would be serious enough. But during and after my university years, I came to see that there was a pattern to the errors and omissions in my education. An agenda was in play. Far from being objective, my textbooks and teachers and therefore my exams and term paper assignments all expressed a consistent point of view, a single story, a *vested interest*. They embedded certain unconscious assumptions in all our minds. They supported a predetermined set of values, a specific alignment of powers and a coherent way of behaviour. In other words, their single, unquestioned story helped form a useful American identity which I, as a good American boy, embraced and inhabited as my own.

A few years later in college, under the influence of a good liberal arts education, my 'American exceptionalism' was repeatedly sideswiped and finally totalled as I read more books, met more people, and travelled to more places around the world where I listened to stories told from the perspectives of others. Now, I must acknowledge that my nation's history is not so exceptional, but rather has much in common with the histories of Rwanda, Sierra Leone, Israel-Palestine or South Africa.[8] Now I must acknowledge that my country's history is both heroic and tragic, glorious and shameful, beautiful and blemished. Now, as my sense of American history has been revolutionised, so has my American identity. You've probably had similar awakenings – more or less rude – that led you to similar conclusions and disorientations. (And if you haven't, may I recommend a liberal arts education?)[9]

Once we acknowledge that there's a big and complex difference between *what actually happened* and *how we interpret, understand and recount what actually happened*, an obvious question presents itself: What effects might this kind of history education – or indoctrination – have on a whole nation of kids as they grow up and take the reins of power in America? How would this or that version of American history tend to shape American identity – who we invade, who we bomb, who we protect, who we welcome, who we shun, who we trust, who we fear?

What is true for Americans is also true for Christians – in the US, but also in Denmark and the UK, in Nigeria and Kenya, in India and Singapore, in Guatemala and Brazil. We Christians will not experience a reorientation of our identity until we are willing to go through a profound rethinking of our history. We will never truly deal with the worst parts of our past by denying or minimising them, but only by facing them, honestly, humbly and fully. That is what the Bible calls *repentance*.

In Kent Nerburn's *Wolf at Twilight*, a Lakota elder powerfully articulates to a Caucasian writer what historical repentance looks like: 'When you look at black people, you see ghosts of all the slavery and the rapes and the hangings and the chains. When you look at Jews, you see ghosts of all those bodies piled up in the death camps. And those ghosts keep you trying to do the right thing.' But the stories of the Native Peoples are still minimised and marginalised, he explains, so 'when you look at us, you don't see the ghosts of the little babies with their heads smashed in by rifle butts at the Big Hole, or the old folks dying by the side of the trail on the way to Oklahoma while their families cried and tried to make them comfortable, or the dead mothers at Wounded Knee or the little kids at Sand Creek who were shot for target practice'.

Until we hear those stories and feel their import, the Lakota elder suggests, others remain *the other*, not *us*; *their kind*, not *our kind*. If we sustain ourselves in an oppositional identity by the way we sanitise our history, if we hold ourselves at a distance from the other, we 'can turn them into slaves or kill six million of them or shoot them into mass graves at Wounded Knee'. If, to put a twist on an old saying, we only learn and tell one sanitised, privileged version of our history, we will repeat the worst parts of it. But if we bring our secrets into the light, according to the Good News we proclaim, we can be redeemed, re-identified, born again.

CHAPTER 10

How Constantine Prepared the Way for Columbus

Once one comes to possess an identity document, one is bound to the ground of that identity document, whether it be about national or religious affiliation, or a particular advocacy cause, and so on. One begins then to be 'attached' to the very ground of such 'identity.' Here a passport symbolizes classification, categorization, homogenization, totalization, genderization, sexualization, racialization, ethnicization, and so forth. The passport fundamentally limits the endless dimension of one's 'neighbors,' one's 'friends,' to a certain 'category,' especially when there is, in our reality, a 'strong' passport and a 'weak' one. Theologians-without-passports intentionally dissociate themselves from the dominant power, practice, or discourse that totalizes, categorizes, classifies an individual person into a stereotypical box, numbers and data. Theologians-without-passports commit themselves to 'make a contribution to the universal community,' to the Reign of God, where every individual human being is equal to everyone else, treated justly, accepted fully as who one is.

Namsoon Kang[1]

If we Christians are taught much Christian history at all, we learn versions that are no less sanitised than my introduction to Christopher Columbus in public school. Take, for example, the historical episode often called 'the conversion of Emperor Constantine'.

Whether it's in Sunday School, youth group, summer camp, a sermon, a confirmation class or a Christian college or seminary classroom, we typically learn that in AD 312, the Emperor had a vision of a cross in the sky, and we're told that the cross had an inscription of three words: 'Conquer by this.'[2] So far, so accurate.

But are we ever encouraged to ponder what these three fateful words meant – perhaps, 'Terrorise by this,' or 'Force conversions by this,' or 'Kill by this,' or 'Expand your violent theocracy by this'? Do these words trouble us?

Are we told that the upright beam of the cross in Constantine's vision was a spear? Is any suggestion ever made that this re-appropriation of the cross by Constantine signals its de-Christianisation and re-Romanisation? Is there any mention, in this context, of Jesus' words about the future of those who live by the sword (or, we might add, spear)? Do we ever see even a shred of irony when the instrument of Roman torture and execution on which Jesus had been brutally killed is once again employed to instil fear and terror, but now, not merely in the name of Rome and its emperor who nailed others to it, but in the name of . . . one who was once nailed to it?

All this becomes even clearer if we imagine a different conversion, one that never happened but could have. Instead of a gold-plated, bejewelled spear-cross with the words 'Threaten and kill by this,' imagine that Constantine had seen a vision of a basin and a towel with the words, 'Serve by this,' or a vision of a simple table of bread and wine with 'Reconcile around this,' or a vision of Christ's outstretched arms with 'Embrace like this,' or a vision of the birds of the air and flowers of the field with 'Trust like this,' or a vision of a mother hen gathering her chicks with 'Love like this,' or a vision of a dove descending from heaven with the words, 'Be as kind as this.'[3] But it was not so.

As with Columbus in 1492, so with Constantine in 312: the ways we retell our history form our identity. Our Christian histó-ries, like our political ones, shield us from the full truth about how we became who we are and, in so doing, they keep us from seeing ourselves as others see us. Our standard histories support an oppositional identity where 'we' are the virtuous ones, the victims, the defenders of truth, the peacemakers, and 'they' are the aggressors, the invaders, the heretics, the evil ones. Some no doubt overreact to this self-defensive history by exaggerating 'our' evil and minimising theirs. But this mirror image of histori-cal distortion doesn't buffer its opposite as intended; in fact, it only serves to strengthen the defensiveness of those who tell the single dominant story with its more familiar distortions.

In seeking to strike a healthy and honest balance in telling our history (a never-ending task, by the way), I'm convinced that we Christians – Western Christians in particular – must acknowl-edge the degree to which our faith has become a syncretised faith, a compromised faith, we might even say a corrupted faith. From Constantine to Columbus to the other Conquistadors to the Colonisers to the present, we have mixed authentically Christian elements of love, joy, peace and reconciliation with strictly imperial elements of superiority, conquest, domination and hostility. We have created a new religion with an identity far different from the one proclaimed and embodied by Jesus in Galilee, or by James and Peter in Jerusalem, or by Paul around the Mediterranean, or by the Christian scholars of the second and third centuries. In other words, what we call Christianity today has a history, and this history reveals it as a Roman, imperial version of Christianity.[4]

The word *imperial*, of course, requires definition. By it I mean a system of thought and behaviour based on empire, which is an integrated system of domination, subordination, expansion and assimilation.[5] In particular, recalling the pivotal story of Constantine's Christian conversion (ambiguity intended), I mean a system of Christian thought and practice that functions within (and often as a fractal of) the Roman Empire's prime model of domination, subordination, expansion and assimilation. Seen in this light, Columbus truly was a faithful Roman-Imperial Christian, however gravely his violent deeds betray the actual life and teachings of Jesus.

If we are to move forward wisely from this point, we can't simply seek to remove those imperial elements from our telling. It's not enough, in other words, to cover up the past and promise to do better going forward. To do so would be to deny and minimise the damage that has already been done, and that kind of denial is, predictably, typical of an imperial mind-set.

So we must not soft-pedal the degree to which these hostile, imperial elements have become an inescapable feature of our Christian history. We must acknowledge that they have played a critical role in creating both Christianity as we show it and the world as we know it. And these imperial elements have also, we must realise, played a critical role in creating us. So we must confess that we are imperial Christian people, part of an imperial Christian faith, and our world has been infused with imperial Christian hostility.

If this imperial hostility is such a deeply embedded element of our Christian identity, we must do the hard work of recounting our whole history in light of it. Doing so will be humbling. It will have the character of a confession. It will force us to stop seeing ourselves as the good guys and others as the bad guys. It will require us to acknowledge, as I did in my blog post after novelist Anne Rice 'quit Christianity', that our religion, like every other religion, is in some real sense *a failed religion.*[6]

Contrary to expectations, these confessions will not prompt us to reject our heritage; they will rather make it possible for us to redeem our heritage and resurrect from it a new Christian identity, characterised by humility, strength and benevolence.

Such confessions will also clear our vision, making it possible for us to see 'the other' in a new light. Take, for example, the way we see adherents of the world's second-largest religion, Islam.

CHAPTER 11

How Constantine Prepared the Way for Today's Headlines

It is my ardent hope that Muslim and Christian religious leaders and teachers will present our two great religious communities as communities in respectful dialogue, never more as communities in conflict. It is crucial for the young to be taught the ways of respect and understanding, so that they will not be led to misuse religion itself to promote or justify hatred and violence. Violence destroys the image of the Creator in his creatures, and should never be considered as the fruit of religious conviction.

Pope John Paul II[1]

Christians from conservative backgrounds like mine have a simple way of telling the story of Mohammed and his spiritual descendants. Our version of Muslim history, deeply embedded in the Roman Christian tradition of Constantine, goes like this: Mohammed was a false prophet who received a demonic vision.[2] He denied key Christian doctrines and created a counterfeit religion that holds people in darkness and will lead them straight to hell unless Christians intervene so they can be converted. His religion spread by the sword, holding people as captives through tyranny and terror. It is (since the defeat of godless communism) the greatest existing threat to Christians and Christianity.[3]

Some might temper this rather harsh depiction, acknowledging that the 'seeds of the Word' can even be sown into that dark and dangerous religion. They might acknowledge certain good elements in Islam. But they will generally follow those concessions with a statement of Christian superiority, suggesting, for example, that the Christian God is pure Reason while the Muslim God is pure Will.[4]

But there is another way to tell the story of Islam. This alternative telling emerges when we take seriously the historical impact of Constantine's vision in 312.

Whatever its source, inspiration or legitimacy, Constantine's vision worked. Constantine and his successors did indeed conquer under the sign of the cross. Constantine's cross image was carried at the head of armies going into battle, as if to say, 'Resistance is futile. You will be assimilated . . . or eliminated.' The Roman Empire became the Roman Christian Empire, and all who opposed the Empire – and its violent imperial ways – were understood to oppose Christianity and Christ.

Imagine yourself as someone outside the Roman Empire, an inhabitant of what we now call Ireland, Germany, Central Asia or Arabia. How would you feel about this Roman Christian Empire whose expansive ambitions include plans to assimilate you? Wouldn't you see Rome and its religion as a threat, ready to conquer you, perhaps kill or enslave you if you resisted, force you to convert if you submitted, and happy to tax and conscript you for its wars if you surrendered?[5] Wouldn't you fear or resent this threatening superpower and its religious chaplaincy?

Now imagine you have had a real spiritual experience, an authentic vision from the God of Adam, Noah, Abraham, Moses and Jesus. You want to live your life as a loyal follower of God, submitting your life to God's will. What should you do? Obviously, you should find the religion that proclaims faith in the God of Adam, Noah, Abraham, Moses and Jesus, and join it. In other words, you should become a Christian. Right?

But on second thought, why would you want to affiliate with the religion of an empire that threatens your security, history, culture and economy . . . and does so in Christ's name? If you do join the religion of the empire, won't your neighbours consider you a traitor or a potential collaborator with the enemy? If Rome attacks, won't they wonder whose side you'll be on? Won't becoming a Christian mean becoming a traitor to your people, your homeland? How will your neighbours ever accept your message from God if it is wrapped up with the military exploits of your most dangerous neighbour? How can you yourself accept a religion promoted and imposed by a violent empire, a regime driven by values and means that contradict the teachings of Christ himself?

In that light, consider the experience of a forty-year-old Arabian nearly three centuries after Constantine. He had a series of visions that convinced him that there are not many gods as all his countrymen believed, but only one. He came to believe that this one true and living God was the same God who had been revealed to Adam, Noah, Abraham, Moses and Jesus. He believed God had spoken to humanity through these great men and that each one's teaching and example should be trusted and followed. God was calling him to bring this revelation to all his fellow Arabs, and to the whole world.[6] What was he to do?

For many reasons, he couldn't become Jewish.[7] Nor could he affiliate with the Roman Christians; that would be tantamount to an act of treason against his countrymen and an act of surrender to a hostile alien force, as we have seen. He had only one option: to articulate his vision of monotheistic faith outside the confines of both Judaism and Christianity. In doing so, he could affirm his affinity with Jews and Christians as fellow believers in one God, and he could commit to non-hostile relationships with them unless they tried to harm or colonise his followers. He could form especially close ties with non-Roman Christians, and he may in fact have done so, especially with the Syrian Christian community then in exile in Arabia.[8]

Now in telling the story in this way, I am not making claims for or against Mohammed and Islam. I am simply suggesting that Constantine gave Roman-Imperial Christians a compelling reason to reject Mohammed (since Mohammed didn't submit to the theopolitical entity Constantine had created) and Constantine also gave Mohammed a compelling reason to reject so-called orthodox Roman Christianity (since Christianity required submission to the Roman theopolitical system). So, we might say, Constantine played a pivotal role in the development of Islam as a separate religion three centuries later. Because of Constantine and his bejewelled spear-cross, the face of Christianity towards Mohammed was a hostile one, and the face of Islam has often mirrored that hostility ever since, as today's newspaper headlines attest.

When we situate Mohammed in this way, just outside the borders of a powerful so-called Christian empire that claimed divine authority to conquer under the sign of the cross, I trust we can interpret Mohammed's choices and convictions in a more sympathetic light.[9]

And when we see later generations of Islamic leaders imitating the behaviour of Roman-Imperial Christian leaders, rivalling and in many cases outcompeting them, perhaps we can interpret their behaviour in a more sympathetic light too. They aren't simply 'them'. They are also a reflection of 'us'.

A brief survey of the history of Christian hostility would include Theodosius who, just several decades after Constantine's conversion, prohibited the practice of any religion other than Christianity even in the privacy of one's home. Around AD 800 came Charlemagne who, with the support of Pope Leo III, aimed to renew the Roman Empire, which had disintegrated and fragmented in the aftermath of a series of brutal barbarian invasions.[10] Among his many exploits on behalf of the *Imperium Christianum*, he imposed the death penalty for all Saxons who would not convert to Christianity.

We might skip ahead to the middle of the sixteenth century, in the age of the Conquistadors, when King Charles V of Spain called together a conference to discuss whether the enslavement of Native Americans was Christian or not. Defending the enslaved Native Peoples was Bartoleme de las Casas. Defending the enslaving Conquistadores was Juan Gines de Sepulveda. Pope Paul III had already declared the Native Peoples capable of receiving the gospel, giving the Spanish conquest an air of exploitation-evangelism. The current question was whether the kind of enslavement Columbus had pioneered would receive official church endorsement.

In the course of his argument, Sepulveda claimed that Christ's parable of the wedding feast (in Matthew 22) required Christians to kill those who resist evangelisation, to which Las Casas replied, 'There is tremendous rashness, then, in presuming to prove by any means of [the wedding feast] parable that Christ commanded his Church that . . . it should use physical compulsion on unbelievers before the faith is preached to them.' Las Casas was echoing the sentiments of a fellow Dominican, Antonio de Montesinos, who had written from the Taino homeland of Hispaniola some forty years earlier: 'I am the voice crying in the wilderness . . . the voice of Christ in the desert of this island . . . [saying that] you are all in mortal sin . . . on account of the cruelty and tyranny with which you use these innocent people. Are these not men? Have they not rational souls? Must not you love them as you love yourselves?'[11] Although the sentiments of Montesinos and Las Casas seem obvious to us now, theirs was clearly the minority report in the era of the Conquistadores. Both Montesinos and Las Casas were ignored. So Sepulveda's brutal protocols continued on, in the name of Christ.

We could go on to explore similar debates in North America among colonial Protestants, debates which continue today, by the way, under the rubric of 'American Exceptionalism'.[12] And we could quickly expand to consider British colonialism in Africa and India, or Dutch colonialism in Africa and Indonesia.[13] We could look at the tragic effects of Christian anti-Semitism through history, and then consider the contemporary impact of Christian Zionism on US foreign policy and its impact on Palestinians under Israeli occupation. Through all these episodes we can trace a common theme: a profound, almost unconscious union between Christian faith and an imperial or colonising mind-set, a mind-set that asserts one group of people has been chosen by God to rule over others, which is closely related to the theological conviction that one group of people – Us – carries God's blessing and favour in a way others do not.[14] Taken further, the chosen become children of God and light; the unchosen, the children of the devil and darkness. In the stark shadows of that duality, how could hostility *not* grow?

For a long time already, voices from the margins – like Montesinos and Las Casas – have been advocating an alternative vision, a minority report. That minority report dares to whisper the dream of a post-colonial, post-imperial Christian identity. Their voices have been systematically suppressed or studiously ignored. But they refuse to be silent. Perhaps the time has come for more of us to listen, learn, confess, change and add our voices to theirs. And perhaps, having done so, we can turn to our neighbours – including the physical descendants of the colonised and enslaved, and the spiritual descendants of Mohammed, Moses, the Buddha and others – and say, 'We're beginning to see it now. We're sorry. We're learning from our history. And at long last, we're changing. We have a long way to go, but we're beginning the long, slow process of repentance.'

Until we face this deep-running current of imperial hostility in our Christian history, we will not be able to forge a robustly benevolent Christian identity. Doing so will be painful. Many will shrink back from it.

But if we face and embrace this pain, new creative possibilities will open before us. We will be able to creatively rearticulate our *core Christian doctrines* in fresh, faithful and profound ways, healing hostility and nourishing benevolence. We will then be able to creatively renew our *essential Christian liturgies* so they fulfil their potential for spiritual formation. And then we will be able to rediscover our *compelling Christian mission*, so we can be energised with a new conviction of who and what we are sent into the world to be and do. To these three creative challenges – doctrinal, liturgical and missional – we now turn.

TWO

THE DOCTRINAL CHALLENGE

Indeed, the word *doctrine*, a word fallen on hard times in contemporary culture, actually means a 'healing teaching,' from the French word for *doctor*. The creeds, as doctrinal statements, were intended as healing instruments, life-giving words that would draw God's people into a deeper engagement with divine things. When creeds become fences to mark the borders of heresy, they lose their spiritual energy. Doctrine is to be the balm of a healing experience of God, not a theological scalpel to wound and exclude people.

Diana Butler Bass[1]

CHAPTER 12

How the Doctrine of Creation
Can Create Humankind(ness)

Old Turtle spoke. 'The world you describe is not the world that has always been, Little One . . . It is because it is so close to a great, whole truth that it has such beauty, and thus the people love it so . . . It is the lost portion of that broken truth that the people need, if the world is to be made whole again.'

'But where is the missing piece?' asked the Little Girl. 'Can we put the truth back together again?'

Douglas Wood[1]

As we've seen, much of the strong/hostile/oppositional identity we find in the Christian faith today springs from the history of Western Roman-Imperial Christianity in the tradition of the Emperor Constantine.[2] This tradition contains incalculable riches and preserves unfathomed values, but it also serves as host for dangerous social and spiritual viruses. What might happen if we were to run our contemporary versions of Christian faith through a debugging program where we scanned for and removed all imperial viruses?

Such a debugging process would no doubt be long, hard, complex and highly contested. Some would mock the process as a futile, simplistic, reactionary, anti-Constantine 'fall of the church' exercise. Some would argue that it was actually God's plan for Christian faith to experience this kind of synthesis, empowering the word of the Lord with Constantine's sword. To remove Roman-Imperial elements, they would argue, would be to reduce or plunder the faith and to oppose God's providence.[3] Others might argue that if we purge Christianity of its imperial viruses, there would be virtually nothing of value left; the religion has little to offer beyond a legitimisation for Greco-Roman philosophy and politics.[4] But many others, and I am among them, would argue that we have no moral option but to run the program, whatever the consequences, in sincere faith and hope that a more healthy, robust, humble, honest and benevolent faith will emerge.

But that wouldn't solve all of our problems. Much of our hostility flows from destructive Roman-Imperial bugs that hide deep in our software, so to speak, but we must admit that some of our hostility also flows from the Bible itself, or at least from our interpretations and applications of the Bible. If we are going to envision, articulate and embody a strong-benevolent Christian identity, we must be willing to critically revisit even those central Christian doctrines we believe to be firmly rooted in the Bible. We must courageously and humbly uncover the ways our doctrines have been used to foster hostility and violence in the past, and then respond in faithful, ethical ways. This will be delicate work, not to be entered into unadvisedly or lightly, perhaps more akin to brain or heart surgery than computer debugging.

You'll notice I didn't say 'we must be willing to *abandon* our central Christian doctrines'. That kind of abandonment, history shows pretty convincingly, produces the weak-benign versions of Christian identity that I am firmly rejecting right along with the strong-hostile versions. Instead of rejecting these doctrines, we need to rediscover, re-envision, and reformulate them in a post-imperial, post-colonial, post-Christendom way.

I am tempted to indulge in a major tangent here – that is, the question of whether 'doctrine as we know it' is in itself an imperial product. Has the very concept of *doctrine* as popularly understood become so full of imperial bugs that it needs to be deconstructed – not just specific doctrines, but the very concept of doctrine itself? Is *doctrine* as popularly understood a tool of imperial control – restricting not only freedom of speech but also freedom of thought, thus promoting exactly the kind of political submission that totalitarian regimes depend upon? Can *doctrine* be rediscovered along the lines proposed by Diana Butler Bass – as a *healing teaching*, drawing from the same etymological root as *doctor*?[5] In other words, can the idea of doctrine itself be reformulated not as an instrument of mind control and social pacification, but as an instrument of healing – including healing from the diseases of empire?

This kind of rediscovery/reformulation process – regarding both specific doctrines and the concept of doctrine itself – has, in fact, been underway for some time, often led, not surprisingly, by Christians who have experienced the downsides of imperial Christianity. From what post-colonial thinkers call 'the subaltern position', from the position of 'others' living under domination, these Christian leaders saw things in the Bible and Christian tradition that others in more privileged positions could not or would not see.[6] These subaltern voices have been joined by growing numbers of people like myself, descendants of the colonisers who live with a range of unearned, inherited imperial privileges conferred by passport, gender, language and skin colour. Guided by our new mentors from among the formerly colonised, we discover that the gospel of Jesus Christ can liberate those who have been privileged by imperial systems just as it liberates the oppressed victims of those systems.

Together, we are seeking fresh understandings of our theological heritage. The pathway forward, we know, must be a path of partnership, not domination or isolation. On this path, many who were last in line in the colonial era move to the front as leaders, and many who were teachers and leaders in the colonial context become students again, learning from those they previously presumed to teach.

What happens when participants in this post-colonial partnership seek to rediscover the core doctrines in Christian theology? How can doctrinal sources of hostility be transformed into resources for solidarity? How can doctrinal instruments of thought and speech control become instruments of healing and liberation?

The doctrine of creation is a logical place to start. Many of us in the West have grown accustomed to hearing the words 'versus evolution' whenever the word *creation* is uttered, because for us the doctrine was important only in relation to centuries-long Euro-American hostilities between faith and science. But when we resituate the doctrine of creation in the context of inter-religious hostility, it becomes incandescent with possibilities for enlightenment and healing.

For example, in stark contrast to many ancient creation myths, Genesis tells us that the universe does not begin in conflict and rivalry among the gods. It begins peacefully, in the creative words, 'Let there be.'[7] Through these words of permission, space and time open up to make room for the new and the other to exist . . . since all creation is, in this sense, 'other than God'. All human beings, together with all created things, have their origin in the same unfolding story of making space for the other. We wouldn't be here if it weren't for the creative hospitality of the God who is host, not hostile, to the other.

Within that spacious story, all human beings share the same divine image. All human beings are, ultimately, sisters and brothers in one human family created in the image of God. As Douglas Wood's profound children's story *Old Turtle and the Broken Truth* makes clear, 'God loves us' is only a fragment of the truth, a dangerous fragment, in fact; it must be reunited with 'God loves others too.'[8] We live within a relationship of diversity without division: we are made on the same creation day as the reptiles and cattle, for example, and we are formed from the same dust. All living things are different but related; distinct but united. Similarly, male and female are not two warring factions; one is not superior and the other inferior: we are different but related, distinct but united.

This creation, then, is a garden of harmony, not a war zone of hostility. It comes equipped, not with oppositional religions that divide, but rather with a naked spirituality that includes and unifies all things in one fabric of creation. Trees and rivers, sky and stars declare God's glory for everyone; exclusive temples and members-only cathedrals are unnecessary. And so, according to our doctrine of creation, we are created by God to live in harmony with God and with all creation in all its wild diversity. We are created for harmony with one another, meaning 'one with the other', male with female, us with them, in dynamic unity without uniformity – different but not divided, distinct but related and unified. What doctrine could better orient us towards a strong and benevolent identity?

Sadly, though, when many Christians hear 'doctrine of creation', they don't think of this stage set for otherliness, hospitality, harmony and solidarity. They think of hostility – between religion and science, faith and reason, creation and evolution, and little more.[9]

The doctrine of creation has been broken into sharp and dangerous shards. It must be put back together again into a beautiful and harmonising whole. In that way, it can become a healing teaching of unimagined power.

CHAPTER 13

How the Doctrine of Original Sin Can Help Christians Be Less Sinful

The doctrine of original sin is a parting glance at the unnecessary nature of what we are ceasing to be.

James Alison[1]

Imagine the doctrine of creation as a beautiful mountain range, visible from our picture window and front porch, a constant inspiration, a timeless reminder of our ancestry and our destiny as well.

Then imagine a fleet of trucks pulling up in front of our home, workers pouring out, chainsaws sawing and hammers hammering, scaffolding rising, clouds of dust and sawdust filling the air. A few hours later the workers clean up and the trucks depart, having constructed a huge billboard that now completely blocks our view of the mountain. On this side of the billboard, original harmony, original goodness and original blessing are only a tragic memory. We can see only garish colours and huge, bold letters that declare UNIVERSAL

CONDEMNATION, UNIVERSAL ALIENATION AND
UNIVERSAL HOSTILITY.

This billboard slogan, many knowledgeable theologians will
argue, is not a proper understanding of the doctrine of original
sin. And I agree. The proper understanding of the ancient
doctrine intends to detour us away from several theological dead
ends and washed-out roads that were encountered in the first
several centuries of Christian history. We would be foolish to
discard the doctrine and waste our time repeating those theological misadventures. Our problem isn't the *proper* understanding of the doctrine: our problem is the *popular* understanding of
it. The two differ greatly and, sadly, holding the former doesn't
automatically undo the damage caused by the latter.

The doctrine of original sin, as *popularly* understood, suggests
that God views all humankind (and, for some, the whole created
order) with hostility because it has lapsed from its original
perfection. According to this popular understanding, God's
particular form of perfection requires God to punish all imperfect beings with eternal conscious torment in hell. So in this
popular view of original sin, God's response to anything that is
less than absolutely perfect must be *absolute and infinite
hostility*.

It might sound like good news, a sort of reprieve, to add that
God forgives and saves a select few. For the select few, what could
be better news than the promise that they will enjoy God's
gracious gift of love and heaven for ever, while their 'unsaved'
counterparts can only look forward to God's absolute hostility
in an eternal hell? Good Christians by the millions believe exactly
this (often under the threat that if they don't believe it, they will
be consigned to an eternity among their counterparts). The

gospel itself is thus a solution to the problem of original sin, understood in this way.

But how do we good Christians handle the heady belief that we are among the select few being saved from original sin? I've spent a lifetime both experiencing and observing the answer.

First, we sing and speak with deep and sincere passion about how blessed and humbled we are to be chosen by God's sovereign grace alone, through no merit of our own. We rejoice with unspeakable joy to know ourselves as objects of God's mercy, and this grateful joy is heightened every time we contrast our bright destiny with the horrible doom of all those who remain objects of God's hostility.

Second, we learn to imitate the complex attitude that we understand God to have towards the fallen/unredeemed/sinners/infidels/unsaved/non-Christians around us. On the one hand, we know God loves them, and so we try to love them, too. But on the other hand, we know God finds them dirty, dangerous, depraved and unacceptable, and so we imitate God's aversion, as we understand it. We try to love the sinners but hate the sin that permeates their lives. Some of us manage that dynamic tension more gracefully than others. Meanwhile, we show to our fellow Christians the same preferential option that we believe God shares: it's our fellow Christians who really matter, to God and so to us. And then we remind ourselves that the unsaved and unredeemed – they matter, too, in the sense that God wants them to join us. If they refuse, then . . . it's complicated.

Third, we translate these learned attitudes into actions and words. We welcome our fellow Christians (at least the ones we have been taught to see as members of our tribe) into our shared inner circle. We are good to each other. We try to conform all our interactions to a high and holy ideal. We fill our schedules with activities related to Christian fellowship. We love us. And what about them – Muslims, Hindus, atheists, Buddhists? For some of us, our aversion to 'the other' carries the scent of fire and brimstone – a furious and fierce hostility that sends us into the world as culture warriors determined to vanquish the godless 'other'. Others of us are more defensive than aggressive in our reaction to those still imprisoned in original sin; they pose a constant threat against which we must protect ourselves with unflagging vigilance, which requires us to create our own schools, radio and TV stations, political parties and amusement parks. For others of us, our aversion has the more refined air of aloofness – we keep our polite distance, minimising contact, holding 'them' at arm's length, observing a kind of spiritual quarantine. For still others of us, our aversion is sweetened with pity, compassion and duty – often motivating us to befriend them in order to evangelise them, in hopes they too can become one of us before it's too late.

Whichever path we take, though, we can be sure that to 'the others' themselves, our doctrine of original sin, at least as popularly understood and translated into attitude and action, does not turn us into good neighbours.

But again, I do not propose we simply jettison the doctrine. Rather, I believe we need to get a fresh understanding of original sin – like the one offered by Catholic theologian James Alison. Drawing from the seminal theories of René Girard, Alison presents a doctrine of original sin that undermines a strong-hostile Christian identity, rejects a weak-benign Christian identity and builds a strong-benevolent Christian identity. I summarise this fresh approach in terms of five key concepts.

1. Imitation: Human beings are by nature imitative (or mimetic) creatures. We aren't born with a large repertoire of instincts as most mammals are; we learn to survive by imitating others – from speaking to using spoons to driving. Even desire is imitative. A child learns what berries to desire as food and what berries to avoid as poison by imitating the desire and aversion of others, just as an adult learns what car to drive or what neighbourhood to avoid by imitating the desire and aversion of others. Mimetic desire drives our survival and our economy as well.

2. Rivalry: When desire is mimetic, predictable problems arise. Whatever you desire, I desire. So if you want that cookie, that bicycle, that girlfriend, that house in that neighbourhood, that status in the community or that fertile farmland, so do I. You start as my model for imitation, but when I compete with you to achieve the object of our now-shared desire, I become your rival (or vice versa).

3. Anxiety: Since I am most likely to imitate those closest at hand, then my parents, my siblings, my spouse or my friends and I can most easily become rivals. And since rivalry often leads to violence, I face a unique threat: not the expected violence of a stranger or an enemy, but the unexpected violence of an envious companion. Not only that, but I may become the perpetrator of violence against those I envy. And since human beings are mimetic by nature, we imitate one another in violence, with disastrous consequences that easily spiral out of control. This threat of spiralling violence produces growing anxiety in any social system.

4. Scapegoating: When social anxiety reaches a critical point, it seeks an outlet. That outlet may be in an explosion of social

disintegration – every person turning on his neighbour. But human societies have repeatedly discovered a less costly, less destructive option. One member (or one subgroup) of the group is identified as different in some way, and that difference provides the reason to exclude, banish, harm or ultimately kill the victim. All imitate one another in shared aversion towards and violence against the victim – or scapegoat – and in so doing, all experience a catharsis of anxiety and a euphoria of unity. Potential disintegration has been replaced with unity, a unity that seems supernatural or magical in its power.[2]

5. Ritualisation: Since a focused release of violence on an innocent victim produces such a useful result, societies find ways to repeat this kind of unifying, cathartic violence pre-emptively, so to speak. In primitive societies, human sacrifice becomes a regular event presided over by a special class of priests. In more ordered societies, animals are substituted for humans, or human victims may be banished, defeated, enslaved or ghettoised rather than killed, and so on. Religious and political systems (and sports leagues) become the curators of our rivalry-management mechanisms. They seek to keep the peace by (a) providing mechanisms for the focused release of cathartic, unifying violence against a scapegoat of some kind, and (b) pronouncing prohibitions on behaviours that would lead to outbreaks of unmanageable, disintegrating rivalry.

How might a fresh understanding of original sin be articulated in these terms? It would say that all human beings are caught in these subtle webs of destructive imitation, rivalry, violence and scapegoating. No sphere of life is untouched by these mechanisms; even our systems of religion and government are implicated. No individual is pristine; all are complicit to some degree. As a result, our very identity as human beings and as individuals has been distorted from the image envisioned in the doctrine of creation.

In this fresh light, the rich imagery of Genesis shimmers and sparkles as never before.[3] Adam and Eve were made to bear the image of God – loving, generous, harmonious, beautiful, hospitable, creative, good. As God's image bearers, they were called to a constructive imitation . . . exercising the benevolent stewardship over creation modelled by the Creator who is host, not hostile, to otherness. But to bear God's image is not enough for them: they want to 'be like God'. They cease imitating God as model and become God's rivals, imitating the serpent's desire for the forbidden fruit.

This descent quickly renders them rivals to one another, too. They are no longer 'naked but not ashamed' in front of one another; they have something to fear. That fear materialises as blame as well as shame as they become one another's accusers.

Their sons play out these destructive mechanisms. Soon sibling rivalry leads to fratricide. Cain is a settled farmer; Abel is a nomadic herder. But East of Eden, difference can no longer exist without division and hostility. So Cain must identify himself over against his brother, who has forged a different way of life and a different form of religion. After murdering the rival other, Cain naturally fears that others will imitate him and do the same to him. Not insignificantly, Cain then builds a city, suggesting that civilisation itself is built on the dirty work of rivalry-driven murderers. Even God seems overwhelmed by the violence of civilisation, wishing the whole creative project had never been started, and seeking to wash it all away.[4]

At Babel, humans seek to overcome difference with sameness (a classic imperial move, by the way), but God intervenes on the side of diversity. The story continues with more rivalry (Sarah and Hagar, Isaac and Ishmael, Jacob and Esau, Joseph and his brothers) and more violence. Slavery enters the story – the dramatic reduction of my brother or sister, made in the image of God, into a tool made in the image of my desire.

And so the beauty of creation – difference without division, diversity with harmony – recedes further and further from human grasp. It might help to think in terms of copying a document or file: all sin today is a copy, an imitation, a replication of this original departure from the aboriginal goodness. In this sense, there is nothing less original than sin because sin is utterly derivative, utterly imitative. We are all implicated in this brutal, devolving unoriginality, and there is no escape from dismal, degrading cycles of mimicry apart from a return to the creative goodness that is even more original than sin.

The book of Genesis would be a tragic epic of despair if it did not hold out exactly this hope in its final chapters. Joseph's brothers play out the script of original sin with vigour – imitative desire producing rivalry leading to violent plots of murder and enslavement. Joseph in the end survives all plots against him, and he forgives and rescues the very violent brothers who at first wanted to kill him. Joseph refuses to imitate the hatred of his rival brothers. Instead, he returns to the imitation of God whose will, Joseph knows, is always benevolent.[5] He steps out of the flow of original sin, so to speak, holding out the hope that with God's help, we can get back to the garden, so to speak, to live in solidarity, not hostility.

So what is a proper understanding of original sin? It is the crisis of identity that emerges as we reject our original God-given name . . . our original identity as soil creatively organised into 'the image of God', within the original harmony and hospitality of creation. Whenever we try to climb above that identity, we fall below it. In grasping at superhumanity, we become subhuman. We become slaveholders who dehumanise others and so also dehumanise ourselves. We become plunderers of the earth who impoverish ourselves permanently in our foolish pursuit of short-term gain. We spin webs of violence in which we ourselves become stuck. We lose our identities as recipients and imitators of the original divine benevolence. We lose our identities as apprentices of God. We lose our identities as fellow creatures in a beautiful creation. Instead, we each forge a distorted, hostile, oppositional identity – rivals with God, rivals with our spouses, rivals with our siblings, rivals with our fellow creatures, positioning ourselves over against creation instead of in and with it.

In this light, the choice between the two trees in the Garden of Eden takes on fresh significance. The tree of the knowledge of good and evil represents a godlike knowing that empowers the consumers of its fruit with the capacity to accuse, to judge and to condemn *the other* as evil and to crown *us* as good. The tree of life, in contrast, nourishes in us the ability to live in benevolent relationship – not accusing the other for being different, not judging or shaming the other for being naked, not condemning the other for being what it is, but rather living with the other in the divine and hospitable harmony of kindness.[6]

I hope it's becoming clear: the popular understanding of original sin too often aids and abets in the expansion of sin. It promotes a dualistic, judgemental, accusatory mind-set that embeds in us an oppositional identity that in turn breeds hostility and rivalry, thus fomenting the very sin it intended to expose and oppose. In contrast, however, a better understanding of original sin exposes hostility and rivalry as the origins of sin, and so prepares the way for us to rediscover a strong-benevolent Christian identity. Instead of a billboard that obscures creation's original harmony, we might think of this understanding as a set of binoculars that helps us peer across the distance to see how good that original goodness was – and to feel it beckoning us, no matter how far we are from it now. This understanding of original sin resurrects rather than obscures the doctrine of creation, and it makes way for a resurrection of every other Christian doctrine, too – resurrecting each doctrine as a healing teaching that reveals our truest identity.

If, in our ancient narratives, a serpent once tempted us to eat from the tree that would allow us to pronounce *us* good and *them* evil, perhaps we need a new narrative today in which a beautiful songbird sings from the tree of life, inviting us to eat again of its original fruit: love, joy, peace, patience, kindness, goodness, gentleness, faithfulness and self-control.

CHAPTER 14

How the Doctrine of Election (or Chosen-ness) Can Help Christians Choose Benevolence

We have just enough religion to make us hate but not enough to make us love one another.

Jonathan Swift[1]

In May 2008, I participated in a gathering in Kigali, Rwanda, in East Africa, a setting of Edenic natural beauty. Scattered among the green hills and fertile farms all around us were museums and memorial sites recalling the hellish genocide that had erupted there fourteen years earlier – an orgy of rivalry, hostility and violence. If there is a baptism into original sin, the Rwandese had experienced it. The Burundians and Ugandans present also knew the depths of human depravity firsthand through recent tragic decades of hostility and violence. Several dozen Kenyans were also present, all of them still traumatised by a recent outbreak of intertribal, postelection violence. Their psychological scars were still fresh, with many of them still living in Internally Displaced Persons camps, their homes having been burned by their neighbours of different tribes.

I had lunch one day with a middle-aged widow who had been the co-pastor of a Pentecostal church in a small Kenyan village. Through tears she told me of the night five months earlier when there was a knock on her door. A crowd of people holding gasoline cans had gathered in her front yard. They told her it was time for all people of her tribe to leave their town. As she escaped through the crowd with nothing but the clothes on her back, she noticed many of her parishioners and, most heartbreaking of all, she saw the co-pastor among them as well. Fires were lit. The house was destroyed. She had been in an IDP camp ever since.

I asked her what her plans were. 'I am going back,' she said softly. 'I have nowhere else to go. That is my village. That is my congregation. That man, even though he is from another tribe, and in spite of what he did, is still my colleague in ministry and my brother in Christ. I will return and rebuild my home. And somehow we must try to be reconciled to one another. With human beings this is impossible, but with God all things are possible.' She paused, then added, 'It may be difficult, yes, and there will be much heartbreak, but reconciliation must be possible.'

The next day I was supposed to address the group.[2] What could I say to people in this kind of pain? Prayerfully and in fear and trembling, I drew stories from the Bible to illustrate seven possible relationships between Us and Them.[3]

Domination: Us over Them – this is the classic imperial/colonial narrative, based on the assumption that *we* can be safe and well only if we are in control.[4]

Revolution: Us overthrowing domination by Them – this is the counterpart to the domination narrative, asserting that we can be safe and well only if *they* are no longer in control. If the revolution is successful, we often adopt the Domination Narrative that formerly animated our oppressors, and they adopt the Revolution Narrative that formerly animated us.[5]

Assimilation: Us absorbing Them – this narrative is based on the assumption that sometimes the best way to eliminate 'Them' is by converting them to 'Us'.[6]

Purification: Us eliminating Them – this is the narrative of ethnic cleansing and genocide that issues this ultimatum: you will either convert (Assimilation) or leave (as refugees) or be killed (via genocide).[7] It often focuses on a small minority and functions as a scapegoating narrative.

Competition: Us competing with Them – in this narrative, we coexist but see one another as rivals. We don't aspire to dominate, overthrow, eliminate, assimilate or expel – just to outcompete and stay in a superior position of competitive advantage.[8]

Victimisation/self-preservation: Us oppressed by Them – this is the narrative of those who have been defeated (by Domination), expelled (by Purification), survived pressures to abandon their identity (by Assimilation) or been weakened and marginalised (by Competition).[9] Survival is the primary focus upon which everything depends.

Isolation: Us apart from Them – whether by migrating to another geographical location or by creating a distinct and insular subculture, this narrative argues for separation and avoidance of the other.[10]

After briefly explaining these common framing stories, I stepped back and invited participants to respond, and the discussion was electric. Members of various tribes in various countries seized upon this new language. It helped them, they said, to understand the tragic hostilities that plagued them. They could immediately sense how these narratives formed strong identities in their tribes and how these strong identities in turn fomented the volatile social and political chemistry in which they lived.

'But is there an alternative?' they asked. 'Is there any other identity that is open to us?' In reply, I directed them to a fresh view of another key Christian doctrine: the doctrine of election or choosing or vocation. This is the doctrine by which we define 'us' as 'the people of God'. In its many popular forms, of course, the doctrine is causing all kinds of mischief and hostility. It serves as a theological justification for the seven hostile narratives we've just considered.

For example, a distorted doctrine of chosen-ness tells many sincere but misguided Christian Zionists that the Jews have been chosen by God to own certain land without concern for the well-being of their non-Jewish neighbours.[11] As a result, these Christians fervently support Israel in a Domination Narrative, justifying the continued military occupation of the West Bank and Gaza. They may even support the Purification Narrative that inspires some Israeli settlers and political parties to drive Palestinian Muslims and Christians from their homes, whether through sudden expulsion or gradual colonisation and appropriation. These well-meaning Christians, often seeking to redress the horrible legacy of Christian anti-Semitism, seem to have forgotten that the Domination script is not the way of Jesus. They forget how sincere Christians in South Africa abused the same doctrine of chosen-ness to justify apartheid, or how

Christians in the United States used the same doctrine of chosen-ness to justify unnumbered crimes against Native Americans and African-Americans, or how Christian anti-Semites through the centuries used this doctrine to justify their unconscionable treatment of their Jewish neighbours in the first place.

Can the doctrine of chosen-ness be reformulated, and if so, how? If we return to the Bible, we see that the original calling of creation is a call to diversity, a call to blessedness, to fruitfulness, and to multiplication 'after their kind'. 'Let there be', then, makes room for an evolving community of perpetual diversity. Each 'kind' has a right to exist – and it has no right to deprive other kinds of their God-given right to exist. We might say that God's original calling to each species was not to domination, revolution, purification, assimilation, competition, victimisation or isolation – but to creative participation in a dynamic and evolving story whose source, unfolding and destiny was in God.

But in the aftermath of original sin (properly understood) in Genesis 3–11, that original vocation to creative participation has been compromised and distorted by rivalry and scapegoating. So in Genesis 12, we find a new paradigm: God calls and commissions Abraham to a new and unique role – to a strong-distinct but non-hostile identity. God calls Abraham to leave his father's house (the source of his identity to date) in Ur (a centre of the Domination Narrative for the Chaldean empire) and to venture into unknown territory – suggestive of the forging of a new identity. In other words, God calls Abraham to become 'other' – other than his father's house, other than the ethnic, political and religious identity into which he had been born. In that other-ness, God promises to make of Abraham's descendants 'a great nation' with a great name – the word *great* suggesting, among other things, the strength of identity we have been grappling with in these pages.

But that great or strong identity isn't cast in hostility to other nations. Abraham's identity is not greatness exploiting others (domination), greatness overthrowing others (revolution), greatness absorbing others (assimilation), greatness excluding others (purification), greatness resenting others (victimisation), greatness separated from others (isolation) or greatness at the expense of others (competition). Abraham's greatness is *for the sake of* others: *And all nations on earth will be blessed through you.*

This calling might sound noble, but it won't be easy. Yes, some will bless Abraham's tribe. But others will curse them – curse them for being different, curse them for resisting empire, curse them for not imitating the typical scripts of 'normal' societal narratives. And so, God says, as others treat Abraham, so they will be treated: *I will bless those who bless you, and whoever curses you I will curse.* But even so, blessing will have the last word: *all nations on earth will be blessed through you.*

Sadly, Christians, Muslims and Jews, for all their differences, have imitated one another again and again in misunderstanding and misapplying this doctrine of chosen-ness. Rather than receiving God's call as a vocation *to be the other for the sake of others*, they have received the call to be *us* controlling, *us* overthrowing, *us* absorbing, *us* distancing, *us* expelling, *us* outcompeting, *us* resenting . . . rather than *us being a blessing to others.*

But doesn't being a blessing imply a kind of superiority? Isn't there a kind of exclusivism, elitism or at least paternalism inherent in being chosen by God? Interestingly, the unfolding narrative of the book of Genesis conspires against this common misunderstanding. After receiving this promise of and vocation to a new kind of identity, Abraham sets out on his journey. After a brief (and non-violent) stay in Canaan, he is forced by famine to Egypt, where he survives through the gracious hospitality of the Egyptians – the one who will be a blessing to others is not above being blessed by others. He refuses to enter into rivalry with his relative Lot and takes the 'leftover' land, giving his potential competitor the advantage of first choice.

When a domination-revolution conflict breaks out and Lot's family is captured in the hostilities, Abraham goes into battle to rescue them and then refuses to be drawn further into the hostile us-them politics of the region. He soon encounters a strange character identified as Melchizedek, the King-Priest of Salem – of Shalom or Peace. Melchizedek shows hospitality to Abraham and blesses him, and Abraham reciprocates with a generous gift. This is an encounter of mutuality, not hostility; of neighbourliness, not us-versus-otherness. Abraham's unique calling doesn't send him into the world with an exclusive, elitist or paternalistic attitude: it sends him out with a strong, benevolent identity.

So in just a few chapters, we see Abraham journeying out of hostile identities and moving into the alternative identity to which God has called him. In the chapters to come, the story gets even more interesting with a second visitation-vocation (15:1–21) and then a third (18:1–15). The story of Hagar and Ishmael is a painful study in otherness, driven by rivalry between Sarah and her Egyptian slave Hagar. (It's not insignificant that the Egyptian people who will forever be known as the enslavers of the Israelites were, in Hagar, first introduced through one who was the enslaved.) When Hagar is treated as a despised 'other' by Sarah, the Lord intervenes on Hagar's behalf and makes a promise to Hagar that shows she is of concern to the

Lord as well: *I will so increase your descendants that they will be too numerous to count.* The Lord names him Ishmael, meaning *God hears* – and Hagar responds by naming God *The One Who Sees Me*.[12] So it must never be forgotten that God sees and hears the other.

Sarah's rivalry with Hagar resurges years later, after she has given birth to Isaac. Abraham is father of both Ishmael and Isaac and is distressed by the rivalry, but God assures Abraham that God will bless Ishmael even if Sarah doesn't (21:13). Again Hagar is driven off, this time with her boy, and again God comes to their rescue.

The whole book of Genesis – and indeed the whole Bible – struggles with this issue of 'us-ness' and 'otherness'. With Ishmael and Isaac as with Cain and Abel, the other is brother, and both are beloved by God. For Isaac to have a unique blessing does not mean Ishmael can't also have a blessing of his own. For one to receive a special vocation from God doesn't mean that others haven't also received their own vocations. Centuries later, the prophet Amos will remind his people of the same truth:

> 'Are you not like the Ethiopians to me, O people of Israel?' says the Lord. 'Did I not bring Israel up from the land of Egypt, and the Philistines from Caphtor, and the Arameans from Kir?' (Amos 9:7)

So to be blessed by the true and living God of all creation is not an either-or thing; it is a both-and thing. God had a unique vocation *both* for Israel *and* for the Ethiopians. God liberated *both* the Israelites *and* the Philistines and Arameans from their oppressors.[13] The doctrine of calling, election or chosen-ness has indeed been abused as a vicious weapon of hostility. But we can rediscover it as an instrument of peace, an instrument of blessing. To do so will require us, like Abraham, to make a radical break with the hostile identities we inherited – identities of domination, revolution, assimilation, purification, competition, victimisation and isolation. It will require us to venture out – 'not knowing where we are going' – learning to embody a new, strong identity, an identity of *mission* and *reconciliation*: blessed to be a blessing, others for the sake of others, giving and receiving blessings with other blessed people, and thus joining God in healing a world torn by human hostility.[14]

CHAPTER 15

How the Doctrine of the Trinity Can Foment Harmony and Unity

For it is in the depths, as Paul Ricouer insists, that we 'touch on something unsaid . . . a mystical ground (*un fond mystique*) of what is most fundamental in each religion and which is not easily translatable into language but rather borders on a common profound silence.' In other words, the best way to tackle the violent tendency within religious conviction is to go all the way down to the source that religion does not master and that refuses to be rendered into dogmatic formulae or ideological manifestos . . . It is in this hearkening to a source beyond and beneath oneself, a superfluity one does not possess or manipulate, that we may find new resources for nonviolent resistance and peace.

Richard Kearney[1]

I was sitting on the balcony of a high-rise hotel room in Southern California. The Pacific Ocean sparkled under a smog-free sky. A rabbi we'll call Sol was enjoying the view with me. I had originally met Sol a few years earlier through a phone call: 'I represent a group of several dozen rabbis,' he'd said, 'who have read all of your books. We would like to meet with you sometime.' I wasn't expecting that! Since that first phone call, we had met a couple of times and a warm friendship had begun. I was in his neighbourhood to speak at a local seminary, so he kindly came by to say hello.

'Sol, we've become good enough friends now that I can ask you something kind of personal, right?' I asked.

'Sure. Anything.'

'What do you think of Jesus? I'm not asking that as a test question or as a prelude to an evangelistic presentation,' I explained. 'I'm just curious.'

'Of course, he was one of ours,' Sol said. 'He was a Jew in the prophetic tradition. And many of my colleagues would agree with me when I say I think he spoke from God and the leaders of the priestly tradition were wrong to reject him.'

There was a pause. We both surveyed the Pacific Ocean shimmering in the afternoon sun. Then Sol continued, 'But look, after two thousand years of anti-Semitism, I hope you won't expect us to get excited about the doctrine of the Trinity anytime soon.'

I hope you can feel the power of his words. Confessing the Trinity served as the litmus test of acceptability in much of European history, forcing Jews into the status of outsiders and outcasts, non-citizens in 'Christian nations'. This exclusion and marginalisation led to ghettoes and pogroms, and eventually to gas chambers.[2] Muslims similarly experienced Trinitarian and related doctrines as a threat, as have Hindus, Buddhists and members of indigenous religions. As a result, many sensitive Christians have concluded that Trinitarian doctrines are irredeemable, that they must be quietly minimised if not outright abandoned. Trinitarian controversies have been so much a part of the problem that Trinitarian thought cannot be part of the solution.

I agree that Trinitarian doctrines have indeed been part of the problem. But I also believe that Trinitarian doctrines – held as healing teachings, not as an imperial loyalty test – can, properly understood and practised, contribute much to the solution.

Few doctrines can surpass the doctrine of the Trinity in either the fervency or the ambiguity with which it is held. The Councils of Nicaea and Chalcedon are seemingly convened all over again whenever the doctrine of the Trinity is seriously discussed, and seemingly orthodox Christians expose themselves – often to their own surprise – as closet adoptionists or Arians, unconscious Nestorians or Apollinarians, or implicit monophysitists or monothelitists. (I'll be interested to hear what fault doctrinal experts will find with something I say about the Trinity in this chapter.) The doctrine of the Trinity has been so central to the Christian faith that to deny it, and sometimes even to affirm it in a new way, has been an excommunicable offence.

As a result, many good Christians – perhaps most – avoid thinking about the doctrine of the Trinity as studiously as they avoid denying it. The less they think about it, the less they'll say about it, and the less trouble they'll get in for misspeaking about it. So, without venturing too far into the conceptual minefields of *homoousios* and *hypostases*, of being and persons, of nature and will, they try to uphold a few basic mysteries – that God is one and in some sense three; that Christ is man and in some sense God; that the Spirit is the Spirit of the Father and the Son but in some sense not reducible to the Father and the Son.

Most Christians understand that the doctrine of the Trinity is historically important, but they seldom understand why. As I've already noted, some suspect that the doctrine is little more than a sinister tool of mind and speech control, used from the time of Constantine to centralise the power of heresy hunters and to test Christian teachers on their submission to church authority. Others simply accept that Trinitarian doctrine is part of the gospel bargain: if you want to go to heaven, here's what God requires you to assent to.[3] Relatively few have grappled with the philosophical, biblical and practical issues that energised Trinitarian controversies throughout Christian history. Fewer still have critically examined how the doctrine has been abused as a weapon against others through history, as my rabbi friend pointed out. And even fewer have imagined how the doctrine could become a bridge rather than a barrier in the future.

What might a strong-benevolent holding of Trinitarian theology look like? For starters we could explore an approach called Social Trinitarianism.

Social Trinitarianism is by no means a new approach: it has its origins in the thought of the Cappadocian Fathers of the fourth century, especially Gregory of Nazianzus. In the eighth century it was further explored by John of Damascus. It has been revitalised in recent decades by a range of theologians including Eastern Orthodox thinkers like John Zizoulas, historic Protestants like Jürgen Moltmann, and Evangelicals like Stanley Grenz, Miroslav Volf and J. Baxter Krueger. At the heart of Social Trinitarianism is the concept of perichoresis, which images God as a dynamic unity-in-community of self-giving persons-in-relationship. The Father, Son and Spirit in this view are not three independent units (or monads) eternally bound together in a larger unity. Nor is God one independent unit with three identical parts. Rather, each person of the Trinity exists in dynamic social relationship with the others, and God is the relational unity in which they relate.

Of course, the term *person* in the previous sentence is a highly technical term. It doesn't simply mean *individual*. Some have employed the term *interdividual* (a neologism attributable to René Girard) to acknowledge how the being of one Trinitarian person is not independent of the others; one couldn't be subtracted, leaving the other two to stand as a Duality, for example. Nor does the identity of one Trinitarian person stand over against the identity of the others so the Father could be defined as 'apart from the Son or the Spirit' or the Spirit as 'apart from the Father or the Son', and so on. Rather, the Spirit is the Spirit *of the Son* and *of the Father*. The Father is the Father *of the Son* and vice versa. So the very idea of *person* is redefined in Social Trinitarianism as 'being in relationship'. A person's relationships with the others, in other words, aren't an accessory to the person who exists apart from them. Those relationships are what and who that person is, and that person cannot be said to exist apart from those relationships. *Being*, then, for God as for us, means 'interbeing', being in relationship, so the three persons of the Holy Trinity are not merely one *with* each other: they are one *in* each other. We might say they are *interpersons* or *interpersonalities*. And, as creatures made in the image of God, so are we.

However interesting this might sound to you (or not), it might also seem so esoteric and so highly nuanced that it can only lead to the rancorous theological quarrels and hostile excommunications that we're trying to escape. But a simple thought experiment can make clear how powerful and reconciling this Social Trinitarian vision of God, personhood and ourselves can be.

First, imagine (recalling the previous paragraphs) God as this 'being as communion', as this loving trinity of perichoresis, a sacred choreography of self-giving, other-receiving; honouring, being honoured; fully seeing the other, fully revealing the self. Imagine (in stark contrast to the hostile narratives of the previous chapter) an eternal one-anotherness who is by nature non-assimilating, non-isolating, non-dominating, non-eliminating, non-overthrowing, non-competing and non-victimised or non-victimising.

Now imagine this God self-expressing in a universe. What kind of universe would this kind of God create? It would not be a universe of independent, isolated individuals or monads (as in the isolation narrative from the preceding chapter) because God is not an independent, isolated monad. It would not be a universe of undifferentiated homogeneity (as in the domination, purification and assimilation narratives) because God is not an undifferentiated homogeneity. Nor would it be a universe of unending rivalry leading to competition, revolution and victimisation, either, because God is not many-in-conflict but three-in-one, unity-in-community. It would not be a universe of duality, stuck in the conflict of one versus the other, because God is one: one one-another.

Clearly, then, this Trinitarian vision of God helps us imagine a relational universe of one-anotherness, community-in-unity, unity-in-community, being-in-interbeing, where benevolence towards the other is at home, and hostility towards the other is foreign, invasive, out of place. To draw from the world of music, this vision invites us to imagine the universe as a wild and wonderful symphony, full of polyphony and surprise, expansive in themes, each movement inspiring the possibility of more movements as yet unimagined, all woven together with coherent motifs and morphing rhythms, where even dissonance has a place within higher, more comprehensive patterns of harmony and wholeness.

Finally, imagine how people in this universe would manifest trust in this triune God. Imagine in particular how people who hold this trust would relate to others who don't understand or hold it. Would they do so by dominating their counterparts and requiring them to assent to their vision by threat of sword or banishment? By rejecting the other and isolating from the other unless and until they see the light? By trying to overthrow or assimilate all their understandings into this one, robbing them of their individuality? Such actions would violate the very spirit or nature of the God these Trinitarians were supposedly being faithful to!

One could only manifest trust in 'this new vision of God as deathless, creative relationality'[4] by manifesting undying, creative love towards those who didn't share the belief. This kind of Trinitarianism, then, compels those who hold it to encounter the other with a bias against hostility and clannishness and a bias towards benevolence and otherliness.[5]

Imagine that! Imagine that vision of the Holy Trinity and how it could convert its holders from their hostile old identities to a robust, energetic, harmonious new identity. God-with-God in community leads us to envision God-with-us in community. And that vision in turn dares us to imagine God-with-them in community. And that expansive vision invites us higher still: to envision

God-with-us-and-with-them in community, which leads us further still to envision us-with-them in community. This approach to the Trinity need not be a litmus test used to legitimise us and delegitimise them. Instead, it can be a gift, offered to others like a poem, not an ultimatum – given not to require assent-leading-to-acceptance or dissent-leading-to-condemnation, but rather to inspire us to reverence otherliness as a theological attribute.[6] At that moment, Trinitarianism becomes not only a healing doctrine but a healing practice.

As I try to take all this in, I go back in my memory to that balcony with my friend Sol. I see us sitting together, pondering and enjoying a sparkling sea that expands beyond all horizons. We are two men of two different religions, united in our awe at the unspeakable, expansive, profound beauty of it all. God is not a doctrine to be mastered but a mystery to be mastered by.

CHAPTER 16

How a Deeper Christology Can Save Christians from Hostility

The New Testament contains what amounts to a genuine episte-mology of love, the principle of which is clearly formulated in the first Epistle of John:

> He who loves his brother abides in the light, and in it there is no cause for stumbling. But he who hates his brother is in the darkness and walks in the darkness, and does not know where he is going, because the darkness has blinded his eyes. (1 John 2:10–11)

> . . . Only Christ's perfect love can achieve without violence the perfect revelation towards which we have been progressing . . .

> René Girard[1]

I had lunch a few years ago in an Afghan restaurant with my Muslim friend Ahmad, who is an imam. I asked him to tell me how he came to be an imam, and what he loves most about Islam. He shared from his heart and I was deeply moved. Then he asked, 'How would you respond to that same question? How did you become a pastor and what do you love about Christianity?' I followed his example and shared from my heart too, beginning like this: 'Well, could I begin by telling you what I love about Jesus?'

When I paused a few minutes later, our eyes met, and I could see my friend was uncomfortable. 'What's wrong?' I asked. 'Did I say something that offended you?'

'Oh, no, no, no, no,' he said. 'I suddenly realise that everything I have heard about Christianity until now I learned from my fellow Muslims, and they passed on to me the misunderstandings they learned from other Muslims. Until now I have never listened to a sincere Christian explain his faith as a love for Jesus, peace and blessings be upon him. I have been so terribly misinformed and I have likewise misinformed others. I feel so sorry, so sorry. From now on, I will more adequately share with my congregation what Christianity truly is, because now I have learned it from a Christian who knows firsthand, not a Muslim who only passes on what he has heard.'[2]

He paused, and then added, 'When you say that you love Jesus, it fills my heart with joy. We Muslims love Jesus, too. We believe Jesus is a great prophet and we love him dearly. So you and I – we have this in common. We both love Jesus.'

At that moment, I could have said, 'But Ahmad, you don't think of Jesus in the same way we do. So your love for Jesus doesn't count.' Then I could have entered into an argument to set him right. Instead, I asked him what it meant for him as a Muslim to call Jesus a great prophet. His response surprised me. Believing that Jesus was a great prophet meant that God was speaking to all humanity through Jesus. It meant that Jesus' word and example must be followed and that God would evaluate us against the measure of Jesus' life and teaching.

As he explained this, I couldn't help but notice an irony. We Christians believe that Jesus was more than a prophet, but that means, all too often for all too many of us, that his life and teaching can be largely ignored. As long as we believe certain things about his divinity, death and resurrection, maybe with some auxiliary beliefs about (depending on our denomination) Mary, Peter or the Bible, we're Christians in good standing, no questions asked. Then I thought of Jesus' own words, 'Why do you call me "Lord, Lord," but do not do the things I say?'

Sadly, too often in church history – and too often today – Jesus has not been a point of contact as he was that day for Ahmad and me. As my friend Rabbi Sol knew all too well from the history of Christian anti-Semitism, Jesus has often been presented as a weapon and a threat, more wolf of God than lamb of God, filled more with the spirit of a hawk than a dove, more avenger of heretics than friend of sinners. Our Christology, however 'high' in theory, has produced in practice far too many Christians with an elevated sense of superiority. And that superiority can only lead to hostility: *My religion is better than your religion. My theology is better than your theology. My God is better than your God. My Jesus is better than your . . . what? Your Moses? Your Jehovah? Your Elohim? Your Mohammed? Your Allah? Your Buddha? Your Atman? Your Great Spirit? Your Gaia? Your Imani?*

The ridiculousness of pitting Jesus as a rival against other prophets or Gods or saviours becomes evident when you try to imagine Jesus himself doing so. Imagine a group of Christians bringing Mohammed to Jesus, and then Jesus questioning Mohammed. When Mohammed's answers don't pass his orthodoxy tests, imagine Jesus washing his hands and turning

Mohammed over to the Christians to execute him. *No, that's not Jesus – that's Pontius Pilate!* Or imagine Jesus dragging the Buddha before a crowd of Christians and commanding them to stone him as a false prophet. *No, that's not Jesus commanding the Buddha to be stoned – that's Jesus standing with the Buddha, defending him from those about to throw stones!* Or imagine Jesus bringing Mohammed, the Buddha, Moses and a panel of leading atheists to the top of a mountain so they can see the whole earth spread out below them in all directions. Imagine Jesus saying, 'I'll let you all share in the ownership of all of this – if only you'll bow down and worship me!' *No, wait a minute. That's not Jesus, that's* . . . You get the point.[3]

The absurdity of these scenarios becomes even more stark when you consider the message of our two earliest Christological hymns, both found in Paul's letters, ostensibly written sometime between AD 53 and 61.[4]

The Colossian hymn presents Jesus in stunning counter-imperial language (not insignificant in light of our faith's tragic identification with the Roman Empire, as we've seen repeatedly already).[5] The hymn celebrates him as the true king or emperor: he is the true image of God, the true firstborn destined to inherit the throne, the true source and purpose of creation, the true head of the body politic, the true embodiment of the fullness of God, the true source of peace and reconciliation. But then the hymn ends with this staggering conceptual coup d'état: while Caesar gains and holds power and enforces the Pax Romana by shedding the blood of all who resist him, Jesus exercises his sovereignty and brings the Pax Christi by shedding his own blood. The power of Christ (and what Jesus called the kingdom of God) is manifest not in hostile conquest and killing, but in benevolent self-giving to the point of death. We must not define Jesus and his kingdom by fitting them within conventional understandings of kings and kingdoms. Rather, we must judge and deconstruct those conventional definitions in light of Jesus and his example.

The Philippian hymn makes a similar point.[6] Christ as a true image bearer of God does not climb to a place of prominence and glory through the normal means of rivalry and conquest. Rather, he descends – down into common humanity, down into servanthood, down into suffering, down into death – even death on a cross. This descending, open-handed humility rather than climbing, clutching pride, this self-giving rather than selfish ambition, this preference for others rather than competitive superiority . . . this is the attitude that honours God, and that God honours, and that in fact reveals the true nature of God. How could followers of this Christ and this God justify treating others with contempt, disdaining them as inferior, rejecting them as other and enemy? How could any of these all-too-common hostilities be done in the name of this Christ?

Where our Christology has been so strong, oppositional and distorted, it's easy to understand why many have advocated weakening our Christology to weaken its hostile distortions. But my hope is that a deeper, more vigorous, more robust Christology will become as much a part of the solution to Christian hostility as the old approaches have been part of the problem. This new kind of strong Christology begins by redefining strength itself in light of Christ's strength-through-weakness, gaining-through-losing, rising-through-descending.

Christ isn't merely one sector of the tapestry of Christian theology. Rather, Christ is interwoven throughout the fabric of every sector. For that reason it's hard to know where to begin and where to stop examining Christology and its impact on Christian identity in a multi-faith world. In a thorough exploration, we would concentrate on key biblical terms, terms that, it turns out, are far more complex, contested and interesting than most of us Sunday School graduates realise: *Son of God*, *Son of Man*, *Lord* and *Christ* for starters. And we would look at the ways those terms have been woven into various doctrines and systematic theologies over history. We would pay attention not only to what was affirmed, but also to what was marginalised or ignored. We would ask tough questions about why Greco-Roman philosophical categories gained such prominence in understanding Christ, and we would question whether those categories must forever and everywhere be considered normative.[7]

For our purposes here, though, we can only scratch the surface by considering how a fresh vision of two Christological doctrines can reduce hostility and strengthen benevolence.[8]

First, the doctrine of the Deity of Christ is affirmed in the Nicene Creed with these words: 'We believe in one Lord, Jesus Christ, the only Son of God, eternally begotten of the Father, God from God, Light from Light, true God from true God, begotten, not made, of one Being with the Father.' The process of arriving at each pregnant phrase of these few brief lines was long, agonising and fascinating, but it remains largely unknown to the average Christian. In contrast, the average Christian seems to arrive at the doctrine of the Deity of Christ in a simple, quick, three-step process: (1) Define God, using the Bible, perhaps assisted by Greek philosophy. (2) Apply this definition of God to Christ. (3) Work out the areas of apparent contradiction or potential misunderstanding that arise.

In this way, on a popular level many Christians understand the doctrine to mean, 'What is true of God is true of Christ,' or 'Jesus is equal to God,' or, put more mathematically (and less theologically), 'God = Jesus: Jesus = God.' Wise Trinitarians would quickly usher us back to the language of one of the creeds, but again, on a popular level, including on the level of religious broadcasting with its massive impact, this approach often frames the doctrine.

There has been an alternative approach to Christology in the Christian tradition, favoured more in the Anabaptist and Quaker communities, and resonant with the Franciscans and the Celts before them. It doesn't contradict traditional or creedal Christology, but it takes another approach to get there: (1) Seek to understand or know Christ (primarily by reading the Gospels in context). (2) Apply this understanding or knowledge to God. (3) Enrich, challenge, adjust, affirm or correct all previous understandings of God in light of Christ.[9]

So where the popular approach takes a pre-existing definition of God and applies it to Christ, this alternative approach challenges preconceived understandings of God and revises them in light of Christ. The assertion shifts the emphasis from 'What is true of God is true of Christ' to 'What is true of Christ is true of God.' Or more simply put, from 'Christ is like God' to 'God is like Christ.'

Again, this might seem like a rather esoteric and trivial adjustment. But consider its importance when we are willing to challenge violent and exclusive conceptions of God in light of the non-violent and inclusive way of Christ. The impacts of this adjustment are radical and far-reaching, and they suggest not a lower or reduced Christology but an equally or – I would say

– an even more robust one. We can trace a similar pattern in regards to a second Christological doctrine.

The doctrine of the incarnation is drawn primarily from the opening words of the Fourth (or John's) Gospel:

> In the beginning was the Word, and the Word was with God, and the Word was God. He was in the beginning with God. All things came into being through him, and without him not one thing came into being. What has come into being in him was life, and the life was the light of all people. The light shines in the darkness, and the darkness did not overcome it . . . The true light, which enlightens everyone, was coming into the world . . .
>
> And the Word became flesh and lived among us, and we have seen his glory, the glory as of a father's only son, full of grace and truth . . . From his fullness we have all received, grace upon grace. The law indeed was given through Moses; grace and truth came through Jesus Christ. No one has ever seen God. It is God the only Son, who is close to the Father's heart, who has made him known. (John 1:1–5, 9, 14, 16–18)

Again, the focus of our investigation prohibits a full engagement with this luminous passage. But please notice three important elements of the text. First, consider the term *Word*. It's fascinating because of its resonances both in Hebrew and Greek thought. In a Jewish context, the passage evokes the Genesis 1 creation story ('in the beginning . . . all things came into being . . . light'), suggesting that the Word is the creative word by which everything springs into existence: 'Let there be.'

To say that this Word became flesh is to say, among other things, that Jesus embodies the divine creativity that makes impossibilities possible and that makes new possibilities spring forth into actuality. It's to proclaim something more far-reaching – and hopeful – than the arrival of a new religious leader or a new religion. It is to proclaim that a new genesis has interrupted business as usual in human history. And what will that new creation entail? Among other things, it will mean a new commandment – that we love one another as Christ loved us. We might say, in other words, that this new creation means an end to the old era of hostility, including religious hostility. 'Let there be love,' it proclaims.

The term *Word* – or *Logos* – is no less powerful in a Greek context. For the Greeks, the logos is the internal logic, pattern or meaning of the universe. For John to proclaim that this logos has been enfleshed in Jesus would mean, in today's terms, that in his story we see the syntax of history, the plotline of evolution, the deep meaning of the surface events, the unified field theory that explains all data.

Many assume that in using this term *logos*, John is fitting Jesus into the standard Greek framework of Logos, much as some Christians fit Jesus into their preconceived notions of God. But I think René Girard was right when he analysed the text differently:

> If love and violence are incompatible, the definition of the Logos must take this into account. The difference between the Greek Logos and the Johannine Logos must be an obvious one, which gets concealed only in the tortuous complications of a type of thought that never succeeds in ridding itself of its own violence.[10]

Girard suggests that John is making the same move Paul makes in Colossians when he turns imperial language on its head, or in Philippians when Paul argues that true glory is manifested not in grasping but in self-giving, not in selfish ambition but in servanthood.[11] It is, in fact, the same move Jesus makes later in John's Gospel when he strips and stoops to wash the feet of his disciples. In the conventional Greek understanding, the internal logic of the universe mandates for some to be slave masters and others to be slaves, for some to dominate and others to be oppressed, for some to be male/superior and others to be female/inferior. In so doing, the Greek logos legitimises a world divided between the powerful and powerless, rich and poor, us and them, the civilised and the barbarian, slave master and slave, male and female.[12] In such a divided, dualistic world, hostility, conflict and violence are . . . logical.[13] Acceptable. Normal.

But according to John, that logos of power is false. John audaciously proclaims that the true logic of the universe – the true meaning or syntax or plotline of history – has been enfleshed in Jesus and dwelt among us, full of glory, full of grace and truth, uttering one commandment only: love. This logos of love reveals to us the true heart of God and therefore the true hidden logic and meaning of the universe. The false, exclusive, dualist logos of power enlightens only the civilised or the philosophical or the powerful. But in Christ, a universal logos – 'the true light that enlightens everyone' – has come into the world.

And so, in a strong-benevolent Christology, Jesus is not lifted up into a pre-existing concept of God or a pre-existing category of philosophy. No: Jesus presents us with a radically new vision of God, a non-violent God, a suffering and serving God, descending and disrupting pre-existing categories, opening up previously unrealised possibilities. And when this benevolent logos comes, full of grace and truth, we do not welcome him. We reject him. We kill him, in the name of our preferred and familiar logos of hostility and violence. And so a crucified logos beckons us from the darkness of our violent past into the new light of a resurrection morning. Again, Girard captures the drama, with its obvious implications for the formation of Christian identity in a multi-faith world:

> The gospel interpretation of the Old Testament can be summed up in this approach . . . the replacement [of] the God that inflicts violence with the God that only suffers violence, the Logos that is expelled . . . When the consequences of this substitution finally come to fulfillment, there will be incalculable results.[14]

Incalculable results indeed.[15]

CHAPTER 17

How the Doctrine of the Holy Spirit Can Empower Our Encounter with the Other

In a very real sense, according to Christian experience and symbolism, the Spirit is given with creation, indeed is the instrument or the power of creation. She is with us from the beginning, grounding and connecting every living being ... I can rest in her ... Utterly mysterious, totally unpredictable, filled and directed by love/compassion, she is the womb in whom I rest and from which I issue moment by moment.

Paul Knitter[1]

I wanted to crawl under my chair.

It was a few weeks after 11 September 2001, and a group of faith leaders in our community just outside of DC pulled together a series of Sunday-afternoon inter-faith gatherings. Our gatherings were hosted at a local mosque – fitting, we all felt, so that Christians, Jews, Hindus, Sikhs, Buddhists and others could experience warm Muslim hospitality in the midst of all the inter-religious fear and hostility of the moment. At our first gathering, we observed the Muslim traditions of removing our shoes and of seating the men in one room and the women in another, connected via CCTV. But our hosts graciously suspended their traditions for subsequent meetings so that we non-Muslims, 'the other', would feel more at home.[2]

At this particular gathering, the imam invited each of us to take five to ten minutes to address this question: *What, according to my tradition, is my duty to my neighbour of another religion?*[3]

It was a great question and all of us had the best intentions, I'm sure. As I recall, the first speaker was a Sikh from India. Perhaps he became temporarily possessed by the spirit of political animosity between India and Pakistan, the native land of the imam, but whatever the reason, he managed to insult our hosts in his very first sentence, even as he raised a valid concern. 'My first duty to my neighbours is not to send them off into another room as second-class citizens, as has been done to the women here today.' Awkward!

The next speaker was a Catholic priest, a good friend of mine. He had laboured for many hours over a brilliant scholarly paper which he read . . . every word . . . in a perfectly flat monotone . . . without looking up . . . even once. It was full of quotes, quotes from popes, quotes from scholars, quotes from encyclicals, quotes from I-can't-remember-where. His ten-minute paper took twenty minutes to read, and every minute was packed full with good information, but I imagine it felt like an hour for those not fluent in academic prose. I can't remember what he said about my duty to my neighbour of another religion. But I can remember being relieved that his paper didn't insult anybody.

Then came a mainline Protestant minister I didn't know. He also read a paper that was filled with a lot of quotes and he also delivered it in an emotionally low-cal monotone. He spoke intelligently of our Christian duty to see Christ in all people, but the illustration he chose was ... questionable at best. It's (almost) always good to quote Dietrich Bonhoeffer, and almost always bad to illustrate a point using Hitler. He managed to do both by saying that Bonhoeffer saw Christ even in Hitler. That was when I wanted to be swallowed up by the floor. The two rabbis – one Orthodox, sitting on my left, and one Reconstructionist, on my right – physically squirmed and furiously massaged their eyebrows as if choreographed. *At least he stuck to his ten-minute limit*, I thought, as he sat down. *And at least it can't get any worse.*

It did. The next speaker was an acquaintance of mine, a Pentecostal pastor with a good heart. He started getting emotional, which the people liked as relief from the previous two speakers. The more emotional he got, the faster he talked, and the speed, combined with his Deep South accent, combined with his generous use of evangelical lingo, meant that he was incomprehensible to most of the folks in the room, for whom English was a second language.[4] (He could have been speaking in tongues, and I don't think they would have known or cared as long as he didn't put them to sleep.) Soon he was shouting something to this effect: 'I love you! I love you all! And because I love you, it is my duty to you, my neighbours, be you Muslim, Hindu, Jewish, Sikh or Buddhist, to tell you that you are all going straight to hell unless you repent and receive Jesus Christ as your personal Lord, Saviour, Healer and Deliverer!'

Ah, I thought, so it could get worse. Next he was quoting John 14:6 and John 10:8, implying that all other religions were false and founded by thieves and robbers. At one point, tears streamed down his face as he told everyone how much he loved them and didn't want them to be in hell for ever. I looked at my watch. Twenty minutes. Now I was rubbing my eyebrows. 'Oh God, let the world just end now,' I prayed. After nearly thirty surreal minutes, he wrapped it up, and I couldn't believe what happened next.

Applause! Extended, loud applause! I was so shocked, I can't remember for sure if it was a standing ovation, but I think it was. What? Were they glad he told them they were going to hell? No – I'm quite certain few had gotten beyond his style to capture his content. Were they just happy for it to be over? Maybe in part. Were they responding to his passion, emotion and conviction? Did the 'I love you! I love you all!' come through so powerfully that everything else seemed unimportant? Yes, I'm quite certain that was it.

I won't bore you with the rest of the speakers, of whom I was next to last. (My point was that my Christian duty is to love my neighbour as myself. That late in the game, I knew that the best way I could practise what I was preaching was by being mercifully brief.) Everyone managed to rally by the end of the hosting imam's closing comments, and all considered the gathering a success, and I suppose it was, in the sense that we all managed to be polite and respectful of each other in spite of our massive displays of awkwardness, insensitivity and cluelessness. More than ten years later, and I'm still cringing right now as I remember all this.

In the days that followed, I kept thinking about my Pentecostal colleague. I kept thinking about the applause he received after he spoke. No, I wasn't jealous. But I knew the response was significant, and I wanted to understand it. Here's part of what I gradually concluded: for him to be himself, to pour out his heart, to unleash his emotion – even more, to rouse his emotion, and to do so in the presence of others of different faiths . . . that was just the gift people needed in the aftermath of 11 September. People needed to cry and shout and vent, not maintain a monotone of surface calm. They needed to rouse themselves towards something other than hostility or fear. In spite of his theological content, that was what this preacher managed to model that Sunday afternoon. I came to believe that my Pentecostal brother did something magical that day – not for me, because I was feeling so utterly responsible for how things were going, but for the majority who (thankfully) couldn't understand what he was saying. He made space for them to *be* human, to *feel* human, to feel *alive*.

And in that very human connection, he communicated real love for the people in the room. He made eye contact with them, not just his manuscript. He wasn't just faithfully representing a tradition or dutifully fulfilling an assignment as some of us seemed to be doing: he was speaking with fervent, sincere love as a human being to human beings.

In so doing, I think my friend revealed three of the deepest secrets of Pentecostalism: humanity, vitality and sincerity.[5] When my friend spoke, he wasn't a 'human thinking' addressing 'humans thinking': he spoke as a *feeling human being* to fellow *feeling human beings* of flesh and blood. He addressed us as human beings who, like him, want and need to stand, shout, laugh, cry, vent, be roused, clap and . . . feel alive. And that vitality – so different from the religious gravity that was all too common among us – became a manifestation of good news: the possibility of something beyond routine existence and heads-down survival, the possibility of joyful vitality and conviviality. And when humanity and vitality are focused outward in sincerity and love for others . . . the condemning content is overshadowed by the spirit, the Holy, vital, loving Spirit.

Pentecostalism in its first dynamic century has helped us see (among other things) what the Spirit can do at the end of long church services with lots of loud singing and louder preaching. In the next century we must discover what the Spirit of God can do outside church services altogether, in the world at large – spreading humanity, vitality and sincerity in the worlds of business and politics, art and culture – not to mention the arena of inter-faith reconciliation. For that to happen, for us to debug and reboot Christian theology as a benevolent rather than a hostile program, we're going to have to give the doctrine of the Holy Spirit – what theologians call pneumatology – a second thought. And a third, fourth, fifth, sixth and seventh, too.

Our first thought of the Holy Spirit, of course, is the realisation that there is a Holy Spirit, and that the Holy Spirit is God-in-us or God-upon-us or God-among-us everywhere and anywhere. Our second thought of the Holy Spirit flows from the first: that the Spirit is ubiquitous – everywhere, always, in all creation. That leads to a third thought, logical and hard to dispute, but too seldom acknowledged: the Holy Spirit pre-exists all religions, cannot be contained by any single religion, and therefore can't be claimed as private property by any one religion.

That means that Pentecostals don't own the Holy Spirit, nor do Christians, nor do monotheists, nor do theists. According to Genesis, the Spirit was active in creation before there were any human beings, not to mention any religions; according to David, we cannot flee from the Spirit even in the grave; and according to Paul (quoting a Greek poet), all human beings live and move and have their being in the Spirit. So we can say that the Spirit is open-source rather than proprietary, and that people (and macaws and bonobos and tortoises and parrotfish, for that matter) are bumping into the Spirit at every turn, whether they acknowledge it or not.

That leads to a fourth thought, even more surprising: *what we call the secular is actually the realm or domain of the Spirit.* The secular – literally meaning the world, the realm outside of church control – isn't profane. Rather, properly understood, it is sacred because the Spirit is and has always been active there, evoking light from darkness, order from chaos, fullness from void, life from lifelessness, actuality from potentiality and potentiality from actuality.[6]

If the secular is sacred, that means the Spirit is at work in what we call secular work in the secular world (a redundancy, by the way). So the scientist studying interstellar dust is investigating the domain of the Spirit, and the Spirit gently 'hovers' over her neurons as they fire a hypothesis into being. The same is true of a palaeontologist excavating a fossil, an executive developing a marketing plan, a stonemason fashioning a chimney, a father changing a diaper, a mother planning a vacation, an engineer designing a solar panel and a bookkeeper wrestling with a budget. And that's as true for a Muslim astronomer, a Buddhist palaeontologist, a Sikh executive, a Hindu stonemason, a Jewish father, a Jain mother and an atheist engineer as it is for a Christian theologian. What may differ is not the presence and benevolence of the Spirit, but the awareness and responsiveness of the individual.

These second thoughts lead to yet another: if the Spirit is ubiquitous and all people are encountering the Holy Spirit simply because we live, move and have our being in the Spirit's domain, we can understand human religions – all human religions, including our own – as imperfect human responses to our encounters with the Spirit who is present in all creation. That is not to deny the presence of unique divine revelation in any one religion, nor is it to affirm that all religions are the same, nor is it to imply that the Spirit should be credited or blamed for everything going on in our religions. Instead, it is simply to propose that each religion, based on its unique location and history, would have a unique, particular and evolving perspective from which to encounter the Spirit in a unique way.[7] That would mean that differences between religions would not necessarily mean contradictions. They could simply mean additional data, expressed in different systems of local imagery and language, based on differing encounters with the same Spirit of God, present in all creation across all time. Not only that, but in light of the wildly different local conditions in which they encounter the same Spirit, we might interpret some religious differences in a new light: rather than saying different (contradictory) things about the same thing, various religions could sometimes be saying different (complementary) things about different (complementary) experiences entirely.[8]

What would that mean for Christian identity? It would mean at least three things. First, we Christians can make a strong claim to have received a real revelation through real encounters with the real Holy Spirit in specific locations and at specific times in creation. Second, we have something unique to offer members of other religions, based on our unique and real encounters with the Spirit. And third, it would mean other religions have something to offer us as well, based on their real and unique encounters with the Spirit. To refuse to receive those gifts would be tantamount to dishonouring the Holy Spirit's work beyond our group's own experience. These second thoughts would prepare us for one more.

If the Holy Spirit is indeed ubiquitous and secular, active in all creation, not just the church, and if everyone in creation can't avoid encountering the Holy Spirit, and if all of our religions potentially contain localised, particular responses to the Holy Spirit[9] (along with lots of other components, such as expressions of rivalry and fear), and if each religion has treasures to give and treasures to receive from the others, then we would expect the Holy Spirit to be moving people in each religion to offer their good gifts to others, and to receive the good gifts offered by others. In other words, we would expect the one Holy Spirit to be moving, working, 'hovering' over each religion – and also in the space between religions, or at the boundaries between them, inviting people into conversation, exchange, even communion, across the boundaries that have in the past separated them.

And that Spirit-work would apply to us, right now. We would expect that in my writing and in your reading of this book, the Holy Spirit would be at work, hovering over us, seeking to lead us out of slavery to hostility and conflict and into a good, free land of benevolence and communion.

In a strange, messy, imperfect-but-real way, that's what I believe the Holy Spirit was doing that 2001 afternoon in the mosque. It happened through all of us, I think. Our shared desire to be together and to communicate intelligently with one another expressed something of the Holy Spirit. But through that

Pentecostal preacher – through him, and no doubt in spite of him to some degree – the Holy Spirit conveyed love in an extraordinary and needed way. Predictably perhaps, his words said, *I'm in; you're out. To be in, you must join my religion and believe what I believe.*[10] But his actions and his manner spoke more truly: *I love you. I care about you. I'm here with you. I'm pouring out my heart to you – in spite of our differences. I'm holding nothing back. I'm taking a risk. I'm being real. I love you.* When the people felt that sincere, uninhibited, overflowing, outpouring love – the primary fruit of the Holy Spirit – the walls came down, and they erupted in applause.

CHAPTER 18

How Faithful Doctrinal Reformulation Can Make Orthodoxy More Generous

Learning from my own intertribal experiences, I had some small understanding that other tribes also used a harmony concept as a foundation for living. I found that each tribe has a word or several words in its own language that broadly represents living in harmony and balance. As far as English references go, some tribes speak of harmony as a way of balance; some refer to the concept as the 'beauty way'; while others may talk of a 'good way' or 'good road' or 'a good path.' Other tribal groups call it the 'blessing way.' The majority of Native American people tend to recognize the concept in their own tribes and in other tribes.

Randy Woodley[1]

I have four children, each wonderful, each beloved. One of them is a cancer survivor. From the age of six to ten, he underwent daily chemotherapy, using the best chemotherapeutic agents available at the time to save him from leukaemia. During the time of treatment, his greatest immediate threat was not the cancer, but rather the chemotherapeutic agents themselves. They were unpleasant, to be sure: they caused vomiting, hair loss, throat lesions, extreme lethargy and mood swings. In addition, they rendered him dangerously vulnerable to common infections. Chicken pox, for example, was potentially lethal. To kill the threat of cancer, chemotherapy threatened to kill him.

As in cancer treatment, so in treatment for religious hostility: the treatment is by no means safe, and it might be considered poison if not for the presence of an even more dangerous threat, which raises an important question: Is Christian orthodoxy so badly infected with so much hostility that it is incurable? Is the patient beyond hope of cure?

Many people answer yes. The only way they see to escape the hostility of Christian orthodoxy is to flee it as a lost cause, to become post-orthodox refugees, either in another religion or no religion. Knowing they don't want to stay among a hostile people, they seek a better homeland, one they hope will be less contentious, less aggressive, less hostile. But chances are, once they arrive, the new identity-territory to which they have fled will have derived at least some of its identity-strength through hostilities of its own (including, perhaps, hostilities against Christian orthodoxy!). And once they've settled in that new homeland, they may not find greater resources for reconciliation and peace than the ones they left behind.[2]

That's why I hope a better option has become clear in the preceding chapters: faithfully reformulating orthodoxy by treating its oppositional, hostile and imperial malignancies. The doctrines themselves don't pose a threat, but rather fast-growing, easy-to-spread mutations of those doctrines. We have to stop those mutations without killing the patient (and before the patient goes on a killing rampage), and so we've considered how that might be done in regard to several key doctrines: creation, original sin, election, the Trinity, the deity of Christ and the Holy Spirit. Many other doctrines deserve similar treatment through similar reformulation. Perhaps, five hundred years after the Great Reformation, we are on the verge of the Great Reformulation.

How, for example, might our atonement doctrines be reformulated in a non-violent, post-imperial, post-sacrificial light – thus addressing the real problem of original sin as we have explored it here?[3] How might the Bible's apocalyptic passages be reformulated so as to yield a non-violent eschatology that promotes hope and constructive action for the future? How might we faithfully reformulate those doctrines of heaven, hell and final judgement so they are no longer malignant? And along with them, how might we reformulate our understandings of Satan and his minions and their principalities and powers that oppress and possess human beings, driving them to subhuman behaviour?[4] How might we reformulate our understanding of the Church and its mission so that we could articulate a more robust ecclesiology that will support a strong-benevolent Christian identity in the future?

Clearly, we've already set the stage for these rediscoveries. The doctrinal reformulations we've already considered have sufficient weight to destabilise the status quo and nudge it towards a tipping point. Already the cat is out of the bag, and already these questions are being raised – in seminary classrooms but also in online discussions, in denominational headquarters but also in pub theology groups and emergent cohorts. Perhaps future generations will consider us to be farther along in the Great Reformulation (or the Great Emergence, etc.) than we ourselves realise.

Doctrines don't exist in a static linear outline where you can take out your outdated eschatology module and replace it with a new updated one, leaving everything else intact. Rather, doctrines cohere and interact in a dynamic system in which each part is related to all the others. When you disturb this kind of dynamic system with the right kind, right amount and right intensity of creative disturbance, the whole system can go through a radical rebooting – what we often call a paradigm shift. On the other side of disequilibrium, the system has the chance to re-establish equilibrium in a creative, robust, generative way.

If the creative disturbance is too limited, other elements in the system will gang up on it and attempt to crush or co-opt the reformulation.[5] Or, in reaction to a successful reformulation, a counter-reformulation might be launched, after which the system may re-establish a version of itself that is even more hostile than before. And if the creative disturbance is too great, the system may collapse altogether, leaving insufficient resources for a resurrection of any kind.[6]

Our challenge is to bring the appropriate amount, kind and pace of creative disturbance to the system, and then to participate in the often messy but always exciting processes of renewal, reform and refounding, depending on the Spirit of God to guide and energise, to correct and reorient, as the reformulation unfolds.

Whatever we do, we must expect and listen to criticism. We must listen to the critics on the right who tell us that we're proposing too much too fast. We must listen to their counterparts on the left who tell us we're proposing too little too slow. We must soberly consider the dangerous potential consequences of collapse – consequences that are partly in the hands of people like us who propose change from the margins, and even more in the hands of those in the centres of power who have more at stake in defending the status quo. And speaking of the status quo, we also must soberly consider the ways that our religious systems are already fuelling the status quo with hostility – between religions, classes, ethnic groups, political parties and nations, and between human beings and the planet as well, all of which can contribute to the ultimate catastrophic collapses: the destruction of our planetary civilisation and our global ecosystem.[7]

These aren't trivial matters! What can we do but speak as best we can, trusting that where we have not spoken strongly enough, others will amplify, and where we have spoken too strongly, others will moderate?

As we play our role in the as-yet-unwritten story, we are acting in good faith upon the doctrines we have already considered. We are trusting that the Creator has built into creation the resources we need for self-correction in this critical moment. We are trusting that original sin, for all its terrifying power, is not more powerful than the more original goodness God has written into the code of creation and of us. We are trusting that God is still calling more and more of us, like Abraham, to leave the Ur of strong-hostile identity and venture out, through the barrenness and insecurity of weak-benign identity, into a fertile terra nova where identities can be strong and benevolent.

We are trusting that that the doctrine of the Holy Trinity models a kind of glorious one-anotherness that we can learn and into which we can be drawn. We are trusting that Jesus – purely non-violent, purely benevolent, purely good – truly is the logos that reveals the heart of God and the ultimate inner logic by which the universe arcs towards justice and peace. And we are trusting that the Holy Spirit is drawing us into insight just as others are being drawn into complementary, supplementary and critically corrective insight. And we are trusting that the Holy Spirit groans within us, as Paul put it, in longings too deep for words, yearning within us for all creation to be liberated from the futility of human hostility and the destruction it unleashes. We are trusting that regardless of the ways the Bible has been abused for hostile purposes, it has unimagined resources for peaceable ones.

If these explorations be deemed unorthodox, we must ask what kind of orthodoxy are we left with? Must we not, in all humility, acknowledge that all orthodoxy is semi-orthodoxy – meaning that none of us can claim to have captured the infinite and inexpressible in our feeble human definitions and expressions? And would that not mean that all orthodoxy is also semi-unorthodoxy, and that every claim to absolute orthodoxy is the least orthodox claim anyone could ever make?[8]

These questions stir a nearly forgotten memory from my childhood. The details are foggy, but I believe I was in the family car, an old Chevy Impala, riding home from church on a Sunday morning. Like any good boy of nine or ten, I was trying to figure out who 'we' were so I could be a loyal member of 'us' and a loyal opponent against 'them'. Something was said in the sermon that morning that moved me to ask a question that is central to the identity of every ardent young fundamentalist: 'Who are the liberals, Mom? They sure must be bad.' 'Liberals believe in the universal fatherhood of God and the universal brotherhood of man,' she said, as if that needed no further explanation.

I don't remember anything else, but that brief moment is frozen in my childhood memory. Why does it stay with me so vividly? The universal fatherhood of God sounded like a good thing. The same with the universal brotherhood of man. (We were entirely comfortable with the universal reference of male pronouns back then.) I'm quite certain I didn't argue or even ask another question. But I must have pondered my mother's reply in my heart in such a way that it just resurfaced, decades later. That may have been the first moment when I felt a twinge of identity conflict in my boyish soul, a feeling that maybe *we* weren't all good and *they* weren't all bad.

We have Jesus to blame for the doctrine of the fatherhood of God, and for its corollary that we are all sisters and brothers in God's creation. There's no better place to reflect on this doctrine than in the parable of the Prodigal Son (Luke 15). The parable, it turns out, is all about identity – after all, what's more primal to identity than one's family?

As we often tell it, the story climaxes when a runaway boy returns home feeling disgraced, hoping to re-enter the household as a slave, and the father graciously receives him as a son. But the real climax, I propose, comes later, when the father slips out of the welcome-home party to speak with the alienated older brother outside. As the interchange unfolds, it's clear that the older son feels every bit as conflicted and confused about his identity as his brother: 'Listen! For all these years I have been working like a slave for you, and I have never disobeyed your command; yet you have never given me even a young goat so that I might celebrate with my friends.' Even though he has remained dutifully at home, he sees himself as a slave, not a son, taking orders, putting in his time.

Both brothers, then, not just one, suffer from an identity crisis. Neither sees himself as he truly is: God's beloved child and connected to his brother in one family. The father's prodigal love to the younger son becomes the means by which the older son could discover how loved he himself is . . . if he would 'have eyes to see and ears to hear'.

But in his alienated and hostile identity, he can't even speak of 'my brother'. Instead he refers to the returned runaway as 'this son of yours'. Then the father cleverly, wisely, tenderly turns the phrase, referring to him as 'this brother of yours'. The primary message of this story, then, is not addressed to rebellious younger sons sowing their wild oats, as we normally suppose. The primary message is addressed to hostile older brothers who feel right and superior and offended, who won't join the party by joining God in welcoming and celebrating 'the other as brother'. The moral of the story runs something like this:

> You can't maintain hostility against 'the other' without also withdrawing from the father who loves both you and the other as beloved children. If you maintain hostility against the other, you stop acting like a son in the same family. You leave your true identity as a son and start playing the part of a slave. When you cut off the other, you're breaking God's heart. God wants you to join him in loving the other as part of one family.

Probably the story should be entitled 'the lost son', not the prodigal son, because it comes packaged with two other stories – of a lost sheep and a lost coin. But the lost son, it turns out, isn't the younger son. When the story ends, that son 'was lost but now is found'. The lost son is the older son. He's the one who doesn't know who he is, where he is or what he's doing. He's the only outsider – placed there by his own refusal to love. And in this, of course, he is a mirror for the intended audience of this triplet of stories:

> Now all the tax collectors and sinners were coming near to listen to him. And the Pharisees and the scribes were grumbling and saying, 'This fellow welcomes sinners and eats with them.' So he told them this parable . . . (Luke 15:1–3)

Would the meaning become clearer if we altered the text slightly like this?

> Now all the Muslims and Buddhists, New Agers and agnostics were coming near to listen to him. And the radio preachers and Bible teachers were grumbling and saying, 'This fellow welcomes non-Christians and eats with them.' So he told them this parable . . .

Could it be that our core doctrines are even more wonderful and challenging than we previously imagined, asking us not simply to assent to them in the presence of our fellow assenters, but to practise them in relationships with those who don't recognise or hold them? Could our core doctrines in this way become 'healing teachings' intended to diagnose and heal our distorted and hostile identities? Could they be aspects of the Harmony Way that restore us to a strong and benevolent identity and unleash in us a joyful desire to converse and eat with the other, so that we once again take our place in the family of God? Could our core teachings be shared, not as ultimata (believe or die!), but as gifts (here's how we see things, and here's what that does for us . . .)?

THREE

THE LITURGICAL CHALLENGE

Our religious self, like our cultural or social self . . . takes shape through an ongoing process . . . of forming a sense of self and then expanding or correcting that sense as we meet other selves. There is no such thing as a neatly defined, once-and-for-all identity.

Paul Knitter[1]

CHAPTER 19

How the Christian Year Can Become More Christian

> I begin the prayer that Jesus taught us: 'Our Father . . .' Who is
> included in this word 'our'? After that first prayer when I said,
> 'God,' there was no way back to unbelief. God was there to
> stay in my life. After this prayer when I said, 'Our God,' there
> was no way back to unbelief either. *The other* was here to stay
> in my life.
>
> Samir Selmanovic[1]

A few years ago I was invited to preach in an old Anglican church
in a rural village in the United Kingdom (further specificity isn't
important). Having arrived early, I had a few minutes to wander
around the church and read the wall inscriptions that are so typical of old British churches. A large inscription from the nine-
teenth century arrested my attention. It honoured a young man
from the parish who had died as a soldier in India, fighting to
maintain the British Empire's control of the subcontinent. The
inscription included words to this effect: 'He bravely fought and

honourably died in service to the crown, the brave son of a conquering race.'

My guess is that most members of that parish pay no more attention to the inscriptions on their walls than they do to dust in the corners or cracks in the ceiling. But as a guest, all the while I preached, that inscription seemed to heckle me from the wall to my left. 'What if a person of Indian descent came to this church?' I wondered. How would he or she feel to be dubbed 'a conquered race'? And how does it feel to be a British citizen, having these words on the wall remind you each Sunday of your colonial past? What does the inscription say to small children as they learn to read, come of age, undergo confirmation? What does the act of ignoring the inscription do to those who ignore it? What would I do with that inscription if I were the priest at this church? Would I try to cover it up? Have it removed? Use it as a teaching opportunity by placing a theological reflection beside it? With all these distracting questions swirling in my mind, I doubt my sermon was very coherent.

The vestiges of imperial Christianity are not always as obvious as this inscription in stone. But they are no less present in most of our churches. Racism, colonialism, exclusivism, elitism and other members of the hostility family often hide camouflaged in songs and hymns, devotionals and prayers, sermons and Sunday School lessons. And it's not only what is said that aids and abets hostility: it's what is left unsaid. For example, I remember preaching in a predominantly Tutsi church in Burundi. After I made an appeal for the Twa people, the nation's oppressed minority, someone came up to me and said, 'The word *Twa* has never been spoken before in this church. It is as if the Twa didn't even exist. Thank you for reminding us that the Twa too are

God's children.' I thought of how many real-world hostilities around the world are similarly protected through avoidance and silence in churches today.

In education, there is something called the null curriculum. It's the between-the-lines curriculum that teaches by what is never mentioned, or by the way the chairs are arranged, or by the way bells ring and meals are served and floors are cleaned and walls are painted (or not). In churches, there is what we might call the null liturgy – the unwritten repertoire of forms and prac-tices that teach without even being noticed. If we are going to reformulate liturgy to reshape Christian identity in the direction of strength and benevolence, we are going to have to address both our explicit liturgy and our null liturgy.

Normally the term *liturgy* is used to describe an order or programme of gathered worship, usually on a Sunday morning. It derives from a Greek word meaning 'public duty', literally 'the work of the people'. I've suggested elsewhere that we could better define it as 'the workout of the people' – where each litur-gical element is like an exercise or apparatus at a gym or health club, designed to strengthen a particular muscle group.[2] Liturgical elements in this broader sense – whether a hymn, a chant, a prayer of confession, a season of the church year, a class or small group, a sermon, or the Eucharist understood in this way or that – exercise different faculties of the soul, and in so doing they strengthen, for better or worse, some form of Christian identity.

As in the case of the inscription on that church wall, liturgical elements can harbour vestiges of racism, colonialism and nation-alism that stand in direct opposition to the gospel. When we sing a popular praise chorus like 'Show Your Power', we can uninten-tionally label and objectify the other, as in 'for our inheritance, give us the lost'. When we faithfully recite a nice, sweet, vague prayer of confession week after week, but never specify what sins we're actually guilty of – institutional racism, complicity with plutocracy, greed, gluttony, ecological apathy or cowardice in response to our call to be peacemakers and justice seekers – we are being liturgically formed in a Christian identity that tacitly supports the status quo.

If we want to move beyond both a strong-hostile Christian identity on the one hand and a sweet, sentimental, benign Christian identity on the other, we must grapple with liturgy in this broad sense, starting with the church year. Imagine the positive impact on Christian identity if we conceived of the church year in fresh ways.

Advent

In advent, we celebrate the coming of Christ as the prince of peace. We cultivate a longing for peace. We highlight the bright promise of his coming – good news of great joy for all peoples everywhere – against the dark realities of our world: competitive religious supremacy, strident neighbour-less nationalism and the misguided sense of privilege, all flowing from a misguided sense of calling. As we look back to the original advent, we also see Christ as still coming to us from the future in perpetual advent. In that spirit of welcome, we urge every heart to prepare him room so earth may indeed receive her needed king and the kingdom he proclaimed.

Perhaps we re-tradition the advent candles around four titles commonly ascribed to Jesus: *Christ* – meaning the promised liberator, who frees us from our endless cycles of violence; *Lord* – the anti-Caesar, who brings peace not by shedding the blood of

Three: The Liturgical Challenge

enemies but by offering himself in love; *Lamb of God* – who comes to put an end to the cycles of scapegoating and sacrifice once and for all; and *Word of God* – who reveals God's character as non-violent, kind and reconciling.[3] Perhaps in this context, we rediscover Mary as the living icon of receptivity to and participation in the new gospel way of life. Perhaps we also rediscover the social, political, economic and theological foment of Mary's Magnificat. And perhaps we re-tradition the idea of virgin birth as a decisive repudiation of the standard patriarchal systems of violent male dominance, evermore associating the saving power of God with the tender care of a mother's love.[4] Such a celebration would give new meaning to the title *Saviour* as applied to Jesus – a fitting focal point for Christmas Eve: Jesus, the firstborn of a new generation of humanity characterised by love, non-violence and solidarity with all, comes to save humanity from what it has become.

Christmas

On Christmas Day, we would celebrate the birth of the man who repudiated the violent path of obsessive taking (which René Girard called *acquisitive mimesis*) and blazed the new path of generous self-giving. Our mutual gift-giving would then echo the self-giving of God in Christ.[5] And the celebration of Christ's birth could become a birthday party, not just for Jesus but also for the new humanity that transcends and includes all previous identities. Imagine, beginning on Christmas Day, the expansive possibilities of the twelve days of Christmas – rescued from the banality of geese a-laying and lords a-leaping: each day devoted to celebrating a different aspect of the love of God for all humanity, starting with the poor, the vulnerable, the last, the least and the lost.[6]

Lent

Imagine the possibilities of Lent as an annual season specially devoted to the life and teaching of Jesus, and an annual call to repentance – to examine and change our lives in light of his kind life and teaching of kindness. Perhaps Lent could take shape around a four-year cycle, with year one focused on the Sermon on the Mount, year two focused on Jesus' interactions with individuals, year three focused on Jesus' parables and year four focused on the meaning of Jesus' signs and wonders or his Olivet Discourse. Or perhaps one year could be devoted to each of the four Gospel writers. Whatever the focus, the purpose would be identity formation as followers of Jesus in his way of peace, justice and reconciliation.

Holy Week

Again, imagine the possibility of Palm Sunday as we ponder Jesus weeping over Jerusalem for its ignorance of the ways of peace. Imagine us lamenting today's ignorance in today's centres of political, economic and religious power: *Oh Washington, Washington! Oh London, London! Oh Buenos Aires, Buenos Aires! Oh Harare, Harare!* Imagine if that yearning for peace framed the week to follow, as we hold up our personal, familial, ecclesial, political, economic and international conflicts to be softened, as it were, by the tears of Jesus. Imagine Monday to Wednesday devoted to specific incidents recorded in the gospel, culminating in Maundy Thursday with Jesus' command to love one another – including stranger, outsider, outcast, betrayer and enemy. What act could more dramatically embody the opposite of violence than the washing of feet? What attitude could more appropriately express the opposite of hostility than humble servanthood? (We will consider the Lord's Supper in an upcoming chapter.)

Then imagine Good Friday, as we ponder the mystery of God identifying not with the torturers but with the tortured; not with the powerful but with victims of abused power; not with those who scapegoat but with those who are scapegoated. Good Friday thus becomes the great celebration of God's empathy with all human suffering and pain. It exposes all violence as anti-God, and reveals God as the one who identifies with all victims of violence. Pondering the cross and the agonising road to it, we acknowledge God's self-revelation in Christ as a suffering victim – not as a dominating victor. In our Good Friday services, then, we defect from the broad and smooth road of violence and domination, choosing the rough and uphill pathway of the cross – choosing to suffer rather than to make others suffer.[7] When we observe the stations of the cross, and especially when we come to the women weeping for Jesus, we hear him saying to us, 'Do not weep for me, children of the twenty-first century, but for yourselves and your children.' In that spirit, we would return to the tears of Palm Sunday, seeing in the suffering of people today the suffering of Jesus, and vice versa.

Then comes Holy Saturday, a day of silence and stillness, an in-between day that I have often felt should be the day devoted to doubt, the day at which we listen to agnostics and atheists and remind them, and us, that they too have a place among the people of God.

Easter

Then Easter dawns. The scandal of Easter was not simply that a supernatural event occurred. Minds in the ancient world weren't divided by the rigid natural-supernatural dualism that forms modern minds. In those days miracles were notable not for *defying the laws of nature* (a concept that was unknown until recent centuries), but for *conveying an unexpected meaning* or message through an unusual or unexplainable medium. What was the scandalous meaning conveyed by the resurrection of Jesus? It was not simply that a dead man was raised. It was *who* the raised man was. Someone rejected, mocked, condemned and executed by both the political and religious establishments was raised. A convicted outlaw, troublemaker and rabble-rouser was raised. A condemned blasphemer and lawbreaker was raised. A non-violent non-conformist who included the outcasts – and therefore became an outcast – was raised. What does that mean about the authoritative institutions that condemned him? What does that mean about his non-conformist message and non-violent ways?

What might happen if every Easter we celebrated the resurrection not merely as the resuscitation of a single corpse nearly two millennia ago, but more – as the ongoing resurrection of all humanity through Christ? Easter could be the annual affirmation of our ongoing resurrection from violence to peace, from fear to faith, from hostility to love, from a culture of consumption to a culture of stewardship and generosity . . . and in all these ways and more, from death to life. What if our celebration of Easter was so radical in its meaning that it tempted tyrants and dictators everywhere to make it illegal, because it represents the ultimate scandal: an annual call for creative and peaceful insurrection against all status quos based on fear, hostility, exclusion and violence?[8] What if we never stopped making Easter claims about Jesus in AD 33, but always continued by making Easter claims on us today – declaring that now is the time to be raised from the deadness of fear, hostility, exclusion and violence to walk in what Paul called 'newness of life'? What if Easter was about our ongoing resurrection 'in Christ' – in a new humanity marked by a strong-benevolent identity as Christ-embodying peacemakers, enemy lovers, offence forgivers, boundary crossers and movement builders? What kind of character would this kind of liturgical year form in us? How might the world be changed because of it?

I can imagine Easter opening a fifty-day period during which we constantly celebrate newness, freedom, change and growth. As we would retell each year the story of the risen Christ appearing in the stranger on the Emmaus Road, so part of every Easter season for us would mean meeting and inviting to our tables strangers, aliens, refugees, people of other religions or no religion at all, to welcome them as we would Christ, and to expect to meet Christ in them.

During those fifty days, we would observe the feast of the ascension. We would do so without arguing over whether a literal Jesus was literally seen literally rising into literal clouds (have that either way you want it). Instead, we would focus on the meaning of ascension – the *actuality* that transcends *factuality*: that Jesus now reigns for us as the non-violent king, the servant-king, the king of love. He has already ascended and has already been enthroned, which is to say that we don't need to wait for some future day to start living by his way. We can, we must, begin the insurrection of resurrection now.

Pentecost

I have always felt that Pentecost is the most underrated holiday. What could be more important than the outpouring of the Holy

Spirit on 'all flesh'? What could be more meaningful for people being saved from hostility than to celebrate the Spirit who empowers us to 'speak in tongues' – to transcend the us-them barriers of language and see all people as one diverse community in God's commonwealth of love? This would be a season to read the book of Acts – a book that is about boundary-crossing from Pentecost (God speaks all languages, not just ours!), to the early church holding 'all things in common' (God reconciles rich and poor!), to the healing of the lame beggar (God welcomes the disabled!), to the resolution of the Jewish-Greek widow controversy (God shows no favourites!), to the baptism of the Ethiopian eunuch (God includes the racially and sexually other!), to Peter's conversion at Cornelius's home (God calls nobody 'unclean'!), and so on.

Kingdomtide

I prefer this name to 'ordinary time' – although the point could be made that living a 'kingdom-of-God life' should indeed be ordinary for Christians. (Some may prefer the term *kindomtide*, to shift from a political/patriarchal to a familial/filial image.) If Pentecost celebrates our joyful immersion into the Spirit, this season instructs us in walking in the Spirit day by day. This is the season to focus on the nine-fold fruit of the Spirit – strong and benevolent in flavour: love, joy, peace, patience, kindness, goodness, gentleness, faithfulness and self-control. This is the season to seek Spirit-empowerment as we learn and practise the specific skills and habits of following Jesus' way – active and deep listening, processing pain into forgiveness and reconciliation, feeling and showing compassion, conflict transformation, pre-emptive peacemaking, serving others, giving secretly, receiving gratefully, returning blessing for cursing, doing good to those who do you evil, withdrawing to pray in solitude. There is plenty here to keep us on the edge of our seats until Advent season begins again.[9]

'What you're recommending here,' you might say, 'is a radical revision of the whole church year! Is that allowed? Is it possible?'

'Yes,' I would reply, 'that is exactly what I am recommending. The deeper question is not whether revision is allowed, but rather whether the church year as it is currently practised is actually working. Is it producing Christians with a strong and benevolent identity? If not, then how, in these critical times, could we possibly justify not revising it?'

Obviously, this is not the kind of project any one person can accomplish in one chapter or even one book. But great liturgical reformers like John Chrysostom, St Francis, Martin Luther, John Calvin, Thomas Cranmer, Charles Wesley, Pope John XXIII and Vincent Donovan have arisen in the past. And I dare to hope and believe that there are, alive today, thousands of women and men, young and old, from the global north and south, east and west, clergy and laity, who have been given the gifts to help us now. If the ancient formula *lex orandi lex credendi* (the rule of worship is the rule of belief) is true, then it is equally true that *lex orandi lex vivendi* (the way we worship is the way we live). If we want to live in greater strength and kindness, then strength and kindness must be more central to our liturgical lives season by season, Sunday by Sunday, year by year.

CHAPTER 20

How Baptism Differs from Sitting on Santa's Knee

Flannery O'Connor conveyed baptism through its exaggeration, in one novel as a violent death by drowning. In answer to a question about why she created such bizarre characters, she replied that for the near-blind you have to draw very large, simple caricatures.

Walker Percy[1]

My second-best educational experience in life (after finger painting in kindergarten) came in graduate school when, under the wise tutelage of Dr Lewis Lawson at the University of Maryland, I wrote my thesis on novelist Walker Percy, whom I had the privilege to correspond with and meet. In addition to inspiring me by his literary example, encouraging me to write and introducing me to the term *postmodern*, which would later become so helpful to me, Percy helped me understand the crisis of Christian identity: the Christian today has 'cast his lot with a discredited Christendom' and 'inherited a defunct vocabulary', he said. What is one to do in such a predicament?

He does the only thing he can do. Like Joyce's Stephen Dedalus, he calls on every ounce of cunning, craft, and guile he can muster from the darker regions of his soul. The fictional use of violence, shock, comedy, insult, the bizarre, are the everyday tools of his trade. How could it be otherwise? How can one possibly write of baptism as an event of immense significance when baptism is already accepted but accepted by and large as a minor tribal rite somewhat secondary in importance to taking the kids to see Santa at the department store?[2]

As an adult convert to Christian faith, Percy knew firsthand that baptism was in its origin far from a 'minor tribal rite somewhat secondary in importance'. On an individual level baptism represented, like death, the end of an old identity and, like birth, rising into a new one. On a public level, it represented a rejection of all current forms of religious identity in pursuit of a new kind of identity.

It's shocking how few Christians realise that John the Baptist didn't invent baptism. He revolutionised it. He turned it from a sign of submission to the religious status quo into an act of guerrilla theatre that protested the religious status quo.

Luke tells us that John was the son of Zechariah, a priest. The priestly class was centred in Jerusalem around the temple – an opulent monument to religious power, success and prestige. Prior to entering the temple, pilgrims to the holy city would undergo a ceremonial washing, part of the elaborate ritual apparatus overseen by the priests. Why a washing? Because pilgrims who came to the holy city from faraway places had (along with other contaminations) undergone polluting contact with 'unclean' Gentiles. The ceremonial washing in Temple-affiliated baths was, then, a celebration of identity – what we might call a conventional or establishment identity: *we* are the clean and legitimate, *they* are the unclean and illegitimate, and *we* must be washed clean from all contact with *them*. There was a theological assumption behind this identity: God loves *us* and finds *them* unclean, smelly, disgusting, dirty, unacceptable. The Temple and its baptisms, then, were ritual enactments to bond adherents to this strong-superior identity: *God is hostile to all unclean people, and through our baptism we separate ourselves from all that is unclean.*

When John comes of age, he does not follow his father into the priesthood as everyone would expect.[3] Instead, he turns away from Temple and holy city and enters the wilderness. It is highly possible that for some time he associated with one of the Essenic communities like the Qumran settlement, the source of the Dead Sea Scrolls. Members of these hyper-puritan communities felt the Temple system was hopelessly corrupted, having (among many failings) struck a compromise with the occupying Romans. In protest, they created separatist communes out in the desert, far from Jerusalem, and there they set up their own religious apparatus – complete with baptismal pools that would be used several times a day. The message is clear: the conventional establishment is just as unclean as the Gentiles, and by separating ourselves from them, *we* stand apart as the truly, *truly* pure. Day after day, bath after bath, adherents bound themselves ever more passionately to this theological claim: *God is hostile towards all unclean people, and through our baptism, we separate ourselves from all that is unclean.*

These anti-establishment communities in this way positioned themselves as mirror images of the establishment they opposed. If the establishment was oppositional, they were hyper-oppositional. If the establishment was puritan, they were hyper-puritan. If the establishment required conformity, they were hyper-conformist – only to a contrasting hierarchy and regimen. If we are tempted to compare the Jerusalem establishment to Roman Catholicism in the Middle Ages, we might see Protestantism as the Essenic counterpart. If we are tempted to compare the Jerusalem establishment to Mainline Protestantism in twentieth-century America, we might see Fundamentalism or early Evangelicalism as the Essenic counterpart. If we are tempted to compare the Jerusalem establishment to Religious Right Evangelicalism in the first decade of the new century, we might see the New Atheism or the Secular Left as its Essenic counterpart. If we critique the former as compromised and institutionalised, we might critique the latter as reactionary and extremist. From a distance, we can see each as a rival whose oppositional, hostile, us-them identity in many ways mirrors that of its opposing double.

Against this backdrop, then, we must imagine John leaving Jerusalem and choosing not to follow in the footsteps of his father in the priesthood. We see him heading east from Jerusalem through the Judean wilderness. But whether or not he stays for a time with the Qumran community, he does not remain with them for ever. Instead, he leaves the rugged hill country and heads north into the rift valley above the Dead Sea, and there, on the banks of the River Jordan, he begins to baptise people.

Remember as you see the crowds gather that baptism already has two established (pre-Christian) meanings. For conventional

Temple adherents, it means separating oneself from Gentiles (people of foreign religions) and conforming to a conventional establishment identity with all its hostilities. For Essenic separatists, it means separating oneself from one's conventional compatriots and taking on a radical, counter-establishment identity with all its hostilities. For both, it means washing away contamination; separation from unclean acts, things, places and people; the establishment of a distinct and oppositional identity. Against that background, what would it mean to be baptised by John in the River Jordan – far from Jerusalem and the Temple precincts, yet away from the isolated Essenic communities as well? What would it mean to be baptised in a public place, in a natural river rather than a man-made bath, in running – maybe even muddy – river water?

John defines the essential meaning himself: he proclaims not a baptism of conformity but a baptism of repentance, which means a radical, far-reaching rethinking of everything. If one was previously formed by a conventional Temple establishment identity, one rethinks that way of life. If one was previously formed by an Essenic anti-establishment identity, one rethinks that way of life. What might have been considered acceptable before – hating Gentiles, hating priests, hating the poor, hating the rich – now seems like a sin to be confessed. What might have been considered unacceptable before – reconciling with enemies, showing kindness to outcasts, putting the needs of people above religious rules – now seems like a good thing. That kind of repenting would determine the kinds of sins people would confess as they descended into the Jordan for baptism.

In Matthew's Gospel, John sees some Sadducees and Pharisees coming for baptism. (They were not friends, by the way – one might imagine John addressing American Democrats and Republicans or British Conservative and Labour today.) His response is fascinating:

> You brood of vipers! Who warned you to flee from the coming wrath? Produce fruit in keeping with repentance. And do not think you can say to yourselves, 'We have Abraham as our father.' I tell you that out of these stones God can raise up children for Abraham. The axe has been laid to the root of the trees, and every tree that does not produce good fruit will be cut down and thrown into the fire. (Matt. 3:7–10)

The epithet 'brood of vipers' was a common expression of the day, meaning malicious or hostile people.[4] John seems to be echoing Jeremiah 46:22, where Egypt is compared to a viper.[5] Drawing from that allusion, John appears to be saying something very powerful – something about identity:

> You are the offspring of malicious, hostile communities. Like Egypt, you oppress and enslave. Who warned you that you need to change? Yes, you might claim to have a clean, pure identity because you are descendants of Abraham, but that isn't impressive at all. What God is interested in is not hostility but fruitfulness.

The violent image of vipers soon contrasts with a peaceful animal image: the Holy Spirit descending as a dove upon Jesus. So the kingdoms of this world – including religious kingdoms – are viperlike and violent; the kingdom of God is dovelike and peaceful. Baptismal repentance means defecting from the former and identifying with the latter.

In Luke's version of the story (3:7ff.), these words are directed towards not just the Sadducees and Pharisees but the crowds in general, and the crowds ask what kind of fruit God wants to see from them. In every case, the response relates to how they will treat others – not with hostility, not with resistance, but with kindness, generosity and justice:

> 'Anyone who has two shirts should share with the one who has none, and anyone who has food should do the same.' Even tax collectors came to be baptised. 'Teacher,' they asked, 'what should we do?' 'Don't collect any more than you are required to,' he told them. Then some soldiers asked him, 'And what should we do?' He replied, 'Don't extort money and don't accuse people falsely – be content with your pay.' (Luke 3:11–14)

So for John, baptism is hardly a second-rate tribal rite comparable to sitting on Santa's knee. It is the radical reversal of identities of exclusion and hostility. It is a defection from all exclusive, hostile and elitist identities – whether they be establishment or anti-establishment in nature. It is a sign that one is repenting of all hostile identities, knowing that those identities can only lead to violent cataclysm. By de-identifying with oppositional identities – by dying to them – one can identify with something new: the kingdom, reign or commonwealth of God – which is a call not to separation and exclusion, but rather to solidarity and reconciliation, as we have seen again and again.

In most of our traditions, Christian baptism is little different from temple baptism. It represents identification with the clean, the orthodox, the good, the 'us'. In some, baptism is more akin to Essene baptism, representing identification with the super-clean, the hyper-orthodox, the holier-than-others, the elite and exclusive 'us'. What would happen if we rediscovered baptism in this alternative way of John and Jesus: discovering a new identity in the transcendent and inclusive kingdom of God, an identity that locates us in solidarity with all people everywhere?

If we reformulated baptism in this way, what kind of cate-chism would prepare us for it? How would that subversive cate-chesis guide us to face and repent of our prejudices, our racisms, our nationalisms, our political and economic antagonisms, our hostilities of every sort? How would it help us discover a new identity as people 'born again' – not entering an elite human ancestry or exclusive religious pedigree, but passing through water and the Spirit so that we are joined once again to all humankind (and to all creation), to be ever marked by human kindness? How would the history of the last two thousand years be different if this understanding of baptism had been sustained?

Baptism in this sense means far more than immersion into Christianity or a Christian religious institution. It signals immer-sion into Christ, so that from now on, inside the identity of Christ, we look out at the other through his eyes, so to speak. It is immersion into the kingdom or commonwealth of God, so that we now see all people from the perspective of this new filial citizenship. 'In Christ' and 'in the commonwealth of God' are far deeper realities than 'in Christianity' and 'in the Christian religion'. Irish theologian/philosopher Peter Rollins captures the difference quite starkly, reflecting on Paul's proclamation that in Christ there is neither Jew nor Greek (religious identity), slave nor free (socioeconomic identity), male or female (sexual identity):

This vision of Paul's is often domesticated by those who would wish to turn this radical vision on its head and claim that he really means we must lay down all earthly identities in order to take up another identity, that of being a Christian. All identities are thus rendered impotent in relation to this unique super-identity.[6]

This domesticated understanding betrays Paul's real meaning, Rollins realises. To truly be 'in Christ' does not mean embracing 'yet another identity', but rather 'lay(ing) down the various identities that would otherwise define us'.

He then recalls Paul's words in Philippians that call us to share the attitude of Christ, who did not grasp or cling to his exalted identity but rather poured himself out, made himself nothing, descending through humanity to servanthood and through servanthood to death as a criminal and disturber of the violence-based Pax Romana. To follow Christ is to share in his radical divestment of identity. He concludes:

> We can even say that in Christ there is neither Christian nor non-Christian . . . The scandalous nature of this radical vision is captured succinctly in the Gospel according to John, where the Christian is described as one who lives in the world (with all of its social, religious, and political divisions) while no longer being of it (not being held fast by them) . . . When this loss of identity is enacted in a liturgical setting, we may call it a suspended space, for in that location one symbolically lays one's identities at the door.[7]

Could you imagine a baptism that carried this radical and subversive meaning? Can you see how this meaning would turn the site of every baptismal font or pool into a modern-day River Jordan, every baptiser into a modern-day John the Baptist and every person baptised into a modern-day agent of the commonwealth of God? Can you see what baptism could be – the laying aside of all hostile identities and the taking up of a new identity in Christ, in which old divisions are replaced by a strong, profound solidarity of human-kindness, shared with everyone?

CHAPTER 21

How Songs, Prayers, Sermons and Sunday School Classes Can Save Lives

Onward, Christian soldiers, marching as to war,
With the cross of Jesus going on before.
Christ, the royal master, leads against the foe;
Forward into battle see his banners go!

Sabine Baring-Gould[1]

I love that old hymn 'All Things Bright and Beautiful'. You're probably familiar with the chorus if you have much history in Protestant churches . . .

All things bright and beautiful,
All creatures great and small,
All things wise and wonderful:
The Lord God made them all.

Some might say it's a little sentimental, but that's true of a lot of our hymns, especially nineteenth-century ones.[2] Sentimental or not, I love the hymn's five verses because each celebrates the beauty of creation, one of the primary ways my own soul experiences and worships God.

> Each little flower that opens,
> Each little bird that sings,
> He made their glowing colours,
> He made their tiny wings.
>
> The purple headed mountains,
> The river running by,
> The sunset and the morning
> That brightens up the sky.
>
> The cold wind in the winter,
> The pleasant summer sun,
> The ripe fruits in the garden,
> He made them every one.
>
> The tall trees in the greenwood,
> The meadows where we play,
> The rushes by the water,
> To gather every day.
>
> He gave us eyes to see them,
> And lips that we might tell
> How great is God Almighty,
> Who has made all things well.

Recently I learned from Peter Rollins that the lyricist, Mrs Cecil Frances Alexander, penned one more verse to the hymn, one that today's hymnals don't include:[3]

> The rich man in his castle,
> The poor man at his gate,
> He made them, high or lowly,
> And ordered their estate.[4]

As I pondered this verse, I couldn't help recalling various stops in my travels over recent years. I've been inside the castles and mansions of some of the world's rich and powerful – eaten gourmet meals, enjoyed scintillating conversation, slept in the finest beds and even relieved myself in bathrooms of shocking opulence. And I have walked among the poor outside the gates of the rich . . . visiting in homes smaller than bathrooms, walking in the faecal mud of crowded refugee camps and squalid squatter villages, sleeping in dingy slums and grim occupied territories where oppression is the norm and the police are just another threat. Having been both inside the castles and outside the gates, if I were asked to sing this verse in church some Sunday, I can only say that I would choke. I would walk out. I don't know if I could ever return to a church where this verse was sung.

Imagine the effects of singing such a verse on the rich – the gratification, the peace, the joy, the sense of divine entitlement. And imagine the effects on the poor – the humiliation, the fury, the outrage or the resignation. What reaction might Mrs Alexander have been hoping for?

The verse descends from distasteful to almost blasphemous as I notice how its language inadvertently parodies Jesus' parable of the rich man and Lazarus.[5] For Jesus, the rich man's apathy about the poor man's poverty was a damnable offence. But even the damned rich man wasn't singing about his privilege as something beautiful and ordered by God! If Jesus were present at the singing of such a hymn, I could imagine him pulling the plug on the sound system in protest.

It makes me wonder whether, in Mrs Alexander's mind, this now-forgotten verse contained the real point of the song. Were all the cute little birds, tiny wings, pleasant summer sunbeams and meadow-play just so much sugar to make a nauseating theo-political, theo-economic message easier to swallow?

At some point, hymnal editors decided that verse needed to be dropped. On one level, I'm glad they did. It must be a step in the right direction to sanitise our hymns, fumigate our prayers and otherwise edit out the residue of our inherited prejudices, leaving us with a bright and beautiful church life that is super-sentimental and saccharine-sweet. Or is it?

After some second thoughts, I wonder if simply dropping offensive elements like these carries the pungent aroma of cover-up, the stale smoke of denial. Considering our history and its anti-Semitism, imperialism, racism, favouritism towards the rich, carelessness or patronisation towards the poor, plundering of the earth and other expressions of hostility – would it be better if these ugly elements of our heritage could be removed from use but still retained somehow in our corporate memory – if only in an instructive footnote or cautionary appendix to the hymnal?

In that same footnote or appendix we could explain what we've learned, how we've changed and why we're trying to be different now. In so doing we would acknowledge that what we do in church can too easily serve the interests of the conflicted status quo and the privileged few. We would thus admit that our liturgies can camouflage injustice. We would face the ways our sermons and hymns can baptise hate and bigotry. We would remember how our holidays and sacred rituals can embed a hostile identity in little children for generations to come. And we would simultaneously confess that we have in the past practised cover-up and denial about the dark sides of our history, and declare our commitment to stop doing so in the future. In so doing, we would form in ourselves and future generations a stronger, wiser, humbler, more benevolent identity.

And from there, the next step would be clear: to replace those elements of our hymns, sermons, rituals and holidays that currently reinforce an oppositional identity with creative alternatives – elements that would help to form in us a strong and benevolent identity as God's creative agents for justice, peace, reconciliation and hope. So we might replace the 'rich man in his castle' verse with something like this:

> All who thirst for justice,
> Who serve among the poor,
> Forging tools for farming
> From weapons made for war.

Or maybe this, keeping with the nature theme:

> Those who save the planet
> From recklessness and greed,
> Preserve endangered species,
> And tend the soil and seed.

If Christian faith in the centuries ahead is to embody a new identity, it will not be enough to sweeten and sanitise our past. Just as the Bible has faithfully and courageously done (as we'll see in the next chapter), we must preserve the ugly, embarrassing and contrary voices of our heritage. Doing so will humble us, but also heal us. We must have the humble courage to side with some verses, prayers and other liturgical resources and against others – not in an oppositional or a hostile way, but in a constructive, identity-forming way. We must understand why Mrs Alexander, God bless her, would pen such a verse and surround it with such sweetness, and we must then look for ways we are doing the same thing – in our songs and hymns, in our prayers and confessions, in our sermons and classes.[6] We must uncover the null curriculum inherent in all we do in gathered worship.

We must do this for adults, and also for children. In so many churches I encounter, serious liturgical renewal is beginning among adults, but the kids are being taught through the same off-the-shelf curricula of the past. Many of these curricula are more hi-tech, flashy and user-friendly than ever, but for all the updates in style and packaging, little thought has been given to the identity they are building in kids.

I was speaking to some staff members from a Christian publishing house recently – more creative, energetic and committed people would be hard to find. I mentioned my special interest in kids' curriculum for Sunday School and confirmation classes. They showed me their most recent curriculum, built around the life of Samson. I couldn't help but be impressed with the lessons they had drawn from Samson's life. Then I asked, 'What do you do about Samson's violence?' They looked puzzled, so I continued, 'I mean, we don't want kids to pull down buildings on their enemies, right? So how do we deal with Samson's violence?' This question had never crossed my mind until recently, and it was clear it was a new question for them as well.[7]

That interaction prepared the way for a conversation with my friend Tracy Radosevic, a gifted biblical storyteller, and one of her mentors, Tom Boomershine, founder of the Network of Biblical Storytellers (a fantastic group more people should know about).[8] I mentioned my concern to Tom: 'You're doing a fantastic job of helping kids and adults learn biblical stories, but what do you do about the violence of so many stories?'

Tom had obviously thought long and hard about this. He said he was becoming more and more convinced that we can't tell stories in isolation – especially violent stories. So we can't tell about David killing Goliath (1 Samuel 17), he said, without also telling the story of God not allowing David to build the Temple because he was a violent man (1 Kings 5). I had never thought of that kind of pairing before. Ever since our conversation, I keep stumbling across example after example of hostile-reconciling pairings as I read and reflect on the Bible.

For example, we can't tell the story about Elijah (1 Kings 18) calling down fire on the prophets of Baal without hearing Jesus' rebuke of his disciples for recommending the same violent response to the 'religiously other' (Luke 9). We can't tell the story of Moses sending people to kill their brothers (Exodus 32) without also telling the story of the Transfiguration, where the non-violent words and ways of Jesus are honoured over those of Moses: '*This* is my beloved son. Listen to *him*' (Mark 9). We can't tell the story of the slaughter of the Canaanites (Deuteronomy 7) without telling Matthew's masterful reversal of that story in Jesus' encounter with the Canaanite woman (Matthew 15). We can't quote 'Jacob I have loved, but Esau I have hated' without also telling the story of Jacob's injustices against Esau, leading to Jacob's climactic need to reconcile with his offended brother, leading to Esau's truly amazing grace to Jacob, leading to Jacob's experience of 'the face of God' in the very one who was supposedly hated by God (Genesis 32–33). The Bible itself, it seems, has in-built reconciling stories to counteract and disarm the hostile ones, but people who want to justify hostility pick the hostile ones and choose to minimise the reconciling ones.[9] (More on picking and choosing in the next chapter.)

How we teach our children really matters, for Bible stories no less than Quranic suras can easily be turned into terrorist weapons. Our stories, sermons, prayers and songs can contribute to liturgies of hostility or liturgies of kindness, forming communities and individuals who translate those liturgies – for better or worse – into their daily lives and into the history of humanity . . . and inhumanity.

CHAPTER 22

How Reading the Bible Responsibly Can Look Irresponsible (and Vice Versa)

One cannot adhere to the Christian faith without a 'decision' in which we take our distance from the 'past'.

Heinz R. Schlette[1]

I was a relatively unknown pastor and author until *Time* magazine included me on a list of influential religious leaders back in 2005.[2] The brief article recounted something I said during a Q & A session at a large Evangelical pastors' gathering the year before. I was asked to declare my position on homosexuality or gay marriage or some related subject. I responded with something like, 'The thing that breaks my heart is that there's no way I can answer that question without hurting someone on either side.'

For all its failings, my not-terribly-inflammatory response accurately reflected a tension I lived in, a tension many of my pastoral colleagues today know all too well. On the one hand, I was the guest of an Evangelical organisation that had an official position against homosexuality. I didn't want to be disruptive or inconsiderate of my hosts, who were trying to bring people together in an atmosphere with a low inflammatory quotient. On the other hand, my inherited conservative thinking on the subject had changed, and I was now working to protect people from discrimination rather than add to it. Caught in that tension, I aimed for a middle path and tried to articulate the tension I felt. As a result, *Time* judged me a potential paradigm shifter with a 'kinder and gentler brand of religion'.[3] A well-known fundamentalist preacher responded to the *Time* article by claiming that in seeking to avoid hurting either my conservative hosts or my gay friends, I was now guilty of 'hurting God'.[4] He judged me unfaithful to the Bible (as he interpreted it) and to God (as he understood God). His comments stirred up a brief hurricane of controversy in the blogosphere. I and others like me were repeatedly accused of 'picking and choosing' the parts of the Bible we liked and ignoring the rest. 'If you want to quote the Bible's verses about love and peace, you also have to quote the ones about hell and damnation,' they said. 'Otherwise you're putting your own authority above the authority of the Bible. So no picking and choosing!'

Some time later, I was surprised to see that one of the world's leading atheists agreed with the 'No picking and choosing' rule, albeit for a different reason. By picking the Bible's love verses and soft-pedalling its hate verses, he suggested, moderate believers give cover to extremists. They help maintain respect for the book their less moderate counterparts will use to inspire and defend violence. In order to deprive extremists of this cover, he said, we must decisively throw out the whole book as a Bronze Age collection of dangerous myths and destructive superstitions.

Just a few months ago, I came across another reference to picking and choosing, one that responded to this atheist's critique. It came from one of my favourite writers, an Irish Catholic philosopher named Richard Kearney:

> So when militant atheists . . . accuse believers of 'picking and choosing,' they are actually accusing them of being *responsible* believers. This is what faith is about: making a choice, venturing a wager, discriminating between rival interpretations in order to make the best decision regarding love and hate, justice and injustice.[5]

So there you have the dilemma: picking and choosing is deemed destructive by both a fundamentalist Christian and an outspoken atheist, but praised as responsible biblical interpretation by a Catholic philosopher (one born, not insignificantly, in a country scarred by religious troubles). Beneath the surface of picking and choosing, Kearney realises, lies the complex art and science of interpretation (hermeneutics, in the language of theologians and philosophers). Interpretation isn't, he makes clear, simply an impersonal, objective, scholarly matter. It is also a profoundly ethical one, and we could say a political one as well. Ultimately, in choosing how to interpret our sacred texts, we pick and choose between 'compassion and murder'.[6] There is no way forward in the pursuit of a strong-benevolent Christian identity that bypasses a lengthy journey through the wild and challenging landscape of hermeneutics.

Hermeneutics is one of the central liturgical practices of the Christian Church. Nearly all liturgies include a sermon in which passages of the Bible are read and interpreted. How can we turn this important liturgical practice towards the formation of strong-benevolent Christian identity?

Artist-theologian Derek Flood understands that hermeneutics means far more than either a facile picking and choosing of our favourite texts or an equally facile taking of everything 'literally'. In an article entitled 'Wrestling with Scripture', he begins where we all must: by acknowledging the hostility and violence of many Bible passages.[7] Passages like 1 Samuel 15:2–3 and Psalm 137:8–9 are lying around like loaded weapons waiting for some fearful or angry interpreters to pick them up and use them for genocidal purposes.[8] Flood flatly rejects traditional attempts to legitimise passages like these. He instead argues for 'a way that allows us to remain faithful to Scripture without needing to defend and promote violence in God's name'. The way forward, he says, is to 'read our Bibles as the Apostle Paul read his'. He then demonstrates how Paul, especially in the epistle to the Romans, reinterprets his sacred Scriptures in the light of God's radical self-revelation in Christ.

Flood graphically displays, for example, Paul's edited quotation of Psalm 18:41–49 and Deuteronomy 32:43 in Romans 15:8–10. Notice what Paul picks to retain and what he chooses to reject:

> For I tell you that Christ has become a servant of the Jews on behalf of God's truth, so that the promises made to the patriarchs might be confirmed and, moreover, that the Gentiles might glorify God for his mercy. As it is written: ~~'I destroyed my foes. They cried for help, but there was no one to save them – to the LORD, but he did not answer . . . He is the God who avenges me,~~

who subdues nations under me . . . Therefore I will praise you among the Gentiles; I will sing the praises of your name.'

Again, it says, 'Rejoice, you Gentiles, with his people, ~~for he will avenge the blood of his servants; he will take vengeance on his enemies and make atonement for his land and people.~~'

The language of divine mercy and promise is retained. The language of divine violence and vengeance is gone.[9] In that simple move, Paul courageously re-articulates the meaning of salvation. It is no longer 'rescuing Israel from peril by killing her enemies', but rather 'the restoration of all people in Christ'.

Flood notes how a respected professor once 'joked that Paul would have surely flunked a seminary class in exegesis'. But no, Flood replies, this isn't a case of Paul playing fast and loose with the Bible. Rather, 'Paul is deliberately flipping the meaning of these passages . . .' Paul's rationale becomes all the more clear in Flood's reading of Romans 3:10–18, where Paul weaves together several Old Testament passages to exemplify the core issues of human evil – all relating to hostility and violence, failing to 'know the way of peace'. (The original passages are cited in brackets.)

As it is written,
'There is no one righteous, not even one;
there is no one who understands, no one who seeks God.
All have turned away, they have together become worthless;
there is no one who does good, not even one.' [Psalms 14:1–3]
'Their throats are open graves; their tongues practise deceit.'
[Psalms 5:9]
'The poison of vipers is on their lips.' [Psalms 140:3]

'Their mouths are full of cursing and bitterness.' [Psalms 10:7]
'Their feet are swift to shed blood;
ruin and misery mark their ways,
and the way of peace they do not know.' [Isaiah 59:7–8]
'There is no fear of God before their eyes.' [Psalms 36:1]

Flood concludes: 'Paul is making a very different point from the original intent of these Psalms. In fact, he is making the *opposite* point – we should not cry out for God's wrath and judgement [on the other], because we are all sinners in need of mercy.' He continues, 'This is not a case of careless out-of-context proof-texting; it is an artful and deliberate reshaping of these verses ... from their original cry for divine violence into a confession of universal culpability that highlights our need for mercy.'

In all Paul's letters we find this same pattern, not sloppy proof-texting to buttress Paul's inherited preferences and prejudices, but a consistent pattern of reinterpretation 'in Christ', whereby his own inherited preferences and prejudices have been revolutionised. In case after case, hostile and violent sections of quoted passages are simply left out so the meaning is artfully and deliberately reshaped according to 'the way of peace', which is the way of Christ. As Flood concludes, 'Paul has disarmed Scripture in Jesus' name.'

In this, of course, Paul faithfully follows his model. In his very first public sermon in Nazareth (Luke 4:18–27), Jesus similarly 'flips the meaning' of Isaiah (61:1–2) by dropping the phrase 'and the day of vengeance of our God'. Lest anyone miss the 'de-hostilisation' and 'de-exclusivisation' of his omission, he then refers to the story of the prophet Elijah who was directed by

God to help a Sidonian woman – an outsider of another religion. And then he adds the story of the prophet Elisha helping a Syrian man – another outsider of another religion. You can imagine the panic in the minds of Jesus' neighbours as they process what their homegrown prophet is saying: *What? Is Jesus suggesting that God loves 'those people – Sidonians and Syrians' just as much as 'us'? Is this 'good news to the poor' universal, for all people, rather than exclusive to members of our religion only? Who does he think he is to betray our elite, exclusive identity like this? This is heresy! Blasphemy! Treason!*

That day in Nazareth when Jesus modelled this deliberately subversive way of reading of the Scriptures, he went right to the heart of us-them oppositional identity. No one should be surprised at the response: hostility. The people who spoke well of him a few moments before (Luke 4:22) now want to kill him (4:28–29). (This, no doubt, illuminates the real meaning of Jesus' words, 'I have come not to bring peace, but a sword.')[10]

Again and again in the New Testament, when people are confronted for being exclusive, hostile or violent, they predictably respond with exclusion, hostility and violence. Consider, for example, the violent response when Stephen confronts the violence of the Sanhedrin in Acts 7. Or consider the incident in the temple (Acts 21–22), when Paul is accused (falsely, it turns out) of defiling their sacred ground by bringing uncircumcised outsiders into it. A mob is about to kill him until some Roman soldiers intervene, and then Paul defends himself. He manages quite a long speech, considering the circumstances, and all seems to be going well until he mentions God sending him to the religiously other. At that, the crowd yells, 'Rid the earth of him! He's not fit to live.' Accepting 'the other' is the one thing that 'we' find absolutely unacceptable, time after time.

The more I read the New Testament, the more clearly I realise that this other-aversion is at the heart of what the gospel calls us to repent of. The old era of us-them thinking and oppositional identity is coming to an end, the gospel declares. In Christ, God is calling us to a path of reconciliation.[11] Walking that path requires us to go back and reread our Scriptures and 'flip them', faithfully picking and choosing – subverting hostility in the strong pursuit of love.[12] Flood concludes, 'Wrestling with Scripture in this way may not be an expression of doubt at all, but an act of faithfulness to both God revealed in Christ, and to Scripture, whose goal is to point to him (Rom. 10:4).'

True, picking and choosing aren't allowed when you're a lawyer dealing with a legal code or constitution. You can't pick Article I.A.3.b and ignore Article 2.C.7.d. But as I argued in *A New Kind of Christianity*, the Bible isn't a constitution. To read, interpret and apply the Bible as if it were a constitution is a category error.[13] It's more accurate to say that the Bible is a library filled with diverse voices making diverse claims in an ongoing conversation. Faithful interaction with a library means siding with some of those voices and against others. (But it also means refusing to remove from the library those voices you don't side with, as we've already seen. The Bible thus facilitates ongoing, open dialogue and debate, not a totalitarian regime of homogenised propaganda.) Siding with some voices and against others isn't simply picking and choosing according to one's own tastes, then. Nor can it be reduced to a simple matter of objective scholarship or logic. Interpretation is also and always a matter of ethics, a matter of the heart and the conscience. So we can expect hostile people to side with hostile voices in the text, fearful people with fearful voices and peace-loving people with peace-loving voices. Interpretation will always to some degree manifest the character of the interpreter along with the meaning of the text.

Jesus pointed out this ethical dimension of textual interpretation one Sabbath day when he dined at the table of a prominent Pharisee (Luke 14). He boldly defied normative Sabbath restrictions by healing a fellow guest. Then he defended his Sabbath violation by appealing to the basic human kindness of all those present: aren't they all decent enough human beings that they would rescue an ox on the Sabbath if it fell into a pit? He made a similar move in another incident involving a man with a deformed hand in a synagogue (Mark 2:25–3:6). In both cases, the compassionate voice of empathy trumps the accusatory voices of condemnation.[14] The same pattern holds true in the Sermon on the Mount. 'You have heard it said,' Jesus says, and then quotes the verses about an eye for an eye, a tooth for a tooth.[15] That kind of retributive justice was once a step up from excessive revenge – ten eyes for an eye, or fifty teeth for a tooth. Now, however, we must take another step up, Jesus says: 'But I say to you, love your enemies.' Of those eight stunning words, the first may be the most stunning of all.

For Jesus, it is permissible to say, 'The Scriptures say . . . *but* I say otherwise,' if the otherwise takes us in the direction of greater compassion, kindness, non-violence and reconciliation. Accusatory retributive justice fades into the past, and a new day of compassionate restorative justice dawns.

Or at least it does with Jesus. It remains to be seen to what degree we Christians today will move forward with Jesus and to what degree we will dig our heels in with the less magnanimous voices in the biblical library.

In our liturgical practice of reading, interpreting and preaching the Bible, we are repeatedly forced to choose between hostility and hospitality, mercy and condemnation, compassion and legalism, forgiveness and revenge, laying down our lives or taking the lives of others . . . page after page, reading after reading, Sunday after Sunday. The way we read, interpret and preach the Bible not only reveals what is hidden in our hearts, but it holds the key for changing or reforming our hearts.

Will the Bible be the sword by which we cut off and threaten 'the other'? Or will the Bible point beyond itself, directing us to Jesus who offers to his disciples the authority to bind and loose (Matthew 16:19) – or, we might say, to pick and choose? For those who choose the latter approach, the Bible is transformed from the sword of combat to the scalpel of surgery – for self-examination and self-critique, exposing our own hostility so that we can join God in compassion for all people and solidarity with the other (Hebrews 4:12–16).[16]

Those of us intent upon forging a strong and benevolent Christian identity in our multi-faith world will be carrying our Bibles with (or within) us. We will read and teach the Bible responsibly and ethically, following the strong and benevolent examples of Paul and Jesus. We will pick all passages that advocate hostility, vengeance, exclusion, elitism and superiority to remind us of where we would be and who we would be if not for Christ. And we will choose all passages that advocate reconciliation, empathy, inclusion, solidarity and equality to remind us of where we are going and who we are called to be in Christ – a precious identity indeed.[17]

CHAPTER 23

How the Table Differs from the Altar

. . . Ricouer offers a startlingly refreshing reading of the Eucharist as a celebration of blood-as-wine, transubstantiation being taken as a sign of life and sharing rather than a token of sacrificial bloodletting. The Eucharistic commemoration of the giving of one's life – 'Do this in memory of me' – thus becomes an affirmation of the gift of life to and for the other rather than an anxiety about personal physical survival after death. In other words, when Christ said 'it is finished,' he meant it.

Richard Kearney[1]

I love the Eucharist. I am not a stickler for the form it takes. Whether accompanied by robes, choirs, smells and bells in a lofty cathedral or enjoyed around a simple table in an intimate celebration among friends, I am endlessly enthralled by the meaning and mystery of the Lord's Supper.[2]

But the Lord's Supper has often been the scene of the church's food fight. When Gentiles as well as Jews, the poor as well as rich, and slaves as well as slave masters were welcomed to the table as equals, you could predict that trouble might ensue. When neither Jesus nor the apostles wrote a detailed rule book or policy manual for the one right way to conduct the meal, you might expect others would try to fill the void. And because one singular desired outcome for the experience was never nailed down, you could anticipate that debates would erupt about its meaning – although the vitriol of those debates does come as a bit of a shock. Now, it's hard to name the ritual without thinking of the hostile language surrounding it – *ex-communication*, the threat of being *dis-fellowshipped*, the *guarding* or *fencing* of a *closed table*, and so on.

When I just referred to the Eucharist as a ritual, I was defining *ritual* as 'an act that employs the body to bond to a meaning'.[3] But what meaning are we bonding to in the Eucharist?

One line of meaning presents the Eucharist as a celebration of hospitality, a table of fellowship and welcome, a means of amazing grace, releasing us from bondage to hostility and reconnecting us through the bonds of human-kindness. It emphasises the table as a place of meeting, of reconciliation, of filial affection, of companionship . . . the place where God and all humanity 'at table are sat down'.[4] In this approach, we bond to the gospel of the reconciling reign or commonwealth of God, proclaimed by and embodied in Jesus, which invites us all into reconciliation with God and one another.

Another line of meaning centres on a sacrificial altar rather than a table – a place where God's hostility towards sinners is pacified by body-and-blood sacrifice.[5] In this understanding, we bond not to Jesus' original gospel of the kingdom of God, but to another gospel, the gospel of penal substitutionary atonement, a doctrine that is as precious and central to many Christians as it is problematic or even repulsive to others.[6] The popular idea of penal substitution works like a rather complex equation. God cannot forgive sin without inflicting punishment and shedding blood, the doctrine teaches, so God is obliged to punish all sinners. Because their offence is against an infinitely holy God, their punishment must be absolute, irrevocable and eternal. All human beings will therefore be damned to eternal conscious torment in hell if God does not provide a substitute upon whom God's infinite wrath can be vented.[7] For those who hold these assumptions, it makes sense to say that God tortured and killed Jesus on the cross so as to be able to vent divine wrath upon a single divine-human representative or substitute rather than all of us.

I grew up with this understanding, and for decades of my life it satisfied me, inspired piety in me and troubled me not at all. Gradually, though, the problematic dimensions of the doctrine nudged me to be more at home with Celtic, Franciscan, Anabaptist, Quaker, Eastern Orthodox, Liberationist and other perspectives that proclaim the gospel (and celebrate the Eucharist) with little or no reference to this atonement theory.[8] I now associate the Eucharist not with the altar of sacrifice (as popularly conceived) but with the table of reconciliation and fellowship. This change in understanding, I now see, produces a change in identity – a change that is highly significant in our multi-faith world.[9]

In the altar-sacrifice framing of the Eucharist, God is hostile towards human beings, and only Christians are exempt from God's wrath. Having given to Jesus their sin and punishment to bear on the cross, and having received from Jesus his imputed merit and grace, Christians imagine this exchange afresh each time they receive the Eucharist. The ritual thus reinforces a view of God's identity (as hostile towards sinful humanity and requiring appeasement or satisfaction), of non-Christian human identity (as deserving utter and eternal punishment) and of Christian identity (as being uniquely acceptable and pleasing to God). It is easy to imagine how this view of God, the 'us' and the other could be translated into action in society and history.[10]

In contrast, in a table-centred eucharistic understanding, atoning or appeasing sacrifices are simply unnecessary.[11] Nothing need be done to appease a hostile God, because through Christ, God has self-revealed as inherently gracious and kind, seeking reconciliation, not hostile and vengeful, needing appeasement. If we need to speak of sacrifice at all, we speak of it in its root meaning: *sacred gift*. So as we gather around the eucharistic table, we bond to a meaning very different from that of the conventional eucharistic altar; we bond to the sacred self-giving of a gracious God.[12] As we remember Jesus, from incarnation to crucifixion (and beyond), we see God's self-giving to the whole world in Christ. Christ himself is God's sacred love-gift to the world.[13] At the Communion table, then, we manifest God's self-giving in Christ. We dramatically receive the sacred gift by eating bread and drinking wine. We take these sacred gifts into ourselves so they nourish us – and more: as food, they *become* us by being incorporated (or incarnated) into our own body and blood. In giving ourselves to be receivers of God's self-giving in Christ, we yield ourselves to the Holy Spirit, to be the ongoing incarnation of Christ, so that his body and blood (separated at death on the cross) are reunited, reconstituted and resurrected in us. God's sacred self-giving to us then invites us to imitation, to respond in kind through our own self-giving to God, to others and to the whole world. And so we present ourselves as 'living sacrifices' to God, and we continually offer to God the sacred gift of our thankful hearts.[14]

Around the eucharistic table, then, we bond to a love story of mutual self-giving. We celebrate our identity as recipients of God's gracious self-giving. And we respond in grateful self-giving by taking on a new identity as the ongoing embodiment of Christ – sent into the world to show the same love to the other that Jesus demonstrated – whether to leper or Pharisee, poor or rich, Zealot or tax collector, Samaritan or Roman or Syrophoenician or fellow Jew.

This table-oriented Eucharist does not minimise Jesus' death. Rather, in 'showing forth the Lord's death', we identify with it, and we let our lives be reshaped by it into cruciformity so as to lay down our lives for others just as Jesus did for us all. In this way, we die with Jesus to the ways of this world – hostility, oppression, violence, hate. And we rise with Jesus as well, to 'walk in newness of life', to live in the ways of love, liberation, reconciliation and human-kindness. So the world for us is no longer a battleground; our identity is no longer as warriors fighting with 'us' against 'them'.[15] No: in the Eucharist we bond to the good news that life is a table, a feast, a banquet, and we are a family, a circle of friends, being nourished together by God's bounty, the fruit of the vine and the grain of the field, all in a spirit of love, mutual service and unity.

In this light, the fact that the original Eucharist occurred on Passover eve is, of course, highly significant. The original Passover was a meal of hope, and hope was especially important in anticipation of what would happen to Jesus on Good Friday.

It was as if Jesus were saying, 'Passover was originally a preparatory meal – preparing for liberation from slavery. In the same way, tonight we are celebrating that a new day is about to dawn, a day of liberation – not just from slavery to Egypt then or Rome now, but from all oppressive systems of domination/enslavement, offence/revenge, rivalry/scapegoating and fear/hostility. Don't be dismayed by the disruption that is ahead. Get ready for your liberation that will arise after the disruption.'[16]

This sense of hope and anticipation is especially strong in Luke, where Jesus says, 'For I tell you, I will not eat it [Passover] again until it finds fulfilment in the kingdom of God . . . I will not drink again from the fruit of the vine until the kingdom of God comes.'[17] So just as the Passover marked a new day of liberation for the Jewish people, Jesus says the Communion meal marks a new covenant – a new covenant of love. Just as Passover was the end of an old identity – as slaves – and the beginning of a new identity – as God's people on a journey – the Eucharist celebrates the end of our old oppositional identity and the beginning of our new identity as God's agents of reconciliation and love.

Paul, of course, picks up on this language.[18] The old covenant under Moses was about law, and those laws created an in group and an out group. The in group, identified by circumcision, Sabbath, diet, temple, priesthood, sacrifice and compliance with a host of other religious laws, is inherently exclusive. For Paul, this law-based exclusivity leads (intentionally or not) to hostility towards the other. In contrast, Paul proclaims a new covenant focused on love, not law, and based on faith, not religious compliance ('law' or 'works'). No wonder, then, that Paul so strongly associates the new-covenant meal of Communion with unity. At the Communion table, the old in-group/out-group hostilities are left behind, and the old walls come down. When Paul refers to Christ as the Passover lamb in 1 Corinthians, he doesn't use the image to evoke penal substitutionary atonement theory, but rather to urge the Christians to leave behind all hostilities – as if they were part of the old life under Egyptian slavery: 'Therefore let us celebrate the festival, not with the old yeast, the yeast of malice [or hostility] and evil, but with . . . sincerity and truth.'

Later in the same letter, Paul returns to the Eucharist, again emphasising unity: we share in one cup, and there is one loaf, which means there is now only one body – not us/them, but all-of-us, united in one new humanity (1 Cor. 10:16–17). He expresses great frustration that cultural and economic differences are still evident even at the eucharistic table (1 Cor. 11:17–22), and then again employs the image of one body with many diverse members (1 Cor. 12). Our differences, he asserts, can increase inter-dependence and mutual respect if only we will follow the more excellent way of love (1 Cor. 13).

Whether gradually or decisively, in order to move from a strong-hostile to a strong-hospitable Christian identity, more and more of us are finding it necessary to migrate from an altar/appeasement-centred understanding of the Eucharist to a table/fellowship-centred understanding.[19] We cannot continue to gather around the altar of sacrifice with its hostile portrayal of God as requiring violence and bloodshed to be reconciled to us. We instead dare to celebrate the festival of love, the feast of Communion, with its portrayal of God as gracious, self-giving and reconciling.[20] As we do, the Communion table will deepen our sense of solidarity with all people, recalling Jesus who loved the outcasts and outsiders and was glad to eat with them, who was not hostile to anyone but was rather a host to everyone. Understood in this way, the table of the Lord fills a unique place in this world: it creates space where we experience a family meal with the other, where *one* and *the other* discover a new identity as *one-another* . . . Jew and Gentile, slave and free, male and female . . . where God and all humanity at table are sat down. In this way, we transcend the hostile rivalries of human politics; we descend beneath the hostile tribalisms of human religions. Scot McKnight says it powerfully: 'The single-most powerful political action Christians "do" is baptism and Eucharist, for in those actions we enter into an alien politics.'

As I conclude this chapter, tears fill my eyes and I am once again overcome with awe at the mysteries and hope proclaimed in a simple loaf of bread and cup of wine. I imagine what it could mean if, in the future, each time we arise from the table of fellowship, we do so more deeply bonded with a new identity in Christ, more fully in solidarity with our neighbours everywhere, more profoundly reoriented and reinvigorated to be sent out into the world with a new agenda, a vital, transforming mission. To that mission we now turn.

FOUR

THE MISSIONAL CHALLENGE

It was granted me to carry away from my prison years on my bent back, which nearly broke beneath its load, this essential experience: how a human being becomes evil and how good. In the intoxication of youthful successes I had felt myself to be infallible, and I was therefore cruel. In the surfeit of power I was a murderer and an oppressor. In my most evil moments I was convinced that I was doing good, and I was well supplied with systematic arguments. And it was only when I lay there rotting on prison straw that I sensed within myself the first stirrings of good. Gradually it was disclosed to me that the line separating good and evil passes not through states, nor between classes, nor between political parties either – but right through every human heart – and through all human hearts. This line shifts. Inside us it oscillates with the years. And even within the hearts overwhelmed with evil, one small bridgehead of good is retained. And even in the best of all hearts, there remains . . . an un-uprooted small corner of evil. Since then I have come to understand the truth of all the religions on the world. They struggle with the evil inside a human being (inside every human being). It is impossible to expel evil from the world in its entirety, but it is possible to constrict it within each person. And since that time I have come to understand the falsehood of all the revolutions of history: they destroy only those carriers of evil contemporary with them (and also fail, out of haste, to discriminate the carriers of good as well). And they take to themselves as their heritage the actual evil itself, magnified still more.

Alexander Solzhenitsyn[1]

CHAPTER 24

How Subversive Friendship Can Change the World

'What a wonderful idea!' the Muslim woman said. 'We need to love our traditions and be faithful to our God; but we teach the beauty and goodness of the other religions too.'

Her Hindu colleague chimed in, 'That is the only way to peace – to be ourselves and to create understanding between all people.'

When I reached my car, I realized that I was crying. I had only rarely felt the power of the resurrected Jesus so completely in my soul.

Diana Butler Bass[1]

Christian mission begins with friendship – not utilitarian friendship, the religious version of network marketing – but genuine friendship, friendship that translates love for neighbours in general into knowing, appreciating, liking and enjoying this or that neighbour in particular. This knowing-in-particular then motivates us to protect our neighbour when he or she is under threat, as a little Rwandan girl understood: just before she was brutally murdered during the genocide, she said to her slayer, 'If you knew me, you would not kill me.'

Friendliness was so essential to Jesus' identity that his critics labelled him 'a friend of sinners', bemoaning the fact that he constantly welcomed the wrong people to the table. Even with his disciples he seemed unwilling to maintain a properly distanced, top-down protocol. Instead, he elevated their connection from authoritarian discipleship to human-to-human friendship. It is far more significant than we commonly realise that the earliest followers of Christ did not call themselves *the Christians*, but rather *the friends*.[2]

That's why I was so pleased to learn that German Reformed theologian Jürgen Moltmann has daringly suggested that the traditional triad of images used to identify Jesus – prophet, priest and king – is seriously incomplete, as Tony Jones explains:

> To [prophet, priest and king], Moltmann adds the office of 'transfigured Christ' to emphasize the aesthetic dimension of the resurrection . . . And then Moltmann adds a fifth office: 'But the fellowship which Jesus brings men [*sic*], and the fellowship of people with one another to which he calls, would be described in one-sided terms if another "title" were not added, a title to describe the inner relationship between the divine and the human fellowship: the name of friend.'[3]

Friendship for Moltmann is a free choice, entered into without obligation because of respect and affection. That free choice differentiates being a friend from being a parent, child, sibling, leader or follower – or a prophet, priest or king: 'friendship is a human relationship which springs from freedom, exists in mutual freedom and preserves that freedom'.[4] In radical friendliness to all, Moltmann says, Jesus welcomes all humanity into the divine friendship, and 'the many-faceted work of Christ . . . can be taken to its highest point in his friendship', for friendship is 'the highest form of love'.[5]

By focusing on Jesus as prophet, priest and king to the exclusion of friend for its first two thousand years, our Christian tradition has no doubt made Christian unfriendliness easier than it would have been otherwise. The next two thousand years could be different if we take Christ's subversive, transformative friendship as seriously as Moltmann recommends.

Since my friendship with that precocious Muslim boy named Aatif, many new friends have come into my life . . . Jews, Muslims, Hindus, Buddhists, New Agers and others – including lots of atheists and agnostics, too. One of the most dramatic of those friendships began in the aftermath of 9/11. Like a lot of churches, our little congregation held a prayer service. While praying, I felt a voice speaking, as it were, in my chest: *Your Muslim neighbours are in danger of reprisals. You must try to protect them.* The next morning, I wrote and made copies of a letter extending, belatedly, friendship towards Muslim communities in my area, and offering solidarity and help if simmering anti-Muslim sentiments would be translated into action. I drove to the three mosques nearby – I had never visited them before – and tried to deliver my letter in person.

The first two were locked tight – no doubt for fear of reprisals, so I put my letters in the mailbox. When I arrived at the third, a TV satellite truck was pulling out. There had in fact been an incident the afternoon before. A Muslim woman – easily identified by her religious dress – was pushed down on the sidewalk, and an angry man stood over her and shouted, 'You're probably glad this happened.' The TV crew had come to get a statement from the local imam about the incident.

As the TV truck pulled out, the automatic gates were closing so I – without thinking – stepped on the gas and rushed my car through the gates. When the imam saw a stranger speeding into his driveway, he ran towards me, motioning for me to stop. I slammed on my brakes, threw the transmission into park and jumped out, leaving the engine still running. I couldn't have been more intimidating to the poor imam!

I clumsily introduced myself as the pastor from down the street, apologised both for my scary entry and for my failure to visit sooner. I then handed him my letter, which he opened and read as I stood there awkwardly. I remember the imam, a man short in stature, slowly looking down at the letter in the bright September sun, then up into my face, then down, then up, and each time he looked up, his eyes were more moist. Suddenly, he threw his arms around me – a perfect stranger who had entered his property in a less-than-sensitive way. I still remember the feeling of his head pressed against my chest, squeezing me as if I were his long-lost brother.

'It means so much to me that you have come,' he said. 'Please, please, please come inside.' I had never been in a mosque before, much less in an imam's office (which was, in case you're interested, a lot like my own office, except much neater, and all the books were in Arabic). My host welcomed me not with hostility or even suspicion, but with the open heart of a friend. And so that day a friendship began between an Evangelical pastor named Brian and a Muslim imam we'll call Ahmad.

A few days later, the youth group from our church made a colourful banner expressing their desire for there to be friendship between the youth of the mosque and the youth of our church. The banner was covered in their names, each handwritten with a coloured marker. (The imam hung the banner in the back of the mosque, where it remained for months.) The women of our church heard about the Muslim lady who had been pushed down on the sidewalk, and in response they made a list of names and phone numbers, offering to accompany any Muslim women to the store or an appointment if they were for any reason afraid. The mosque began hosting community dinners to which our people were invited along with people from other faith communities in the area, and many of us have warm memories of delicious Pakistani food shared in the basement of their well-appointed mosque.

The friendship between our congregations grew through a series of inter-faith dialogues we organised (one of which I described earlier), and Ahmad and I began meeting for lunch every month or so. Ahmad wasn't, back in 2001 and 2002 anyway, much for phone conversations, and he didn't have an e-mail address back then. He followed more traditional and humane ways of staying in touch – by visiting me in person. If Ahmad wanted to talk about something or arrange for our next lunch meeting, he knew one place one day each week where I could be found – Sunday mornings at church. So that's when he would drop by, fully resplendent in his traditional garb.

Some people were, I imagine, a little shocked at first to see a Muslim cleric walking through the church lobby as people chatted over coffee and bagels. But because our congregations had developed a friendship, he was soon recognised and welcomed.

Several times, I remember someone coming up and whispering in my ear, 'Brian, your imam is looking for you.' There was something wonderfully right about Ahmad feeling so at home that he could come and find me before or between services on a Sunday to schedule our next lunch meeting.

Both Ahmad and I have moved away since then, and I imagine that contact between the two congregations has waned, which is understandable. But I also know that many people at the church will forget neither the hospitality they experienced from the mosque nor the sense of blessing that came from our friendship, so they won't hesitate to resume contact again when needed. Ahmad and I are on opposite sides of the country now, so we can no longer meet for lunch, but I got an invitation to the wedding of one of his daughters not long ago, after which I called him and we had a great conversation. And he has an e-mail address now, so next time I'm in his new city I'll e-mail him and do my best to schedule a visit. I know we'll have a great meal, and our friendship will pick up right where it left off.

Imagine what might happen around the world if more and more Christians rediscover that central to Christian life and mission is what we could call subversive or transgressive friendship – friendship that crosses boundaries of otherness and dares to offer and receive hospitality. Imagine what could happen if our experience of Communion around the Lord's table on Sundays motivated us, like the Lord himself, to enjoy table fellowship with 'the wrong people' all through the week. Imagine the good that could happen – and the evil that could be prevented from happening – if more Jews, Muslims, Hindus, Christians, Buddhists and others cross the roads and other barriers that have separated them, and discover one another as friends.[6]

The apostle Peter had one such experience in the book of Acts. Peter had a deeply rooted resistance to otherness . . . even after three years of daily contact with Jesus, even after the miracle of Pentecost (revealing that God is equally fluent in every language), even after the Spirit transcended boundary after boundary in the early church. It took a vivid dream sequence to convince him to accept hospitality from 'the other', a Gentile man named Cornelius. Through their encounter, both Peter and Cornelius (and his household) experienced the Spirit.

Here's what Peter said as the experience unfolded: 'You are well aware that it is against our law for a [person of my religious background] to associate with or to visit a [person of another religious background]. But God has shown me that I should not call anyone impure or unclean.' Then, after hearing more of the story of his hosts, he added, 'I now realise how true it is that God does not show favouritism but accepts from every nation the one who fears him and does what is right' (Acts 10:28, 34–35). Peter realised in their encounter that the good news of Jesus subverted and transcended the old laws of insider-outsider, us-them, sacred-profane, clean-unclean.

Even after this experience, Peter slipped back into his old ways, and it took a former Pharisee named Paul to confront him about his hypocrisy.[7] Following Peter's checkered example, the Christian faith has over the centuries repeatedly gained and lost ground in our willingness to participate in transgressive friendship. I've felt the ambivalence myself, knowing that if I befriend 'them' – whether they be the denominationally, religiously, sexually, culturally, economically, ideologically or politically other, some of 'us' will be suspicious of me. But time after time, when I dare to risk friendship across barriers, I experience the Spirit just as Peter did with Cornelius. I've come to accept it as axiomatic: *a Christian moves towards the other in friendship.*

Three words capture the heart of that kind of liberating, transformative and subversive friendship. First, it's a friendship of *companionship* – ritualised in the Eucharist, to be sure, but actualised whenever we break bread and drink wine (or tea or coffee or whatever) with a friend of another faith. Second, it's a friendship of *conviviality*, not just of coexistence. It's not just a matter of talking together about religion, but more of living together, sharing the gifts of life together – attending one another's weddings and funerals and birthday parties, even sharing in one another's holidays (with appropriate respect and understanding).[8] And third, it's a friendship of *conspiracy*.

The word evokes people whispering in one another's ears, speaking of plans and plots that must be kept secret because one would be punished for announcing them aloud. To whisper such plans requires us to be so close as to breathe one another's breath. And so it was when Ahmad and I sat in a restaurant sharing a meal, or when a rabbi friend and I commiserated about the hardships of congregational leadership on a long drive, or when a Hindu activist confided to me his struggles with the caste system in India, or when an atheist and I took a walk in a park together and shared our common dreams for a better world. In each case, our friendships were conspiratorial ... seeking to overthrow the current regimes of hostility, opposition, exclusion, fear and prejudice, not only dreaming of that better world but rehearsing for it, practising it through the give and take of our friendship. Together we were plotting goodness.

In recent years, I've met people all over the world who are discovering the surprising joys of subversive friendship: two moms, Soraya and Nadyne – one Muslim and one Evangelical Christian – whose children modelled for them the possibility of 'playing together' subversively[9] . . . Samir, a former atheist/communist/Muslim who became a Seventh Day Adventist pastor and now helps lead a faith community that comprises sub-communities of many faiths[10] . . . Mark, a former religious-right politician in the United States who realised he had become an anti-Muslim bigot and who subsequently became so dedicated to Christian-Muslim friendships that the US government accused him of associating with terrorists[11] . . . Jeff, formerly a funda-mentalist/charismatic Christian pastor who repented from his anti-Muslim ways and now teaches Christians and Muslims to love and understand one another as neighbours[12] . . . Nita, a Christian woman in a Muslim country who was welcomed into a Muslim feminist group because she, as a Christian and a woman, wanted to share in their struggle against domestic violence.

I've met scores of people involved in these subversive friend-ships of companionship, conviviality and conspiracy . . . but the world needs millions more. So if you aren't already involved in at least one of these friendships, I dare you. It's one thing to say you love humanity in general, whatever their religion; it's quite another to learn to love this or that specific neighbour with his or her specific religion. So, do you have a Sikh neighbour, a Hindu co-worker, a Muslim business associate, a Buddhist member of your PTA, a New Age second cousin? Invite them into companionship over a cup of tea or coffee. Ask them ques-tions. Display unexpected interest in them, their traditions, their beliefs and their stories. Learn why they left what they left, why they stay where they stay, why they love what they love. Enter their world, and welcome them into your world, without judgement. If they reciprocate, welcome their reciprocation; if not, welcome their non-reciprocation. Experience conviviality. Join the conspiracy of plotting for the common good together.

That's what I imagine Jesus, Moses, the Buddha and Mohammed would do if they met one another along the road. When we cross the road to meet one another as friends, in some way, perhaps, they do, too, through us. Perhaps their story is not yet over but continues to unfold in us.

CHAPTER 25

How God's Commonwealth of Peace Confronts Earthly Empires of Hostility

> The Church, therefore, exhorts her children, that through dialogue and collaboration with the followers of other religions, carried out with prudence and love and in witness to the Christian faith and life, they recognize, preserve and promote the good things, spiritual and moral, as well as the socio-cultural values found among them.
>
> Pope Paul VI, *Nostra Aetate*[1]

Jesus didn't start a school. Nor did he start a denomination or an institution. If anything, he started what we would call a community organising movement . . . a movement supported by a privately funded NGO with an all-female board of directors.[2] He recruited twelve core volunteers to lead the movement. They were a diverse lot, almost comically so at times – pairing a zealot like Simon with a tax collector like Matthew, or linking an impulsive activist like Peter with a mystic-poet like John. Enhanced by this diversity, their influence extended to a larger network of committed allies that numbered in the hundreds – and eventually thousands.

What did the movement do? They travelled from village to village, much like a political campaign, spreading their message, looking for 'people of peace' and organising them into small groups, feeding the hungry, healing the sick, offering hope to the depressed, promising freedom for the oppressed, confronting the oppressors and conversing with questioners and critics. Sometimes they organised what we might call outdoor festivals – complete with teaching and food for thousands. Sometimes they staged what we would call public demonstrations – a march into Jerusalem, civil disobedience in the Temple. Often they engaged in quiet, behind-the-scenes relationship building, meeting with an amazing range of people.

One night they might meet privately with a respected religious leader like Nicodemus or Simon, both members of the Pharisee party. Another evening they might eat with a despised tax collector like Zacchaeus or Matthew and their equally despised friends, enemies of the Pharisees. In between, they might spend time with a variety of social outcasts – including foreigners like the Syrophoenician woman, marginal outsiders like the Samaritan woman and isolated social outcasts like the Gadarene demoniac and a host of lepers and beggars. In short, they were like yeast, kneaded into the dough of society, and by their faithful and active presence they changed the world.

After Jesus' death, his disciples continued this same pattern. They extended their travel routes far beyond Judea and Galilee, aiming for 'the uttermost parts of the earth'. But their pattern was the same: meeting people, spreading their message through word and deed, occasionally stirring up controversy and even a riot or two, all the while recruiting and organising a wild array of people into groups that would continue their mission after they moved on.

Paul's evangelistic trip to Philippi, described in Acts 16, provides an interesting model of their movement-building work — a model that can inspire and inform today. Paul is accompa- __ Luke and maybe others. They arrive in Philippi — their first engagement with an official Roman colony. The kingdom of God, we might say, is encountering the empire of Caesar for the first time on Caesar's own turf. The Pax Christi is encountering the Pax Romana.

The little team of emissaries meets a group of women on the outskirts of the city, and one of them, a businesswoman named Lydia, hosts them. Soon, they encounter a slave girl who makes a lot of money for her owners as an occult fortune-teller. On seeing the band of travellers, she shouts, 'These men are slaves like me, but slaves of the Most High God! They will proclaim to you the way of liberation!'[3]

Paul eventually becomes annoyed (whether at her insistent shouting or at her plight, the text doesn't make clear), and he frees her from the occult spirit, after which she is incapable of continuing her fortune-telling work. This, of course, enrages her owners, who stir up a mob and bring Paul and Silas before the local authorities. Their speech is fascinating:

> These men are troublemakers, disturbing the peace of our great
> city. They are from some Jewish sect, and they promote foreign
> customs that violate our Roman standards of conduct. (Acts
> 16:20–21 *The Voice*)

What might the 'foreign customs' in question be? No doubt they are referring among other things to the custom of respecting slaves as equal human beings.[4] Few things could disturb a Roman colony more than challenging the slave-based economy upon which the 'peace' of the entire Roman Empire depends. The magistrates quickly do the bidding of the powerful economic interests (sound familiar?), breaking their own laws by stripping, beating and imprisoning Paul and Silas without due process. Upsetting a slave-based economy is a dangerous thing!

That night, Paul and Silas lie in the highest-security section of the local jail. There, severely beaten and chained, they sing songs – probably an act of protest as well as piety, as if to say, *The Romans have imprisoned our bodies, but our spirits are still free to worship the God who liberates slaves!* An earthquake occurs – as if to symbolise the earth-shaking radicality of the liberating message Paul's team proclaims – and the chains and gates of their imprisonment are unlocked, again, highly symbolic of their liberating mission. The jailer rushes in and, seeing the open gates, he assumes the prisoners have escaped. He immediately pulls out his sword to kill himself, which reveals the deep fear he experiences as part of the Roman domination system: he would rather die than be thrown into the prison he manages.

When Paul and Silas tell him they haven't escaped – that they are voluntarily remaining in their cells – the man is shocked, falls to his knees in front of his prisoners and cries out, 'What must I do to be liberated?' Not insignificantly, he uses the same word that the slave girl has used.

Paul and Silas say something like this: 'You live in the fear-based system of the Lord Caesar. Stop having confidence in him

'When!' I shouted, just as my cup was about to overfloweth.

He laughed. 'Are you sure you don't just want to empty out the tea and I'll start again?'

'No, this will be fine, thank you,' I said primly.

He laughed again as he sloshed a generous measure of whiskey into his own mug. *What nice dimples you have.*

I held my mug aloft. 'Cheers.'

'Bottoms up,' Jack agreed, as he clunked my mug with his own.

There was a moment of strained silence, filled only by the merry crackling of the logs on the fire. I broke it.

'I don't suppose you happen to know who that woman in the photo is?'

'Do I what? That would be my granny, Mary Power. She used to live here.'

'Really? That's a lovely idea, keeping a photo of her in the cottage. What was she like? She looks pretty formidable.'

'Oh, by God, she was. Ruled my grandfather with an iron fist. A true matriarch.'

Hmmm, I mused. *I wouldn't mind being a matriarch myself one day.* I had a feeling I'd be very good at it. My family were always telling me how bossy I was.

'Did you know her well?'

'God, yes. I spent half my childhood here. Granny used to mind us a lot of the time. It wasn't easy for my mother, running the pub and raising seven boys.'

I bet it wasn't.

'She was great, was Granny Power. Wouldn't let you away with a thing, mind you. And she always smelt of roses. That's what I remember best about her. Every time I smell roses I think of her.' He looked away, seemingly a little embarrassed by this revelation. 'Anyway,' he said, 'what do you think of the cottage?'

'Oh, it's gorgeous,' I said enthusiastically. 'I just love the way it's been done up. I'd really like to get the name of the interior decorator.'

Jack, who had been in the process of taking a gulp of his Irish tea, spluttered it down his fleece and all over the coffee table in front of him. He narrowly missed the edge of my skirt. I jumped and stared at him in surprise. Then I realised that he was laughing. His laughter was replaced by embarrassed coughing as he leapt up to get a cloth.

'Are you all right?' I was concerned. Usually, even I didn't poison my visitors with my refreshments this early on in the proceedings.

'Fine, thanks. Jesus, that was pretty disgusting. Sorry about that. Here, lift up the tray and I'll wipe it up properly.'

I lifted objects out of his way as he cleaned up the spillage as thoroughly and efficiently as a professional housewife. I was temped to offer him a pinny (or perhaps a bib).

94

'Now!' He finished his clean-up with a flourish and a satisfied smile. Then he looked down at his fleece and frowned.

'I'll have to do something with this too.' He pulled the garment over his head in one swift movement, and as his T-shirt rode up I was treated to a flash of his delectable six-pack. He caught me checking him out and I looked away quickly, but not so quickly that I didn't notice a glint of satisfaction in his eyes. *He did that on purpose*, I thought.

He went over to the sink and started rinsing out his fleece, his back to me. He was wearing a plain grey T-shirt. I thought disloyally of the way the sleeves of Paul's T-shirts flapped around the tops of his arms like flags. Jack's biceps were barely contained beneath his sleeves. And those buns! Like two ripe peaches in a handkerchief. By God, I could do him some justice! I was reminded of the scripts for bad American porn movies (I'd once seen a documentary about them):

Heroine: Oh, Chip, have you been working out?

Hero: Come over here, honey, and find out for yourself!

I was still trying to come up with a cunning plan to get him out of the rest of his clothes (nudge his arm next time he took a sip, so he'd spill the rest of the tea; throw the contents of my cup into his lap while pretending to look at my watch; turn on the central heating, so that the combination of that and the blazing fire would force him to strip off;

hell, just throw him fully clothed into the shower) when the real man, having completed his ablutions, sat down beside me again. Was it my imagination or was he sitting closer this time? The hairs on his arm brushed gently against mine, making me shiver.

It was my turn to spring to my feet. 'Music! Why don't I put on a CD? What would you like to hear?'

He looked up at me and smiled a slow, lazy smile. 'Something mellow.'

Mellow, I thought as I made my way to the stereo in the bedroom. *Mellow. Does he mean something smoochy?* What did I have in my extensive (not) collection that was mellow?

Paul always jokingly called my motley selection of CDs 'the Best-of collection'. Almost every single one was a 'Greatest Hits' or 'Best of'. I reasoned that this made practical good sense: what was the point in buying an album unless you were sure you liked at least seventy-five per cent of the songs on it? Anything less was a pure waste of money. I was aware that this attitude made musical purists such as Paul shudder as if someone had just walked across their graves, but I was unapologetic. I pushed away all further uncomfortable thoughts of my boyfriend (boyfriend? what boyfriend?) and, instead, concentrated hard on my musical selection.

Tina Turner. Prince. The Beatles. The Eagles. Fleetwood Mac. *The Best Love Songs Ever* (definite no-no). *The Soppiest Lurve Songs in the Universe.*

Chaka Khan. *Hits of the Screaming Sixties. The Greatest Soul Classics of All Time. Now That's What I Call Music* 4, 6, 17 and 43. I was uncomfortably aware of just how uncool, unhip and downright middle-aged my collection was. At last I happened upon a copy of Blur's *Greatest Hits* that I had acquired accidentally on purpose from Paul (who?). It didn't occur to me at the time that it was perhaps a tad disloyal to play this in the circumstances (what circumstances? I wasn't doing anything).

I found a song I liked, about a bloke from the city who goes to live in a house in the country, and turned the volume up several notches before returning to Jack.

'That all right?'

He screwed up his face. 'I don't really like Blur.'

'Okay. Let's try something else.'

I went back into the bedroom and began calling out the names of CDs at random. He stopped me at George Michael's *Greatest Hits*, Volume I.

'Oh, that's a great collection. Play that.'

A man after my own heart! Paul always went mad when I tried to play this particular CD.

I returned to the couch and, without looking at Jack, took a swig of my 'tea'. I winced. I think my mug had received a top-up while I wasn't looking. The bad American porn movie was still running in my head:

Heroine: Are you trying to get me drunk, kind sir?
Hero: Do I need to, young miss? (Probably not.)

97

I took another sip. Not only did I have a very pleasant warm strip running from my throat to my heart; a nice, fuzzy sensation was also beginning to develop across the crown of my head. I looked across at Jack. I thought his eyes looked a little blurry around the edges too. There's nothing like a few home measures to get the party started.

'What were you laughing at, anyhow?' I asked him.

'Hmm?'

'When you spewed whiskey-tea all over the furniture.'

'Oh, that.' He smiled enigmatically and took another sip. 'I know the name of the interior designer.'

'Really? Who?'

'Jack Power.'

In my less-than-alert state, it actually took me a few seconds to work out who he was talking about. 'Jack Power? Oh, you mean ... Oh!'

He nodded.

'You're kidding! You?'

'The one and only.'

'By yourself?'

'By my own self.'

'Wow! I mean, I don't mean to sound so amazed,' I said, sounding amazed. 'It's just that you're – well, I mean, you're a farmer.'

'A man can wear many different hats, you know.' This time he was definitely slurring his words.

I pondered this revelation for a while.

'You're not really a typical farmer, are you?'

'A typical farmer being?' His eyes seemed to lose their good-humoured haze, and he was no longer slumped but sitting upright on the edge of the sofa. Oops. Now I'd done it.

'I mean ... well, you know – the usual image of a farmer is, like....'

I trailed off, unfortunately not drunk enough to be immune to embarrassment. Jack continued to look at me, long and hard.

'You mean when I came here tonight you expected me to have a piece of straw sticking out of the side of my mouth.'

'No, not at all, that's not –'

'Perhaps you'd be happier if I said "Begorrah and begob" every now and then.'

I was silent. I couldn't tell if he was joking or not. His eyes looked kind of angry to me. He got up. Without taking his eyes off me, he slowly eased off his boots. Then his socks. A shiver of fear and anticipation prickled up and down my spine. Then he started to roll up his trouser-legs. What was he doing?

Then, to my amazement, he planted his feet wide apart and gripped the material of his T-shirt just below his shoulders, as if holding on to an imaginary pair of braces. And then he started to sing.

'Old McDonald had a farm, E-I-E-I-O,
And on that farm he had a cow, E-I-E-I-O.

99

With a moo-moo here, and a moo-moo there,

Here a moo, there a moo, everywhere a moo-moo ...'

On every 'moo', he kicked his leg up in the air. This was so unexpected that I dissolved into a fit of giggles. Oops, looks like our Lainey's drunk again....

He stopped singing and joined me on the couch, laughing somewhat manically. We eventually managed to calm down. Jack leant across and wiped away the tears that had formed on the outer corners of my eyes with his left thumb. His right arm had somehow ended up across the back of the couch, practically around my shoulders. *Perhaps this would be a good time to tell him I have a boyfriend*, I thought.

'You have a lovely laugh, you know.'

Tell him!

'And lovely hair, too.' He stroked a thick strand of my hair, which had long since escaped from its sedate ponytail. I gulped. I appeared to have lost all power of speech. His face drew even nearer to mine. I was nearly knocked sideways by the hot smell of alcohol off his breath. He must have been drinking whiskey neat for some time.

Then, without warning, Jack leapt off the seat and started pulling on his socks and boots as if he was late for an urgent appointment.

'I have to go, Lainey. Thanks for the tea.' He had a strange, almost wild look in his eyes.

'That's all right. Thanks for the whiskey. And the logs.' I knew I must look and sound confused. I followed him to the front door, which he was already holding open with a strange, hunted look on his face. Had I done something wrong? Maybe he just had to be up early to feed the chickens.

'See you.' He bent to kiss me on the cheek. I moved my head at the wrong moment and he got me on the ear by mistake. Before I had the chance to consider whether to kiss him back or not, he was out the door and in his jeep. Surely he wasn't going to drive home in that state? As the car skidded on the gravel of the driveway and disappeared with a screech down the hill, I realised that, in fact, he was. I also realised that his father had probably taught him how to drive. What could I do? I could hardly invite him to stay the night.

As I staggered into the bathroom, I could have sworn that Mary Power threw me a disapproving look. *Leave me alone, Mary.* Somehow managing to stay upright, I hiked up my skirt and pulled down my tights and knickers. As I peed, I kicked the tights off my feet and sang happily to myself. 'And on that farm he had a pig, E-I-E-I-O. With an oink-oink here....' I collapsed into drunken giggles again.

I got up and flushed, then slumped over the sink and looked up into the mirror. Oh, no! Horror of horrors! I had panda eyes! I must have rubbed at them in my drunken state and smeared mascara everywhere. No wonder Jack had run off in fright. I looked like a zombie. And as for the hair … my fringe had morphed into a parody of an Elvis quiff.

For the second time that night, I went to bed without getting undressed. I knew I should probably spend some time beating myself up about my behaviour – which had been entirely inappropriate for someone who was supposed to be a girlfriend – but instead I pulled a Scarlett O'Hara and decided to think about that tomorrow.

Chapter Eight

Fortunately, I overslept, so I didn't have time to agonise about Paul the next morning. I was too busy agonising about the fact that I was going to be late for my first morning in Ballyknock District Court. Luckily, the courthouse was directly across the road from the office, so I just had time to grab the relevant summons and charge over.

What a dive! I'd been in nicer garages. The courthouse consisted of one massive, high-ceilinged room. I was to find out later that there was no heating and no toilet – lack of facilities seemed to be a common problem in Ballyknock. The judge's raised seat was high up at one end of the room, and beneath this was what looked like a giant's dining-room table. This was where the solicitors and court reporters sat. At the back of the room were a few rough benches for hoi polloi – clients, criminals, kids on school trips and nosy members of the public. To the right, another set of benches held various members of the local constabulary. The first people who caught my eye were the two gardaí who had come to my aid on the Night of the Rats. As I came in, they nudged each other and whispered to their colleagues. A few of them started to smirk.

Fantastic.

'All rise.' The court registrar entered the room, followed by the district judge – who, true to type, looked like a grumpy old bollix.

Even more fantastic.

I rushed to find myself a seat, and squeezed in at the end of the table beside a bulky, red-headed man. The judge sat down and so did everybody else. He surveyed the courtroom from his elevated throne – all the better for abusing you from a great height, my dears.

The redhead leaned over and whispered into my ear, 'Are you Tyrone's new solicitor?'

I nodded. 'Lainey Malone.'

'Brendan Ryan, the local competition.' I vaguely remembered Tyrone mentioning him. He was the only other solicitor based in Ballyknock. Judging by his friendly smile, he didn't seem too fazed by the idea of a competing firm.

104

He really was an odd-looking man. Did I mention his hair was red? Well, it was positively on fire. It was the type of ginger that little kids sometimes have but usually grow out of. It occurred to me that perhaps it was dyed – but no, surely nobody would dye his hair that colour on purpose? I also guessed it hadn't met with a comb in the last forty-eight hours. He hadn't grown out of his freckles, either. They were scattered all over his face and his hands; they were on his lips, on his eyelids and practically up his nose. He looked like a join-the-dots picture. He was wearing a chunky orange cardigan, buttoned up the wrong way. His wife must have knitted it for him; there could be no other explanation. The ensemble was completed by a tweed jacket that had seen better days. If he hadn't been such a hulking man, he would have been in imminent danger of being mistaken for a leprechaun.

'DPP v. Paddy Murphy,' called the registrar. That was one of mine; I had to plead guilty to a traffic offence. I jumped to my feet and rattled off my spiel, trying to sound sincere in my apology on behalf of my client. As I sat down, Brendan Ryan rose to his feet beside me.

'And I'd like to welcome Ms Lainey Malone to Ballyknock on behalf of the Kilkenny Solicitors' Association. I'm sure we're all looking forward to working with her.'

Oh, no. Tyrone had warned me about the country tradition of welcoming new solicitors on their first day in court. I'd thought I might be able to get away without it, but obviously not.

Brendan Ryan sat down and a senior-looking police officer stood up. 'And I'd like to welcome Ms Malone on behalf of the Kilkenny gardaí. We hope she'll be very happy here.'

I nodded my thanks.

And then the judge spoke. 'Yes, Miss Malone, you're very welcome. We've already heard a lot about you. I understand you're going to keep us safe from all the vermin in the town.' The judge flashed me a sarcastic smile, and explosive snigger-ing broke out from the garda benches. I looked quickly around the table and saw that most of my so-called colleagues were either laughing or trying not to. Even Brendan was suppressing a smile. Well, wasn't this just fan-bloody-tastic?

Welcome to Ballyfuck.

By the time I finally escaped from that damn court-room, it was well after three. I heaved open the ugly wooden doors of the courthouse and breathed in the fresh air as if I were a lifer being released from prison. What a criminal waste of a day. At least I didn't have far to travel back to the office.

I pushed open the door of Tyrone Power & Co. and did a double take. The office seemed to have been converted into a crèche. There were children everywhere – horrible, snotty-nosed little kids tampering with the equipment. I let out an angry roar – which I didn't have to fake.

'What's going on here?'

All the little tykes (there were five of them) stopped what they were doing and turned to look at me, eyes wide with fear.

'Get out now, all of you. This is a solicitor's office. Adults only!' My voice rose several decibels. One of the little girls looked as if she was going to cry.

'Lainey! I didn't hear you come in. Were you stuck in court all this time, poor lamb?' Patricia emerged from my office bearing several reams of photocopying paper. 'Have you met my kids? Well, they're not all mine, I'm minding the two girls for a neighbour, but the boys are mine – Tommy, Christy and Mikey.'

Ah yes, Mikey. He of Coco Pops fame.

'Say hello to the nice lady.'

Silence. Patricia shoved her boys in the back and they reluctantly greeted me. It was obvious that they weren't convinced that I was a nice lady.

'I'm sorry for shouting at them, Patricia. It's just that when I came in I saw all these kids running around the office, and I didn't see you, and I thought – well, I don't know what I thought.'

'That's quite all right. I suppose it must have been a bit of a shock. The kids are doing some photocopying for their school project. I hope you don't mind.'

'No, that's just fine.' *Frankly, my dear, I don't give a shit.* I headed unenthusiastically into my inner office, feet dragging considerably.

'You take the weight off, and I'll bring you in a nice cup of coffee and one of those scones I promised you.'

'That would be heaven, Patricia. Thank you.'

She smiled and closed the door. I slumped into my chair, folded my arms on the desk and sank my head down into them, like a child taking a nap.

I'm tired, my head hurts and I want to go home – partnership or no partnership, Jack Power or no Jack Power (I've frightened him off anyhow). I missed my flat, I missed my friends, I missed my old office. I missed Paul's moaning. And now I'd just yelled at a bunch of little kids. *God, just get me out of this godforsaken shit-hole.*

I jumped and sat up straight as the door opened. Patricia placed a coffee and a scone in front of me. The scone was spread liberally with red jam.

'I hope you like raspberry jam.'

'I love it, thanks.'

I waited for her to leave, but she continued to hover expectantly at the door. I realised I was meant to sample the fare before she left. I took a bite.

'Mmm. This is just delicious.' I didn't have to lie. 'Did you make the jam too?'

'Yes. It won first prize at the Mivik show, you know.'

'Congratulations. It's lovely.'

Patricia continued to hover. Now what?

'Have you tried any of Bridie Power's jam yet?' she asked casually.

'Yes, she gave me a pot of strawberry.'

'So she didn't give you any of her raspberry, then?'

'No.'

'Hmph. Didn't think so. She only came third in the raspberry.' Patricia smiled triumphantly and left the room with a flourish. Good Lord! Get me back to Dublin, where nobody cared about prize-winning jam. What was next? Giant-marrow competitions? Quick-draw knitting-needles at dawn? I wasn't able for this. I was going to ring Tyrone and tell him I couldn't cut it. First thing in the morning.

I was still in a fouler when I got in that night. If I'd had a cat or a dog, I would have kicked it. Instead, I had to be content with kicking off my shoes and slumping onto the couch with a heavy sigh. And then I screamed. For there, sitting on the rodent-deterrent – you know, the thing that was meant to repel rodents – looking right at me, bold as brass, was a little grey mouse.

'I don't fucking believe this!' I drew my feet up onto the couch, lest a little furry creature run across them, and rooted around in my bag for my mobile. I was all for communing with nature, but this was bloody ridiculous.

'Hello. Seamus Murphy Pest Control.'

'Oh, hello. This is Elena Malone; I'm calling from Power's Cottage.'

'Ah, yes. Nice to talk to you, love. How are things?'

'Not good. I'm sitting here looking at a mouse.'

'Are you sure it's a mouse and not a rat?'

'Perfectly sure.' *Jesus Christ!*

'Well, that's great.'

'I beg your pardon?'

'You see, love, if you've got mice, that means the rats have gone.'

'And I'm meant to be pleased with that, am I?' I could feel the fury building up in my chest and getting ready to explode out of me like an alien in one of those sci-fi films. Just to annoy me even further, Seamus Murphy laughed good-naturedly.

'Don't worry. I'll come up first thing tomorrow morning and fill in a few holes for you, love, no extra charge. But do you know what I'd really recommend?'

'Surprise me.'

'A nice ferret.'

He wanted me to get a ferret! A glorified rat with extra-sharp teeth. I thought wildly about a programme I'd seen years ago, about old men in an English village competing to see which one of them could get the most live ferrets up the legs of his trousers. They would tie the ends of their trouser-legs with bits of twine so that the ferrets couldn't escape. I wanted no truck with such animals.

'I know a man who breeds them. I could get you a really good price on one.'

'I don't *want* a ferret. I'd rather have mice.' My eyes were fairly bulging out of my head at this point.

110

'Well, a cat, then.'

'Do you really think so?' The anger drained out of me, leaving only despair. Just then, the biggest spider I had ever seen in my entire life ran across the floor in front of me like a disembodied hand.

'Yes. You leave it with me, love. I'll have you sorted with a grand cat in no time.'

'Thanks.' I hated cats.

I hung up and sat staring into space. My eyes filled with tears of frustration. I screamed again, this time out of irritation rather than fear, and hurled my mobile across the room, where it collided with the rough plastered wall and landed with a clatter on the slate tiles. That was effective. Not only did I have mice, I now had a busted mobile too.

And I had no hope of getting any sleep tonight, either.

And it was still only bleeding Tuesday.

Roll on Friday.

Chapter Nine

The rest of the week crawled by at a snail's pace. I didn't hear a peep out of Seamus Murphy, rat-catcher extraordinaire. I didn't see hide nor hair of Jack Power, either. Looked like I'd blown that one.

I could barely contain my excitement as the train pulled into Dublin's Heuston Station that Friday evening. I was practically jumping up and down in my seat, as if I were suffering from a severe kidney problem. I was the first passenger out of her seat; I was standing at the carriage door about five minutes before the train drew to a halt.

Paul had arranged to pick me up from the station. I couldn't believe how much I was looking forward to seeing him – although I supposed that, at this point, it would be a treat for me to see any of my Dublin friends. With delight, I stepped onto the platform and walked rapidly towards the exit.

There he was.

My heart melted at the sight of him. He was standing at the end of the platform, a lone figure wearing the long black coat I had bought him for his last birthday. He didn't wear it all that much; I think he secretly disliked it. He was self-consciously clutching a bunch of white flowers. Now this *was* remarkable. Paul didn't do flowers. He thought they were impractical. Why spend all that money on a bunch of weeds that were going to be dead within a fortnight? On the few occasions I had received flowers from him, he had sent them via Interflora so that he wouldn't have to go through the mortification of being seen carrying them. As I got closer, I realised they were lilies – my favourite. As I got closer still, I could see his big soppy grin.

'Hey, you.' I reached up and hugged him close, squishing the flowers in the process. I leaned back and smiled up at him. 'Who's the lucky girl?' I asked, nodding at the bouquet.

'These are for you.' He thrust the lilies awkwardly towards me, as if I were a royal princess and he were the shy four-year-old girl who had been nominated to present them to her.

'They're gorgeous. How did you know that lilies were my favourite?'

'Is that what they are? I didn't know.'

113

Typical Paul, spoiling the moment with honesty. He couldn't lie to save his own life. Still, the effort had been made.

'Mmm.' I stuck my nose deep into the lilies and took a deep sniff. Of course, they had no scent. (What is it with flowers nowadays? They never have any smell. In my day….)

'They smell heavenly.' I, on the other hand, had no problem lying when I felt the occasion merited it.

'Do they really? I couldn't get any scent from them.'

'You must be getting a cold.'

'Do you think so?'

'Definitely. You should take a Lemsip before you go to bed tonight.' I could go on lying all night if necessary. It was no hardship.

'Will you make it for me?' He smiled, almost shyly.

'We'll see.'

We started to walk towards the car park. Paul had wrapped his arm around my waist, and I could feel him looking down fondly at the top of my head. I turned and smiled happily at him. His smile turned to laughter as we moved into a more brightly lit area.

'You have pollen all over your nose.'

I stopped and swiped ineffectually at my proboscis.

'Here, let me.' Paul removed a handkerchief from the top pocket of his suit jacket. It was clearly

114

spotless and neatly pressed and folded. Anybody else would have thought that he got 'a woman' in to do his laundry for him. I, however, knew that he had done it himself.

Paul carefully folded the handkerchief into a small triangle and set about wiping the pollen off my nose. I tried not to laugh at the look of intense concentration on his face. Out of the corner of my eye, I could see passers-by staring at us. Let them stare. Paul, who usually cared so much about the opinions of others – including complete strangers – seemed oblivious.

He caught my eye and saw that I was laughing at him; he stopped rubbing my nose and looked all self-conscious and vulnerable. I couldn't resist reaching up and kissing him lightly on the mouth. He stared down at me for what seemed like the longest time. Then he cupped my face in his hands and brought his lips down on top of mine – not hard, just sweetly insistent. The barest flicker of tongue ghosted between my parted lips, causing a particular tingle that I hadn't felt in an age.

He stopped, at last appearing to remember where he was. Quite frankly, I was amazed that he had forgotten himself for so long. Usually Paul only indulged in public displays of affection when he was drunk. And I hadn't tasted alcohol on his mouth, only mint. I was further amazed at how nice this was. It was almost like one of our early dates – only better, because now I knew him.

'Is it gone?'

'Is what gone?'

'The pollen off my nose, silly.'

'Yes, all gone.' He stuffed the hanky into his coat pocket (it wouldn't do to replace a dirty, crumpled handkerchief in the top pocket of his suit jacket) and put his hand on my shoulder, propelling me towards the car park more quickly this time.

Paul had secured a late booking in The Paddy Field, my favourite Chinese restaurant – no mean feat on a Friday night. No doubt he had used the name of his firm to secure special privileges. The owners were clients.

The host was all smiles. 'Smoking or non-smoking?'

'Smoking,' I said.

'Non-smoking,' said Paul, at exactly the same moment.

We turned and looked at each other. The host looked away. I could see Paul weighing me up. Then, with an audible sigh, he turned back to the host.

'Smoking it is.'

I made sure he didn't see my triumphant smirk as I marched ahead of him towards our table. I had been prepared to stage a fake tantrum. I felt entitled. I'd had a hard week.

I settled my happy bum into my chair as Paul took off his coat.

'Jesus Christ!' he exclaimed.

'What is it?' Had he changed his mind about the smoking already?

'There's pollen everywhere.'

Sure enough, Paul's black coat was streaked with bright-orange pollen, and so was his suit jacket. He took out his trusty handkerchief and started to rub at it, which only made the stains worse. He cursed under his breath.

'Don't worry, you can get them dry-cleaned.'

'I've just got it dry-cleaned. I only put this outfit on clean today.'

This outfit. Excuse me.

'Well, we'll try to do a job on it when we go home, then.'

'It must have happened when you hugged me.' He flashed me a testy look.

'I see – so it's my fault, is it?'

'I didn't mean that.'

Yeah, right.

'It's just that – Jesus, I'll never get this crap out. That's the last time I'm getting you flowers.'

Charming!

'Oh, for God's sake, Paul. Sit down and stop making a show of yourself. Everybody's looking at you.' That usually worked. Paul looked around worriedly and sat down at last. And things had been going so well…. The honeymoon was over already.

'Let's order. I'm starved,' I said, eager to change the subject. I had that familiar heavy, weary feeling that I'd been experiencing all too often, of late, in

Paul's company. Why did we keep on having such stupid rows over nothing? It was as if we were at cross-purposes all the time. I had hoped that tonight would prove an exception – but apparently it wasn't to be.

I perused the menu as if it were a legal document. Of course, it was much more important than that. Paul looked amused (thank God).

'Surely you know that menu off by heart at this stage. You always order the same thing anyway.'

'Well, maybe I fancy a change. And don't call me Shirley.'

Good humour restored. For now.

'Shall we order a bottle of wine?'

'I can't drink, I'm driving.'

'Oh, come on, Paul, let's get hammered. I'm really in the mood. Leave the car in town tonight. We can get a taxi, and you can collect it tomorrow.'

'You know I hate doing that. It's too much hassle.'

I shrugged. The waitress approached to take our order. Her vibrant ginger hair clashed spectacularly with the scarlet kimono she was forced to wear. She looked like she knew it, too.

I went for my usual lemon chicken (Paul had been right).

'And would you like some wine with your meal?' the waitress asked in a thick Louth accent.

'Yes, please,' I said.

'No, thanks,' said Paul, at precisely the same time.

118

'We'll have a bottle of the Chilean red, please.' I could feel him glaring at me, but I refused to look at him; I continued to smile pleasantly at the waitress.

'I told you I was driving tonight,' Paul said, when she had gone.

'I know. You'll be able to have one glass anyway, and I'll have the rest.'

'Are you sure that's wise?'

'No, Paul, I'm not sure it's *wise*,' I spat, 'but I don't feel like being wise. I've had a shit week, and I just want to chill out and have a few drinks and a nice relaxing time with my boyfriend. Now, is there anything wrong with that?'

'No. No, of course there isn't. I'm sorry, Lainey. Tell me all about your week. I want to hear everything.'

And the thing was, he really did. That was one of the great things about Paul: he was such a good listener. He sat there with his chin on his hand, not saying much, but paying rapt attention as I waxed lyrical about all my woes and grievances. He even laughed in all the right places and asked relevant questions. At times like this, I could almost fool myself into believing that I had the perfect boyfriend. Almost.

'So,' he asked me later, as I was tucking into my slab of pecan pie (worth three million points in the Weight Watchers handbook), 'what do you want to do next weekend?'

'Oh, I don't know. Nothing special. I'll probably be knackered again. What do you want to do?'

He gave me a funny look. 'I thought I might book a weekend away somewhere. In the circumstances.'

In the circumstances. Oh, dear.

'Yes, I think it'd be a great idea to go away for our anniversary.'

'I can't believe you forgot, Elena.'

Elena. Whoops!

'I didn't forget.'

'Yes, you did.'

I reached out and placed my hand on his. It lay beneath mine like a dead fish. It was very tough at times, going out with such a sensitive man. Served me right for taking up with a Cancerian, I supposed. Paul was so easily hurt, and I was getting so tired of walking on eggshells whenever I was with him. Half the time, I really didn't understand why women wanted sensitive men. Give me an insensitive lout any day of the week.

'I'm sorry, Paul. I've just had a million and one different things on my mind, what with the move and everything…. I'd love to go away with you. How about Kerry?'

'Whatever.'

'Please don't be mad with me.'

'I'm not mad with you.'

I'd have liked to believe him, but, judging by the way he was brutally stabbing his lemon meringue pie with his fork (classic passive-aggressive behaviour), it seemed unlikely that I'd been forgiven.

'I think you've killed it.'

'What?' He looked up at me, a sulky expression on his face.

'The pie. I think it's officially dead.' I gave him a big smile, so he would know I was joking. He looked down again and put down his fork. I could tell from the way his dimples were half-showing that he was trying not to break into a grin.

'Do you want coffee?'

'No, let's just get the bill and go home.'

Ah. Home. Now, what home would that be, exactly?

'Um … did you want me to stay with you tonight, then?'

'Course I do.' Paul looked alarmed. 'You weren't thinking of going back to your flat, were you?' His eyes were wide with hurt.

'Oh, God, no!' I said quickly.

'Yes, you were,' he said accusingly. 'I can't believe you'd rather go back to Bimbo Central than stay with me.'

'Bimbo Central? Thanks very much. It's nice to know what you really think about me and my friends.'

'I wasn't talking about you and Hazel. I meant the other one.'

'Christiana has a name, you know.'

'Bloody stupid name, if you ask me.'

'That's rich, coming from someone whose girl-friend was named after a Russian ice-dancer.'

He laughed in spite of himself. Emergency averted.

'Oh, you haven't forgotten that we're having lunch with my parents on Sunday?'

'No, I haven't forgotten. I'll be there.'

Paul got on remarkably well with my parents. This freaked me out no end.

'And Annie is home from China.'

'Brilliant.' This seemed to cheer him up even more. He got on great with Annie, too.

Maybe he was just going out with the wrong sister.

Chapter Ten

Paul and I headed over to my parents' house at about one that Sunday, after staying the night in my apartment for a change. We had spent most of the evening sitting on the couch, drinking wine with Hazel and listening to her give out about Chris and her boss. She left for the office at around noon; there was no stopping her, hangover or no hangover.

I voiced my concerns to Paul on the way over. We were driving along in my beautiful car, which I'd retrieved from the garage the previous day – no more smelly hackneys for me. It felt so good to be back behind the wheel. I smiled and stroked the dashboard lovingly as I drove along. My baby!

I tore my attention away from the Audi to talk

to Paul, who was sitting stiffly in the passenger seat beside me, waiting for me to make a mistake.

'How does Hazel seem to you lately?' I asked.

'She's cracking up.'

'You think so too? Why didn't you say anything to me?'

'It's obvious to anyone with two eyes in their head. She's out of control.'

'Mm. You should have heard the way she spoke to Chris last weekend.'

'Well – I wouldn't let that worry you too much.' Paul couldn't understand how anyone could be alone with Chris for five minutes without blowing a gasket. 'Jesus, Lainey! You just went through a stop sign without stopping.'

'It's Sunday lunchtime. There's no one on the road.'

'Even so. I thought you were supposed to be an officer of the law.'

'Oh, shut up. I'm off duty.' And with that (but without indicating, as Paul kindly pointed out), I swung into the cul-de-sac where my parents lived.

Home was a four-bedroomed, two-storied, detached dwelling in the leafy suburbs of south County Dublin, distinguishable from the other houses in the estate only by the colour of the garage door and the number of shrubs in the front garden. I pulled up alongside my father's Volvo. He disapproved heartily of my choice of vehicle; something about standards, I think it was.

My mother answered the door, all floaty scarf and Yardley perfume.

'Come in, come in, you're most welcome.' She planted a resounding kiss on each of my cheeks and then held me by the shoulders and examined my face.

'It's great to see you, Elena. But you look tired. Have you been taking that tonic I gave you?'

'Yes, Mum.' *You mean that vile stuff I poured straight down the sink?*

'And Paul. Long time no see. Let me have a look at you. Handsome as ever! You've filled out a bit, too. It suits you.'

Life isn't fair. Who ever heard of a woman being told that she's filled out and that it suits her?

'Dinner will be ready in two ticks. Go into the sitting room and keep your father company.'

'Where's Annie?'

'Tatiana's only getting up now, would you believe. She says it's the time difference, but if you ask me, that's just an excuse. She was always a terror to get out of bed in the mornings.'

Everything but my father's legs was obscured by *The Sunday Times*.

'Hello, Dad.'

He peered around the side of the newspaper.

'Ah, hello.' He put the Business section to one side and rose stiffly to greet us. 'Good to see you again, Paul' – he shook his hand – 'and you too, Rosie.' He patted me on the shoulder and sat back

125

down in his armchair. He looked so out of place in the ultra-feminine, rose-chintz living room that it was almost laughable.

'You all right, Dad?'

He sighed and shook his head. 'I was just reading about the shocking state of the economy. You two young people don't know how lucky you are to have secure jobs. Just be sure you hold on to them.'

Here we go....

'I'd give my company another six months at the most. Things are looking very bad.'

My father: the ultimate prophet of doom and gloom. For at least the last twenty years, he had been predicting the bankruptcy and closure of the firm where he worked.

'You've been saying that for ages, Dad, and nothing bad has happened yet.'

'Oh, but things have never been this serious. You mark my words.'

Words duly marked. There was no use arguing. Besides, he enjoyed talking this way; why spoil his fun?

'Lainey!'

The atmosphere in the room instantly lightened.

'Annie!'

I hadn't seen my sister for six months. We hugged each other tightly.

'You look fantastic.'

'So do you. What did you get me?' It was a time-honoured ritual.

'Don't worry, I have a pressie for you upstairs. And one for you, Paul.' She grinned at him.

Tatiana is brilliant. We're five years apart – close enough to make us close, not close enough to make us rivals. It probably helps that we look completely different: I inherited the blue-eyed, blonde looks of my father's family, while Tatiana has my mother's dark curly hair and brown eyes. She's a lot taller than me, too, with a chest like a shelf.

As soon as I was born, she took it upon herself to look out for me. She had been my mini-mammy for as long as I could remember, ever ready to beat up any kid who had the bad judgment – and bad luck – to tease or torment me.

'How's Beijing?' asked Paul.

'Overcrowded,' she smiled, 'but apart from that, it's great.'

She was taking a well-earned two-year sabbatical from teaching Home Economics to Irish teenage boys. It wasn't only the school kitchen that they had managed to burn out. Teaching English to Chinese businessmen had turned out to be a far more rewarding and civilised experience.

'It's high time you came back home and found a nice Irish boy to marry.' This was from Dad, of course.

'There's another six months to run on my contract. I might think about coming home then,' she replied good-naturedly. She had always been more patient with Dad than I had. Still, I could probably have had patience with him too if I'd lived thousands of miles away and only had to see him twice a year.

'About time, too. I need someone to look after me in my old age.'

'Don't worry, Dad. We'll find a lovely nursing home to put you in. I have one in mind already.'

You should have seen his face. We broke into peals of laughter. It was always fun, ganging up on him like this.

He muttered under his breath as he got up from his chair and went to the bay window.

'I see you're still driving that fancy car of yours, Rosie.'

'Whose car should I be driving, Dad?'

'Don't get smart with your father. Remember whose money put you through college.'

Tatiana made a face behind his back, and I bit back more giggles.

'Did you ever get that steering-wheel lock I was telling you about?'

'Um – not yet.'

'Why not?'

'Because there's already an alarm on my car.'

'Do you really think those fellas would let the likes of an alarm stop them? They can get into anything they want to nowadays. There was a documentary about it last week on the English channel. Did you see it?'

'No.'

'I saw it,' said Paul. 'It was fascinating.'

Congratulations, Paul O'Toole. You have just won yourself two hundred brownie points!

My father gave Paul an approving look. 'Don't you think she should get herself a wheel lock, son?'

'I do, yes.'

Traitor.

'You hear that, Rosie? You should listen to your young man.'

'What my "young man" doesn't know is that there hasn't been a car stolen in Ardskeha in the last ten years. I know because I checked. The locals don't even lock their car doors, for God's sake.'

'Well, you don't want to be the first in ten years, do you?' Dad nodded sagely.

'I wonder what Mum's doing in there. Dinner should be ready by now.' Tatiana the peacemaker strategically changed the subject.

I took her cue. The last thing I wanted to do was ruin Annie's homecoming by having one of my regular spats with Dad. 'I'll go see if she needs any help.' On my way out to the kitchen, I bent down and hissed in Paul's ear, 'Lickarse!'

I heard Mum before I saw her. She didn't see me; she was fully occupied in dancing and humming around the kitchen with a bowl under her left oxter and a whisk in her right hand. The kitchen was flooded with the strains of beautiful classical music, which mingled wonderfully with the pungent smell of burning. With the instinct that had been

129

bred into me over the twenty-nine years that I had been my mother's daughter, I headed straight for the cooker and simultaneously switched it off and opened the oven door. I coughed, waving frantically in an effort to disperse the plumes of black smoke, and removed a distressed-looking chicken from the oven.

My mother didn't appear to notice. She was transfixed by the portable television that she had nagged my father into installing on top of one of the presses. I glanced up just in time to see Katarina Witt execute a particularly skilful triple toe-loop (or maybe a double axel – who knew? Mum did, of course).

'Mum,' I said gently. It didn't do to be too harsh in these situations. 'What are you doing? The dinner is getting burnt.'

The music took a dramatic turn, and Mum gripped my forearm.

'Bizet's *Carmen* on ice!' she said urgently. 'Rita lent it to me! It's fabulous, Elena – you have to see it! Just give me a minute, it's almost over.'

I looked at the tears streaking down my mother's rapt face. There were funny stripes where the salt water had come into contact with her cream blusher. She always got a bit weepy while watching ice-skating ('I could have been a contender…'). I prised the ceramic mixing bowl from underneath her left arm, noticing that one end of her floaty scarf had been trailing in it.

'Here, give that to me. You'll never get the cream to thicken if you keep crying into it like that. Why aren't you using the electric whisk that Dad bought you for your birthday?'

'Hmph! Electric whisk, indeed! The old bollix knew I wanted an aromatherapy starter kit. I'd like to tell him where he can shove his bloody whisk!'

'Mum!' I was scandalised. It was okay for me to use language like that, but she was my mother, for God's sake. A little decorum, please!

'Besides, I can't hear the music over that thing.' She wiped each eye with the corner of her apron and showed signs of starting to compose herself.

'Come on. I'll help you bring in the dinner.'

'No, no. You go inside and tell everyone to sit down at the table. I'll be quicker doing it myself.' I doubted it.

I stuck my head around the living-room door. 'Dinner's up, ladies and gentlemen. Take your seats at the table, please.'

I followed Tatiana, Paul and Dad as they filed into the dining room. The best crystal and china had been dusted off for the occasion. We all automatically sat in our allotted places, like programmed robots.

'I bet she's watching that *Carmen* tape again,' Dad said to me. I shrugged. 'I knew it. The dinner will be burnt, you mark my words.'

'I hope you all like your chicken well done,' Mum said gamely as she swished into the room, carrying a plate in each hand.

131

'Blackened chicken is one of my favourites, Mum,' said Tatiana. Mum smiled fondly at her and exited the room again.

'I knew it,' said Dad. 'I'm going to confiscate that bloody telly.' I noticed that he waited until Mum had gone before he said it.

Paul, who, along with Dad (the two men, don't you know), had received his food first – a dubious privilege in the circumstances – shot me a very worried look. My hidden hand patted his knee comfortingly under the table.

'Just do your best,' I whispered, smiling at him sympathetically.

Mum came back in with the rest of the plates and set them down with a flourish.

'Now, everybody – enjoy.'

We'd try. We really would.

'Would you like some gravy, Paul?' said Mum pleasantly.

I administered a swift sharp kick to Paul's ankle. *I wouldn't recommend the gravy today, sir.* Luckily for him, he got the message.

'No, thanks, Mrs Malone. I don't take gravy.'

'For the last time, call me Teresa. I won't say it again. Now, will you have some butter instead?'

I sensed Paul glancing over at me quickly. When no kick was forthcoming, he answered, 'Yes, please.'

The general rule in the Malone household was that anything that came straight from the packet and didn't require any input from my mother was safe enough.

'Well, isn't this lovely?' said Mum, beaming around at all of us. 'My whole family together.'

Except that Paul isn't one of the family, I had to restrain myself from reminding her. Although I knew she badly wanted him to be.

Down at the other end of the table, my father snorted, no doubt to convey his opinion that, no, this burnt offering wasn't lovely at all.

'Oh, Tatiana, you have to watch *Carmen* on ice. It's superb. I know you'll just love it,' my mother gushed.

Annie nodded her head affably, chewing her piece of chicken for the forty-eighth time.

Mum had been trying in vain to get us interested in ice-skating since we were old enough to stand. Tatiana, with her gangly legs that were far too long for her body, had been the first disappointment. I had disappointed approximately five years later, by delivering repeated impressions of the Sugar Plum Elephant every Saturday at the Dolphin's Barn ice rink.

'We haven't had a decent meal in this house since you got your hands on that blasted video,' snapped Dad.

'Oh, shut up, Joe.' Water off a duck's proverbial. 'Oh, Elena – don't leave the house today without taking that book I borrowed from Christiana. I've had it so long it's getting embarrassing.'

'I wouldn't worry, Mum. She's probably forgotten all about it.'

'What's the book?' Poor Paul was doing his best to make polite conversation. He never really knew what to say when confronted by mad people.

'It's about reincarnation. Fascinating! Do you believe in reincarnation, Paul?'

'Um, no. Not really.' He looked sorry he'd spoken.

'Who does Christiana think she's the reincarnation of these days?' asked Tatiana.

'Marilyn Monroe. That's why she's gone platinum-blonde again.'

'Interesting. She always goes for someone glamorous, doesn't she? Last time I was home she thought she was Kylie Minogue.'

'But Kylie isn't dead – is she?' My father sounded worried, and then looked embarrassed. He had been very taken by those gold hot pants.

'Don't worry, Dad; Kylie hasn't kicked the bucket. But that wouldn't matter to Chris.'

Dad and Paul exchanged a look. It was easy to interpret: *Women! Completely bonkers!*

Just then, Mum gave them further confirmation. 'Oh, girls, I forgot to tell you. I'm being made a Reiki Master next week!'

'Really?'

'I don't know why you're surprised. Hasn't she been bossing me around for years?' Dad had a point.

'Being a Reiki Master has nothing to do with bossing people about, as you well know, Joe

Malone. I wish you'd let me try it out on you. Your energies are all blocked, you know. No wonder you're such a grouch.'

'Paul …' Dad determinedly changed the subject. 'Have you given any more thought to buying a property?'

'Yes, I have.' Paul smiled at my father in relief: at last, a chance to discuss a normal, sensible topic that he knew something about. His pleasure was to be short-lived, however. 'I have my eye on an apartment on the Quays.'

'No, no, no.' Dad shook his head solemnly. 'A property like that won't hold its value once the bubble bursts, you mark my words. And all those apartments were literally thrown up; they'll probably collapse at the next strong gust of wind. No, what you need to invest in, son, is a good solid property with a few years on it, down the country somewhere. Forget Dublin. I'd go for somewhere in the south-east if I were you. In fact, you know what?' He said this as if the idea had just that second popped into his head. 'The area that Rosie is living in would be perfect.'

Oh, here we go, I thought. *Why doesn't he just go the whole hog and offer Paul a dowry to take me off his hands? I'd suggest one hundred camels. They're all the rage this season, you know.*

'I'll certainly think about it.' Paul smiled politely and turned his attention back to the Brussels sprout that he had been attempting to saw in half

135

for the last five minutes.

'Mum? How long did you cook the sprouts for?'

'Oh, I don't know. Why do you ask?'

'Well, they're a bit hard.'

'They're like bloody bullets,' said Dad helpfully.

'You're not supposed to cook vegetables for a long time. It takes all the goodness out of them.'

'All the goodness in the world isn't going to benefit you if you can't bite into the damn things in the first place.'

'Mum. Dad. I have some news for you.'

All eyes were on Tatiana, sprouts forgotten.

'I'm getting married.'

She certainly knew how to pick her moment.

There were a couple of seconds of shocked silence, and then Mum squealed and ran around the table, throwing her arms around Tatiana's neck from behind and almost throttling her. She was closely followed by me.

'That's great news, Annie! Is it that guy you wrote to me about?'

Annie nodded happily, then looked over expectantly at my father. 'Dad?'

'That's great, Annie. But who are you marrying?'

'He's one of my students. I've been teaching him English.'

Dad sat like a statue. 'What's his name?'

'Chen.'

We all watched in morbid fascination as the colour drained from Dad's face.

'You mean he's a Chink.'

'He's Chinese, yes.' Tatiana's tone was cool and her expression hardened as she spoke.

'Oh, no, Annie. You can't marry a Chink.'

'Dad, please don't use that term. I'm marrying Chen and that's all there is to it.'

'But he's from a totally different culture. I bet he's not even a Catholic.'

She ignored this. 'I have another bit of news.'

We all looked at her again.

'I'm pregnant.'

My mother squealed and strangled Tatiana once more. My father sat like a thundercloud at the head of the table.

'Well, I hope for your sake that you're not expecting a girl, or you'll be forced to abort.'

'Dad!'

'Joe!'

We all glared at him angrily. He threw his napkin on the table and got up. 'I'm going to get a take-away. I've had enough of this muck.'

He stopped at the door and looked back at Tatiana.

'I hope you're proud of yourself, Miss. You're the first fallen woman in the Malone family.'

We all sat in silence until we heard the front door slam. Then Tatiana started to sob uncontrollably.

'Fallen woman!' she said between sobs. 'Where does he think he is? The Bible?'

Mum cradled her in her arms. 'Don't worry, dear. He'll calm down once he gets used to the idea. Now come into the living room and I'll give you a nice Indian head massage. It'll make you and the baby feel a whole lot better.'

I sighed. There was nothing like a good Sunday roasting.

Chapter Eleven

I was so happy to be driving my beautiful car again. I turned the top down and the radio up; it was playing a song about going to visit the countryside and eating lots of peaches. Yes, having my car back made returning to Ballyknock just about tolerable. At this rate, I might even make it to the end of the week. In fact, I was almost glad to get away from Dublin for some peace and quiet. Warring flat-mates, Neanderthal fathers, hormonal sisters ... after what I'd been through, handling a few mice should be a doddle.

And speaking of mice ...

Patricia came into my office shortly after five on Monday evening.

'Do you have any spare boxes in here?'

I gestured to a container of flat archive boxes balancing against the far wall. She took one of them and expertly made it up. I reflected, not for the first time, that whoever invented them there boxes must be a zillionaire several times over. Wish I'd thought of them.

'I have a surprise for you,' she twinkled as she went back into the office.

What could it be? One of her famous fruit bracks? Her secret recipe for prize-winning raspberry jam? My very own pinny? I shouldn't scoff, I admonished myself; she really had been very kind to me.

I had been wrong on all counts. Approximately ten minutes later, Patricia burst through my office door holding in both hands that very same box, although this time it clearly wasn't empty.

'There you go!' She plonked it unceremoniously on top of the file I'd been working on.

I was filled with instinctual, childish delight at receiving a present, any present. 'What is it?'

'It's the answer to all your mouse problems.'

Just then, the box moved. All by itself, you understand. I noticed that the lid had been Sellotaped down on either side and that several large holes had been punched into it.

'What's in there?' Delight was turning to apprehension.

'Look through the lid and see for yourself.'

'It's not a ferret, is it?'

She laughed. 'See for yourself.'

I cautiously stood up and peered through the holes. From the depths of the box, two round green lights glowed eerily up at me. I jumped back in fright as the lights moved swiftly to the top of the box and an object like a fur and leather pin-cushion, with five pins stuck into it, shoved itself out of one of the holes.

'It's a cat, isn't it?' I said with ill-concealed disgust.

As if in reply, the box emitted a low, guttural yowl.

'It doesn't sound too friendly.'

'She's just scared, poor little cratur. So would you be if somebody took you away from your home and stuck you in a box for no good reason.'

She had a point. Still, I was confused. 'Where did she come from? I mean, did you have her hidden in your drawer all day long, or something?'

'Begod, no, child. Seamus is after bringing her around in his car. He tells me she's a feral cat that his wife – that's my sister Dorothy – has been feeding for the last couple of years. She's just weaned her last set of kittens.'

So the rat-catcher had come up trumps after all.

'What do I owe him?'

Patricia laughed her head off at this particular gem. 'Cats don't cost anything.'

'They do in Dublin.'

'Sure they're all half-mad up there – no offence, lovey.'

141

'None taken.'

'I mean, the countryside is overrun with cats; I'm certain Seamus and Dorothy are only delighted to be getting rid of this one – not that they're trying to dump her on you,' she added quickly. 'It's just that they have about thirteen cats as it is, between the house and the barns. And you're in desperate need of a cat, as far as I can tell. And they tell me that this one is a grand little killer.'

Great. 'What's her name?'

Patricia looked at me as if I were losing my mind. 'I don't think she has a name. "Cat", I suppose.'

That was original.

'Here, I'll carry her out to the car for you.'

I packed up and followed Patricia and the box out to my car. As Patricia started moving, the cat started meowing. At least, I think that's what it was doing. I didn't know much about cats, but surely that was no ordinary meow. It was more like a baby's plaintive cry – a distress signal if ever there was one.

I clicked open the doors, and Patricia went to put the box in the back seat.

'No, no, no! Not in there.'

She turned and looked at me in surprise.

'You can put it in the boot.'

She shrugged and moved to the back of the car. I shook my head in amazement. A cat, in the back of my Audi – sacrilege!

The cat kept up its pitiful mewling all the way home. If anything, the sound became louder and more insistent. There was another noise, too; a kind of knocking. I was torn between sympathy and alarm.

I finally pulled up outside Power's Cottage and approached the boot with caution. *Easy does it....* I slowly opened it. *Holy shit!*

Like a bat out of hell (or a cat out of hell), a small bundle of dark-brown fur catapulted itself past me and disappeared into the depths of the garden. I couldn't even tell in which direction she flew.

But that was the least of my problems. A second later, my nostrils were assaulted by a pungent stench. *Oh, Jesus!* I covered my nose in disgust. I might not have been the world's greatest feline expert, but I knew cat piss when I smelt it. Thank Christ I hadn't let Patricia put her in the back seat. *Horrible little animal,* I thought. *I hope she never comes back.*

I forgot all about the cat until I was leaving for work the next morning. There on the doorstep, placed dead-centre on the mat, was a decapitated mouse.

There was still no sign of her when I was getting ready for bed that night. Feeling very foolish, clad only in fleece-lined pyjamas, slippers and a torch, I advanced into the darkness.

'Cat! Where are you, Cat?'

No response.

I moved out onto the road. At times like this, I was glad I didn't have many neighbours. I wished I knew more about cats. How did one find a cat that didn't want to be found? I swept the beam of the torch in random arcs about the road.

'Here, kitty, kitty!'

I hadn't told Patricia about my predicament. I was hardly going to admit to losing the creature ten minutes after she had been given into my custody. *How's the cat settling in? Oh, just fine, thank you....* If she didn't turn up soon, I'd have to pretend she'd got run over by a car or something. As far as I knew, cats were always being run over. Okay, so I lived on a road where there was, on average, one car every sixty minutes; the moggy got unlucky, that was all.

Increasingly desperate, I walked up the boreen towards the old derelict schoolhouse. It was with some effort that I quelled the impending feelings of creepiness.

'Meow,' I said quietly into the darkness.

I couldn't believe I was doing this. If only Iseult could see me now.

'Meow,' I said, louder.

Still nothing.

'Oh, this is ridiculous.' I turned on my slippered heel and headed back to the cottage.

'Meow.' This time it wasn't me.

'Meow?' I replied.

'Meow.' There it was again. I wasn't imagining things.

I nearly lost my life as something warm and soft rubbed against my left leg. In a blind panic, I dropped the torch, which began to roll down the hill, illuminating alternate patches of road and hedgerow as it went. I chased after it as if my life depended on it, scenes from *The Blair Witch Project* flashing alarmingly through my head.

I caught up with the errant torch and directed the beam uphill. Sure enough, there was the cat, eyes glowing like green candle-flames in the darkness. She was just sitting there, all casual: *What's all the fuss about?*

'Meooow,' she said as she ran towards me, tail aloft, wrapping herself around my legs again.

Relieved, I almost ran back indoors, the cat padding delicately along beside me. I placed a bowl of cat food on the kitchen floor and watched as she enthusiastically tucked into it. On impulse, I leant down and stroked her back a few times. The cat reverberated like the engine of an expensive sports car.

'You're not so bad,' I told her, and took myself off to bed.

It was the last week of September, and the Indian summer was drawing to a close. I had come to an executive decision to make the most of the few bright evenings that were left to me: I headed off on a constitutional every day after work. This evening, the sky looked uncertain. I changed into my walking gear quickly, before it could make up its mind for the worst.

There wasn't much else to do down here. Since I'd moved down to Ballyknock, my social life during the week had deteriorated dramatically. In my previous incarnation as a Dublin solicitor, there had always been someone to meet after work for a drink or a meal; even if there wasn't, there was always Paul and/or Hazel and/or Chris to hang out with. Hell, if I got really desperate, I could even visit my parents. Right then, I'd have killed for an evening in with the old dears. I was sick of watching TV; even I had a limit to how many soap operas I could follow simultaneously. In my boredom, I'd taken to having one-sided conversations with Mary Power on the wall. She hadn't started to answer back yet, but I believed it was only a matter of time.

I was so wrapped up in nostalgia for my ex-social life that I failed to notice the clouds gathering overhead. My first clue to the impending downpour was when a large raindrop landed squarely on the bridge of my nose. Then one on my hand. Then one on my forehead. Then another. And another. In sixty seconds I was soaked to the skin. A grand soft day, thank God.

Damnation. I must have been two miles or more away from the cottage – I had a bad habit of setting off on a long stroll and forgetting that I'd have to walk the same distance back again. I turned and started to run. In hindsight, this was ludicrous; I was hardly fit enough to run two metres, let alone two miles. No sooner had I begun than a large black bird, probably a crow, burst out of a hedgerow and flew directly into my path – most likely looking for shelter too. Momentarily startled, I lost my footing and fell heavily to the ground. I felt my right ankle going. *Shit!*

I must have looked a sight, sitting on the rain-sodden ground, groaning and massaging my ankle ineffectually. It really hurt. What was I going to do now?

As if on cue – in one of those rare instances of serendipity – I heard the sound of a far-off engine. It was definitely drawing closer. Thank goodness. Surely the driver would stop and be a good Samaritan. I strained my ears. Not a car; something larger. A truck? A jeep? A tractor, even?

A blue crock of a tractor emerged dramatically out of the mist and drew up beside me. Jack looked down in obvious surprise that the bedraggled lump of clothing at the side of the road was in fact a human being, and that, furthermore, it was me. He switched off the engine and jumped down lithely.

'Lainey! What are you doing out here?'

'Oh, you know. Just having a rest.' The rain was still bucketing down around us.

'Are you hurt?'

'It's my ankle.'

'Here, let me have a look.'

He knelt down in front of me and, taking my ankle firmly but gently in his hands, laid it on his knee. He undid the laces of my new state-of-the-art hiking boot and smiled.

'Thinking of going rock-climbing, were we?'

'I didn't have anything else to wear,' I replied sulkily.

Jack eased off the boot and began to manipulate my ankle up and down, left and right. At one point I let out an indignant squeal.

'Nothing broken. Probably just a sprain.'

'Just a sprain, is it? That's easy for you to say. It bloody well hurts. What makes you an expert, anyhow?'

'I'm not, but my brother gave me a few tips.'

'I didn't know you had a brother who's a doctor.'

'I don't. I have a brother who's a vet.'

'Oh, well, I'm very flattered to be compared to a heifer.'

He ignored me. 'Come on. Let's get you in out of the rain.' He hoisted me easily up into the air, like a new husband about to carry his bride over the threshold, shoved me inelegantly into the cab of the tractor and jumped in beside me.

'Now, we'll have you home in no time.' He looked over at me as he started up the engine. 'Jesus, girl, you look like a drowned rat.'

'Thanks a lot.'

'Don't mention it.'

The tractor took off at its top speed of ten miles an hour. At this rate, I might make it home by Christmas. I shivered.

'Cold? Here. Cover yourself with this.' Jack handed me a tartan blanket that stank ferociously of sheepdog. Not wanting to appear ungrateful, I draped it delicately across my knees, trying not to visualise the dog hairs and possibly even fleas that were transferring themselves to their new home – my clothes.

Despite my somewhat harsh words, I was weak with gratitude. What would I have done if he hadn't come along? I glanced slyly across at him when I thought he wasn't looking. I was wrong. He was looking. He smiled easily and openly at me.

'You all right?'

I nodded. 'Thanks.'

'Don't mention it. Maybe you can do the same for me someday.'

What? Save him in my tractor? I doubted it.

The sudden downpour had ended as abruptly as it had started. In typical perverse Irish-weather fashion, the sun had come out again. An almost perfect rainbow, in all its vivid glory, straddled the countryside before us. Everything looked beautiful after the rain – like a woman's eyes after crying: washed clean.

Jack looked good after the rain, too. I wished the wet look suited me that well.

'The view is pretty good from up here.' I meant it. I could see far more than I'd ever seen in my car or on foot. I could practically see right into people's bedroom windows, for a start. Usually, I was only able to nose into the first storey of people's houses.

149

'I'm telling you. People underestimate the charms of a tractor.'

'I'd say it's a real babe magnet, all right.'

Jack laughed. 'You'd be surprised. I'm not doing too bad today, anyway, am I?'

He gave me a bird's-eye tour of the countryside. To the right, a field of lazy beds – rows and rows of ridges, used for growing potatoes at the time of the Famine. To the left, the recording studio of a reclusive rock star. (Really? Rich, famous people chose to live here?) Up ahead, the gate lodge of the estate of the Master of the Hunt. I craned my neck, as instructed by Jack, to make out a herd of deer. 'And see those horses over there? See that little brown one with the bandy legs? A two-time Derby winner.' He was munching happily on a clump of grass, bathed in golden autumn sunshine. I never would have guessed. I searched for signs of security precautions, but there were none.

We reached Power's Cottage, and I wondered how on earth I was going to get down off the tractor. Without saying anything to me, as if he were a fireman and I needed rescuing from a burning building, Jack placed his left arm under my right armpit and his right arm beneath my knees, and swung me out of the tractor and onto the ground. I winced as my injured foot made contact with the earth.

'Keep your weight off it.'

He hauled me into the house and deposited me outside the bedroom door.

'You'd better get out of those wet clothes. Let me know if you need any help.'

'I'll be all right.' I closed the door, hobbled over to the bed and sat down heavily. I could hear noises coming from the kitchen: Jack filling up the kettle, Jack cleaning out the fire. I glanced at myself in the dressing-table mirror. My cheeks were flushed and my eyes were unnaturally bright. I must be getting some sort of fever.

I emerged ten minutes later, hair roughly blow-dried, dressed in pyjamas, a towelling robe and bed-socks. Oddly enough, I wasn't embarrassed by my appearance. Flames were already leaping out of the hearth.

'Here. Sit yourself down.' Jack guided me over to the couch, where I sat as instructed. He handed me a mug of tea. 'Do you mind if I go into your bedroom for a second?'

'No – but ...'

He emerged from the bedroom with my duvet, which he proceeded to cover me with, tucking it right up to my chin. All that was left exposed was my face and the hand holding the mug of tea.

'Now ...' He looked down at me seriously. 'Do you think you need a hot-water bottle?'

'I'm fine, Jack. Couldn't be cosier.'

He grinned. 'Never let it be said that Jack Power doesn't know how to treat a girl.'

Never let it be said, indeed. He was like some hero out of a romantic novel. Were farmers meant to be this smooth?

He was so nice. So funny. So gorgeous…. So what was he doing here with me? I banished the renegade thought immediately, before it had time to take root.

His next good deed was to bandage my ankle. He took a first-aid kit – which I hadn't even known existed – from under the kitchen sink, and wrapped my foot up like a mummy. I was relieved I'd happened to shave my legs in the shower that morning. Pity about the chipped nail-polish, though.

'You're to go to the doctor first thing tomorrow. You won't be able to drive so I'll take you.'

'What, in the tractor?'

'If you're good, I'll bring the jeep.'

So Jack Power brought me to the doctor the next morning ('a slight sprain'. Slight! The man was clearly a quack). Then he collected me from work that evening and took me home. As he was leaving (he had to bring the cows in from the field), he turned and looked at me strangely. I felt awkward in his company for the first time in the two days.

'Are you doing anything this Saturday night?' he asked.

Tell him.

'I'm going to Kerry for the weekend.'

'Oh? Whereabouts?'

Tell him.

'A hotel close to Sneem.'

'Oh. Who are you going with?'
Tell him.
'My boyfriend.'
Told him.
Jack nodded slowly, as if understanding some-thing.
'Well … I hope you have a nice time. I'll see you soon.'
'See you next week sometime?'
He waved, without looking back at me, and sped off down the hill in the jeep.
Come back!

Chapter Twelve

The chosen location for our anniversary weekend was an elegant country-house hotel on the Ring of Kerry. I made my own way down on Saturday morning, the Audi cautiously hugging the cliff road. The spectacle of the waves rushing at the harsh coastline and flinging themselves against spiky black rocks was so awe-inspiring that I almost ended up in the ocean on two occasions.

It was mid-morning when I swung through the impressive wrought-iron gates of the hotel. I drove slowly, taking in the lush, well-kept vegetation and the ancient native trees. Paul's car was already parked in front of the hotel. He must have left his flat in Dublin at five in the morning, or some such ungodly hour. He'd probably been for a swim, had a back rub and played two rounds of golf already. All I wanted to do was sit in one of the plush reception rooms with a coffee and a smoke and read the papers. Hotels with activities were wasted on me.

I opened the door of room 101 with the key they had given me at reception – a proper key, not one of those stupid cards that never work. The room was everything I had hoped for and then some. A four-poster bed! I'd never slept in a four-poster before, but I'd always wanted to, ever since I'd read 'The Princess and the Pea' at the age of six. I sat on the edge of the bed, giggling as I bounced up and down and took in my surroundings. The décor was wine and gold, rich and royal. Original paintings of the Kerry countryside adorned the walls and each piece of furniture was an obvious antique – not that I knew much about these things, but I knew quality when I saw it; not a stick of over-varnished MDF in sight. There was even a writing desk. I kicked off my shoes, padded over and started fiddling around with all the little compartments. Hotel pencils and sheets of writing paper had been laid on. Maybe I'd even start writing that novel I was always thinking about – but later. There was still the bathroom to explore.

I turned on the light to reveal a pristine black-and-white bathroom, striking in its contrasting modernity. There was a bath with all the jacuzzi trimmings (I could be a floozy in the jacuzzi) and a shower that would comfortably fit two people (at least). But these details barely registered: I was magnetically drawn to the freebies adorning the sink. I noted with excitement the Crabtree & Evelyn shampoo, conditioner and body lotion. And then there were the shower caps, and soaps in fancy flowery boxes. Lovely. I looked around, wide-eyed, to see what else I could steal when I was leaving. There was a fluffy white bathrobe hanging on the back of the door…. No. I'd never have the nerve. I'd be glancing nervously in my rear-view mirror all the way back to Ballyknock, expecting a squad car to pull me over at any second: 'Where do you think you're going with that bathrobe?' I had always been a good, law-abiding citizen. I'd love to claim that this was for moral reasons, but actually I was just terrified of being caught.

I selected a soap, a shower cap and two body lotions and was about to transfer them to my bag when I was interrupted by the sound of a key turning in the lock. Guiltily, I threw the contraband behind me into the bathroom, where it landed with a clatter in the sink. I posed casually in the doorway, leaning my left hand against the frame, my right hand on my hip. It was Paul. I loved the way his face broke into a genuine happy smile the second he saw me.

'You're here!' He kissed me warmly.

'You're in a good mood.'

'I'm just pleased to see you. When did you get here?'

'About half an hour ago.' More like ten minutes – but who was counting?

He looked at his watch. 'What time did you leave?'

'About seven.' It had been more like eight. I'd had to wrench myself from my cherished Saturday-morning lie-in.

'Really? The traffic must have been awful.'

'Oh, it was. Terrible. I got stuck behind a tractor coming out of Ballyknock, and there was a bad pile-up just outside Cork, and, would you believe, there were loose horses on the road in Clonmel....' I trailed off as it became obvious that Paul was no longer listening to my excuses (just as well, too). He was hunkered down beside his sports bag, pulling out clean clothes.

'Were you swimming?'

'Yeah. I did about fifty lengths. The pool's fantastic. Maybe you'll come down with me tomorrow morning?'

'Yeah, maybe. Do you fancy an early lunch? I'm starved.'

'Sure. Just give me a few minutes to shower and change.'

I looked on appreciatively as Paul whipped his T-shirt over his head and stepped out of his shorts. Mmm ... I'd almost forgotten about his footballer's legs. I stood in the doorway of the bathroom, watching him prepare for his shower.

'What happened here?' He was picking the body lotions out of the sink and lining them up properly again, as nature intended.

'I don't know. They must have fallen.'

As Paul turned on the jet of water and stepped into the shower, I was struck by a brilliant idea. Mentally hugging myself with excitement, I went back into the bedroom and rapidly stripped off, throwing my clothes onto the bed or wherever else was convenient. I tiptoed back into the bathroom, loosening my hair as I went, and drew back the door of the shower, startling Paul.

'What are you doing? I'm having a shower.'

'I just thought you might need your back scrubbed.' I smiled up at him in what I hoped was a suggestive fashion, and felt vaguely foolish.

Stepping into the shower, I closed the screen behind me. Paul looked at me, his brow furrowed, uncertainty clouding his eyes. I ignored this and looped my arms loosely about his neck, pressing my breasts against his chest. This, at least, had the desired effect.

'Let me wash your hair,' I said.

'What do you want to do that for?'

'I just want to. Let me wash your hair this once, Paul. Please.'

I had recently read in a well-known women's magazine that washing your partner's hair (even if he didn't have all that much of it) was a sure-fire way of establishing intimacy. I squirted a blob of

Paul's medicated, masculine-smelling shampoo into my hand and began to spread it over his head. I rubbed it in, using each and every finger to massage his scalp, until it looked like he was wearing a white foam wig. I removed the shower nozzle and started to rinse. As I did so, I accidentally dislodged Paul's shaving kit from the shelf; unfortunately, it landed slap bang on his big toe.

'For fuck's sake!' He hopped onto his other leg.

'Sorry.'

But the fun didn't end there. As he hopped, a soapy rivulet ran straight into his eye.

'Oh, Jesus!' He rubbed frantically at it.

Without saying another word, I replaced the shower-head and got out. I grabbed the nearest towel and exited the bathroom, leaving a trail of soapy footprints behind me.

An all-too-familiar phrase played once again in my mind.

Why do I even bother?

Lunch was a frosty affair – and I'm not talking about the ice-cream pie for dessert. I was in a bad mood because I felt I'd made a fool of myself. Paul was in a bad mood because I'd failed to apologise for injuring his toe/injuring his eye/ruining his shower. He could go fuck himself if he thought *I* was going to say sorry to *him*.

I think he sensed this; he was the first to thaw out.

'The food's lovely here, isn't it?'

I shrugged.

'Better than that over-priced restaurant for posers that Chris made us go to.'

He was trying to catch my eye, but I deliberately wouldn't let him. I was in a sulk.

'Will we go for a walk after lunch – explore the grounds?'

'You can do what you want. I'm going to stay here and read my book.'

We ate in silence for a couple of minutes. Then Paul said, 'I got you an anniversary present.'

'What is it?' *Damn!*

A smug smile played about his lips. 'Will I go and get it?'

'Do what you like.' I knew I was being ridiculously petulant, but I didn't seem able to stop myself.

He went out to his car and returned a minute later, carrying a large oblong box wrapped in silver paper and decorated with a bright-red bow. At first I thought it might be a dozen roses, but when he placed it in my arms I realised it was too heavy for that. A sawn-off shotgun, perhaps? A stick to beat the lovely lady with?

With that familiar Christmas-morning feeling, I ripped open the silver paper. I saw Paul wince; he hated the way I wasted wrapping paper. You could never use a piece again after I'd got my hands on it.

I finished unwrapping and stared down at the box in my lap.

'What is it?' I already knew the answer. I just didn't believe it.

'It's that steering-wheel lock your father mentioned last week. It's an amazing gadget. Look, I'll show you what it can do.' He removed it from my lap and started playing around with it, like a total fucking anorak.

My vision blurred, and for one crazy moment I thought I was going to cry. *Don't be ridiculous, Lainey. It's not as if that innocent steering-wheel lock is a symbol of everything that's wrong with your relationship....* I realised that Paul had stopped enthusing about the thing and was addressing me again.

'Don't you like it?'

'I love it, Paul. It's so romantic. I got you those cufflinks you wanted. They're in the car. I'll get them for you later. Right now, I'm going for a walk.'

'I thought you were going to stay and read.'

'There's been a change of plan.'

'Give me a second and I'll come with you.'

'I'd prefer to go on my own.' I walked out of the restaurant without looking back. There must have been something about my manner that prevented Paul from following me.

A fucking steering-wheel lock. Was I going out with my father or what?

I needed time to think.

I felt a lot better after spending a few hours on my own. The hotel grounds would have soothed

161

the most troubled of hearts.

I met up with Paul for dinner, which was a much jollier affair than lunch. We were entertained during our meal by a pianist, who – in between beautifully played classical pieces – told the most outrageously filthy and funny jokes. The wine flowed even more beautifully than the music, and by the time we were onto our coffees I was in great form.

I had begun to talk seriously about accompanying the pianist with my superb singing voice when Paul decided it was time to go to bed. He pushed me along the corridor to our room, his hand firmly on the small of my back, guiding me when I started to veer off course. He shushed me now and then, when the strains of my marvellous rendition of 'My Way' threatened to disturb the inhabitants of the other rooms.

In room 101, I flopped down on the bed and watched the ceiling spin. I heard Paul locking the door behind us and shielded my eyes when he turned on the bedside lamp. I felt him lie down on the bed beside me. Even though my hand was still covering my eyes, I could tell he was looking at me. I felt hot breath on my neck. Gentle fingers stroked the skin of my clavicle rhythmically. I gave myself over to the sensation, stretching my supine body luxuriantly on the bed. The fingers travelled further down, tracing the outlines of my breasts and following my curves from ribcage to waist to hips. Hot, insistent lips pressed down on my mouth. I kissed them back gently, aware of the fingers starting to unbutton my top. I lay almost rigid, a knot of anticipation tightening in my stomach.

And then I heard the sound of a zipper. I looked out through my fingers; Paul was tearing open a condom and preparing to assume the position. Oh, no. Too soon. I sat up on the bed, and he looked at me in surprise.

'What?' he said to the expression on my face.

'Let's have some fun first.'

He frowned. 'I thought this was fun.'

'It is,' I said urgently, grabbing at his arm, 'but look – we have this whole hotel room at our disposal. A four-poster bed, for God's sake. When are we going to have the chance to sleep in a four-poster again?'

He shrugged.

'Not to mention the mirror in the wardrobe at the end of the bed.'

Still nothing. All I seemed to be doing was making him look uncomfortable. I pressed on regardless.

'I have a pair of silk hold-ups with me. Why don't you tie me to the bed?'

'I don't know, Lainey –'

'Oh, come on. This bed is perfect for it. You can even blindfold me if you want.'

'Why? So you can pretend that I'm somebody else?'

'Oh, don't be daft, Paul. It's nothing to do with that. It makes the sensations more intense, that's all.'

'So you've done this before, then.'

I blushed. 'Might have done.'

'Who with?'

'For God's sake, Paul. I had other boyfriends before I went out with you – you know that. Now are you going to tie me up or not?' I already knew the answer.

'We don't need all that kinky stuff, Lainey. We love each other.'

Did we?

I climbed over to the other side of the bed and got under the covers.

'What are you doing? Don't you want…?' Paul put his hand on my shoulder.

I shook it off. 'No, I don't want. I'm going to sleep.'

I lay stiffly under the covers, staring at the edge of the bedside table, until Paul eventually got under the covers himself and turned off the light. Some anniversary weekend this had turned out to be.

I lay there, wide awake, staring into the gloom, for what must have been an hour. Shortly before I fell asleep, Paul whispered my name.

'Lainey.'

I didn't answer.

'Lainey? Are you awake?'

Just pretend you're asleep.

'I love you, Lainey.'

It was two o'clock the following day, and we were having afternoon tea. This consisted of cheese, ham and turkey finger sandwiches – with the crusts cut off, of course – and home-made fruit scones, still warm from the oven, served with real butter on a silver butter-dish, strawberry jam and whipped cream. I wondered how Bridie and Patricia would rate the jam; it tasted pretty good to me, but, then again, I was no expert. This was all washed down with coffee or tea, depending on your preference, served in a little antique silver pot. But the *pièce de résistance* of the entire afternoon-tea experience was the dessert of the day: strawberry mousse on a perfect, light piece of sponge, served on a silver cake-plate.

Did the people serving us not realise that we were only plebs who would have settled for a lot less?

I sat with my face obscured by the Living section of the *Sunday Independent*. I wasn't really reading it; I just wanted to avoid looking at Paul, who had his nose buried deep in the Sports section. Every now and then he would make some comment about speculation over the new manager of the Irish soccer team, and I would say 'Mmm' in response.

At one point, I looked across at him. Was he really that oblivious to what was going on in this relationship? He acted like we had no problems. Was it all a big macho show, or did he genuinely think we were doing okay?

I was considering another (solitary) walk when a shadow fell across me.

'Hello, Lainey. I thought it was you.'

I looked up to find that the owner of the shadow was an ex-boyfriend of mine.

'Oh. Hello, Eric.' I sucked in my stomach involuntarily.

Eric had been my first love. I had met him when I was nineteen and in second year at UCD, and we had been inseparable until almost the end of third year. At least, I had followed him around with puppy-like devotion, waiting for him to throw me the odd scrap of affection whenever it suited him. It tended to suit him on Saturday nights and whenever he fancied a quick blow-job. He was the type of man who takes the spark out of a woman and then dumps her because she's lost her spark. In short, he broke my hymen and my heart.

I realised he was looking expectantly at Paul.

'Eric, this is Paul. Paul – Eric. We knew each other in college.'

Paul stood up and shook hands with Eric, and the two of them sized each other up. I could tell that Paul had immediately copped who Eric was. I had told him a little bit about Eric, but not too much, as Paul had a tendency to become insanely jealous for no good reason. He knew, however, that Eric had been my first proper boyfriend and that he had been the captain of the rugby team in his last year in college. The latter fact in particular irked him no end.

'Romantic weekend away from the Big Smoke, is it?' Eric asked me.

'Something like that. You?'

'I'm down with a few of the lads. Golf.' He gestured to three men who were gathered around the bar, similarly attired in tank tops, baseball caps and stupid-looking trousers.

'Do you play, Paul?'

'I do, as a matter of fact.'

'Are you in a club?'

'Clontarf.'

'Really? Nice course.'

Paul looked pleased.

'What's your handicap?' Eric asked.

'Ten.'

'Not bad.'

'Yours?' I knew he wouldn't be able to resist.

'Three.'

Paul was crestfallen; there was no other word to describe the expression on his face. Eric smiled that smug smile that brought me back a decade in time. *So you're still a self-satisfied bastard, then.*

'What are you doing with yourself these days, Eric?'

'I'm a management consultant.'

'Really? I didn't know a degree in history and rugby qualified you for that sort of thing.'

He laughed. 'You'd be surprised what it qualifies you for.'

He'd put on a couple of stone – most of it beer, no doubt – since the last time I'd seen him. Not that I could talk: I was considerably softer around the edges

167

too. And was it my imagination, or was he already thinning on top? I sincerely hoped so. He had always been so vain about his shiny black tresses.

In college, Eric's hair had been shoulder-length. For some reason, in those disastrous romantic formative years I had been wildly and irresistibly drawn to long-haired lovers, especially if they had beards. Maybe I thought that if they resembled Jesus Christ they were less likely to use and abuse me, or maybe I'd just fancied Robert Powell when he played Jesus of Nazareth. Most of these boys were the type who would invite me up to their rooms to show me their poetry – and when they got me up there, they actually wanted to show me their poetry (always terrible angst-ridden mush). Eric, however, had wanted to show me something entirely different.

Back in the present, I tried to imagine him with a comb-over.

'Better be off. It was nice seeing you again, Lainey. We must meet up in Dublin some evening for a few scoops.'

'Yes. We must.' *Not.*

'Bye, then.'

'Bye, Eric.'

He went back to his cronies. I shook my head and resumed reading the book reviews. I wondered what I had ever seen in that prat, and it was a good feeling.

After a while, I glanced over at Paul. His face was like thunder.

'What's up with you?'

Paul continued to glower.

'Come on, spit it out.'

'You know what's wrong,' he spat.

'No, Paul, I don't know. Did Arsenal have the crap kicked out of them by Man United again?'

'I just can't believe you did that.'

'Did what?'

'He asked you out, and you said yes! Right in front of me!'

'Oh, come off it, Paul. I was just being polite – and so was he.'

'No. It was more than that. He obviously still fancies you. I suppose you used to tie each other up and have lots of showers together.'

'Oh, don't be so ridiculous.' I slapped the newspaper down on the table, picked up my bag and stalked out to the lobby. I pressed the button for the lift about fifteen times, as if that was going to make it come any quicker. At last the empty lift arrived and I got in. As the doors began to slide shut, I saw Paul running towards me.

'Hold the lift. Press the button. Elena!'

Ha! I watched the door slide shut on Paul's stunned features with satisfaction.

Back in room 101, I began to fling my possessions – which were scattered to the four corners of the room – into my overnight bag. The key sounded in the door and Paul came in.

'I hope you're proud of yourself.'

169

He was greeted by a stony silence.

'That was very mature – not holding the lift for me.'

That did it. I threw down the blouse I'd been holding and rounded on Paul. Looking back, I think I might even have shoved him in the chest once or twice; I was in such a blind rage, it's hard to recall. What I do remember is the expression of shock on his face.

'Mature? Don't talk to me about mature! You're the most immature, uptight, anal, sulky, annoying, pathetic son of a bitch I've ever had the misfortune to meet, and I want nothing more to do with you – nothing! Did you hear me? I'm going to walk out of this room, and I never want to see you again!'

I paused to see if my words were having the desired effect. If the desired effect had been to make a grown man cry, I had succeeded admirably.

'Paul – Paul…. I didn't mean it. I just lost my temper.'

But it was too late.

Paul walked over to the bed, as if in slow motion, and sank down heavily. His face was a distinctly unhealthy grey-white, and his eyes were wide and glistening with unshed tears that he may not even have been aware of. I felt as if I'd shot a newborn fawn at point-blank range.

In desperation, I sat down on the bed beside him and put my arm around his shoulders. He didn't respond, didn't sink comfortably into me like he usually did.

'You don't want to go out with me any more, do you?'

'Paul, I ...'

'You don't, do you?' He turned and looked me in the eye. At that moment, the one thing I wanted to do more than anything else was to lie. But I couldn't.

'I don't think it's working out.' Why was there no better way to say it? Why did it sound like such a cliché?

He stared at me for about ten seconds, then hauled himself up off the bed as if he'd just run a marathon.

'Tell me what I need to do to change your mind.' He went to the window and looked out, his back to me, evidently trying to compose himself.

I crumpled further down onto the bed and hid my face in my hands, trying to block out this terrible scene. Maybe if I couldn't see it, it wouldn't really be happening.

'Just tell me what I have to do,' he said again.

What could I possibly say? That I wanted him to change his whole personality, become a different person entirely, be more fiery, flamboyant, challenging, passionate, dangerous? That just wasn't him. He was good, safe, kind, considerate, reliable Paul. Boring Paul. That was all there was to it. He just wasn't what I'd imagined myself ending up with. He was an accountant, for God's sake; what had I expected? Who ever heard of a dangerous accountant? But how could I tell him this?

Instead I came out with, not exactly a lie, but a half-truth.

'It's the constant rowing, Paul. Over absolutely nothing. I can't handle it any more.'

'But we can sort that out. I'll make a big effort. I promise.' He half-turned to look at me, renewed hope in his eyes.

This visible glimmer of hope alarmed me more than anything else. Because I already knew for certain that it was misplaced.

'It's not just that,' I said quickly. 'It's the jealousy and suspicion – like just now, with Eric. I need to be allowed to have a past.'

'I know, Lainey, and I'm sorry. I just can't stand the thought of you being with anyone else.'

He was facing me fully now. I found the naked truth in his expression unbearable. I had to get out of that room.

I recommenced packing. It didn't take long – two minutes at the most. (What with all the palaver, I didn't notice until I got home that I'd forgotten all the freebies.)

I stood in the centre of the room, jacket on, bag on shoulder. Paul was still staring out of the window.

'You're really going, then?' His eyes were open as wide as they could go and there was a choked-up quality to his voice.

I nodded.

'You won't even stay and try and work things out?'

'No, Paul. It's over.' And still the clichés came

thick and fast. I felt as if I were in a play. But the words were shocking to my ears, too. I hadn't intended to utter them this weekend.

I walked over to him and put my hand gently on his arm. He wouldn't look at me.

'Don't.' His voice sounded funny. Thick.

'I'll give you a call during the week to see how you are.'

He nodded out the window.

There was nothing else to be said.

I checked out.

I'd like to point out, here and now, that my decision had absolutely nothing to do with Jack Power.

Chapter Thirteen

At least the cat was pleased to see me. She was sitting on the gate, waiting for me, when I arrived back at Power's Cottage. She proceeded to wind herself around my legs at least thirty times. I knew she only wanted food, but her enthusiastic welcome helped me to feel a little better about myself. When she'd finished eating she jumped up on my knee, looked up at me in what I chose to believe was an adoring fashion and purred so loudly that I had to turn the TV volume up several notches. She dug her claws into me rhythmically, making herself a nice comfy bed, and rubbed up against me as if in ecstasy. I stroked the back of her head.

'Good Cat,' I said. 'I can't keep calling you Cat, can I? What's your name? Is it Smudge?'

The cat stared up at me solemnly. I'd seen prettier felines.

'Is it Patch? Brownie? Kitty? Sheba? Blossom? Slinky?'

As soon as I said 'Slinky', the cat upped her purring by several decibels.

'Slinky,' I said again.

This time she rolled over onto her back, paws quivering in the air, furry stomach exposed.

'Slinky it is.'

That week I was to close the sale of the first house in the new estate in Ballyknock. I was acting for the builders; Brendan Ryan – he of the mad red hair and copious freckles – was representing the buyer. He seemed to have grown several more freckles since I'd seen him last, but he was still wearing the exact same ensemble.

He led me up a dark, narrow staircase to his office. The first thing I noticed upon entering the room was a fishing-rod leaning up against the wall. The second thing I noticed was a dog sitting on an antique chaise longue in the corner.

I decided not to ask.

'Take a seat.'

I sat down on what appeared to be an ancient, gnarled dining-room chair. The dog's seat looked a damn sight comfier.

'How have you been getting on?' asked Brendan.

'Very well, thanks.'

'I've got the money here. Will I just call out the documents and you can hand them to me?'

'Fine.' He clearly wasn't going to introduce the dog. So the dog decided to introduce himself.

He jumped off his throne and made a beeline for me, tail wagging frantically. Brendan continued to ignore him. I didn't have that option: the dog placed his chin in my lap and gazed up at me imploringly with soft, droopy eyes. Any second now, he'd start to drool on the documents.

'Hello, doggy.'

His tail thumped repeatedly on the carpet.

Brendan smiled. 'So you've met my friend, then.'

'Yes. What's ... I mean ...'

'You want to know why I have a dog in my office.'

'Yes.'

'He's a stray. He's been wandering around Ballyknock like a lost soul for the last few weeks. He decided to attach himself to me, poor mutt. Follows me everywhere. Trouble is, I can't take him in. I've already got three Dobermans at home; they'd make mincemeat out of him.'

'What's going to happen to him?'

'I'm taking him to the dog shelter this afternoon.'

'Really? But won't they ...'

'Put him down if they don't get a home for him within five days? Yes.' Brendan was looking at me carefully.

I looked down at the dog, who now had his paw on my lap. He panted up at me. He almost

176

looked like he was smiling.

And that was how, in the space of a fortnight, I managed to achieve the following:

- Acquire one cat
- Acquire one dog
- Lose one boyfriend.

I had been putting off ringing Paul all night. It was amazing what you could find to do around the house when you were trying to avoid doing something unpleasant. The removal of dust from upper shelves suddenly became a matter of life and death. But I could stave off the evil moment no longer. It was 9.45, and Paul went to bed at about ten on weeknights. Besides, my head wouldn't get a moment's peace until I took the dreaded plunge.

Holding my breath, I speed-dialled Paul's number.

As is so often the case in life, the thing I'd wasted so much precious time worrying about never came to pass.

I got Paul's voicemail. I left a short, formal message, saying that I'd just rung to say hello and to see how he was, and that I'd call again next week if I didn't hear from him in the meantime. Not that I expected to hear from him. He was probably there, screening his calls. If I'd been him, I wouldn't have wanted to speak to me either.

I felt a strange sense of anticlimax. All that adrenaline that my body had been producing in preparation for my conversation with Paul was going to waste. I decided to ring the flat.

Hazel answered, sounding frazzled and bad-tempered.

'Hello, who is this?'

'That's a fine way to answer the phone.'

'Oh, it's you.' She sounded relieved. 'I thought it was another of Chris's idiotic friends. I'm not joking, that girl needs to hire her own receptionist.'

'Don't tell me you two still haven't made up.'

'Oh, we have – sort of. It's just those morons she surrounds herself with.'

'Well, I'm glad to hear you're friends again, because I'd like to cordially invite you both down for a weekend in the country.'

'When?'

'This weekend.'

'I can't, Lainey, I have to –'

'Don't tell me you have to work. I don't want to hear it. You can't work every weekend of your miserable life.'

'But I have a huge deal on.'

'You always have a huge deal on.'

'But –'

'I won't take no for an answer. When's the last time you went away for the weekend?'

Silence.

'You see? It's so long ago, you can't even remember.'

'Well … I suppose if I worked late on Friday night, and came in early on Monday morning, I could just about swing it.'

178

'Great. Now do me a favour: give Chris a shout and see if she's free.'

I heard Hazel putting the receiver down on the hall table, then knocking on what must have been Chris's bedroom door. The background music (Shakira? surely not) ended abruptly, and I heard Hazel's low, muffled tones, followed by Chris's excited squeals. A few seconds later, Hazel picked up the phone again.

'She says she'd love to come to Ballymuck this weekend.'

'Brilliant. I can't wait. Only tell her she'll get her head kicked in down here if she keeps calling it that.'

'I'll warn her. She says she's sorry she can't come to the phone, but she's meditating.'

'To Shakira?'

'Don't go there. Is Paul coming down too?'

'You haven't heard, then.'

'Heard what?'

'Haven't you spoken to Paul this week?'

There was a sharp intake of breath. 'He proposed!'

'Far from it. Didn't he tell you? We broke up.'

'No! I don't believe it. We had lunch together today in the canteen and he didn't say a word. I even asked him how you were, and he said you were fine.'

'That's Paul for you.'

'I suppose you broke it off.'

'What makes you say that?'

'You've always had the upper hand in that relationship.'

'That's ridiculous.'

'Oh, please! You've so had the upper hand it's not even funny.'

Had I? It was easy when you didn't give a toss.

'So you dumped him, then.'

'Well – yes.'

'The poor thing! He must be crushed.'

'Like you said, he seemed all right.'

'That's just Paul being Paul.'

'I suppose. You will be extra-specially nice to him for a while, won't you?'

'Of course. One of us has to be.'

'Now, that's not fair. You wouldn't want me to stay with him out of pity, would you? Keep stringing him along?'

'Yeah, yeah. You have a point. But – fuck it, anyway: you two were my only successful set-up. Now I'm down to nil again.'

'I didn't realise you were keeping score. Never mind. If you're good, I'll let you set me up with another dodgy accountant type as soon as I've got over this one.'

'Promise?'

The things I did to pacify my friends.

The dog smelt of old women's houses. I'd have given him a bath, but I didn't have the time: it was almost four o'clock, and Hazel and Chris were due

180

to arrive any minute. They were a good three hours late already – something about Hazel having had to go into work that morning.

I looked down at the dog. The dog looked up at me, one ear pointing to the clouds, the other to the ground. He was black, apart from four mismatched white socks, a white bib and half a white face. He looked like he'd got on the wrong side of one of those machines the Corpo uses to draw white lines on the road. There was a bit of sheepdog in there, all right, and goodness knows what else; judging by his matted dreadlocks, he might have been part Rastafarian. I had spent a good part of the afternoon trying to come up with a name for him, using the same tactic I'd used for Slinky the cat, but I wasn't having much luck finding a name that he'd respond to. I had learned one thing, though, in the short time we'd spent together: he might have been a carnivore, but he had a vegetarian's soul.

He woofed at the sound of a car coming up the hill. Sure enough, I spotted Chris's new purple Beetle in the distance. Hazel called it a bubble car, and then commented cruelly, 'What kind of car would you expect a bubble-head to drive?'

When Hazel got out of the car, I was shocked at her appearance. She was still wearing her work gear and glasses – she used to wear contacts all the time, but she seldom bothered these days. She looked like she could do with a good hairbrushing – and, not meaning to be cruel, a good airbrushing. There was nothing wrong with her features; it was just that her skin was so sickly white that it was practically green, magnifying her dark shadows and blemishes. She'd probably been up all night working again. What I wouldn't have liked to say to that boss of hers, given half a chance…. Still, there was no guarantee that her unhealthy appearance wasn't due in part to Chris's driving/choice of music/ conversation on the way down.

'Your house is so dinky and *cute*!' squealed Chris. 'It's just like a little doll's house.' She caught her breath sharply, and her eyes widened as far as they could go – sure signs that she had just had a wonderful idea. 'I know! Why don't you get it thatched? It would be just like one of those perfect country cottages in the fairy tales. And you could paint it pink!'

'She'll be asking you if it's made of gingerbread next,' said Hazel.

'I'll suggest it to Tyrone next time I'm talking to him. Come and see the inside. Here, let me help you with your bags.'

Chris handed me the smallest of her set of Gucci cases and lugged the other two along on either side of her slender frame. She didn't do travelling light. Hazel, on the other hand, seemed to have brought one Superquinn plastic bag.

'Come on, Terence. We're going in.' Chris appeared to be addressing the dog, who was yelping in pure joy, his tail wagging as if it were about to come right off his body.

182

I put my arm around Hazel's shoulder as we walked into the house.

'You all right?'

'Yeah, fine.'

Didn't look like it.

We decided to go for an exploratory walk while it was still bright. I begged Chris to put on a pair of wellies, or at least sensible walking shoes, but she insisted on wearing the ultra-pointy-toed boots that she had purchased the previous day in Carl Scarpa. She brought her camera with her, too – a massive, professional-looking contraption that she wore around her neck. Something to do with her latest film project.

Before long, we came across a field of cows. Inevitable, really, but I thought Chris was going to have a fit.

'Oh, oh, I love cows! I haven't seen one since I was a kid.' She started taking photos, from many different angles, of a large cow that was staring at us from behind a hedge. All Hazel and I could do was look on, me in amusement and her in exasperation.

'Here. Take one of me and the cow.' Chris thrust the camera at Hazel.

'No,' Hazel said flatly, leaving no room for argument.

'Give it to me.' I took the camera and Chris lined up beside the hedge, posing prettily. 'Come on,

Terence,' she called the dog over, 'you can get in the picture too.'

'Why do you keep calling him Terence?'

'Because it's his name.'

I took several shots, until the cow started mooing like something out of a cartoon, causing Terence – I mean the dog – to dance in circles around Chris's feet and bark annoyingly.

'You know,' said Chris in hushed tones, as if someone might be lurking in the hedgerows, 'that cow might look innocent, but I once knew a man who was gored to death by a bull.'

'You knew him after he'd been gored to death, did you?' asked Hazel.

Chris gave her a dirty look. 'I knew *of* him.'

We headed back before long. Chris's feet were killing her. A red tractor came up the hill towards us; as we moved to the side of the road, to let it pass, Chris had the misfortune to step in a fresh, steaming pile of cow dung.

'My new boots!' she squealed.

'Don't worry, love,' shouted one of the men on the tractor as they drove by, 'it's great for the hooves!'

Three hours later, we were all three ready to go out for the night.

'How do I look?' Chris emerged from the bedroom and gave us an exaggerated twirl.

'Um … are you sure you won't be cold?'

'I never feel the cold.'

184

Let me start from the bottom up. Chris was wearing her new boots (which she had cleaned), Burberry tights, cut-off denim shorts, a revealing white T-shirt (no bra), a short indigo denim jacket and, to top off the ensemble, a Burberry baker-boy cap. I glanced at Hazel uncertainly, but she just looked resigned. It's not that I wasn't used to Chris's outlandish outfits; it was just that they didn't seem so out of place in Dublin. I didn't think Ballyknock was quite ready for this.

'What are we waiting for? Let's go and give those Ballymuck boys a good seeing-to.'

I gulped. 'Chrissy?'

'Yessy?'

'You know how this isn't a big city like Dublin?'

'Of course.'

'Well … things are a little different down here. It's not like Temple Bar. I'd really appreciate it if tonight you were a little bit more – how shall I say it – *restrained* than usual. Do you think you could do that for me?'

'No problem. You just point out the men you fancy, and I'll steer clear.'

'No, Chris, that's not what I mean. It's just that they all know me down here. They all know I'm the local solicitor. I can't really go mad. And you can't either.'

'Where's the fun in that?'

'I'm not asking you not to have fun. Just – well, could you just tone it down a little?' I indicated 'a little' with my thumb and forefinger.

She regarded me seriously, hands on non-child-bearing hips.

'Okay, then. Seeing as it's you.'

'Thanks, Chris.' I breathed a deep sigh of relief.

Beside me, head buried in a magazine, Hazel muttered, as if she was talking to herself, 'You'll be lucky.'

Chapter Fourteen

I couldn't get over the number of bodies crammed into Power's Select Lounge and Bar that Saturday night. Heaving, it was. I realised we might even have trouble getting seats – a problem I hadn't expected to encounter in Ballyknock.

The pub looked better at night. The dirt was less visible. A session was in full swing somewhere to our right. The musicians appeared to be in a side room, but it was hard to tell, as the entrance was obscured by several very able-bodied farmer types.

We received many a curious stare as we fought our way to the alcohol. I was relieved to see Johnny Power's friendly face behind the bar; I'd been starting to feel out of my depth. And there were Shem and Tom Delaney of the Rusty Teeth, sitting on the very same stools they'd occupied the first time I'd entered the pub. The thought that they'd been there ever since flitted across my mind. Perhaps they were Superglued to their stools by the seats of their pants. They were permanent fixtures and fittings, like the old photos and Guinness ads on the wall.

Johnny greeted me like an old friend. Any friend of Tyrone's ...

'What are ye having, girls?'

'I'll get this,' piped up Chris. 'Three Cosmos, please.'

'What was that?'

'Three Cosmopolitans, please.'

'We don't sell magazines here, love. Try the newsagent's.'

Chris frowned at Johnny. It was hard to know whether he was serious or not. His expression was entirely deadpan.

I whispered into Chris's ear, 'I think you should try ordering something else.'

'Do you know how to do Sex on the Beach?'

'I do, love. Just give me a minute and I'll go and get me wellies.'

This time he *was* joking. Tom Delaney shook with gravelly laughter into his pint. Shem just stared at Chris, open-mouthed, like the little boy in the film when he sees E.T. for the first time.

Chris glanced back uncertainly at me and Hazel, who actually looked like she was starting to enjoy herself.

'Three Sexes on the Beach, please, Johnny,' I said. Or was it Sex on the Beaches?

'Why didn't you just say so in the first place?' He grinned at me as he took down the glasses, obviously enjoying this game of 'Let's make fun of the city folk'. He saw me glancing around for a seat.

'Why don't you join the missus over there? She's waiting for her pals to arrive.'

As we carried our drinks over to Bridie's table, Chris whispered to me, 'This place is very odd.'

I almost didn't recognise Bridie, resplendent as she was in a spangled top and high heels. She was seated at a small side table, with a dark-haired man.

'Well, is it yourself, Lainey? Sit down, pet.' She pulled out a chair for me.

I introduced the girls, and Bridie introduced the man at her side. 'This is my youngest, Matt.'

Matt nodded by way of greeting and smiled easily at the three of us. Not bad.

'You're the vet,' I said.

'And you're the solicitor.'

'You look very young to be a vet.' Now, that was a stupid thing to say.

'And you look too young to be a solicitor.'

'Thanks.'

My reflexes forced me to check his finger for a wedding ring. He wasn't wearing one. Still, this didn't prove anything; he might have lost it up a cow's arse.

It turned out he was twenty-seven, and two years

out of veterinary college. He wasn't unlike Jack in appearance – the same ocean-coloured eyes – but his colouring was darker: his hair was black and crinkly-looking, and he had that complexion peculiar to some Irish people, where they can have a tan and loads of freckles at the same time. (Although a tan in Ireland in October is impossible without the aid of artificial means or foreign travel.)

Bridie had the same dark colouring – although her hair was somewhat enhanced at this stage. Tonight, her eyes were emphasised by two bright-blue streaks of 70s-inspired eyeshadow.

No sooner had this thought entered my head than Chris said to Bridie, 'Are you going to an Abba tribute concert later on?' Under the table, Hazel and I kicked Chris in the right and left leg respectively. Above the table, Matt spluttered into his pint.

'Ow! What did you kick me for?' Chris looked dazed and confused.

Luckily, Bridie didn't get the reference. 'What a funny thing to say, child! I do like Abba, though. I'm going to see one of those letting-on Abba bands when they come to Kilkenny at Christmas.'

Bridie – the disco queen.

'Really?' Chris was wide-eyed. 'I'd love to go to that.'

'Well, you should get yourself a ticket and come down for it.'

'I think I will.' She looked very excited.

I heard Hazel hiss into her ear, 'Whatever you do, don't tell her you were Agnetha in a previous life.'

'I wasn't going to,' Chris replied sulkily.

Hazel changed the subject, just to be on the safe side. 'Will we go inside and listen to the music?'

So we did.

Along the way, Chris whispered to me, 'Do you think I should tell Bridie that the 70s-revival look is over? I wouldn't want her to make a fool of herself.'

I looked into her serious, frowning face.

'I think you should probably just say nothing.'

Chris led the way into the music room. The musicians and their groupies looked at her like the escaped lunatic that she was. Luckily, Bridie and Matt were with us to make the introductions and validate our presence. There was Eamonn, who played the fiddle; George, on the mandolin; Paddy, on drums and the occasional vocal. There were three accordion players, each operating at a different level of expertise. One of them, Dixie, was eighty-two years old, although he looked twenty years younger. He'd had his squeezebox since he was ten. When he played, he moved his mouth around in time to the music, as if he were sucking a toffee. An elegant blonde lady who answered to the name of Diane played the piano; then there was Conor on the bodhrán, and Margaret on the guitar. They very quickly forgot about us and turned their attention back to their reason for being there – and, very possibly, their reason for being: the music.

Without saying a word to each other, the mandolin player and one of the accordionists began to play a reel, at exactly the same moment. How did they know? Possibly they'd been playing together for so long that they knew which tune came next in the set. Perhaps they communicated by eye contact, or body language.

The music gathered momentum, growing in force as the other players joined in, each member involuntarily tapping a foot in time with the music. When the reel was finished they moved seamlessly into a jig, and then into another reel. At one point, Conor went to the bar, and Matt took his seat, picked up the bodhrán and started playing, as if it was the most natural thing in the world to do. The music leaped, whirled, galloped like a living creature. It acted like a drug or a prayer. Its cycles reminded me of ancient monks chanting: you didn't understand what they were saying, but you were sure it was something very deep and mystical and involving God in an important way.

At last the set ended, and all the spectators clapped enthusiastically. The players smiled happily at one another, their faces aglow with excitement and exertion. They knew with certainty that they were part of something good.

There was a short break for drinks, and then Paddy, the drummer, was called upon to sing. He delivered a stirring rendition of 'Red-Haired Mary'. Everyone who knew the words – which meant everyone except me, Chris and Hazel – sang along with the chorus. I badly wanted to know the words.

'Jack, you go next,' Paddy shouted towards the doorway when he'd finished.

'Yes, come on, Jackie,' several voices chorused.

My head swung towards the door. Jack was filling the doorway with his gigantic presence – he was what the locals called 'a hardy root'. Fancy Jack Power being here tonight, in Power's pub, of all places.

A feeling that might well have been glee swelled dangerously in my chest and threatened to escape from my throat in the form of a girlish giggle. I managed to quell it in the nick of time and transform it into a pleasant smile.

Look at me, I silently urged the massive figure in the doorway. *Look at me. I'm here. Waiting for you.*

You know how you can feel it when somebody is staring intently at you? You turn to look, although you don't know why; and there they are, staring. Jack's head turned slowly towards me, and we had one of those eye-locking movie moments. So I hadn't been imagining it, after all. It had been such a long time since I had experienced a frisson like this. It felt lovely. We seemed to stay like that for an age. I thought surely everyone in the room must have noticed, but they were too busy shouting out their requests. I tore my eyes away and stared at the

193

floor. An empty pack of cigarettes and a discarded crisp packet.

'"Some Say the Divil is Dead"!'

'"Me Mother She was Orange"!'

'"Ride On"!'

'"The Men Behind the Wire"!'

'I know what I'll sing. May I?' Jack gestured to Margaret, who handed him her guitar. He pulled up a stool, sat down decisively and fiddled around with the instrument, tuning it to his satisfaction.

And then he started to sing Paul Brady's 'The Island'. You could have heard a cigarette butt drop. Every time he sang the line about making love to the sound of the ocean, he looked right at me. I swear to God!

(Where was the nearest ocean, anyway? Now probably wasn't a good time to ask.)

When he'd finished his song and the applause had died down, he squeezed onto the bench beside me. We didn't say anything, our thighs were touching.

'Mattie, you're next.'

Matt shook his head modestly.

'Come on, boy. Give us an oul' tune.'

All eyes were on Matt as the room fell silent once again. He half-closed his eyes and seemed to be focusing on a place many miles away. Then he started to sing 'Danny Boy'. I'd always hated that song – I'd associated it with the start of boxing matches. Until now.

In a voice of almost unbearable sweetness, Matt

brought his audience on an unforgettable trip from glen to glen and down the mountainside. I must have heard the song hundreds of times; how come I had never once noticed the poignancy of the lyrics? Maybe it took a talent like Matt's to bring them to life. As the song drew to a close, I furtively wiped a tear from the corner of my eye. I suspected I wasn't the only one.

There were several moments of silence, followed by a cacophony of whoops, claps and cheers. Jack leaned over and whispered into my left ear, 'Talented little shit, isn't he?'

I turned and looked at him in surprise. Did I detect a trace of bitterness?

'You're not exactly devoid of talent yourself, you know.'

It was true. He was good – only not as good as Matt.

'Do all your family sing, then?'

'Yeah. Either that or play an instrument.'

I was struck by an exciting idea. They could be Ballyknock's answer to the Corrs, or the Nolan Sisters – only with good-looking boys instead of good-looking girls. I could be their manager! (The Power Brothers. Haven't you heard of them? They're huge in Turkey, you know.)

More drinks were bought all round, and somebody offered me a cigarette.

'No, thanks, I don't smoke,' I said without missing a beat. Now why had I said that?

Who was I kidding? I knew exactly why. I'd said it because Jack didn't smoke. He was the healthy, outdoorsy type. I had employed a similar tactic with Paul in the early days; it had lasted three months. The snag here was that Hazel was sitting to my right.

'Can I have a fag, Lainey?' she said.

'What are you asking *me* for? You know I don't smoke.' I shot her an urgent look.

'How come you've got a full pack of Marlboro Lights in your handbag, then?'

I whipped my head around to see if Jack was listening. Luckily, he was conversing with his number one fan – his mother.

'Give me a break, please, Hazel.'

'Why should I? It's obvious now why you dumped poor old Paul.'

'Don't know what you're talking about.'

She arched an eyebrow at me. 'Do I look stupid?'

Unfortunately for me, that was the last thing she was. *Damn! Why did I have to invite her down this weekend, anyway?*

'I'll buy you a Black Russian if you keep your mouth shut.'

'Two Black Russians.'

'Done. That's what I love about you accountants. You're so easily bribed.'

'Just one of our many sterling qualities.'

I reluctantly tore myself away from the heat of Jack Power's thigh and went to the bar. Chris was serving. How had that happened? She had removed her Burberry cap and had haphazardly inserted about ten of the pink, little-girl hair-slides that were sold behind the bar into her wispy blonde strands. I hoped she'd paid for them. She was chatting enthusiastically to Shem, who was now wearing a Burberry baker-boy cap.

'Lainey!' she exclaimed, her face animated. 'Look at Shem. He has a Burberry coat!' She leant right across the bar, her feet no longer touching the floor, and opened Shem's overcoat to reveal the brown tartan lining.

'I bought it thirty year ago on a trip to London.'

And hadn't washed it since.

'Isn't he very stylish?'

'Oh, very.' I was sure Burberry would be using him in their next ad campaign. His was exactly the kind of image they were trying to convey.

'Did you want a drink?'

'Two Black Russians, please.'

'Are they both for Hazel?'

Now, how did she know that?

'How did you know that?'

'I'm psychic, aren't I?'

Psychotic, more like.

'I'd better make them both doubles, so.'

I didn't argue as she turned and started rattling various bottles. Shem watched, captivated; no doubt he was delighted with all the attention he was receiving from this young thing. He turned to me and grinned toothlessly.

'She pulls a grand pint, so she does.'

'That's not all she's good at pulling.'

'What was that?'

'Nothing.'

Tom of the Rusty Teeth had disappeared. I checked the floor under his stool, half-expecting to see him lying there in a pool of beer, but there was no sign of him.

'Two Black Russians.' Chris clinked the drinks down in front of me with a flourish.

'Don't you mean two outrageously camp Russians?'

The drinks were a sight to behold. The glasses were frosted, and each contained at least five cocktail umbrellas and a cocktail stick heavily laden with bits of orange and lemon and maraschino cherries. I paid Chris, anticipating my return to Jack's thigh.

'Are you coming back over, or what?' I asked her.

'Yeah, I'll come with you. See you later, Shem.'

Shem looked disappointed as Chris ducked under the counter and followed me into the music room.

The session was in full swing again, the room even more packed than before. I stood uncertainly in the doorway, a drink in either hand. I needn't have worried. Jack looked up and smiled, as if he'd been expecting me. He patted a tiny space on the bench to his right. I'd never get my backside in there. I fought my way towards the gap and plonked the drinks in front of my blackmailer.

'Two Del-Boy specials, Madam.'

Hazel didn't hear me. A red-faced man in his fifties was telling her how many head of cattle he owned. I turned my attention to manoeuvring myself back into my seat.

'You can sit on my knee if you like,' Jack said. It was a silly, flirtatious thing to say, but it still made me blush. Why didn't he ever blush? I wanted him to blush.

'You're okay.' I squeezed in – just about. I do think he could have made the effort to scooch up a little more. We were so close now that I was conscious of his every breath.

Nothing was said for the next while as everyone was carried along on the waves of the music. Only Chris and Bridie continued to natter. At one point, I heard Chris recommend sparkly blue nail-polish to Bridie, on the basis that it would exactly match her eyeshadow. She also thought it would be the perfect shade to wear to the Abba tribute concert. Bridie seemed delighted with the suggestion.

At one point, Johnny Power came in to collect empty glasses. He took one look at the piano stool, which happened to be empty just then, sat down on it and began to play. He stayed for three and a half songs. The empties piled up and there was no one serving behind the bar, but nobody seemed to care.

I wasn't a bad pianist, you know – even if I said so myself. My mother – after she had got over her initial disappointment that I wasn't going to be the next Jayne Torville – had sent me to piano lessons from an early age. Tatiana had been sent to trumpet lessons, for some strange reason. I had always been convinced that all that huffing and puffing accounted for her extraordinary chest development. All I'd got for my trouble was nimble fingers – handy if I ever decided to move over to the other side of the law and become a pickpocket, but otherwise entirely useless.

I had always quite enjoyed my piano lessons. My teacher was great – ever so slightly bonkers; unbeknownst to Mum, she rewarded me with sweets every time I did well. What I *hadn't* enjoyed was being dragged up, like a hapless heroine from a Jane Austen novel, to perform at family gatherings – a fate worse than death, to a teenager. These experiences had put me off playing for years. But tonight, I could feel my fingers itching to tinkle the ivories for the first time in ages. Maybe later on, after a few more drinks....

The set ended, to another raucous round of applause.

'Someone give us a song!'

'Me, me! I want to sing next.'

I froze. I felt Hazel freeze beside me. We exchanged a look of abject horror as Chris got up and pushed back the tables to clear a space for herself – a very bad sign. She stood excitedly within a circle of curious locals.

'Join in if you know the words.'

And then she launched into her version of Kylie's 'Can't Get You Out of My Head', complete with dance moves from the video. Chris was one of those rare people who really do dance as if no one is watching.

I couldn't look. I covered my eyes with both my hands. Okay, so she could just about hold a tune; but, my God, I'd never live this one down. I could feel Jack shaking with silent laughter beside me. About a minute into the number, I ventured to peek out between my fingers. I had to see the audience's reaction for myself. I glanced around at the incredulous expressions. Some of the men did look genuinely fascinated, but I suspected this was due to Christiana's short shorts and bra-less state more than to her musical prowess.

And then something very strange occurred. Someone started to clap. Judging from the direction of the sound, it may have been Bridie. I felt Jack join in beside me. The clapping spread like a Mexican wave. And then came the next chorus.

'La la la, la la la la la …'

This time it was definitely Bridie, singing along in her wavery old-lady voice.

'La la la, la la la la la …'

It was Matt. I took my hands away from my face and looked around the room.

'La la la, la la la la la …'

Johnny Power.

'La la la, la la la la la …'

Tom Delaney of the Rusty Teeth.

Then they were all singing. I could scarcely believe my eyes, or my ears. I had to hand it to her: the chick was a hit.

Eventually the night had to draw to a close. It was three in the morning, after all. For the first time in my life I had been in a lock-in, and I hadn't even noticed. The local garda sergeant, sitting congenially up at the bar, didn't seem to have noticed either.

Jack and I turned awkwardly to each other. I think I might have been more awkward than he was. I met his gaze with some difficulty.

He smiled at me. 'How long are your friends staying with you?'

'The rest of the weekend.'

'Is it okay if I call you during the week?'

Does the Pope shit in the woods? 'Yeah. Fine.'

'Talk to you then.'

'Okay. Bye.'

A swift kiss on the cheek (his lips, my cheek), and then he was gone. Just like that.

I decided I'd better go retrieve my guests.

Hazel was pissed. But it was nice pissed, not aggressive like at my going-away. She sat dozing happily in the corner of the music room – all the musicians had long since departed – a half-smile playing about her lips. The Black Russians had done the trick.

'Come on. Let's get you home to bed.' I tugged at her gently. She protested slightly before allowing herself to be shepherded towards the exit.

Now where was Chris? I asked Shem, who was up on his barstool, chatting to the sergeant.

'She left half an hour ago with young Mattie Power.'

He looked disgusted. Must have thought he was in with a chance.

Chapter Fifteen

Chris still hadn't shown up at eleven o'clock the next morning. I wasn't especially worried. I was working on my infamous mixed-grill special, the only 'meal' I could actually cook without screwing up. I was even wearing a pinny, which my mother had bought me in the vain hope that it would turn me into a cordon bleu chef by some strange feat of osmosis. She should have known better; we come from a long and illustrious line of bad cooks.

Hazel had just joined me. She was curled up on the couch reading yesterday's *Times*. She looked up suddenly and stared at the wall above the fireplace.

'Who *is* that old biddy? She keeps staring at me. It's giving me the creeps.'

I explained about Mary Power.

'Well, if I were you,' said Hazel, 'I'd stick her in a drawer. I don't know how you can bear it. Especially when you're on your own here at night.'

I didn't tell her that I sometimes chatted to the picture when I got lonely, and that I found it strangely comforting. Neither was I going to admit that I sometimes asked Mary a question before I went to bed and that, when I woke up the next morning, hey presto, I had the answer – waiting for me on my pillow, as it were. (Miraculously, this included legal advice.)

Hazel was wearing the most extraordinary pair of pyjamas. They were pink and fleecy, and the legs didn't stop at the ankles but encased her whole feet, like a giant baby-gro. I was on the verge of asking her where on earth she'd come across this item when the relative silence of the morning was disturbed by the sound of a car coming up the hill.

I looked out of the window, and my heart performed a little somersault as I recognised Jack's jeep. What was he doing here? He wasn't meant to contact me until next week. I started to panic as I visualised the state I was in. But – hold on …

The jeep pulled up outside the house. That wasn't Jack in the driver's seat; it was Matt. And out of the passenger door jumped Chris, still resplendent in last night's outfit.

'Bye, Matt! Thanks for a lovely night!' Chris waved merrily at him and ran up to the front door of the cottage. Matt grinned back at her and then gave me a wave as he spotted me peeking out of the window at him. *Damn! Busted!* How embarrassing – for me, that was; he didn't look the least bit fazed. Not an ounce of shame between the two of them! I would have been mortified.

I let Chris in. She bounded into the house, causing the dog, who had been fast asleep in his corner, to leap to his four furry paws and bark frenetically. The peace of the morning had now been officially shattered.

'Did you have a good time, then?' Was that bitterness or sarcasm in Hazel's tone? Either one was wasted on Chris. She slumped down on the couch beside Hazel, arms and legs splayed, and stretched luxuriantly like Slinky the cat.

'I,' she said, pausing for dramatic effect, 'have just had the night of my life.'

'Really?' I was suddenly extremely interested. I threw down my spatula and sat on the arm of the couch beside Chris. 'Tell us more.'

'Omigod. How can I possibly begin to describe the experience?'

'Try!'

She sat up abruptly, hands placed neatly between Burberry knees. 'Well. First of all, girls, did you know that he's the seventh son of a seventh son?'

'No!'

'Don't tell me you believe in that old baloney,' said Hazel dismissively – although, if you ask me, she looked pretty interested in spite of herself.

Chris ignored the remark. 'He has healing hands!' The triumphant statement hung suspended in the air. Hazel and I exchanged confused looks.

'What's that got to do with last night?'

'Well …' She lowered her voice, drawing us in. 'He knows *just* what to do with his hands and *exactly* when to do it. I'm telling you, girls, no nook or cranny was left untouched. Every time I thought of what I wanted him to do – he just did it. It was like he could read my mind.'

I was enthralled. Hazel looked as if she might start drooling at any second.

'And as for his tongue! Every crevice licked to perfection.' Chris slumped back into the couch like a Victorian damsel swooning. 'I've never known a man to do such things with his tongue. Not ever. And I've been with quite a few men, as you know.'

We knew, all right. A cast of thousands.

'And as for his –'

'Oh, please. We really don't want to hear this. We're just about to have sausages.'

Speak for yourself, Hazel! 'I want to know.'

Chris closed her eyes and placed her hand over her heart. 'It was just beautiful. The whole experience. Simply sublime.' She sighed. 'It was like being touched by the hand of God.'

Hazel snorted. 'How can you compare a tawdry one-night stand to a religious experience? I've never heard anything so ridiculous.'

Chris studiously ignored her again. It was

becoming something of a habit. She turned to me. 'Lainey, you should give him a go. You won't regret it.'

'I will not "give him a go"!' I tried to look indignant but ended up laughing. I thought of Jack and wondered if such skills ran in the family....

'I'm telling you, you don't know what you're missing.'

'Are you seeing him again?'

'Don't be daft.'

Silly me.

'And you too, Hazel. When was the last time you had a good seeing-to?'

I looked on in horror as Hazel's features contorted in fury. 'I don't need "a good seeing-to", thank you very much.'

'If you ask me, that's exactly what you need. Stop you obsessing about that job of yours.'

'Well, I'm very sorry, but we can't *all* work in pathetic nothing jobs and get paid exorbitant sums for doing fuck-all.'

'Hazel! That's enough.'

But there was no stopping her. 'And just because you get sluttier and sluttier every day doesn't mean that we all have to act like out-and-out whores.' And with that she slammed out of the room, leaving two open-mouthed women in her wake.

Just then, a loud, insistent wailing sound erupted out of thin air. It took me a few seconds to recognise it as the smoke alarm.

That was all I needed. Burnt sausages.

As it turned out, neither Hazel nor Chris got to sample the charred remains of my breakfast. Hazel packed immediately and demanded that I drive her directly to the train station. Chris was gone by the time I got back. I didn't know it then, but it was the last time I was to see them together for a long time. Looking back, I should have known. It was inevitable, really.

Jack rang me on Tuesday. Perfect timing. If he had called a day later, I would have had no choice but to turn him down for that weekend. Wasn't that one of the Ten Commandments of the new dating rules? Or did the fact that the pace of life was slower in the countryside mean that he could have got away with ringing me on Wednesday? Anyway, we weren't going out at the weekend – not yet, anyway; we were going out on Wednesday night. Hold on – I had agreed to that, just one day in advance! I began to panic. He was going to think I was some desperate tart.

This kind of obsessive nonsense ran round and round in my head like a hamster on one of those wheels, never stopping, going nowhere. It had been a long time, you see, since I had 'dated' anyone. I had become so comfortable in my little routine with Paul. I tried to cast my mind back to the early days of our romance.

Paul had come along at a time when I had just started to attract men again after a long barren period. It was as if I suddenly began producing a strange and powerful pheromone. I knew love was in the air; I just didn't know who with. I had felt Paul coming. About two weeks before I met him, some mysterious force had compelled me to buy several sets of decent underwear, despite the fact that I'd had no use for such garments for well over a year.

But had I experienced this heady mixture of excitement and high anxiety with Paul? If so, I certainly couldn't recall it now. I had been happy, sure; but, right from the very beginning, it had been like wearing a comfy pair of slippers. I never worried that I was saying the wrong thing. There were no mind-games. You always knew where you were with Paul. He rang when he said he was going to ring, showed up when he said he was going to show up. Good old steady, reliable Paul.

Not that I was accusing Jack of playing mind-games. It's just that I wasn't sure how much he liked me – what he wanted from me. And it had been the longest time since I'd experienced this not entirely unpleasant out-of-control sensation. I had known from the start that Paul was in love – big-headed as that may sound. How had Hazel put it? I'd always had the upper hand.

But times had changed. Paul hadn't returned any of my calls. I was secretly relieved; what would I have said if he had? I rang and left messages on his machine when I knew he'd be in work or at soccer practice. It eased the guilt – somewhat. From time to time I asked Hazel how he was getting on. 'Fine,' she'd say.

Fine. What did that mean? Her obsession with her job had turned her into a lousy informant.

I got a 'lovely surprise' that Thursday. Mum and Dad, who had been in Cork for a few days, were going to drop in and pay me a visit on their way home. If I was 'very lucky', they might even be persuaded to stay the night.

The house was in bits. And I only had an hour to do something about it. These days, I didn't just have to contend with my own impressive capacity to make a right royal mess; Terence was even dirtier than I was.

I had discovered that, though there were many advantages to owning a dog, a clean house was not one of them. The biggest advantage was an ecstatic welcoming committee when I came home in the evening; if only I were as wonderful as he thought I was. There was also the incentive to get off my fat, blubbery arse once in a while to bring him for a walk. Then there was his uncanny ability to tell when I was down in the dumps. He would rest his chin heavily in my lap and look up at me imploringly with his brown Smartie eyes – although he did tend to do this quite a lot around dinner-time, so his motives may not have been entirely pure. He was also excellent at hoovering crumbs up off the carpet. A more dubious plus: I'd be lying on the couch, half-asleep; I would be vaguely aware of a wet, snuffly sound, but before I could sense any real danger, a sloppy wet lick would be administered to my nose and mouth. Completely disgusting, but it never failed to make me laugh. I knew that a lot of the locals, Patricia being a case in point, thought I was insane to give a dog the full run of the house; but what would be the point of having a dog for company if I was inside all the time and he was outside?

The downsides to owning a dog: hair all over the carpets, mucky paw-prints on the kitchen floor and, last but not least, the fragrance of Eau de Canine permeating the entire cottage.

I decided to tackle the smell first. I threw open every window in the house and steeled myself as the chill November air filtered in. Then I sprayed half a can of emergency air freshener through the entire building, making the cat flee in terror. Disgusting stuff, I thought as I choked, but this did qualify as an emergency.

Next job: hoover the carpet. Easier said than done; the pathetic hoover that had come with the cottage had all the power of a travel hairdryer. I attempted to vacuum up all traces of dog. In the end, I had to give this up as a bad job.

I spent the next forty-five minutes in a frenzy of scrubbing, wiping, dusting and polishing. Well, actually, I didn't really polish; I just sprayed the polish into the air to make it smell as if I had. I had read this handy household tip in a magazine once, and it sounded very clever to me. All I needed now was some of that spray that made it smell like you were baking bread, and the illusion would be complete.

I was just slipping on the last clean pillowcase, whilst simultaneously shoving junk under the bed with my foot, when Dad's Volvo pulled into the driveway. I literally wiped the sweat from my brow and surveyed my handiwork proudly. Result! Nobody would ever have known that a slob lived here.

'Elena! You look wretched, my dear. Did you have a tough day at the office?'

'Something like that, Mum.'

'Rosie.' Dad nodded at me and followed Mum into the house, carrying what looked suspiciously like an overnight bag. 'You do look a bit rough.'

Thanks. 'Cup of tea?'

'That would be lovely.'

My mother is a very generous woman. On this particular occasion, she had brought me the following presents:

- A cookbook; another to add to my pristine and rapidly growing collection
- A pot plant; yet another for me to kill. I'd give this one two weeks
- A plastic Virgin Mary key-holder that had been blessed in Medjugorje ('I'll have to check with Tyrone before I go hammering things into his

213

wall'). How she managed to reconcile her religious beliefs with her New Age mumbo-jumbo,
I could never understand.

Dad had just brought himself. He sat in the
nearest armchair and read his newspaper as Mum
nattered on.

They didn't want a meal – God, no – tea and biscuits were grand. They'd stopped off for pub grub
along the way. Oh, wasn't this cottage charming? So
quaint, yet so tastefully decorated. The wooden
ceilings were so high – very attractive feature, but,
of course, so difficult to keep clean. No wonder I'd
had such difficulty in reaching those old cobwebs in
the corner. (*What cobwebs? Oh, shit.*) And just one
more thing – I wasn't to take this the wrong way,
but, next time I was expecting visitors, it really
would be a good idea to hoover up the dog hair.

Talking of said dog, I let him in at my mother's
request, and he immediately set about re-destroying
the carpet. His attempts to ingratiate himself with
his new grandparents were as shameful as they were
successful, earning him four Jammie Dodgers.

'What's his name?'

'Terence.'

The dog woofed softly in approval. It was a
stupid name, if you asked me, but he seemed to
like it. I had tried all week to get him to answer to
Jasper, but no: Terence it was.

As Mum cooed over Terence, it occurred to me
that my father was being unusually quiet.

'What's up, Dad? Tired after the journey?'

'Your father's lost his job. He's been made redundant.'

Dad visibly winced, although he didn't look up – just turned another page.

'Oh, my God! I'm sorry, Dad. That's terrible.'

'Ah, it's not so bad. I'll get a good package out of it.' He still didn't look up.

Imagine. After all these years, his prophecies of doom and gloom had finally come true. I'd have to get him to help me pick this week's Lotto numbers.

'Are you going to look for another job?'

Dad was sixty.

'I haven't decided yet. I might treat it as an early retirement.' He looked up at me this time, as if seeking approval.

'That's not a bad idea,' I said.

Mum tutted. 'It's a terrible idea. What's he going to do all day long?'

I stared at her in surprise. She sounded really angry, as if it were all Dad's fault or something.

To change the subject, I launched into an account of 'my life in the country'. I wasn't long into a description of Patricia and Bridie's vicious jam war when Mum interrupted.

'Have you heard from Tatiana lately?'

'We e-mail each other about once a week.'

'Hmph. You're lucky. We haven't had so much as a phone call since your father chased her back to China.'

'I did not chase her anywhere, woman. She decided to go back early of her own accord.'

'Only because you made it clear she wasn't welcome in her own home.'

'I did no such thing. I just told her a few home truths.'

'Oh, you're impossible. You make sure you hold on to Paul, Elena. Never marry a man who'd rather make his family miserable than admit he's in the wrong. Now I'm going to bed. Elena, show me my room, please. And I'm not sharing with that man tonight.'

Since it was a two-bedroom cottage, I had no option but to let Mum bunk down with me. After ranting on about Dad for an hour, she finally fell into an exhausted stupor.

Thank God they'd be gone tomorrow when I got home from work.

I lay there for at least another hour, unable to drop off. I wasn't thinking about Mum. I wasn't thinking about Dad, or about Annie. I wasn't even thinking about Jack, for a change.

I was thinking about Paul.

I should have told my parents about our break-up. It had been the ideal opportunity. But somehow I hadn't been able to bring myself to do it. I had to come to terms with it myself first. Before that night, I'd thought I had; but evidently not. Realistically, I don't know why this surprised me. We had been together a full year. I supposed these things took time to get over, even when you were the dumper and not the dumpee.

Poor Paul.

I had made him a dumpee.

Chapter Sixteen

As I stood at the edge of the frosty hurling pitch, that Sunday morning, I forced uncomfortable thoughts of my problem parents out of my mind. I chose to focus instead on the fabulous Thai restaurant that Jack had taken me to the night before. Who knew that such a place existed in the wretched provinces?

Let's face it: I had to focus on something other than my current reality. What the hell was I doing there, anyway? I had to be mad (madly in love?). Jack had no clue what a huge compliment this was. Paul had never succeeded in dragging me along to one of his precious soccer games. I had sacrificed not only my essential Sunday-morning lie-in, but also my customary leisurely brunch accompanied by *The Sunday Times*.

Apparently this match was, and I quote, 'vital'. Vital to what, exactly, I had no idea. In my opinion, all sports were only as important – or unimportant – as you chose to make them. Despite the best efforts of a thermal vest, two jumpers, my winter coat, a scarf, a pair of gloves and a woolly hat, I was still fucking freezing.

It was official: hell had frozen over.

This had better be bloody well worth my while.

I was considering slinking back to the warm cocoon of my bed when the pitch was suddenly invaded by fifteen – twenty – twenty-five – thirty pairs of milky-white legs. They were so white as to be practically offensive. Where were my Ray-bans when I needed them? The effect was heightened by the minute 70s-inspired shorts that the players were wearing. Jack's team wore green and gold – matching socks and all; the other team was clad in red and white. Some players wore helmets; more didn't. I watched, mildly interested, as they ran around the mucky pitch, slicing the still morning air with their hurleys and hitting imaginary *sliotar*s between the posts.

Jack ran over to where I was standing. How he recognised me I'll never know; the only parts of me not buried under five inches of wool were my eyes and nose. And I was seriously considering covering them up too. Who needed to breathe? I was more

219

concerned about frostbite. I had visions of icicles forming on my brows and lashes and the liquid part of my eyes freezing over. I kept blinking, just to be on the safe side.

Jack was all smiles, as usual. 'Lainey, you came! Thanks. I know this isn't your scene.'

I pulled the scarf down past my chin. 'Rubbish. I love hurling. Wouldn't miss this for the world.'

He looked at me doubtfully. 'See you after?'

'Definitely.'

He ran off to join the other twenty-nine masochists running half-naked about the pitch.

Just then, a gust of wind sawed right through me. *Jesus Christ!* I looked around at the other spectators. Amazingly, there were about sixty of us now, standing around the sidelines, freezing our butts off. I knew why I was there; what was their excuse? They couldn't all fancy Jack.

A man in black blew his whistle, and the battle commenced. To pass the time, I tried to work out the rules. I knew all about soccer, by osmosis; this couldn't be very different. Another load of eejits in pursuit of a differently shaped ball. I wondered if the offside rule applied to hurling too. Paul had spent many an hour trying to explain this particular piece of male nonsense to me, until I was blue in the face and he was purple.

I did my best to follow the intricacies of the game. My confusion wasn't eased by the fact that most of the players were called P.J., D.J. or J.J. –

except Jack, of course; oh, and Matt, who was playing on the same team. It was clear from the outset, even to my untrained eye, that Mr Healing Hands was the best player on the pitch. Jack had been right: he was a talented little shit. Jack was good, but Matt was better.

Jack's team – Ballymuck Rovers, or whatever they called themselves – took an early lead, largely due to Matt's striking prowess. Another thing hurling and soccer had in common: all the hugging. Jack and a large blond man jumped on each other enthusiastically, even though neither of them had scored that particular goal. Typical repressed males: sport was the only way they felt capable of expressing their affection towards one another.

The game wasn't half as boring as I'd feared. It was fast-paced and, quite frankly, alarmingly dangerous. I had played hockey in school, and that could be vicious enough at times; but at least the hockey sticks were kept relatively close to the ground. Here, every second swipe of the hurleys barely missed a head. In fact, just before half-time, one poor soul took an almighty whack on the nose. It started to pump blood, but nobody took a blind bit of notice – including the bloke with the bloody nose. It made Premiership players with their grazed eyebrows look like complete wimps.

Two male spectators standing close by commented that it was probably broken, but not to worry: that was the fifth time J.J. had got his nose broken, and

221

it had set funny the last time, so this would probably improve the look of it anyway. So there you
had it: not so much a broken nose as a blessing in
disguise.

The crowd were even more entertaining than the
match. The first year I qualified as a solicitor, I
worked almost exclusively in criminal law. This
meant I spent my days in courtrooms, police stations
and prisons, often in the company of drug addicts
and hardened criminals. But never in my life had I
heard bad language the likes of what I heard on the
side of that hurling pitch in Ballyknock.

A man who must have been a coach or a
manager paced up and down the sideline next to
me. The air above his head was electric blue.

'Come on, ye fuckin' little bollixes! Would ye
ever get the fuckin' *sliotar* over the fuckin' bar? It's
fuckin' hurlin' you're meant to be playing, not
fuckin' table tennis…. Oh! Great fuckin' hurl! …'

The half-time whistle blew, and a smattering of
applause broke out amongst the spectators. I
clapped too – at least, I took my hands out of my
pockets and brought them together several times. I
couldn't actually feel them at this stage.

The two teams separated into huddles, psyching
themselves up for the second half. I stamped my
feet and fantasised about hot chocolate topped
with fresh cream and real chocolate shavings.

Then they were off again, with renewed vigour.
('That's the ball! Great fuckin' hurl! He's a tasty

player, all right! Come on, P.J., give 'em hell!') The game was just beginning to flow again when a skirmish broke out. I didn't see the incident that caused the row, but, for some reason, D.J. punched P.J. in the gob, causing him to fall backward onto the ground. D.J. then jumped on top of P.J.'s chest and attempted to throttle him. At this point, J.J. took it upon himself to intervene, trying to pull D.J. off P.J.. He got an elbow in the kidneys for his trouble, which made him crumple like an accordion. Then, all of a sudden, there were about ten players in the melée, flailing and kicking and punching. It was great – just like a barroom brawl in a Western.

It took a while for the ref to restore order. He booked five players and sent two of them off. I was about to lead a chant of 'Who's the Bastard in the Black', which was the only proper football song I knew, but I thought better of it (my reputation as a respectable local solicitor, etcetera, etcetera). One of the players sent off was P.J.. He limped forlornly off the pitch, a lone warrior, blood streaming from his mouth, holding one of his teeth tenderly in his left hand. Not to worry, said the man beside me. He still had at least four left.

Jack's team won. Of course they did. The players walked, limped and crawled off the pitch, covered in varying shades of blood and muck. Even if you had missed the whole match, all you had to do was look at their expressions to tell who had won and who had lost.

An exhilarated Jack called out to me, 'Are you coming to Power's?'

I nodded. Why not? A hot toddy was definitely in order.

Half an hour later I was happily ensconced in Power's pub, a freshly showered Jack sitting beside me. He was practically glowing with fitness after his morning's exertions. An aura of rude good health surrounded him. Me, I was just glad to have the feeling back in my extremities.

'I'm afraid I have a confession to make,' Jack said.

'What?' I was immediately on my guard.

'I brought you here today under false pretences.'

I frowned. 'Go on.'

He sighed. 'The mammy wanted me to invite you to Sunday lunch.'

'Really? Why?' I was fishing now.

'She wants to get to know my new girlfriend better.' His expression was deadly serious.

'I'd like to meet your new girlfriend too. Let me know when she gets here.'

'Don't tease. Will you come for your dinner?'

'Sure.'

He drained his pint glass and rose to his feet. 'Come on, then.'

'What – now?'

'It's two o'clock. We don't want to keep the family waiting.'

The family? Oh, no.

I nearly ran back out of the Powers' kitchen the second I walked in. Did I happen to mention that Jack was one of seven brothers? Well, they were out in force that afternoon. Along with various wives, girlfriends and partners.

'This is Paidi, the eldest, his wife Joan and their three lovely children. And this is Mickey Joe and his wife Molly – Molly's expecting in June. Jimmy and Mags. Gerry and Anne. Little Timmy ...' Timmy was a mere six foot – the runt of the litter. 'And you already know Matt.' I smiled and nodded at all and sundry. *Thanks, Jack.* Talk about the deep end.... I felt in imminent danger of drowning.

Luckily for me, after a few initial curious glances, 'the family' turned their attention back to the food. Johnny stood at the head of the table (which they must have had specially made to accommodate everyone), carving the meat like the father out of *The Waltons.* He just winked at me. Soon I was ignored completely as everyone lost themselves in the aromas and juices of Bridie's unsurpassable roast, excellent spuds and flawless gravy – a far cry from my own mother's burnt offerings. I made a mental note never to cook for Jack.

When everybody had finished, two of the wives/girlfriends automatically got up and cleared away the dirty plates, Bridie doled out generous helpings of home-made trifle from an industrial-sized bowl, and we all tucked in again.

225

A toddler with a snot-encrusted nose had taken a shine to me. She clung to my leg and stared up at me, finger in nostril. I tried not to let this put me off my dessert.

Her slightly elder brother was also a nosy little blighter. 'Are you Jack's girlfriend?' He gazed up at me solemnly.

My face turned the same colour as the sherry trifle – minus the custard and cream. Although the family were pretending to concentrate on their food, I could sense that every pair of ears in the room was pricked up, dying to hear my answer.

'No. I'm just his friend.'

'Then why is he holding your hand under the table?'

'Danny!' The child's mother, clearly horrified, jumped up and dragged her son away from me by the arm. 'Don't be bothering our guest. Go out and play with your new bike.'

'But he was –'

'Do what you're told. Scoot!'

The mother shot me a pained, apologetic look as she returned to the table. I, in the meantime, had invented a new shade of puce. The brothers exchanged knowing smirks. Matt audibly sniggered. I made a mental note to kill Jack, if I ever made it out of there alive.

Various women got up again to clear away the dessert bowls and make the tea. I was unsure what was expected of me – being female and all – so I started to get up to bring my bowl to the sink. Several women immediately descended upon me, removed the bowl from my hand and pinned me back down in the chair. It seemed I was getting a special dispensation because I was new. I wondered what Bridie had done before her sons' partners came along. Had she done everything herself? The idea was horrifyingly plausible: the Irish Supermammy fulfilling her sons' every need. Yet another generation of Irish men ruined. If Jack expected that kind of treatment from me, he could feck off.

At last the tea had been consumed and it was time to go. I tried not to run. Bridie saw us to the door.

'That was gorgeous, Bridie. You could open your own restaurant and charge whatever prices you wanted. Thank you for inviting me.' Sometimes I almost nauseated myself.

But it was the right thing to say. Bridie beamed with pleasure. 'Oh, not at all. You're welcome any time. Any friend of Jack's …' She twinkled.

I turned on him as soon as we were out of earshot.

'You bastard!'

'What?' He was all fake innocence.

'That was a terrible position to put me in. I nearly died when I saw them all sitting there.'

'But you knew I had a big family.'

This was a valid point, so I decided to ignore it. 'That's not the point.' (What was the point?)

'Don't you like my family, then?'

'Don't be silly. They seem very nice. You should have given me more warning, that's all.'

'But it went really well.'

'Do you think so?'

'Yeah, absolutely. You made a great impression.'

'Really?' I was desperate to believe him. Quite pathetic.

'Yes. They all loved you.' He reached over and wrapped his massive arms around my waist.

What can I say? I was disarmed.

Chapter Seventeen

I went out with Jack twice during the following week. The chaste kisses on the cheek turned into slightly less chaste kisses on the lips. Still no tongues. Still no touchy-feely stuff. My body was a throbbing mass of frustration. It was just that I fancied Jack so much. I wanted to jump his bones every time I saw him. I suppose I should have been glad that he was so respectful, but respect was the last thing I wanted. Aretha Franklin and I would have to agree to differ.

So I decided to let him know what he was missing and go to Dublin for the weekend. Alone. It wasn't just a tactic; I felt as if I'd been neglecting Hazel and Chris lately, even though they'd only just been down. Hazel had rung a couple of times the week after they'd gone back, leaving desperate messages, begging me to come to Dublin for the weekend. I had shamefully ignored these messages, for two reasons: I needed a break from all their rowing, and I had more important, Jack-shaped fish to fry. But that couldn't be right. I wasn't the kind of woman who dumped her girlfriends the second an interesting man came along.

Was I?

It was with some trepidation that I let myself into the flat in Dublin that Friday night. A kindly neighbour had agreed to feed Slinky. Terence wasn't with me. I couldn't really visualise him in our tiny apartment; he'd knock everything over with his tail. Mum had generously agreed to have him any time I was in Dublin. My parents had a huge, old-fashioned, suburban garden; Terence was probably digging up bulbs and urinating on rosebushes that very second. I did suspect my mother of an ulterior motive. If she agreed to dog-sit, it meant I had to call in and see her – twice. Not that I resented her ploy. She already had one estranged daughter; I knew she'd never survive another one. She had tried to coax me into staying the night, but I had stubbornly refused. Any sign of clinginess tended to send me packing in the other direction.

So there I was, in the hall of the flat.

'Anybody home?' I called out as I sifted through the pile of junk mail beside the telephone. There was no reply, but I could hear strange music emanating from Chris's room. It sounded like many monks chanting. She was either meditating or engaged in a very strange orgy; you never knew with her. The pungent scent of joss sticks hit me hard in the nostrils as I passed her door. I went into the sitting room.

'Hello!'

I experienced a very funny feeling in my tummy. Something similar to the sensation of going down in a lift.

'Hello.' I couldn't see myself, but I knew the colour was draining from my cheeks.

'Long time no see.'

'How have you been?'

'Fine.' There was that stupid word again. Encompassing everything, signifying nothing.

Paul was seated on one of the high stools by the breakfast bar, nursing what looked like a mug of coffee. He seemed comfortable – physically, anyway; he had changed out of his work gear and his jacket lay slung across the couch.

What was he doing here? I searched his face for clues. Inscrutable. All I could think of was the last time we had seen each other – me the cold-hearted bitch, and him the broken man. He didn't look broken today. He just looked like ... well ... like Paul.

'How are your parents?' he asked.

That was good. Neutral topic. Talk about family. 'Fine. They ask about you all the time.'

'You haven't told them that you dumped me, then?'

Gulp!

Again, his facial expression was completely unreadable.

'No. I haven't told them.' My voice came out small. Humble.

Not that it would have made any difference if I had. They would just have gone on about him even more – what a grand, upstanding young man he was, every parent's dream son-in-law; what was I thinking of, letting him escape, when I wasn't getting any younger, or for that matter any thinner?

'How's your mum?' I asked. Resume politeness. Ignore awkwardness.

'Oh – you know. Just the same. Mad as a fruit.'

I nodded sympathetically.

Paul's mum was a religious lunatic. She went to Mass every day and twice on holy days. You couldn't move in her house without knocking over a statuette of the Blessed Virgin or a headless Child of Prague. Once a year she went on a two-week sun holiday: Lourdes one year, Fatima the next. (The year before, in Fatima, her rosary beads had turned to solid gold because of all the heavy-duty praying.) She did indulge in the odd long weekend, mind you. Lough Derg or Croagh Patrick. I suspected she flagellated herself when there was no one home, and wore dresses made out of sackcloth – whatever that was.

Paul was an only child (probably the result of the one and only time Mrs O'Toole had had sex). His father had run off with a stripper (I kid you not) when Paul was five years old. You couldn't blame the poor guy, really. It was rough on Paul, though. He hardly ever mentioned his dad. All I knew was that he lived in England and that they never saw each other.

When he was six years old, Paul had tried to crucify himself in the back garden. He had found a few bits of plywood and some rusty nails left behind by his father. He'd had to be rushed to Accident and Emergency. It was a wonder he was as sane as he was. And no wonder he was so fond of my family. Okay, they were mildly dysfunctional at times, but at least they weren't completely barking. We were what our middle-aged neighbours called 'a lovely family' – husband an executive, wife a home-maker; 2.4 daughters, one a teacher, the other a solicitor; went to Mass every Sunday.... You never know what goes on behind closed doors.

I had made a bad impression the one and only time I had been invited to Paul's mother's house for dinner. My first boo-boo had been bringing a bottle of wine with me. Alcohol was strictly forbidden in the O'Toole household (Paul's mother still thought he was a Pioneer). I had felt like saying something sarcastic about the blood of Christ, but had managed to restrain myself. My next faux pas had been sitting down to dinner without washing my hands first ('Cleanliness is next to godliness, Elena!'). But, most heinous crime of all, I had started to eat before saying grace. I hadn't been back to the house since. This arrangement suited all parties – the mother, the son and the unholy girlfriend.

To tell the truth, I'd always been a bit miffed that I hadn't been able to charm Paul's mother. My other boyfriends' parents had all loved me – even when said boyfriends hadn't. They'd considered me a nice, sensible girl with prospects and good child-bearing hips; a little prim and proper, perhaps, but surely that was a good trait in a prospective daughter-in-law. And I came from a good family, too – whatever that meant.

But that was all in the past, and it was high time I concentrated on the present, which was sitting on a stool and staring at me in a distinctly cool manner. I wasn't accustomed to being on the receiving end of such a stare from Paul. It was disconcerting; it made him seem like a stranger. I had seen hurt in his eyes before, sure; anger, annoyance, impatience. Love. But never this cold, calculating appraisal.

I took a deep breath. 'You never returned my calls.'

'You always rang when you knew I'd be out.'

This was getting worse. Of course, I didn't blame him. I felt sorry for him, really. I'd moved on to a new and better relationship with Jack. He was all alone.

'Look, Paul, I know you're angry with me, but if you've come here tonight for a row, I'm not –'

'I haven't come for a row.'

'Then what –'

With her usual impeccable timing, Chris burst through the door. 'Oh, hi, Lainey. I didn't hear you come in. Hi, Paul. How long have you been here?'

What? Surely she had let him in?

'Is Hazel in her room, then?'

Paul and Chris exchanged a funny look.

'What is it?'

Another funny look. Then Chris said, 'Haven't you heard? She said she'd ring and let you know.'

'Let me know what?'

'Hazel moved out. She left on Monday.'

'But why?' A stupid question in the circumstances, I know, but I'd had quite a shock.

'We had another row.' Chris's tone was flat, matter-of-fact. She started to busy herself around the kitchen.

I sat in silence for a minute or so, absorbing this news.

'Where's she gone?'

'Back to her parents.'

'I suppose we'd better advertise for a new flatmate.'

'No need. It's all sorted. I've got somebody already.' Chris smiled proudly.

'Oh?' Surely we should have discussed it first. 'Anyone I know?'

As if on cue, we all heard the bathroom door opening. And then the footsteps in the hall, growing louder. And then the door slowly opening.

And in walked Iseult.

Oh. My. God.

'Hello, Elena!' She beamed.

'Hello, Iseult!' I beamed back.

I was going to fucking kill Chris.

I knew that wasn't fair. How was she supposed to know I hated Iseult? Hadn't I always pretended – for diplomatic reasons – that I liked her, that I didn't in fact think she was a shallow, vacuous, vicious carbuncle of a human being? All that had happened here was that my own hypocrisy had come back to slap me hard in the face. Still, I wished Chris had discussed it with me first.

Could this evening possibly get any worse?

Apparently it could. Iseult padded over to Paul, placed her long, elegant, lightly tanned arms about his neck, kissed him on the lips and said, 'Sorry to keep you waiting, darling.'

Darling?

My brain was performing cartwheels at this stage. A billion questions flew about inside my head, threatening to collide into one another. *How long has this been going on? What does he see in her? Why does she have to keep stroking his head? Has she met his mother yet? (Obviously not, or she wouldn't still be with him.) Has he completely lost his senses?*

Iseult was going all out to mark her territory. She

236

fluttered around Paul, cooing and touching him. Skinny bitch! Why didn't she just pee on his shoes and have done with it? Paul, in the meantime, was looking distinctly uncomfortable. He caught my eye on one occasion and quickly looked away. I badly wanted to retreat to my bedroom, but I wasn't going to give Iseult the satisfaction. I preferred to bite off my nose to spite my face. I resolutely sat down on the couch, turned on the TV and stared mindlessly at the screen.

'Paul….' Iseult's voice was wheedling and needlessly loud. 'Will you help me put my necklace on?'

'Sure.'

I knew I shouldn't look, but I couldn't help myself. My eyes were inextricably drawn towards them, as if to a horrific car accident.

Iseult had somehow managed to manoeuvre her body in between Paul's knees, her back to him. She held up her hair with one hand, exposing the nape of her neck. She met my eye gleefully.

Paul's face was a study in concentration. I watched him fiddling around with the delicate catch of the necklace, his brow furrowed.

'There.' He succeeded in fastening it, and Iseult let her hair fall back down over her neck. She turned and kissed him on the mouth.

'Thank you, darling.'

Paul failed to respond, either physically or verbally. I could tell he was conscious of the weight of my stare.

After what seemed like several aeons, the two lovebirds gathered up their jackets and made to leave.

'Bye, guys. Oh, hold on, Paul – I just need to pay a quick visit to the bathroom.'

What, again? I sincerely hoped that the poor girl didn't have diarrhoea.

Paul was left standing like a spare part in the centre of the room. He shifted uneasily from one foot to the other.

'Lainey?'

'What.' I didn't look up at him.

'I'm really sorry if this was awkward for you. I wanted to meet in the pub, but Iseult said she'd prefer to meet here.'

I bet she did.

'You see, she gets nervous waiting for people in pubs on her own.'

Yeah, right. That girl had never been afraid of anything in her entire life.

I looked up at him. 'Don't worry about it, Paul. You two go out and enjoy yourselves. No hard feelings on my part.' I could have won first prize in a fake-smile competition.

'Night, then. Night, Chris.'

And he was gone.

I felt Chris looking at me.

'You all right?'

'I need a drink.'

Several vodka smoothies later, I was nearly all right. It was just like old times.

Minus Hazel.

The row that had broken the camel's back sounded laughably pathetic. Chris had used the last of the milk to make a 'health drink'. When Hazel came into the kitchen to fix herself a coffee and discovered that there was no milk left, she went bananas.

'And I was just about to go down to the corner shop to replace it.'

'I'm sure you were.'

'I was!'

'I believe you, Chris. I wasn't being sarcastic.'

'Oh – sorry. Well, I was. And I told her so. I even offered her a glass of my health drink to tide her over until I came back, but she just went mental.'

I could picture the scene. Chris's health drinks were evil-smelling concoctions made of stuff like wheatgrass juice, tripe and diced frogs' legs (I made the last two up).

'So I said, "Calm down, Haze," and she went absolutely bonkers and said not to call her Haze ever again, that she wasn't a bloody air freshener. Then she stormed out. About half an hour later I heard the front door slam. I just peeked into her room, and half her clothes were gone –' She could tell this just by peeking through the bedroom door? '– and so was the suitcase she keeps on top of her wardrobe. Then, when I got home late the next evening, the room was empty and this note had been shoved under my bedroom door.'

She leaned over to the coffee table, picked up a crumpled piece of paper and handed it to me.

Gone to parents. Won't be back. Ever. One hundred euro enclosed to cover my share of upcoming bills. If more owed, please send details to parents' house.

The note was unsigned.

Was that it?

'Did you try and contact her or anything?'

'No,' Chris said. 'It was lucky Iseult could move in right away, otherwise we would have been stuck paying Hazel's share of the rent until we found a replacement.'

'Yes, I know. But it might have been better to leave it for a while – let the dust settle. Maybe we could have convinced her to come back.'

Chris shook her head vehemently. 'No way.'

I stared at her in surprise.

'I'm glad she's gone. I don't want to live with her any more. The last few months have been awful. You don't know the half of it, Lainey. I was on the verge of moving out myself.'

I was gobsmacked. This was Chris, who never got ruffled about anything – who always seemed blissfully unaffected by slights and insults.

'The only reason I lasted so long was that she

was hardly ever here. She worked late every single night – she was never in before nine – and she'd go into the office every Saturday and Sunday morning. When she *was* here, she'd go round the place slamming doors and biting the head off me every time I opened my mouth. And that's not all. Remember how fussy she used to be about her appearance?'

I nodded. I remembered, all right. Although she dressed even more conservatively than I did, Hazel was fastidious when it came to her looks. She got her hair trimmed and the colour touched up every six to eight weeks, without fail, and she got a monthly manicure, facial and eyebrow-pluck. Her clothes were always immaculate – there was never a stray hair or a speck of dust on the black trouser suits she wore for work. Her morning preparations had frequently had Chris and me banging on the bathroom door in frustration.

'Now she only seems to shower every few days,' Chris told me, 'and she hardly ever bothers to wash her hair. As for make-up – forget it.' And this was a woman who used to get a Christmas card every year from her beauty therapist.

I shook my head silently. I had known things were bad, but I hadn't realised they were *this* bad. Of course, I should have known. If I were a proper friend I *would* have known. But I had been wrapped up in my rapturous thoughts of Jack. I thought of the frantic phone messages that I'd ignored, and cringed.

'I'll ring her first thing in the morning.'

Chris shrugged. It seemed that the treatment she had suffered at Hazel's hands over the last few months had deadened any sympathetic feelings she might have had. And they'd been so close!

I felt compelled to remind Chris of how warm and witty and fun Hazel had once been. 'Do you remember our holiday in Majorca?'

Chris smiled faintly at the memory.

'We had such a brilliant time,' I said. 'Remember that night Hazel got high and took over the karaoke bar? She wouldn't let anyone else have the microphone.' The poor girl didn't have a note in her head.

'She wasn't so uptight in those days, either,' said Chris. 'She had it away with two different Spanish waiters that fortnight.'

'Oh, yes! What were their names again?'

Chris frowned. 'I think they were both called José.'

'I think you're right.'

Maybe all Spanish waiters called themselves José, to avoid complications and future identification.

'Talking of having it away, have you given Matt a go yet?'

'No, I have not. And will you stop talking about him as if he were a fairground ride?'

'He's the best ride I've ever had.'

'Well, it won't be happening. Remember his brother Jack?' I smiled shyly. 'I've been seeing him.'

'Really?' Her face was a study in amazement.

242

'Yes, really. What's so strange about that?'

'Nothing, I suppose. I wouldn't have thought he was your type, that's all.'

Not my type! Since when was a kind, funny, muscle-bound love-god not my type?

'Lainey?' Chris's voice was childlike as she changed the subject. 'Am I very difficult to live with?'

'Well – you play your music too loud sometimes. But, apart from that, no.'

'Hazel says I am. She says I'd try the patience of Job.'

'That's not true. You're a brilliant flatmate. Hazel's just not herself at the moment. I wouldn't take anything she says right now to heart.'

After a few moments' silence: 'Who's Job?'

'Bloke in the Bible.'

'Was he very patient, then?'

'Must have been.'

I was silent again. And worried. Very worried.

I sighed. 'What are we going to do?'

'I think we should have one more vodka smoothie and go to bed.'

Chapter Eighteen

I rang Hazel's home number first thing in the morning. Her dad answered. No, Hazel wasn't there, she'd gone into the office. There was no point talking to him – he was a big eejit; I asked for Hazel's mum, but she was out shopping.

I rang Hazel's office number and got her voicemail. Then I tried her mobile and got her voicemail. Sometimes I hated technology. I even went into town and tried to go to her office, but the security guard – jobsworth bastard – wouldn't let me in.

I tried to contact her again on Sunday but got nowhere. Frustrated, I decided to go and spend some quality time with my parents. Anything was better than hanging around the flat, waiting to be assaulted by Iseult. I got the hell out of Dodge.

My mother was literally bursting with news and gossip. Not only had my first cousin in the States given birth to twins (Shawn and Shannen. Eek!), but – wait for it – Tatiana and Chen were coming home for Christmas.

I greeted this piece of information with mixed feelings. Sure, it would be great to see Annie again, and I couldn't wait to meet her new man; but I hoped he knew his kung fu. He'd need it when Dad got his hands on him. It wasn't every day that one of Dad's precious daughters became a fallen woman.

I didn't voice my concerns to Mum. It would have been mean, when she was so elated by the news. She was already planning to enlist Chen's help to feng shui the entire house. (That should improve Dad's mood no end.) She was also swotting up on Chinese medicine so she'd have something to talk to him about. I felt sorry for the poor bloke already.

I asked how Terence had got on for the last two nights.

'Oh, famously! He was a bit excitable after you left, but I gave him a shiatsu massage and he was grand after that. And you're not to take this the wrong way, now, but he was a little mucky, being a country dog and all, so I gave him a good shampoo and he's all the better for it.' She let Terence in from the back garden and he charged into the sitting room, tail and legs and tongue flying. He was euphoric at the sight of me, even though I say so myself. The mutt smelt like the perfume counter in Boots. He was wearing a tiny green bow above his right ear. It wasn't Mum's fault. She was only used to dressing girls. I'd remove the bow as soon as we got back to Ballyknock. I didn't want the other doggies to make fun of him.

I entered the working week feeling as if I'd had no break. The weekend's revelations had taken their toll. I knew it wasn't reasonable to be so affected by Paul's new relationship – I mean, he had the right to go out with whomever he wanted; I had relinquished my claim. No doubt it was just a reflex reaction to feel so rotten. We'd only been apart a wet week. That Iseult certainly couldn't be accused of letting the grass grow under her feet. Come to think of it, neither could Paul. It had hardly been a decent mourning period.

Luckily, I had Jack's attentions to look forward to. I was keener on him than ever and felt an urgent desire to see him again – to make sure he still liked me; to have my worth affirmed. It must have been the weekend away that did it. Absence *did* make the heart grow fonder, after all.

I hoped it made the dick grow harder too.

I decided to give him one more opportunity to make his move. If he didn't, I was going to make it for him.

When a pleasant Tuesday evening ended with no more than a polite kiss, I resolved that Thursday night was going to be The Night. My very limited stockpile of patience had exhausted itself.

I invited Jack to dinner at 'my place'. Why, I hear you wonder, did I do that, when a) I couldn't cook and b) I had sampled his mother's amazing food?

Well. Apart from desperation, the reason was that I'd temporarily forgotten that I no longer lived in Dublin and, as a result, was no longer within spitting distance of Marks & Sparks. Preparations for previous dinner parties had involved a swift trip to Marks, after which I bunged everything I'd bought into the oven for however long it said on the packet. Pretty foolproof – even for me. Now what was I going to do? Mild panic started to set in. I even considered taking a half-day on Thursday so I could drive up to Dublin, stock up on provisions and make it back down to Ballymuck in time for dinner. That was Plan A. Too stupid, even for me. Plan B involved a mixed grill … no. I couldn't possibly do that. But if he was still around for breakfast the next morning … I decided to stock up on rashers and sausages, just in case.

Eventually, a café in town saved the day. I discovered in the nick of time that they sold some of their delicious produce. I emerged on Thursday evening with a lasagna, a quiche and a cheesecake. I could just about handle salad and garlic bread myself – with the aid of Superquinn.

So that was the food sorted. What about me? I rushed home to commence preparations. By the time I'd bathed in rose-scented bubbles and sprinkled myself with matching rose talc, I felt like a Turkish delight – hopefully, good enough to eat. Good enough to melt in Jack Power's mouth. I dressed, made up my face and pinned up my hair with more care than usual. I decided on a messy chignon kind of affair, with a few carefully contrived tendrils escaping at the side. That way, he could fantasise about taking it down. Maybe I should wear my reading glasses so that he could take them off too (But, Miss Malone, I had no idea you were so beautiful…).

I smiled at the result in the mirror. 'Tonight's the night, honey child.'

As I peered at my reflection, checking for flaws, I caught Mary Power's eye in the mirror. I turned to face her – her dark, mysterious eyes staring right into me, as usual; that enigmatic Mona Lisa half-smile.

'I suppose you don't approve of this kind of behaviour, do you?'

Funnily enough, she didn't reply. Encouraged, I continued.

'I'm not a slag, you know. I really like your grandson. I might even marry him someday. But times have changed and people don't wait until they're married any more. He's being a bit slow off the starter's block, and I'm just giving him a little push in the right direction. A woman has her needs – you know that.' It sounded daft, but I felt like I owed her an explanation. It was her house, after all.

If Mary Power was unhappy with this, she certainly wasn't letting on. Satisfied, I resumed my attempts to make the house look respectable. I had just removed the worst of the dog hair from the carpet – and dimmed the lights so that the rest of it wasn't too visible – when the jeep pulled into the driveway. Jack made his entrance, a bottle of wine in each hand.

'I'm starved. Let's eat!' he proclaimed loudly.

I couldn't argue with that.

You may have heard women of a certain age say of a man, 'He made me feel like a teenager again.' Well, that goes a little way towards describing how I felt about Jack Power that night. (Not that I was a certain age, you understand. Only twenty-nine and a half. A mere pup!) For the first time, I felt uneasy in his presence – tongue-tied, unable to be myself. I don't know if he noticed. He kept the conversation going, in any case, with that easy charm of his.

Finally, dinner demolished, I bit the bullet and suggested that we adjourn to the couch. He agreed without any hint of awkwardness. He'd probably been in this situation a zillion times before.

At this stage, we'd managed to polish off both bottles of wine. I offered him an Irish coffee, which he accepted. That part of the plan was going okay, anyway – the part where I got him so sozzled that even *he* wouldn't consider driving home. There wasn't exactly a taxi rank in the vicinity. However, the other part of the plan, which involved me remaining relatively sober so that I could be in control of the situation and my faculties, had gone horribly pear-shaped. Obviously, a big, rebel part of me had decided I needed double-Dutch courage.

We curled up on the couch with our coffees. The log fire crackled comfortingly before us, and Mary Power looked down imperiously from above. I had to congratulate myself at least on the setting of the scene. You could almost imagine you were in a log cabin in the Canadian wilderness. All that was missing was the sheepskin (mooseskin?) rug – something upon which Jack could throw me and make mad passionate love to me.

After a while, he took the glass out of my hand and placed it on the floor beside him. 'Here. Snuggle up properly.' He grabbed my legs by the knees and swung them up so that they rested across his legs.

'Now. Isn't this cosy?' he said, handing me back my glass.

Yes, it was. Very cosy. And very nice. In ordinary circumstances I would have been delighted with this result. But tonight was no ordinary circumstance. Did I mention that tonight was The Night?

I sat quietly, only half-listening, as he chatted away. I was conscious of the rain rattling against the Velux, the wind whipping around the corners of the cottage, Jack's proximity and body heat…. It took me a few moments to notice that he'd stopped talking.

I tore my mesmerised gaze away from the fire and looked into his ocean-coloured eyes. The flames were reflected in them, lending them an eerie, flickering glow. All at once I felt afraid. Jack looked deadly serious.

In what seemed like an agonisingly slow movement, he leant over and brushed my lips with his. That one feathery touch sent sensations shooting around my whole body. Several tortuous seconds passed, in which I was aware of nothing but his hot breath on my face. Please, sir, can I have some more?

I wasn't disappointed. He brought his lips down onto mine again. This time the kiss was long and soft and deep. He pulled away again – but only for the briefest moment. Then he brought his hand up and cupped my face, kissing me again and again and again. All the time the kisses grew stronger. Longer. More probing. In no time, his massive hands were on my neck – my shoulders – on my breasts, moulding their shape. I arched my body into his, making strange little whimpering noises.

I pulled away without warning.

'What is it?' His voice was husky and urgent.

Without saying a word, I pulled my top over my head and unhooked my bra. He stared for a few seconds and then pounced, alternately feasting his hands and his mouth on my breasts. All sorts of feelings were surging through me. I writhed on the couch beneath him, thinking I was about to explode.

When I couldn't take any more, I wriggled free and stood up. Looking down at him, I held out my hand.

'Let's go inside.'

Jack hesitated. Something strange flitted across his features. It might have been fear, but I couldn't be sure.

'What's wrong?' I said. 'Don't you want to?'

'No, it's not that.' He took my hand and allowed me to lead him into the bedroom.

Once inside, I closed the door, grateful that I'd fixed the lighting earlier so that it was soft and flattering. I hastily removed the rest of my clothes and jumped under the covers to hide my naked body. Jack stood at the end of the bed. He looked uncertain. I patted the space of duvet beside me in what I hoped was an inviting manner.

He put his hands on his hips and looked at the floor. 'I don't know, Lainey.'

I sat upright in the bed. 'What don't you know?'

'Is this a good idea? I don't want to rush you.'

I relaxed. 'Is that all? Don't worry. You're not rushing me. I'm ready.' And had been for the last month. I patted the bed again.

Jack removed his shoes slowly and – I hoped this was only my imagination – almost reluctantly. He lay down beside me, on top of the covers. He was flat on his back, one hand behind his head, his eyes fixed on the ceiling. I leant over and rained soft kisses all over his face. No response. I tenderly unbuttoned his shirt, exposing his flawless torso. I gently kissed his chest and treated it to feather-light strokes. He didn't stir. I unbuckled his belt. He was motionless. It was clear that he didn't have a gun in his pocket, and neither was he pleased to see me.

'Jack ... what is it?'

I draped myself across his body in what I hoped was a seductive manner, my thigh pressing against his thigh, my nipples brushing against his. I kissed him on the mouth, hopefully – desperately.

'Jack,' I whispered. His name hung in the air. Still he wouldn't look at me. With an exasperated sigh, I rolled over onto my own back so that our bodies were no longer touching. What was going on? I didn't understand.

We lay beside each other in mutual silence. The inches that separated us could have been miles. Eventually, Jack made his move: he kissed me lightly on the cheek and got up off the bed. I watched impassively as he dressed himself. When he was fully clothed, he turned and looked down at me.

'Lainey.'

I didn't reply.

'Lainey, answer me.'

'What.' I hadn't meant the word to emerge from my mouth in a vicious hiss, but it did.

'I'm sorry, but that was just too soon for me.'

Oh, you poor delicate flower.

'I would have been happy with just a snog tonight, and then we could have met up for lunch tomorrow, or something.'

My apologies for being such a slut.

'I mean, it's not as if you don't have quite a nice body….'

Quite a nice body? Don't do me any favours.

'I didn't have a condom, anyway.'

I did. Thanks for asking.

'And I have a very early start tomorrow. I'd be much better off sleeping in my own bed tonight.'

Don't let me stop you.

Jack paused for a few seconds.

'Good night, then.'

I didn't reply.

'Lainey. I said good night.' He sounded almost angry. Accusing. As if it was I who had ruined everything.

'Good night,' I said tersely.

He seemed satisfied with this. He left.

I listened for the desolate sound of the front door opening and closing; then the door of his jeep, the slam echoing into the night; then the jeep taking off down the hill, the noise of the engine growing fainter and fainter. Then I pulled the covers up to my chin, turned my face to the wall and cried my eyes out.

Chapter Nineteen

I didn't sleep much that night. Neither was I afforded those few moments' grace you sometimes get when you wake the next morning, as yet blissfully unaware of your problems. I recollected last night's debacle the second I regained consciousness. I groaned inwardly and curled up into the foetal position, wishing I were a tiny infant again with no problems or responsibilities.

I felt sick to my stomach when I thought about the events of the previous night. It wasn't just the humiliation – although, God knows, that was acute enough. It was also the utter demise of hope. I hadn't realised until now that I'd had my hopes pinned on Jack to such an extent. I'd really thought that this was It. That he was The One. I shook my head at my own stupidity – imagine still believing in The One at my age. *You're nearly thirty, Lainey. For God's sake, cop on to yourself. You're meant to be sensible, together, pragmatic....* The thing was, up until that point, I had assumed that I was all these things. But no. It transpired that, when it came to the male species, I was as clueless now as I had been at eighteen.

Grey light filtered in through the curtains. I heaved myself out of bed, even though it was still too early to get ready for work. I couldn't stand to lie there any longer with just my self-destructive thoughts for company. I dragged myself into the kitchen – carefully avoiding Mary Power's gaze – and cursed loudly at the sight of the flotsam and jetsam of the night before. It was like returning to the scene of a crime, seeing the telling evidence of the disaster that had occurred in that very room. Maybe I shouldn't touch anything, just cordon off the whole area until the love police arrived and carried out their investigation. They could draw a chalk line around my body: the victim. Verdict: crime of no passion.

Unable to bear looking at the scene any longer, I rapidly began to clear away the dirty plates and glasses. Seldom had I felt such enthusiasm for a cleaning task that didn't have a deadline attached to it (imminent arrival of visitors, for example). But how else was I to start the process of putting it behind me?

This task accomplished – you'd never have guessed he'd been there – I made myself an almost solid cup of coffee and forced myself to drink several glasses of water in order to counteract the damage I'd inflicted on my thumping head. I was sure I was having some kind of minor brain haemorrhage. The coffee was comforting and revived me somewhat.

Next, I took a long hot shower to wash off his scent, such as it was. I was about to dress myself when I decided, in my infinite wisdom, that I hadn't yet been tortured enough. I walked slowly towards my full-length mirror. Gazing directly into my own bleary eyes, I let the blue towel I was wrapped in fall into a cloth puddle at my feet. Then I began the delicate process of dissecting my body, inch by inch, to work out which particular part of me had so disgusted Jack.

Jack.

I could barely bring myself to think – let alone say – his name.

It's never an easy thing to do, stare at one's naked body in the mirror, with nothing to hide behind. The unflattering early-morning light flowed through the window and added to the horror. Every flaw was laid bare, exposed in all its glory: the stretch marks on my breasts; the slackness of my stomach muscles; my dimpled buttocks; and, worst of all, my raw-sausage-meat thighs. As I pummelled the mottled flesh, I reached levels of self-hatred that I hadn't thought possible. I resolved never to let a chip or a morsel of cream bun pass my lips ever again. The next time Jack Power laid eyes on me, I'd be a svelte supermodel. Then he'd be sorry. I'd have him crying into his beer.

When I'd finished putting myself down, I got dressed for work. I considered ringing in sick, but what was the point? The last thing I needed was to hang around the house all day with nothing to do but think. So I braved the cold. I braved the wind. I braved the driving sheets of rain. And I went into the office and tried to be brave.

When I look back on those few weeks leading up to Christmas, I don't remember all that much – just a kind of Ground Zero of the soul. What I do remember is that the bright, crisp, promising days of early December had given way to a deluge of almost biblical proportions. The whole country-side was afloat, the sky was on the ground and my walks with Terence had become few and far between. Sunny south-east, my arse.

Work was manic – young couples anxious to get into their new homes by Christmas. Normally this attitude irritated me somewhat, but this year, I was almost pathetically grateful for it. I threw myself headlong into my work; I came home most evenings feeling as if my brain had been sizzled on a frying-pan, sunny side down. And my eyes felt sore and overheated, like overworked electrical appliances. But this suited me just fine. Work I knew. Work I could do. Work I was good at.

Men, I clearly wasn't good at.

Disastrous relationships from my past that I hadn't dwelt upon for years came back to haunt me, like ghosts of Christmas past. I wasn't even going to try any more. From now on, it was lesbianism or the nunhood for me.

In all this time, I didn't see hide nor hair of Jack Power.

And then, all of a sudden, it was Christmas. Thank God for Christmas.

I didn't really care if Dad murdered Chen. I was just happy to be away from Power's Cottage and Ballyknock and all its associations. To be in familiar surroundings with the people I'd known since birth was strangely comforting.

I buried myself in Christmas preparations. Mum was delirious with excitement at the prospect of Annie's homecoming, and I allowed myself to be carried along on her wave. Let's face it, I had nothing else to get excited about.

Since each of my parents had asked me approximately twelve times if Paul would be coming over for Christmas, I had no choice but to finally tell them the terrible truth. They were both devastated. You'd think I'd dumped them too. Of course, I could hear the subtext in their heads: I was as good as thirty now, and ne'er a suitable match in sight.

Even though they had the good sense not to voice this concern, I was as indignant as if they had said it to my face. Did I have a sell-by date stamped on my forehead or something? Invisible, indelible: *Consume this woman before the thirtieth or she'll start to go off, begin to smell.* That was me – over-ripe. Soon young men would offer me their seats on the bus. I'd start buying bumper packs of Mass cards.

Mum bombarded me with endless questions about the whys and wherefores of the break-up. 'Why don't you invite him around anyway?' she suggested. I could see the plotting and scheming going on behind her eyes. I silenced her by telling her that Paul had a new girlfriend and that she was a very glamorous fashion editor. That shut her up.

Dad's only comment was a barely audible mumble to the effect that he supposed that now I was going to take up with some foreigner too. Mum turned on him fiercely and warned him once again that if he caused any trouble while Chen was a guest in their house, she'd divorce him. Dad hid behind his newspaper for protection. I didn't blame him. My mother could be pretty terrifying when it came to the protection of her children.

At least now that Annie was paired off and knocked up, some of the pressure would be taken off me. Mum and Dad's thoughts would be distracted from my impending spinsterhood. I considered telling them about Jack (not all the gory details, you understand), just to prove that there was life in the old dog yet, but they were disappointed enough already.

We went unashamedly overboard with the decorations. This year we had many new additions to our usual tacky streamers, baubles and twenty-plus-year-old decorations that Annie and I had made in primary school (sections of egg carton sprinkled with glitter. I think they were meant to be bells). My parents had been to Long Island earlier that year, to visit the then-expectant mother of twins Shawn and Shannen (eek!); while they were there, they'd stocked up on all kinds of out-door lights, including a sparkling reindeer and an illuminated plastic Santa. Mum and I were ludicrously proud of our efforts and fully believed that our house resembled the famous Budweiser ad. Dad, however, informed us that our home was in danger of being mistaken for South County Dublin's answer to Amsterdam's red-light district.

So we were all set. The excitement had nearly reached fever pitch by Christmas Eve, when Annie and Chen were due to arrive. Dad went to the airport to meet them, in his newly hoovered Volvo. Terence was wearing his reindeer-antlers headband. Mum and I busied ourselves putting out little bowls of peanuts and crisps, to the accompaniment of *Christmas with the Rat Pack*. The aroma of mince pies and mulled wine filled the air. (You must be able to get a spray for that too.)

By the time we heard the car pulling into the drive, we had been waiting for such a long time that I'd begun to worry that Dad had taken a detour into the Dublin mountains to kill Chen and bury his finely chopped body. But no: there was Chen, strolling through the front door, smiling easily at everyone. At least, I thought it must be him.

'Lainey, this is Chen.'

It was.

I hugged Annie fiercely. Chen was instantly over-powered by Mum, who started clucking all over him: 'Let me take your coat…. You must find it dreadfully cold over here…. Are you tired after your journey? … Would you like a drink? A nice pint of sake, perhaps?'

'Mum, sake is a Japanese drink,' said Annie, in amused exasperation.

I was in the process of following them into the sitting room when Annie grabbed me urgently by the elbow and dragged me back into the hall.

'Has Dad said anything to you about Chen?'

'Not really. He's been warned to be on his best behaviour, on pain of divorce.'

She let out a deep breath. 'Thank goodness for that.'

'How was he just now in the car?'

'Silent.'

'Better than violent.'

She nodded. Just then, Dad brushed past us carrying two suitcases. We both automatically flashed him a smile.

'What are you two up to?'

'Nothing.' A reflex response that dated back to our teenage years.

Christmas Eve that year in our house was something of a success. Dad behaved impeccably – the super-civil host – while Mum kept the conversation going by firing round after round of ever more probing questions at the travellers. Poor Chen looked quite overwhelmed – so much so that, after only a couple of hours, Annie suggested that they should go to bed because of the jet lag. If you ask me, they were only trying to get out of the game of charades.

I had convinced my mother to let the visitors sleep in the same bedroom. She had agonised about it until I'd pointed out that Annie was already up the duff, so what harm could it possibly do?

She stopped her future son-in-law as he was about to climb the wooden hill to bed.

'Chen, if you don't mind, tomorrow after dinner I'd love to get your expert opinion on a few ideas I have up my sleeve. I want to re-design the kitchen so that it's auspicious from a feng shui point of view.'

'Okay. But only one problem …'

'Yes?'

'I think that feng shui is … How you say?' He glanced at Annie for help. 'A lot of bollix.'

There were a few moments of silence; everyone was frozen to the spot. Then, from the deep recesses of the living room, came the sound of Dad's roaring

263

laughter. Then we all started to laugh, like at the end of an episode of *Scooby Doo*. I knew then with certainty that everything was going to be all right.

My mother went into paroxysms of delight upon discovering that Chen was Catholic (she had been too afraid to ask before) and would be only too delighted to accompany the family to Christmas-morning Mass. So, after the great annual present-opening ceremony around the tree (Chen's presents were impressively apt – and expensive), we all trotted down to the usual half-past-eleven service.

The church was packed. Everyone was in good form and showing off their new clothes. The sermon was light on the fire and brimstone, as befitted the day that was in it. But still I couldn't help thinking that the priest spoke too slowly. You'd think I could be patient for one hour out of my life, but the truth was, Mass bored me to tears. The fact that I hadn't been since last Christmas hadn't boosted the novelty factor. The choir, however, were superb and performed a wonderful rendition of 'A Spaceman Came Travelling' – again. It was like Christmas déjà vu. Apart from the Chinese bloke standing to my left. And apart from Annie's burgeoning bump.

The night before, when Dad was out of the room, she had shyly shown us the five-month-old swelling, which she was keeping discreetly hidden beneath voluminous jumpers. It was weird, in a nice sort of way. Her boobs, which I hadn't thought could possibly get any bigger, were even more enormous than usual. She confided that she now had to order her bras off the Internet (I'd long suspected that breasts that big only existed in cyberspace).

Christmas dinner was the traditional roast turkey with all the trimmings. Surprisingly, it didn't come out burnt. This was due in no small part to the mysterious disappearance of the remote control to the kitchen TV. It had taken all my skills as a lawyer to convince my mother not to attempt aromatic duck as an alternative Christmas dinner. I couldn't, however, stop her from putting a bottle of soy sauce on the table along with the gravy. When she brought out two bowls of prawn crackers, purchased from the local Chinese take-away, for the starter, Annie, Chen and Dad collapsed into fits of giggles. This was very interesting for me; I'd never seen my father giggle before and hadn't thought he was capable of it. Chortling, maybe; chuckling, perhaps; but giggling?

After dinner, Mum caused further hilarity by suggesting that Chen entertain us all with 'some origami tricks'. He politely declined, after explaining that origami was in fact an ancient Japanese art.

'Chen isn't at all what I expected,' Mum confided as we stacked the dishwasher.

'What were you expecting?'

She paused, a dirty plate suspended in mid-air. 'I

don't know. Just something ... different.' She sounded disappointed.

I knew exactly what she had been expecting. I had seen the copy of *Shogun* on her bedside table. She had expected Chen to arrive at the door in full samurai costume, sporting a long ponytail, like Richard Chamberlain in the mini-series. Never mind that the samurai were Japanese; that was what had been in her head.

Mum's disappointment was in direct proportion to Dad's approval. I was quite proud of the way he was handling himself. Here was a man who had envisaged his daughters marrying nice, respectable Irish lads, preferably professionals, preferably with parents who came from the West – a pair of doctors from Sligo would have been ideal – yet here he was, taking his exotic future son-in-law to his bosom. Mind you, it didn't hurt that Chen was a rampant sports fanatic. He was especially fond of Manchester United. Normally Dad wasn't too fond of Man U fans, accusing them of jumping onto the bandwagon of success. He supported West Bromwich Albion himself – out of sheer bloody-mindedness, I suspected. He may well have been their only supporter in the entire country. But his surprise and delight that Chen knew anything at all about soccer more than made up for Chen's support of the Red Devils.

And, furthermore, Chen was just *dying* to learn all about the rules of Gaelic football. The two men disappeared off into Dad's study for an hour and a half after dinner (while the dishes were being done). I was eventually told to go 'rescue' Chen and fetch them both in for a game of charades, but he didn't look in the slightest need of rescuing to me. Some Gaelic match was playing, unnoticed, in the background. Chen and Dad were well into their second six-pack and, heads close together, were loudly discussing the current Middle East crisis. They both looked as if they were enjoying themselves no end.

'What are you watching?'

They looked up at me in surprise, and I felt as though I was intruding.

'A video of the last time Galway won the All-Ireland.'

'I didn't know they had colour in those days. Anyway, come on; you're wanted for charades.'

Chen hadn't played before, but he picked up the rules quickly enough. Dad went first. He stood up, in his new Debenham's jumper and Farrah slacks ('slacks' – a word second only to 'gusset' in ugliness). He may have been staggering a little. He held up five fingers.

'Five words,' we all roared.

He made a motion as if he were reeling in a fishing-line.

'Film,' we all shouted.

He held up one finger.

'First word.'

He made a 'T' sign.

267

'*The Day of the Triffids.*'

Dad was visibly crushed. 'How did you know?'

''Cause you do that one every year,' said Annie. 'Now it's my turn.'

So she hoisted herself up and acted out 'the Battle of the Bulge', pointing to her stomach for the final word. Dad in particular found this hysterical. Then we played Trivial Pursuit, boys against girls. They thrashed us, due to Chen's superior knowledge of – well, everything, really. Then he taught us how to play five-card stud poker. The stakes were high: the pool was five euro. Dad was the biggest winner of the night, happily raking in his shiny one- and two-euro coins as if they were real Las Vegas chips. I'd seldom seen him so happy. I almost felt sorry for the memory of Paul. Even in his heyday, he had never made such an impression.

I wondered what he was doing right now.

It was well into the wee hours by the time we all went to bed – a little drunk, a little tired, but a lot happy.

Chapter Twenty

That family get-together was exactly the tonic I needed. The only snag was that I had to return to Ballyknock sooner or later. Christmas was over; the glitter had long since been washed away by the rain, the fairy lights extinguished. I felt like a discarded Christmas tree put out for the bin-men.

My charming little cottage in the country had never seemed bleaker. I was sick with longing for the comparatively bright lights of Dublin. I even rang Tyrone and begged him to let me come back. But he convinced me to stay. It was only for another six months – no time at all; and the spring wouldn't be long coming; and he needed me down there; and he'd make it worth my while.

So I stayed.

January can be the most unforgiving of months. The prospect of spending the remainder of the winter in Ballymuck seemed to me that year to be the worst kind of endurance test. My walks with Terence had become more or less non-existent; most days I couldn't bring myself to step outside the relative safety and warmth of the cottage into the harsh, hostile winter landscape. Everything seemed so – dead. I just battened down the hatches and prayed for the early onset of spring.

Then there was the danger of bumping into Jack at any moment. I didn't think I had the strength right then to handle the mortification. But I kept a constant lookout for him. Every time a car sped up the hill, my and Terence's ears pricked up simultaneously. Whenever I turned my trolley into the next aisle in the local supermarket, I expected him to be there, peering at me from amongst the vegetables. But he never was.

You see, I still held out some hope for him, in a teeny-weeny corner of my heart. Surely all the good times we'd had couldn't be obliterated by that one unfortunate night? I knew, deep down, that I'd give him another chance if he'd have me.

But I needn't have worried my little head about running into Jack Power. I was in the office one afternoon in mid-January. My concentration was broken by Patricia, who had been hovering around for some time now. She was fiddling around with the filing cabinet in a manner I recognised as meaning that she wasn't actually looking for a file but had something on her mind.

'Can I help you with anything, Patricia?'

'Oh, no, love. I've just this second found what I was looking for.' She plucked a file arbitrarily out of the cabinet. She moved towards the door and then, as if struck by a sudden thought, turned to face me.

'By the way ...'

'Yes?'

'I was wondering if you'd heard how Jack Power was getting on in New York.'

'Excuse me?'

'Bridie was telling me at Christmas that he'd gone to New York for six months, and I just thought that since you and he were very ... close....' She trailed off in a kind of fascinated embarrassment.

I stared blindly at the file in front of me. I didn't even have the wherewithal to cover up and pretend I'd known all about it. I thought I might be sick.

'I'm sorry if I spoke out of turn, love.'

Patricia closed the door gently behind her and left me alone with my racing thoughts. She might have been nosy, but she wasn't mean; she wasn't the type to revel in another person's discomfort.

New York? Why? For what? With whom? When had this been decided? He'd never once mentioned it to me. Had my thighs been so off-putting that he'd had no choice but to quit the country forthwith?

New York.

Six months.

Well, that was that, then, wasn't it? Gloom descended on me like a heavy grey blanket.

Then, one night in February, Paul phoned. Surprised? Me too.

'Hi, Lainey.'

'Paul!' I was so lonely that it was lovely to hear his familiar voice.

'Am I disturbing you?'

'No, not at all.'

'I checked *EastEnders* was over before I rang.'

I laughed. He remembered my addiction. He ought to; he'd suffered it for long enough.

'Do you still watch it?'

'Of course.'

'Thought so.'

There were a few moments of silence.

'Look, I won't beat about the bush. I'm ringing about Hazel.'

'What about her?'

'She's been admitted to St Catherine's Hospital.'

My blood turned to ice.

'Has she been in an accident?'

'No, St Catherine's. It's a psychiatric hospital.'

'Oh, Jesus Christ. What happened?'

'I'm not sure. Some sort of breakdown, I think.'

When I failed to reply, he continued, 'Have you spoken to her recently?'

'No.'

Hazel had made it abundantly clear that she wanted nothing to do with me. My initial worries for her had soon turned to hurt and feelings of rejection. I had only managed to get her on the phone once. Before she'd speak to me, I'd had to go through the ordeal of listening to her mother coercing her into taking the call. Even then, she'd been cold and evasive and had cut the conversation short. I had sent her a Christmas card, asking her to contact me over the holidays, but she hadn't even sent one back.

'Lainey – you all right?'

Paul's voice pulled me back from my thoughts. I realised I must have been silent for at least a minute.

'Yes, I'm fine.' Which was more than could be said for Hazel. 'Is she allowed visitors?'

'Yes. I'm going to see her on Sunday –'

'Can I come with you?' I interrupted.

'Course you can.' He sounded pleased.

'It's just that I'm afraid I'd bottle out if I had to go on my own.'

'You don't have to explain. I didn't much fancy going on my own either.'

'Does Chris know?'

'I don't think so. I haven't told her, anyway. I thought it'd be better coming from you.'

We arranged a time and a place to meet on Sunday. The second he hung up, I dialled the number for the flat. Iseult picked up.

'Hello.'

'Hi, Iseult, it's Elena.'

'Sorry – who?'

'You know – your flatmate.' *Bitch!*

'Oh, Elena! I'm so sorry!'

Yeah, so am I. Sorry I have to share a flat with a snobby cow like you. 'Can I speak to Chris, please? It's important.'

'I don't know. I'll just check and see if she's available.'

Who did she think she was?

'Christiana!' I heard her call out. Iseult was in the habit of calling everyone by their full names. This suited me fine, as I only liked my friends to call me Lainey.

'Lainey!' Chris sounded out of breath.

'Chris, I'm ringing about Hazel.'

'What about her?' Her tone instantly became cool and hard.

'You haven't heard, then.'

'Heard what?'

'Chris, she's in a mental hospital.'

There was a long silence, on the other end of the phone, which I didn't try to interrupt.

'When can we go and see her?'

Paul, Chris and I met outside the gates of St Catherine's that Sunday morning. I felt ill with nerves, as if I were about to go into a very important exam. My jitters weren't calmed by the sight of St

Catherine's. Gothic wasn't in it. It was like something out of Mary Shelley's *Frankenstein* – an ugly, sprawling old building dominated by a tall, sinister tower. Was that where they kept the worst of the loonies?

Was Hazel up there?

The sense of desolation was compounded by the waves crashing angrily against the shoreline. St Catherine's was situated right on the brink of the sea. Land's end. The colour of the waves reflected the sludgy grey sky. I was reminded of Alcatraz. I looked around suspiciously, expecting to see men in uniform patrolling high barbed-wire fences with vicious-looking Alsatian dogs. Strangely enough, there were none. There was just an imposing wrought-iron gate, which we went through without so much as giving a password.

It was weird, but we were all dressed in black. You'd think we'd planned it. Paul was wearing the black coat I'd bought him for his last birthday – bright-orange pollen stains long gone. We all had matching white faces, too.

We asked for Hazel at Reception. We were given directions – there was nobody available to escort us – by a pretty, smiling girl who seemed totally out of place in her surroundings. Where was Nurse Ratched?

Halfway down an impossibly long corridor, we came across an obstruction. Up ahead was a stationary vehicle – it looked a little like a golf buggy, but it was laden down with various domestic supplies – driven by a man who was clearly an employee. He was talking to someone we couldn't yet see.

'Ah, come on now, John. Be a good man and get up out of the way. You're always doing this.'

'No,' said another voice. 'Not until all my demands are met.'

'Come on, man. You have to let me by. They're totally out of bog roll on Ward 3.'

We drew close enough to see that there was a man – presumably an inmate and not another employee – sprawled across the floor, impeding the progress of the buggy. He saw us, too.

'Halt! Who goes there?'

Luckily we had reached our stairwell and didn't have to get past him. We all ducked in through the door and burst out laughing like a gaggle of silly schoolkids. I felt terrible, laughing at the afflicted – but it was funny. And God knows we all needed something to laugh about just then.

We ascended the stairs to the second floor. Was it my imagination or were our footsteps becoming slower?

We saw the sign for Hazel's ward up ahead. Thank God. But – oh, God … what would we find in there?

Paul was about to push the door open.

'Stop!' It was Chris. 'I'm sorry, but I don't think I can go in.'

'It'll be okay. It's only Hazel.'

'I know. But I'm sorry, I really can't.'

I looked at her white, pinched face.

'Okay. You don't have to. Just stay here and wait for us.'

I pushed open the door.

'No!' Chris almost shrieked. 'I'm not staying out here on my own.'

So we all three went into Ward 4. It was a long, narrow room with beds on either side. Thankfully, all was peaceful – perhaps the inmates had just received their meds. We scanned all the faces, looking for a familiar one, half-hoping not to find it.

I was beginning to think we were in the wrong place when Chris exclaimed, 'Over there!' and pointed to the very last bed on the left.

Sure enough, there was Hazel. A little paler and thinner than usual, but Hazel just the same. Her bed was beside a grubby-looking window out of which she was staring. *That'll suit her,* I thought ludicrously. *She always likes the window seat on planes.* She was sitting quietly, knees up, covers half off. She wasn't rocking to and fro. She wasn't wailing. She wasn't wearing a straitjacket. She was just Hazel.

As we reached her bed, she turned towards us and gave a little start.

'Hello,' I said.

A mixture of emotions fought for precedence on her face: pleasure, anger, shame.

'What are you lot doing here?'

'We've come to see you, silly.'

There was an awkward silence, which we filled by presenting her with our ridiculous gifts. I had brought along a bag of fruit. Well, that was what I normally brought to patients in hospital. Was it the done thing to bring fruit to someone in a mental hospital? Could they cause injury to themselves or others with a finely sharpened banana? Paul presented her with a gossip magazine and a packet of Mikado biscuits (10% extra free). Chris bore a big white plastic bag, which I discovered – too late – contained her top ten self-help books. This gift seemed woefully tactless, somehow. I steeled myself for a vicious reaction, but I needn't have worried: Hazel accepted each gift with an almost eerie absence of emotion. I got the impression I could have handed her a live lobster and she wouldn't have batted an eyelid. With monumental effort, I blinked back tears. It was like a light had gone out inside her; as if the Hazel I knew had been taken by body-snatchers and replaced by this insipid stranger.

It was Paul who broke the silence.

'What happened to you, Hazel?'

I stiffened. Surely that was too direct. But, quietly and calmly, she began to tell us what had happened.

Hazel had got to the point where she was working every single weekend. She hadn't had a day off in three months. Her working day began at seven and ended at eight. In the final weeks, things had got very hairy indeed. Her first glimpse of the office building each morning reduced her to tears. She knew she was in real trouble when she was in a department store one lunchtime, buying tights for work, and went to the toilet; they happened to use the same hand soap that was in the office toilets, and the smell made her vomit.

It had all come to a head one morning when her boss had summoned her into his office and given her a right bollocking in front of two of her colleagues. She hadn't answered back. She hadn't responded at all. She'd just turned and walked out of his office and out of the building, stopping only to collect her bag and coat. She'd kept on walking until she reached her parents' house, six miles away. There she'd walked straight up the stairs to her room, got into the bed of her childhood and slept for eighteen hours. When she woke, her distraught mother, unable to get any sense out of her, had called the family GP, who had sent her straight to St Catherine's.

'So here I am,' Hazel concluded flatly.

It was lucky a nurse approached just as she was finishing her story, because not one of us had the first clue what to say. The nurse silently handed Hazel a tablet and a small plastic cup half-filled with water, then plumped up the pillows and left as silently as she had arrived. Hazel swallowed the pill and looked at me defiantly.

'It's only an antidepressant.'

I nodded.

'I'm not mad, you know.'

'Oh, I know.'

She stared at me long and hard, trying to work out whether she could believe me. Seemingly satisfied, she tore her eyes away and went back to looking out of the window. A sea view. How nice.

Paul and I exchanged glances.

'How long will you be … staying here?' he asked.

'I can leave whenever I like,' she said sharply.

'Oh, I know – I didn't mean –'

'The doc thinks I should stay for another week.'

We all nodded sagely.

'Maybe we could all meet up when you're back home,' I ventured. 'I mean – as soon as you're feeling up to it.'

She shrugged. 'Maybe.'

Paul looked at me again. 'I guess we'll be going now.'

I nodded. She certainly didn't seem keen on having us there any more.

'What'll you do for the rest of the day?' It was the first time Chris had spoken.

'Oh, I have a very full afternoon ahead of me. First an hour of basket-weaving, followed by a spot of finger-painting. Then I have my electric shock therapy to look forward to.'

Chris looked horrified.

'She's only joking.' I dragged her gently away from the bed. Optimism reared its pretty but naïve head. The old Hazel was still in there somewhere.

'I'll give you a ring at home in a week or so.'

'Whatever.'

As we moved away she lay down, presented her back to us and pulled the covers up to her ears.

The collective relief as we left the ward was palpable. Walking considerably faster than we had on the way in, we managed to reach the corridor leading to the exit without further mishap. Just as we were about to reach the light at the end of the tunnel, a chilling scream rang out. I thought it came from the tower. Mrs Rochester! Chris ran the final few yards. It took all my willpower not to run after her.

Fifteen minutes later we were seated in a coffee shop, close to St Catherine's but mercifully out of sight of the tower. We sipped our lattes as if they contained the elixir of life. Nothing much was said for some time; we were all caught up in our private thoughts. Then Chris spoke.

'Imagine,' she said, 'all along, everyone thought that I was the mad one.'

We didn't try to deny it.

Right then, Chris seemed to be the sanest person I knew.

Chapter Twenty-one

After what seemed an eternity, the harsh days of winter softened into the sky-blue days of spring. It didn't take as much effort on Terence's part to get me tramping the roads of Ballyknock of an evening. In fact, these walks proved to be the perfect antidote to a busy day at the office.

It was the end of March. The clocks were just about to go forward or back or whatever it is they do at that time of year. I luxuriated in the gentle spring sunshine as it bathed my eyelids. It felt like a long-lost friend that had been away on an extended trip, possibly to Australia.

The hedgerows around Ardskeha were studded with wild violets and little, yellow, star-like flowers (what were they? I'd have to look them up) – Easter colours. The Easter bunnies abounded, too; a young rabbit seemed to appear around every bend to torment Terence. Luckily he was too dumb or too slow to catch any of them, although he put up a great show of delirious barking and chasing each time. He probably ignored them when I wasn't there.

As I ambled contentedly, I was aware of an old, familiar scent intermingling with the usual sweet aroma of fresh cow-pat. An unmistakable green smell.

It was growth. New growth. The countryside was coming alive before my very eyes.

Trees that, a couple of short months ago, had appeared gnarled and close to death, hunched and bent against the wind like ancient folk, were now covered in sticky, lime-green buds. I had never before been so viscerally aware of the changing of the seasons, the renewal of life. The natural world had only been sleeping.

I was happy to let Terence lollop up ahead. A lead seemed mean and unnecessary in the circumstances. I spotted him every so often, excitedly sniffing a rock or a clump of grass and then cocking his leg against it in ecstasy. I was marvelling at his doggy world, filled with a myriad of scents that I was totally unaware of, when I heard the harsh sound of an engine up ahead. At first I thought it was a piece of agricultural machinery in a nearby field – the sound was raucous enough – but it was getting louder all the time, coming closer. Obviously a vehicle of some kind. I shouted several times at Terence to come back, but he studiously ignored me, intent on some new, exciting smell. He continued to stand stock-still in the middle of the road up ahead. The vehicle drew closer and closer. In a panic, I began to run towards him.

'Terence!' I yelled.

But I was too late. A red Peugeot careered around the corner and connected with Terence's vulnerable little body. There was a terrifying yelp and a sickening thud as he was catapulted into the air, to land in a crumpled heap at the side of the road.

There was a rushing sound in my ears. After being glued to the spot for a few interminable seconds, I began to run again, but this time I seemed to be running in slow motion, each leg weighing a tonne, feeling like I was trapped in one of those bad dreams where you're being chased by a monster and your legs betray you by refusing to work properly.

As I reached the scene of the accident, Johnny Power emerged from the driver's seat and ran over to where Terence lay.

'This your dog?'

The only response he got was incoherent babbling. But it told him everything he needed to know.

'You should have had him on a lead.'

I felt a surge of fury. 'And you shouldn't have been driving like a bloody lunatic!' It came out as a screech.

He looked at me in alarm, then took off his jacket. 'He's still alive, anyhow. We'll take him to Mattie. He'll know what to do.'

I looked down fearfully at Terence. He was alive, all right – for the time being. His bewildered eye stared skywards, like that of a dying fish on a trawler.

I looked on uselessly as Johnny wrapped Terence tenderly in his anorak and placed him on the back seat.

'Get in beside him and I'll drop ye down to the surgery.'

In a slightly less maniacal fashion – although this difference would not have been discernible to the untrained eye – Johnny drove back down the hill to the village. In the surgery, he masterfully bypassed the queue, Terence in his arms, a distressed me in tow.

'Sorry, lads,' he said by way of explanation, 'but you can see he's in a bad way.' The motley collection of cat, gerbil and budgie owners nodded their heads in concerned unison.

Johnny marched straight through a door marked 'Surgery', and I followed him. Matt was inside, finishing up with his last patient. He didn't appear at all surprised by our impromptu appearance.

'Put him down here.' He gestured to an examination table. 'Gently does it.'

He began to poke and prod at Terence's limp body.

'Hmmm ... lost a lot of blood.'

I noticed with horror a rapidly expanding dark stain on Johnny's anorak.

'Can you make him better, please?' I sobbed.

The two men turned to look at me, somewhat embarrassed by my tears. I was too far gone to care.

'I'm going to have to operate. Do you have pet insurance?'

I shook my head. I'd never even heard of it.

'Don't worry about the cost. I'll look after it,' said Johnny.

As the kindly veterinary nurse led me gently out of the room, I heard Matt say, 'Jesus, Da. Not another one.'

The next forty-eight hours were crucial. Isn't that what they always say? They were nightmarish, in any case. I was amazed at how tightly and how quickly that scruffy little creature with the lopsided ears and crooked arse had wrapped himself around my heart. The thought of Terence experiencing distress or pain was unbearable to me.

But somebody up there had been looking down on us. A few days later he was well enough to come home, sporting a large bald spot on his side, in the centre of which was a scar. Around his neck was one of those ridiculous-looking upside-down-lampshade contraptions, meant to prevent him from pulling at his stitches. He also wore a bewildered expression and carried with him a prescription for plenty of TLC.

He went to the kitchen, whimpered pathetically and circled three times before settling onto his cushion in the corner and promptly falling asleep. Slinky – who normally regarded him with the disdain that her naturally superior species reserves for canines – crept up to the sleeping Terence, sniffed delicately at his stitches, licked them a few times, and then curled up beside him and fell asleep herself, all the while purring loudly. I took the opportunity to pop down to the supermarket.

Paul had a theory that you could tell a lot about a person by the contents of his shopping basket: whether or not he's a keen cook, for instance, or how healthy his lifestyle is. That was why I was concerned to find that I'd bought one bottle of vodka, one packet of chocolate biscuits and five cans of gourmet dog food. I knew what impression this must have given my fellow shoppers: that I was a sad, lonely, alcoholic spinster, with an eating disorder and only an animal to keep me company.

As I drove home, I had a vision of myself as an old woman. My hair was still long, but now it was pure grey and straggly. I was unmarried and childless, with fifty cats – all descendants of Slinky. My neighbours shunned me, and their kids called me 'the mad old cat woman' and performed knickknacks on my door. I was still living in Power's Cottage.

But that was ridiculous. I'd be back in Dublin in four months' time – back to the vibrancy and the hectic social whirl of my former existence. I had already passed the halfway point in my time of incarceration in the Irish countryside. It was down-hill all the way from now on. I had another, alto-gether more pleasant vision, this time of myself (in present times) on a high nelly bicycle with a basket attached to the handlebars. The basket overflowed with fragrant wild flowers. I wore a long summer dress and open-toed sandals. My hair fanned out behind me and the cool breeze caressed my tanned face as I freewheeled down the hills of Ardskeha.

My pleasant reverie was interrupted by the realisation that a car was looming up ahead. I felt immediate irritation. It was a particularly narrow strip of road; I knew from experience that, if the driver of the other car failed to pull in sufficiently, my beautiful baby's paintwork would be badly scratched by the scrub growing in the ditch. It was a jeep; good – that meant the driver had no excuse not to pull in good and far.

Except he didn't. With great annoyance, I regis-tered the angry scraping noise as the branches made lethal contact with my left wing. As I drew alongside the jeep, I prepared to give the driver a dirty look at the very least. But my anger immedi-ately dissipated when I saw that it was Matt, local hero and saviour of dogs. We lowered our windows simultaneously.

'How's it going?' he called.

'Good, thanks. How are you?'

'Great form. I've just been up at Power's Cottage. I was in the area, and I thought I'd call in and see how Terence was doing.'

'Sorry we missed you.'

'I can come back with you now, if you like.'

'Well – okay, then.'

An excuse to refuse him had been on the tip of my tongue, but I could see that would have been churlish. It was nice of him to take the trouble of calling in on Terence. And, apart from the fact that I owed him the hospitality, it would do me good to have the company. I'd been spending far too much time on my own lately; if I wasn't careful, I'd end up a bona fide recluse and my fantasy of being a wild-haired old crone would come true. Besides, if I didn't invite him back (although, come to think of it, he'd invited himself), I'd only end up eating all the biscuits by myself.

Matt executed a highly illegal U-turn on a hairpin bend and followed me back home. Once inside, he made a beeline for Terence, who was still curled up in the corner, looking woebegone. When he saw Matt, however, he began to thump his tail feebly against the floor and rolled onto his back to have his tummy tickled. Even Slinky – who normally fled when a stranger came into the house – stayed in her curled-up position beside Terence and purred like a motorbike when Matt rubbed her head.

I made Matt a mug of tea and he sat back on the couch, crossed his legs casually and smiled at me. I smiled back.

'I really can't thank you enough for everything you've done for Terence.'

'My pleasure.'

'I heard you stayed up all night with him after the operation.'

He shrugged. 'It was the least I could do. I couldn't let another animal be sacrificed on the altar of my father's Peugeot.'

'Does he send a lot of business your way, then?'

'Like you wouldn't believe. The man's lethal once he gets behind the wheel of that rust-bucket.'

I settled back comfortably in the armchair, tucking one foot up beneath me. 'Anyway, I just wanted to let you know how grateful I am.'

'Really? How grateful would that be, then?' He was still leaning back on the sofa, his body totally relaxed, his eyes intent.

I frowned. 'Very grateful, of course.'

'Grateful enough to come to the races with me next week?'

'What?'

'You heard.'

'But … No – I'm sorry, next week isn't good for me.'

The cheek of him! What did he think I was – some sort of prostitute who paid for services rendered with sexual favours? What did that make Terence? My pimp?

'Ah, come on. You must get lonely up here on your own all the time.'

'No,' I lied. I could hear the temperature of my voice drop by several degrees. 'And I don't need your pity, either.'

'Who said anything about pity? I'm merely trying to extend the hand of friendship.'

Yeah, right. I was willing to bet that wasn't all he wanted to extend.

'Look, Matt … no offence, but I'd feel weird going out with you, after being with Jack.'

The mere mention of his name made me blush deeply, and it occurred to me that maybe Matt knew all the intimate and embarrassing details of our last night together – although that didn't compute: he'd hardly have asked me out if he were aware of the full horror of my thighs.

'I don't see what Jack's got to do with it. He fecked off to the States, didn't he? I wouldn't feel any loyalty to him if I were you.'

'It's not a question of loyalty. It's a question of … of morality.' I alighted on the word triumphantly.

Matt gave a small laugh and settled even more comfortably into the sofa. 'Is that all?'

'Yes. That's all,' I said coldly. He uncrossed his legs and began munching a chocolate biscuit. He didn't seem perturbed in the slightest. If I'd been him, I'd have been cringing with embarrassment; in fact, I would have been out the door minutes ago. To add insult to injury, the traitorous Slinky leapt up onto his lap and proceeded to make a little nest for herself. It had taken me a fortnight to

get her to sit on my knee. He was like St Francis of
Assisi – although, as far as I knew, St Francis hadn't
had a reputation as a womaniser.

Maybe I was being a little unfair.

'Look, Matt, I'm not trying to be a bitch here.
It's just that – two brothers … it just seems a little
sick to me. And then there's Chris.'

He looked at me blankly.

'Chris,' I said. 'You know, Christiana. Small,
blonde, bonkers – that night in Power's….'

'Oh, Christiana!' he exclaimed, the penny dropping. 'Why didn't you say so in the first place?'

'My name's Elena, by the way.'

He grinned. 'I know your name. And I promise
I'll still remember it next week when we come back
from the races.'

I looked at him disdainfully, I hoped, but by
now he was staring off into the middle distance
and chomping on another biscuit.

'How is Chris, anyway?'

'Why? Do you miss her?'

'Does she miss me?'

'I doubt she even remembers your name.'

He laughed, drained his mug and leaned forward, his hands clasped loosely between his knees,
a discommoded Slinky mewing in disapproval.

'Look,' he said, 'if it makes you feel any better, I
can state categorically, as my Granny Mary is my
witness –' He gestured to the great lady above the
fireplace. '– that, if you come to the races with me,

it won't be a date.'

'No strings attached?'

'There'll be no sex on the cards whatsoever. I give you my word. Even if you beg for it.'

I couldn't help laughing at that. I was won over.

'Oh, all right, then – since you put it like that … I'd love to go to the races with you.'

Matt fell back into his seat as if exhausted. 'Jaysus. I had no idea lawyers were such hard work.'

He got up to leave, taking one more biscuit for the road. 'I've got to go and see a man about a cow. You keep a good eye on Terence, and give the surgery a ring if you have any concerns. I'd hate to think I'd missed a good night's sleep for nothing.'

He paused at the front door. 'I suppose a good-bye kiss is out of the question?'

'Get out,' I laughed.

When his jeep was no more than a tiny dark-green dot at the bottom of the hill, I closed the door and went back inside.

Incorrigible.

Still, I didn't feel quite so lonely any more. The crone fantasy now seemed a distant memory, and I was speeding down the hill on my bike again.

Chapter Twenty-two

It was a pet day.

I'd never been to the races before. Did I have to wear a hat? I researched the matter extensively by asking Patricia, fount of all knowledge on things local.

'A hat is optional, lovey. It's nice to wear one, but they still let you in if you don't. And it doesn't have to be too formal, either; you don't need to look as if you're going to a wedding.'

I took the information as gospel. Tyrone had been right: there was nothing – but nothing – that Patricia didn't know about local custom, and it came in very handy on the most unexpected occasions.

My millinery choice was made considerably easier by the fact that I only had one hat. It was a wide-brimmed, floppy straw affair, very Pimms and lemonade on the lawn. I usually just plonked it on my head when I was sunning myself in the garden; but I had a long, pink, raw-silk scarf that I could tie around it in a floppy bow, which would be perfect on this occasion. Since the day was so gorgeous, I decided to wear with it a long, pink summer dress, which was getting its first outing of the year, and strappy sandals with two-inch heels – quite high for me. I tied my hair back into a loose ponytail at the nape of my neck and applied light make-up. I was as pleased as I could be with the result.

Matt picked me up at the allotted time and complimented me excessively. Proceedings were already in full swing when we arrived at the racecourse. I couldn't get over the throngs of people milling about. Styles ranged from smart casual to elegant formal. I was relieved not to feel out of place.

Like his brother, Matt seemed to know everyone – although, among the people greeting him, the ratio of women to men was quite worryingly high. Some of these women kissed him on the cheek before eyeing me up and down speculatively. *No, I felt like shouting at them, I'm not his latest bit of fluff!*

But I was glad to have him with me, just the same. I felt woefully unqualified to place bets on my own. The bookies were all in one area, a bewildering array of men of various ages in varying styles of caps and overcoats, all willing and able to take your money off your hands. They all kept their takings in what looked like oversized handbags that were made of battered leather, as if the men and their bags had been on the circuit for years. They each had a child-size blackboard on which they wrote mysterious figures – they might as well have been hieroglyphics, for all the sense they made to me. Every so often, one of the men would look at something through a pair of binoculars and change one of his figures. It was baffling yet fascinating.

I allowed Matt to place my bets for me, but I insisted on picking my own horses. He suggested that we study the form first. I pretended to know what this meant. I soon found out that it involved, in part, watching the animals being led around a paddock prior to the race. I chose my first horse on the basis of its sweet expression and a charming white blaze on its nose. Matt gave me a strange look.

'You can't pick a horse just because it's pretty.'

I stuck my nose haughtily in the air. 'That's not the only reason. I have a feeling about this horse.'

He shook his head before selecting an ugly, vicious-looking brute that I'd never have chosen in a million years.

His horse galloped to an easy victory. Mine took a tumble at the first fence.

'Was that the feeling you had, then?' Matt inquired.

296

'What?'

'That the pretty horse was going to fall at the first fence.'

'Oh, shut up!' Smart-arse. I'd show him.

For the next race, I decided on Serena's Lad. I chose him because I'd once owned a guinea pig called Serena, but I pretended to Matt that it was because he had good, strong-looking legs.

'Strong-looking legs, eh?' He looked at me doubtfully. 'Are you sure you won't go for that chestnut filly – number eight? I'd say she could do the business all right.'

'No.' I shook my head firmly. 'Serena's Lad it is.'

'Have it your way.'

I had it my way.

I had considerably more success this time. Serena's lovely Lad soared athletically over the first two fences before refusing at the third, sending his jockey flying. Meanwhile, number eight, the chestnut filly, flew home to a decisive victory.

'Two out of two,' said Matt as we went to collect his winnings – again. Was there nothing that this man did not excel at?

I took his advice from then on and finished the day with a tidy little profit. I got so caught up in the cycle of studying form, placing bets, watching races, going to the winners' enclosure – where the steam rose off the horses' bodies like smoke – and eventually winning, that I forgot all about lunch. Most uncharacteristic. It wasn't until late afternoon, as I was standing behind a woman who was wearing a hat made of a manipulated wire coat-hanger and pink and white marshmallows, that I realised how hungry I was.

'Hungry?' It was Matt, reading minds as usual.

I thought we'd head to one of the many food tents, but no; Matt had a surprise in store.

'Wait here and prepare to be impressed,' he instructed me.

He disappeared off in the direction of the car park, and reappeared five minutes later carrying a gigantic basket.

'I hope you like picnics.'

Did I what! I followed him to a pleasant green area, a little way from the general noise and mayhem. We settled down in the shade of a massive copper beech, the sunlight dappling over us through the leaves.

The picnic hamper contained one bottle of Moët & Chandon champagne (lightly chilled), one bottle of freshly squeezed orange juice, one large bowl of green salad, one cheese board comprised of five different types of cheese, four swans made of choux pastry and fresh cream, and one punnet of peaches. Matt had also brought along two champagne flutes, cutlery, napkins, paper plates and a blanket to sit on.

We clinked glasses that were bubbling over with Buck's Fizz.

'I don't know what to say, Matt. You've outdone yourself.'

'As long as you enjoy it.'

I did. What is it about eating outdoors? The food somehow tastes so much better. I helped myself to salad, cheese and two swans. The combination of late lunch and early-summer sunshine ensured that the champagne bubbles went straight to my head, stopping off on the way only to tickle the inside of my nose. I took my hat off and let the sun beat down on my face. My eyes began to close.

'Here, lie down,' said Matt. He gently pulled me back until my head was resting in his lap. (You've heard the expression 'like putty in his hands'?) He began to stroke the hair around my brow. After a while, I felt him loosening my ponytail and pulling it out of its bobbin.

'That's better,' he said quietly, as he started to run his fingers through my emancipated mane.

I knew I should stop him, but I simply didn't have the willpower. The combination of his rhythmic fingers grazing my cheek and neck, the twittering birds, the buzzing bees, the scent of fresh-cut grass, the sunshine, the champagne … I seemed powerless to resist. I comforted myself with the thought that, if he expected me to behave like Chris, he had another think coming.

It was a few minutes before he spoke.

'We forgot the peaches, Elena.'

'I'm stuffed.'

'Have one. They'll only go to waste.'

I made to get up, but he pressed me down again. 'I'll get it for you.'

Eyes still closed tightly against the sun, I listened to Matt rummaging around for the peaches. When the rustling noises stopped, I held out my hand; but nothing materialised in it. Instead, the warm, sweet-smelling, fuzzy skin of the peach was held lightly against my lips.

I took a bite. The skin yielded easily and my mouth was filled with intense softness and sweetness. The flesh of the peach melted onto my tongue and the juices slid down my throat. Once I'd swallowed, I felt the fruit pressed against my lips once more. I took another bite. This time, some juice squirted out and landed on my cheek; I could feel it dribbling down my face towards my chin. I reached my hand up to wipe it away, but Matt caught it.

A shadow fell across my face and I felt hot breath, then a peculiar sensation as his tongue delicately licked the juice from my face. I froze. When the peach was held to my lips for the third time, I hesitated for a long moment before sinking my teeth into the flesh again. No sooner had I swallowed than Matt brought his lips down on top of mine. I responded urgently and hungrily, drawing his tongue into my mouth.

He stopped abruptly and offered me more peach. Then more kisses. More peach. More kisses. Soon there was no peach left.

'You want another one?'

I nodded greedily and we did it all again,

although this time the bites of peach were smaller and the kisses longer.

When I caught myself silently willing Matt to take off my dress, I pulled myself together and moved away. I sat up and looked around, as if I'd forgotten where I was. Just to recap, I was in a field, contemplating fornication.

The sun momentarily popped its head behind a cloud, and this was enough to fully break the spell. I stood up and brushed the crumbs off my dress, then busied myself tidying up the plates and glasses, too embarrassed to look Matt in the eye; but soon everything was cleared up, and I had no choice but to look at him. He hadn't moved. He was half-lying, half-sitting, his weight resting on his elbows, his ankles crossed. He stared up at me intensely, his eyes like rockpools.

We were both startled by the sudden sound of a giggle. I gasped and whipped my head around, just in time to see two young girls run off from behind the copper beech.

'Hey, you two!' Matt called after them. 'Lizzie O'Donnell and Kate Murphy! I'm going to tell your mothers on you – spying on people like that!'

This just sent the girls into further kinks of laughter. We watched them sprint off until they had disappeared into the crowd.

'You know them?'

'Lizzie's a cousin of mine and Kate is Patricia's niece – you know, Patricia who works in your office.'

Patricia's niece! That was all I needed. The details of my illicit affair would be all over Ballyknock by sundown.

But what was so illicit about it? We were both free agents, consenting adults, etcetera, etcetera. If I hadn't recently broken up with Matt's brother, everything would have been marvellous.

'Shall we go and put a few more bets on?' I was keen to disrupt the highly charged atmosphere.

'The last race finished fifteen minutes ago. Didn't you hear the announcement?' His voice was ever so faintly mocking.

No, I hadn't heard it. I wonder why.

'We could go down the local,' Matt said. 'That's what most people do when the races finish. Should be a laugh.'

I scratched my cheek, twiddled the buttons on the front of my dress, fiddled with the ribbon on my hat. Then I retrieved my bobbin from where it lay on the picnic blanket and tied my hair back into the most formal ponytail I could manage in the circumstances.

'No offence, Matt. Thanks for everything. I've had a lovely day – the races and the picnic and everything …' I trailed off momentarily. 'But I'm pretty tired now, and I really don't feel like going to the pub. Could you drive me home?'

That sounded very sensible, didn't it? Reasonable and polite, too. I knew Matt was studying me carefully. I half-expected him to object, but he didn't.

'Right you are. Let's go.' He climbed to his feet, bundled up the last of the gear and held out his hand to me. I took it shyly, hoping that nobody would see us as we walked back to the car – ironic, considering what we'd just been up to.

Back in the jeep, I had the worrying thought that Matt might be reading more into my request to be brought home than there was to be read. He wasn't expecting a night of squelching passion, was he? Just to be sure, I kept my arms and legs tightly crossed for the entire journey and directed my knees pointedly away from him. I gazed resolutely out of my window, ostensibly to admire the gorse as it blazed against the sky and clashed magnificently with the grass. I spoke only when spoken to, and my replies were as polite and as proper as I could possibly manage.

Power's Cottage. I glanced nervously at the man in the driver's seat. *Please don't make this difficult....*

Matt smiled and leaned his forearm across the back of my headrest.

'I'm not going to be invited in, am I?'

'Um ... well, as I said, I had a lovely day, but I'm –'

'I know. You're tired.'

'Yes.'

'I'll give you a call.'

I nodded in response, got out of the car and watched as he drove down the hill. Then, feeling as if I'd had some sort of lucky escape, I went into the cottage and shut the door behind me.

Chapter Twenty-three

Sleep came more easily than I had anticipated. I still felt half-drugged. It wasn't until the next morning that I attempted a full post-match analysis. It wasn't easy. Where was Johnny Giles when you needed him?

To backtrack a little, I woke early – early for a Sunday morning, that is – and, struggling into my dressing-gown, wandered barefoot into the small conservatory. It was already sauna-hot in there. Another glorious day loomed ahead, and I had nothing to fill it with. But that was okay. I had always had an infinite capacity for doing nothing – a generous navel to contemplate. If I were ever to write an honest CV, I'd list 'doing nothing' as my main hobby. I'd probably dress it up, call it meditation or something.

I drove down to the shop and returned with a blueberry muffin and the Sunday papers. I made proper coffee and settled down for a morning of complete rest and relaxation. Only my mind had another agenda. That was when the analysis began.

What was it about these Power men? There had been a time – not so long ago – when I'd had complete control in all my relationships; when I hadn't felt like a tiny, insignificant feather being blown along by every gust of wind life sent my way. I hated this feeling – but I was surprised by the realisation that I loved it too.

I also realised, that morning, that I was still smarting badly from the humiliation I'd suffered at Jack's hands. I'd never before been so thoroughly rejected by a man, and now I saw that it had shaken my confidence to the core. Any belief I might have had in my own physical attractiveness had been diminished significantly. It would be nice to tell you that I had too much self-esteem to be adversely affected by the insensitive actions of one man, but that didn't appear to be the case.

And surely Matt knew about that awful night. Men talk about these things as much as women do, and the two brothers were close. Several times, yesterday, I'd only just managed to stop myself from asking Matt how Jack was getting on. I badly needed to know why he'd done what he'd done.

Embarrassment and pride were the only things that had stopped me from asking outright.

But there was something else holding me back – from Matt, that is. I felt as if I was on the brink of something – what, I wasn't sure; as if I was about to take a plunge into dark and mysterious waters, like a mermaid who would never be able to go back to living on dry land. I didn't know whether I was ready to burst out of my safe mould. It wasn't foreboding I felt; only fear.

So I did what I always did when confronted with a perplexing situation. I made a list. I can't remember all the details now, but it went something like this:

Title: *The Continuation of My Relationship with Matthew Power*
Subtitle: *Provided, of course, he wants to pursue a relationship with me*

Pro
- *Chris says he's great in the scratcher*
- *Less likely to end up as sad old crone*
- *Could be fun*
- *Got nothing better to do*
- *He's a spectacular kisser*
- *He saved Terence's life*

Con
- *He slept with Chris*
- *Polite Ballyknock society will be scandalised*

306

- *I strongly suspect that he may only be after one thing*
- *He gets around a lot – what if I catch something?*
- *I don't know if I could face another rejection*
- *He's Jack's brother*

Usually, such an exercise served to clarify the situation; but this time, as both lists were precisely the same length, it merely added to my consternation. Maybe I was looking at this from the wrong angle. A little comparing and contrasting might be in order.

Matt
- *Exciting*
- *Fun*
- *Good-looking*
- *Puts together an amazing picnic*
- *Chris says he's great in the scratcher*

Paul
- *Kind*
- *Fun (when he wants to be)*
- *Reliable*
- *Good-looking*
- *Down-to-earth*
- *Honourable*

I immediately scribbled out the list in frustration. This was getting me precisely nowhere. What was the point in comparing the two men, anyway? Paul was part of my past now. I threw down my pen and took a sip of my lukewarm coffee. I idly watched a pair of bluetits collecting strands of Terence's fur with which to line their nests. How cute – and how strange, that little bits of Terence should be up goodness knows how many trees in Ardskeha.

My pleasant musings were rudely interrupted by the telephone.

'Hello?'

'Morning, Lainey.'

'Morning, Matt.'

'What are you up to today?'

'Don't know yet.'

'Fancy a walk?'

Hmmm … what to do? If only my lists had produced a more conclusive result…. Oh, feck the lists. It was a beautiful day. Why let it get away?

'All right. What time?'

Another summer dress, this one in shades of blue and lilac, was resurrected. No hat or heels required today.

It was a walk. Just an innocent walk. Then why did I feel so guilty – as if I were betraying someone?

Matt arrived at ten past two. White T-shirt, dark canvas jeans; crinkly black hair, tanned, freckly face and forearms; knowing blue-green eyes. He wasn't as tall as Jack, nor as well built. He was more lithe – wiry. He moved with a cat-like grace. I'd never

308

come across a man so comfortable in his own skin.

We decided to walk around Ardskeha. There seemed little point in going elsewhere when you'd be hard pushed to find scenery that stunning. Hand in hand – as if we were a couple – we walked up and down the boreens. Matt helped me over stiles into fields where he'd played as a child. I walked barefoot on the grass. He pointed out the tracks the foxes used. He showed me a badger's den and a rabbit warren. He told me the names of all the wild flowers and trees I'd been wondering about, and which insignificant-looking weeds were hiding cures for common ailments. He seemed so perfectly at home, so totally in synch with his environment.

We were back at Power's Cottage before I knew it. Matt looked at me expectantly. How on earth was I going to avoid asking him in this time? The truth was, it just felt too dangerous to have me, Matt and a double bed in close proximity.

I had a brainwave.

'Why don't we sit outside? If you set up the tables and chairs, I'll sort the drinks.'

'Sure. Where do you want them?'

'Over by the cherry tree.'

Down at the bottom of the old-fashioned garden of Power's Cottage was a massive old cherry tree. In full bloom, as it was now, it resembled a giant, fluffy pink canopy. The blossom wouldn't last much longer; even now, the slightest breeze made pink petals rain down like confetti.

Luckily, I had some old-style lemonade in the fridge (alcohol was a definite no-no today). I made up a pitcher, with plenty of ice and fresh lemon slices, and carried it out to the garden, along with two glasses. Matt had set up two wrought-iron garden chairs and the matching table just beyond the shade of the cherry tree. He was staring up into the branches.

'I have a lot of happy memories of this tree,' he said as I set down the pitcher. 'I spent a lot of time in this garden when I was a kid. My granny used to mind me and Jack after school. We spent hours up in that tree – playing *Star Trek*, mainly. Jack always got to be Captain Kirk because he was the eldest. See that funny lump in the bark?'

I nodded.

'That was the throttle. You could get up to warp speed nine if you pressed it hard enough.'

I merely nodded again. To be honest, I was a little uncomfortable at the casual mention of Jack's name.

Matt had stopped talking, and his attention was fully focused on me once again. 'You know, I'm sure he didn't mean it.'

'You're sure who didn't mean what?' I knew exactly who and what he was talking about.

'Jack. Whatever he did or said to you. I'm sure it was nothing personal.'

'What do you know about it?'

'Nothing. But I do know that Jack has a lot of issues he needs to sort out.'

310

'Issues'? What manner of psychobabble was this? Did Jack's 'issues' excuse his shoddy behaviour that night? His intimations that I had dragged him to bed against his will? His comment that my body was 'quite' nice?

Matt must have recognised the cynicism in my face. 'Don't be too hard on him, that's all. He's a nice guy really.'

I used to think that too.

As the sun shone down on our heads, we each drifted off into our own silent reverie. It was almost too hot to make conversation on this lazy, sunshiny Sunday afternoon. I watched drowsily as two butterflies performed a mating dance. They were like free-floating petals come to life. They teased and chased each other for a full minute before disappearing over the wall into the neighbouring field.

At one point, I offered Matt some food.

'No, thanks. I'm not that hungry yet.'

Yet? How long was he planning to stay? He didn't expect me to cook for him – did he? But my alarm was soon dispersed by the sun's rays, and I drifted off pleasantly again.

After a while, I felt Matt move his chair closer to mine. Then, without a word, he gently lifted my lower legs by the calves and laid them across his lap. Next, he eased off my sandals and began to massage my feet, one at a time. I didn't object, because a) I'd just got a pedicure and b) it felt like heaven. Like

311

the floozy I was so obviously becoming, I let him continue. I decided I liked being a floozy. I didn't even get worried when his hands travelled up past my ankles and onto my shins, and then my knees.

But my eyelids did jerk open when I felt his hands slide under the hem of my dress and onto my lower thighs. I looked at him and gulped.

'What …' I had to clear my throat before I could continue. 'What are you doing?'

His eyes were frighteningly intense. And then he spoke the sweetest words that have ever been spoken by a man to a woman. Words that, without even realising it, I had been waiting to hear from a man all my adult life.

'Anything you want, Lainey. I'll do anything you want.'

My pulse racing in my ears, I stood up and held out my hand. Matt silently took it and allowed me to lead him under the heavy pink branches of the cherry tree. I leaned my back against the trunk and pulled his body in to mine. Our kisses continued from where they had left off the day before, although they were more frenzied this time. I took both of his hands in mine, kissed them passionately and then placed them at the top of my dress. He instantly got the message and began urgently opening the buttons down the front.

I had a glorious feeling of being exposed and liberated, all at once. We were outdoors, yet hidden; in danger of being caught, yet safe. The only things now separating Matt's naked hands from my naked body were a front-loading white bra and a cotton white thong. These barriers were soon disposed of. What followed was a flurry of physical sensations, of an intensity I'd never experienced before. Wherever I arched my body, Matt's fingers or mouth or delicious tongue followed. The rough bark of the tree against the skin of my back. The sunlight dappling through the branches against my front. The petals falling down onto my bare breasts. I almost felt at one with the universe. I certainly felt at one with the tree.

As soon as Matt was as naked as I was, I coiled my legs around him. Instinctively knowing what I wanted, as I had known he would, he hoisted me up off the earth, and I wrapped my legs around his waist.

With each thrust, a shower of pink petals rained down on our pink bodies. The tree would soon be as naked as we were. I felt like I was in a scene in a Bollywood movie – only X-rated. And then the pink explosions went off in my body and my head.

So, you see, I needn't have worried about Matt trying to get me into bed after all.

313

Chapter Twenty-four

I didn't go to work the next day. I wasn't sick; I was in a daze. I would have been a liability in the office, staring into space and making stupid mistakes that I'd only have had to rectify the next day.

So I stared into space at home instead. I took a break from staring at lunchtime, for a sandwich and the Ricki Lake show. Tabloid TV – the modern-day version of throwing Christians to the lions. The title of today's show was 'Get Your Hands Off My Brother, Mother'. It featured a selection of tarts and hos who had taken liberties with more than one male member of the same family. A black colossus of a woman in the audience shook her chubby finger at one of these women and called her a 'hoochie mama'. Was that me? Was I a hoochie mama? I wasn't exactly sure what it entailed, but I could tell by the woman's tone that it was no compliment. I began to get the heebie-jeebies. What had seemed so right yesterday now seemed so wrong....

I switched channels and watched an appalling Australian medical drama instead, but I couldn't get the chilling thought that my life was turning into an episode of *Ricki* out of my head. I might as well up sticks and move to a trailer park in Sweet Home Alabama. And how weird that that show should be broadcast today, of all days. There was definitely a message in there somewhere.

I looked up at Mary Power, who regarded me sternly.

'Oh, shut up,' I said loudly, making Terence jump. 'It's your fault for having such attractive grandsons.'

I felt marginally better for having pinned the blame on somebody else. But blame for what, exactly? I was single. Matt was single. Jack was in New York. Chris wouldn't give a toss. She'd just want to compare notes.

My guilt magically evaporated when Matt picked me up that evening. Later on that night, at twilight, with a brook babbling beside me and bats swooping low overhead, I became at one with a large, flat rock.

I honoured the office with my presence the next morning. I strolled in at about half past nine. My hair was down and still wringing wet after my long and luxurious shower. I'd decided to let it dry naturally for a change. Pity I couldn't have another day off and let it dry in the sun. Sun-dried hair – almost as delicious as sun-dried tomatoes. My face was ever so slightly tanned and free of make-up. I wore a navy skirt and a white linen blouse, open at the neck; I'd noticed in the car that I'd forgotten to iron one of the sleeves, so I'd just rolled them up. My legs were bare; I just couldn't face tights today.

I cherished the look on Patricia's face: amazement tempered with disapproval, overshadowed by burning curiosity. It was the first morning I'd been in the office later than her since I'd started work in Ballyknock. Oh, she was polite enough. She even told me my hair was nice down. But I noticed she didn't bring in scones for at least three weeks.

Mid-afternoon, I had a call from Tyrone. As usual, he was introduced by the nasal and noxious tones of Barbed Wire.

'Can you hold for Mr Power, please?'

'Yes, Barb.'

For goodness' sake, how long had I worked for him? And that cold bitch still announced him as if I were a stranger.

Tyrone came on the line, voice booming as usual. I instinctively held the receiver several inches away from my ear.

'Lainey! How's the form?'

'I'm in great form, Tyrone, thanks for asking.'

'Delighted to hear it. You sound it, too. Listen, I'm coming down to pay the Ballyknock office a visit.'

'When?'

'Tomorrow.'

Holy shit! 'Thanks for the notice. You wouldn't be coming down to check up on me, by any chance?'

'Lainey Malone! What a question. Don't you know I have the utmost faith in you?'

'Do you, now? Sorry for insulting you, so.'

'Apology accepted. I just feel the urge to visit the furthest outpost of my empire.'

'Your empire? Excuse me!'

'So I'll see you tomorrow at nine. Oh, hold on – Barb wants a word.'

'With me? About what?'

'How would I know? See you.'

He put me through to his illustrious secretary.

'Barb. What can I do for you?' She was probably going to warn me to stay away from her man.

'Actually, Elena, it's a little awkward….'

What was this I was hearing? Was the great Barbed Wire unsure of herself?

'It's about Tyrone.'

I thought so.

'He puts on a good show, but he's been very unwell lately.'

317

'Really?'

'Yes. He's been working his fingers to the bone, trying to get everything sorted so he can move down to the country. He's overdoing it. He won't listen to me any more. Maybe you'd have a word with him – see if you can convince him to slow down a little.'

'I'll certainly try.'

'And another thing....'

'Yes?'

'Don't let him smoke. He tells me he's off them, but I know he sneaks the odd fag every now and then.'

'I promise I'll keep an eye on him.'

'Okay, so. Bye.'

'See you.'

'Oh, Elena?'

'Yes?'

'Thank you.'

'You're welcome, Barb.'

How about that? Not so cold after all.

Patricia and I spent the rest of the afternoon in a frenzy of tidying and organising. Bins were emptied, desks were cleared, miscellaneous post was filed – Patricia was even keener to impress the boss than I was. I completed several odious legal tasks I'd been putting off, astounding myself with my new-found motivation.

Tyrone arrived at quarter to nine the next morning and began a frighteningly thorough investigation of every file in the office. Equally frightening was his appearance. He had aged an unnatural amount since I'd seen him last. Gone were the chubby, prosperous, fat-cat cheeks; the skin was pulled taut over every contour of his face. I didn't say anything until we were at lunch. He'd taken me out for posh nosh in the local golf club. He couldn't wait to begin exercising his membership rights.

'You've lost weight,' I blurted out over coffee.

'Thanks. I'm thinking of giving up this solicitor lark and becoming a model. What do you think? They say it's never too late for a change of career.'

I purposefully kept my expression stern. 'I don't mean it in a good way. You look gaunt – sick, even.'

'Well, the doctor told me to cut out the fatty foods, so I did.'

'Are you sure that's all it is? You're not working too hard?'

'Have you been discussing me with Barb?'

'Don't be so paranoid. It's as obvious as the nose on your face. You've been pushing yourself too hard, as usual. You know what the doctor said: you have to start taking things easier.'

He shrugged my comments away. 'The harder I work now, the quicker I can get down here and relax. And the quicker you can move back to Dublin. That is what you want – isn't it?'

'I suppose. But I don't want you half-killing yourself in the process. That would defeat the whole purpose.'

Tyrone fished around in his pocket and pulled out a pack of Benson & Hedges.

'No!' I almost yelled. 'You're not allowed.' He looked at me oddly and I quickly amended, 'I mean, you can't smoke in here. It's a no-smoking area.'

'Then why is there an ashtray on the table?'

I was momentarily stumped.

'Well, it's just that I've given up and it's too much of a temptation to be around anyone else smoking.'

'But you still have an ashtray in your office.'

'It's for clients,' I said, thinking quickly. 'In case they get stressed or upset and need to light up.'

He scanned my face. I made sure I didn't look too triumphant as he put the cigarettes back in his pocket.

'You *have* been talking to Barb, haven't you? That's why she asked me to put you back on to her yesterday on the phone.'

'She might have said something.'

I waited for the legendary Tyrone Power temper to flare up, but he just grinned at me. 'Amn't I the lucky man, to have two such gorgeous women looking out for me?'

I breathed a sigh of relief. I hadn't made him angry.

'Because you're looking great, Lainey. I've never seen you look so well. Country living must agree with you.'

I considered this new concept in surprise. Maybe it did suit me. Although I'd also recommend regular sessions with Matt Power to induce a sense of total well-being.

'As a matter of fact, you look like the cat that got the cream.'

'Do I really?' I smiled. Like the cat that got the cream.

'Wouldn't be anything to do with Mattie Power, by any chance?'

That wiped the smile off my face. I hadn't realised that the Ballyknock grapevine swung all the way to Dublin.

'How did you know about that?' I couldn't play it cool.

He laughed at me. 'A little Bridie told me.' He was enjoying this, evidently getting his own back.

'Whatever happened to poor old Jack? I heard you were seeing him before Christmas.'

Had he, now? He'd never let on before.

'Bridie's terrified you're going to send another of her sons off packing to the States.'

The cheek!

'What are you doing – working your way through the whole lot of them?'

'No!'

'And what about that Dublin lad you were seeing – Peter, wasn't it? You brought him along to the company barbecue that time.'

'Paul.'

'Paul, that's it. Nice lad. What did you do with him?'

I shifted uncomfortably in my chair. When was this barrage of personal questions going to end? This was the one drawback of being on good terms with your boss.

Tyrone sensed my discomfort and took pity on me. 'All right, all right, I'll shut up now. But seriously, Lainey … can I give *you* a bit of advice?'

'What?' I was wary.

'Just be careful with young Mattie. I mean, don't get me wrong, he's a grand chap and I'm awful fond of him; but – well – he's a bit of a lad, if you get what I'm saying. All right for a good time, but don't get too hung up on him.'

I blushed furiously. 'Don't worry, I won't.'

'Glad to hear it. Now come on – back to the office. We've got work to do.'

Chapter Twenty-five

Tyrone returned to Dublin, and I did my best to return to some semblance of normality. Easier said than done, with Matt on the scene. I mean, one-night stands are so demeaning. That's why it was so imperative that I should see Matt again. And again. And again.

We took full advantage of the long, mild spring days and dined *al fresco* most evenings. Over the coming weeks, I became at one with a meadow (Matt made daisy chains for my ankles, wrists, neck and waist), a deep green forest (on the forest floor amongst the bluebells), a hay-shed (it was raining. Fun but a bit prickly), a tree-house (he was the type of man who would try to get you up a tree rather than into bed), a waterfall (highly recommended) and the back of his jeep (reminiscent of teenage years. It was quite chilly that night).

You might wonder how – with all this excitement going on – I could drag myself away to Dublin for a weekend. I had two reasons for going. The first one was that Tatiana had given birth to a baby girl. No, she hadn't been forced to abort when they had found out that she was expecting a girl; no, Chen hadn't insisted that the child be deposited in the nearest orphanage while they tried to conceive a son and heir; no, Annie hadn't been forcibly sterilised so she couldn't have another child. When I rang and spoke to Chen, he wept tears of pure joy.

My parents, too, were beside themselves with happiness. They were travelling to Beijing on Monday to visit mother and child. I wanted to see them before they left, and to give them presents for Annie and my new niece – LuLing. I was now Auntie Elena. How strange.

The family home was in uproar. Cases were packed, unpacked and repacked. Piles of ironing loomed high on the kitchen counter. My mother rushed around in a blind panic, crossing items off lists with a red Biro and adding new items with a blue Biro. My father sat in his armchair, quietly reading a book entitled *How to Survive an Aeroplane Crash: One Hundred Tips*. I gently pointed out that his choice of reading material could hardly alleviate his fear of flying, but he just said, in a very solemn voice, 'There's no harm in being prepared, Rosie.' The eternal Boy Scout.

My mother reported that he was driving her demented. I thought it best to refrain from commenting that she'd been demented for years, probably since long before she had met him. It wasn't just his failure to assist in the holiday preparations that was driving her to distraction – although he probably thought he was preparing, in his own special way.

Since he'd retired, his mission had been to find himself the perfect hobby. First there had been bridge. Mum didn't mind that – it got him out of the house and meeting new people – but his interest waned after a few short weeks. Then there had been the photography. Dad had reportedly bought thousands of pounds' worth of equipment ('Think of it as an investment, Teresa') – and that obsession had lasted exactly twelve days (she'd been keeping count). I meekly pointed out that this would come in handy to take pictures of LuLing, but Mum was not to be dissuaded from her frustration. Then he'd been all set to take up wood-turning ('It's something I've wanted to do my whole life, Teresa'); Mum couldn't even get the car into the garage any more, what with all the equipment; and had he produced so much as one bowl? I think you know the answer. His latest passion was for home brew. You couldn't get near the airing cupboard for pipes and bubbling cauldrons. It was the last straw when Mum discovered that all her clean knickers smelt of beer.

Of course, she just wanted him to go back to work. He was clearly invading her territory.

After about an hour, I couldn't wait to vacate the premises. Before I left, I fed Terence and shut him out in the back garden. It was for his own good. Witnessing such a high level of domestic un-bliss couldn't be good for him.

This brings me to my second reason for travelling to Dublin on this particular weekend. It seemed that Hazel was finally ready to face the world again. Chris, Paul and I were meeting her for lunch.

I was the second person to arrive. Hazel was sitting alone in a booth at the back of the café. I tried to quell my nerves as I walked towards her. The last time I'd seen her, she'd been in St Catherine's.

Hazel looked up from her menu just as I reached the booth. She smiled weakly.

'Hi, Lainey. It's good to see you.'

I struggled to control my emotions as we embraced. It felt like squeezing a bag of bones. As I settled in opposite her, I tried not to make it too obvious that I was scrutinising her face for clues. Was this the old Hazel? The new Hazel? (The mad Hazel?) She was wearing her glasses. Her hair was down and unadorned, but freshly washed; her face was devoid of make-up, but she'd lost her deathly pallor. She was wearing jeans and a pale-grey top, simple and pristine. In other words, vintage Hazel.

'You're looking well,' I told her, relieved that I didn't have to lie.

'So are you. I love your hair.'

'Thanks.' I was bashful. I'd decided to leave my hair loose again today. It now extended halfway down my back. A few days before, I'd taken a few strands on the left-hand side and worked them into a plait. Matt had liked it. Now the hairstyle was making its maiden voyage to Dublin.

I was about to ask her how she *really* was, when the others arrived – or, I should say, the others plus one. Whose bright idea had it been to bring Iseult along? Hazel's first foray back onto the Dublin social scene, and somebody had to bring along her nemesis. I glared at Paul and he looked away, embarrassed. There was no point glaring at Iseult, because she was talking shrilly into her mobile phone, and there was no point glaring at Chris because – well, because she was Chris.

Paul and Chris hugged Hazel as if she were breakable. Then Chris turned her attention to me.

'Lainey! What have you done to yourself? You look amazing. Let me have a look at you.'

Had I really looked that bad before? And was the fact that Chris thought I looked amazing actually a good thing? Before I could decide, Chris – much to my embarrassment – forced me to get out of my seat and give her a twirl.

I was wearing a long, floaty skirt that contained all the colours of the universe in a vivid haze, and a simple white linen top with ruched sleeves and a lace-up neck. My boots were tan suède, and my short, fitted jacket matched them. I wore giant gypsy-style earrings and colourful bangles. Chris heartily approved.

'I've never seen you looking so good. If you were showing a bit more leg, you'd be perfect.'

Showing plenty of leg herself, she clambered into the seat beside me.

I was aware of Iseult, still talking loudly into her phone, looking me up and down. She was speaking at her assistant.

'No, no, no, Samantha. I told you not to listen to that one; she wouldn't know Prada from Primark. You should always do what *I* tell you. The whole thing will have to be re-shot. The hippy-chick look went out with the Ark.' She snapped her mobile shut.

'Hi, Elena.' She bared her teeth at me; it was probably meant to be a smile, but it reminded me of a programme about sharks I'd recently seen on the National Geographic channel. She proceeded to kiss everyone, once on each cheek. What was all this continental-style kissing? I must have missed its introduction. Had it been brought in with the euro? Irish people couldn't be doing with all this kissing stuff. It wasn't natural.

Paul sat next to Hazel, opposite Chris and me, and Iseult squashed in beside him. As Hazel, Chris, Paul and I ordered coffees and sandwiches, Iseult ordered salad and mineral water and loudly informed us that she'd just returned from a photo shoot in the Caribbean. Puke!

A situation that could have been horribly awkward was made less so by Chris's blessed aimless chatter. She was very excited because the company she worked for was going to allow her to direct her first short film. She was undaunted by the prospect, despite the fact that she had not the first clue what the film would be about. She did have ideas, however – plenty of them, each more outlandish than the last.

Hazel was unusually quiet – although who knew what was usual in these circumstances? She seemed afraid of the crowds of people in the restaurant. Maybe we should have picked somewhere quieter. But it was Grafton Street on a Saturday afternoon; quieter didn't exist. Her body language was different, too. She sat holding her coffee mug in front of her face, gripping it tightly in both hands, her eyes darting from side to side. She was aeons away from the cool, calm, collected Hazel I knew so well – the girl who could sum up a person in one succinct phrase, thereby reducing me and Chris to tears of laughter. At least her eyes had lost that eerie, faraway look.

The East European waitress brought over Iseult's order. Iseult held up the bottle of water that had been placed before her and shook it from side to side, pinky finger extended.

'Excuse me. What's this?'

'You ordered a bottle of water, did you not?'

'I ordered a bottle of still water, dear. As in no bubbles. *Capiche?*'

'I am very sorry. I will get you another bottle right away.'

Iseult rolled her eyes in despair. One just couldn't get the staff nowadays.

'That kind of thing drives me mad. Oops – sorry, Hazel.' She held her hand up to her mouth and tittered.

Hazel and I exchanged a look that was just like old times. I glanced at Paul, but he was concentrating hard on his sandwich. He appeared oblivious, but I knew him and I knew he must be uncomfortable, to say the least.

How could he stand being with her? Okay, she was good-looking. And, God knows, not an ounce of fat clung to her taut thighs. But, really, was that adequate compensation for everything else he must have to put up with? And, even more worrying, what did that say about me? A lot of men routinely go for a certain type – just look at Rod Stewart. Was I the same type as Iseult? I knew we didn't look alike, but…. What a horrifying thought. I'd have to ask Hazel when she got a little better. I could hardly ask Chris. (Hey, Chris? You know your friend, the complete pain in the arse? Please tell me I'm nothing like her.)

I wasn't mad about the effect she was having on

Paul, either. He'd barely acknowledged me since they'd arrived. The odd thing was, I kept catching him looking at me; but every time I tried to meet his gaze, he looked away a split second too soon. Was he not allowed to so much as look at other women any more?

Why did he have to bring her along, anyway? The more I thought about it, the more annoyed I got. How on earth were we supposed to have a heart-to-heart with Hazel when Cruella DeVil was breathing down our necks?

As soon as there was a lull in the conversation (Chris had taken the first bite of her sandwich), I said impulsively, 'Paul, how are things with you?' I was determined to draw him out.

'Um … like what things?'

'Well – work. How's work? Not doing crazy hours, I hope.' That was very tactful of me in the circumstances, wasn't it?

'No more than usual. Although I've had a few late nights recently.'

'You'd need to watch that,' said Hazel quietly. It was one of the first times she'd spoken. 'You don't want to end up like me.'

This silenced everyone – everyone, that is, except Iseult.

'Well, I think Paul is absolutely right to work hard at his career. You don't get anywhere these days without ambition. And it's especially important for someone in Paul's position.'

331

What position was that, exactly? Under her thumb?

As Iseult uttered her words of wisdom, one of her arms went around Paul's neck and the other travelled under the table to his knee (I hoped). She snuggled up against him coquettishly, staring at me. *Oh, stick it up your swiss, you stupid bitch!* I had a good mind to mention Matt. I probably would have done, if Hazel hadn't known that he'd already shagged Chris. And there was no guessing what Chris herself might come up with. No, I was better off keeping schtum.

We finished up our sandwiches amidst much mindless small talk, the blander the better.

'Coffee, Paul,' said Iseult.

'Yes, please. I'd love another cup.'

'No. Coffee, Paul. I want a decaf. And get me two sachets of sweetener.'

Nobody moved.

Then Paul turned his head slowly towards her and said, 'I'm sure the waitress will be around any minute to take your order.' His face was set like stone.

Iseult started to say something else, but thought better of it and closed her mouth. I resisted the urge to raise my clenched fist in the air and shout, 'Yes!'

They left not long after that. Iseult didn't really say goodbye; she was too busy barking orders at the long-suffering Samantha again. Paul trailed behind her, fury and embarrassment intermingling on his features.

'I'll give you a call next week, Hazel. Bye, Lainey, Chris.'

Chris had to go too. She had an urgent jam-and-funk-dance class to attend. I got out of my seat to let her pass. As she moved out of Hazel's earshot, she said to me, 'He's good, isn't he?'

I reddened. 'What are you talking about?'

'We both know who I'm talking about. Told you he was exceptional. And I'm glad to see you using that hair and those tits at last. High time. It's a sin to waste such God-given talents.' She smirked at me, and pranced off to go jamming and funking for the afternoon. Flabbergasted, I returned to my seat.

'What was all that about?' asked Hazel.

'Oh, nothing. Just Chris being Chris. Anyway … alone at last. We can talk properly now.'

Except the thing was, I couldn't think of a darn thing to say. I wanted to act normally, I really did. But things *weren't* normal, and there was no denying it.

'Are you going to keep living at home for the time being?' I tried.

'Yes. It's the best place for me right now, I think. Mum and Dad have been brilliant.' She stared off into the blue yonder, as if recalling how great her parents had been.

'And how about work? You're hardly going back to that hellhole.'

'God, no. Not that they'd have me back.'

'Their loss.'

Hazel laughed without humour. 'It's nice of you to say so. But I don't think they'd see it that way.'

'Well, they should. You worked damn hard for that miserable shower of shites.'

She took a sip of coffee. 'It doesn't matter any more. It's in the past. I have a job interview next weekend, anyway.'

'Really? For where?'

She had applied for a position as a part-time bookkeeper in a small, family-run firm. Of course, she was completely over-qualified for the post, but her therapist thought it would be good for her. Imagine – sane, logical, sensible Hazel had a therapist.

'You see,' she explained to me, after a while, 'like I was saying to Laura – that's my therapist – the other day, I feel like I've been lied to all my life.'

'By who?'

'Oh, I don't know. Nobody. Everybody. Society, I suppose. I mean, I've played by the rules all my life – and look where it's got me. I was told to work hard in school, so I did. "Keep at the books," my father used to say. So I did. And I got a good Leaving Cert and I went to college, and my parents were so proud…. I was the first in our family to go to college. Did you know that?'

I nodded encouragingly.

'So I decided to study accountancy. I was always good at maths, and it seemed like a sensible, practical option. I mean, people will always need accountants. And it meant I'd be considered a professional. Me! So I worked really hard and got all my exams. I came third highest in my class. Did you know that?'

I shook my head. No, I hadn't known that.

'So then I get my first proper job, and it's damned hard work, but I don't mind. I'm prepared to put in the long hours, you see, because I want to do well. And I do. I get promoted. Then I decide to move on to that last dump of a place. Worst move I ever made. But I kept working hard, and at first I didn't mind. I thought I could cope. I sacrificed everything for that job – my social life, my health, my relationships. Do you know how long it's been since I've had a proper boyfriend?'

'How long?' Actually, I knew, but at this point her questions were purely rhetorical. I didn't like to interrupt her when she was on a roll.

'Five years.' She held up her open hand for emphasis. 'Five – long – years. Do you remember that idiot Dinny?'

'Yes.'

'Well, he was my last boyfriend. Just think of it – that fool! And what were they for? All those sacrifices?'

I shook my head.

'For nothing, that's what. Study hard. Go to college. Get a good job. Work hard. Lick the boss's arse. Put off getting married. Put off having kids. And for what? Fuck all. I tell you, Lainey, it's all a load of bollix. I would have been better off pissing around in secondary school for five years and then working as a checkout girl. Or going to Australia for a year. Most of my friends did that. Why didn't I? Will I tell you why?'

She banged her fist on the table.

I nodded, fearful now that the floodgates had been opened. The couple at the next table had stopped talking and were eavesdropping avidly.

'Because I thought I was being the smart one, that's why. I thought, *I know! I'll stay home, work hard and get ahead while those other poor fools back-pack around Australia. They'll never get on in their careers.* That's what I thought. I mean, how smug can you get? Look at them now – thriving. And look at me. I've fucked up my life good and proper.'

'No, you haven't, Hazel. Don't say that.'

'But I have. What accountancy firm would have me now? I just walked out on my last job. I didn't even give notice. I'd be afraid to ask them for a reference – God knows what they'd say about me. And what man's going to want me now? I've been in the nuthouse, for God's sake.'

'Any man would be lucky to have you.'

'You must be kidding. Besides, it wouldn't be fair of me to inflict myself on a fellow human being at this time. And that's the other thing.'

There was another thing?

'I'm almost thirty-one. What chance do I have of ever becoming a mother?'

'Hazel! You have loads of time. Look at Annie. She didn't meet Chen until she was thirty-four, and she didn't have LuLing until she was thirty-five.'

'I suppose so.' This pacified her somewhat. But then: 'That's the feminist movement for you.'

What did the feminists have to do with it?

'They con you into believing that you're going to be completely fulfilled by a career, and that you can put off motherhood forever. But it's all damn lies. Look at all those women in their thirties on IVF programmes. They were lied to as well.'

The couple at the next table were preparing to leave. The woman was looking at Hazel strangely. All of a sudden, she came over to us and said rapidly, 'I couldn't help overhearing, and I agree with everything you've said. The best of luck to you.' She held out her hand.

Hazel shook it, a bemused expression on her face. Then the woman practically ran out of the café, seemingly overwhelmed by her own impulsive behaviour. Her boyfriend scampered after her, looking equally self-conscious. Hazel and I looked at each other and burst out laughing.

'What was all that about?' she said.

'Well, it was a vote of confidence, anyway.'

'Why didn't you tell me I was talking so loudly?' She looked sheepishly around at the rest of the punters sitting close by, but they were all ignoring us.

'There's an alternative career for you. You can become a motivational speaker.'

Still laughing, we ordered more coffee. I stirred my latte thoughtfully.

'That Iseult is a piece of work, isn't she?'

'You can say that again.'

'What on earth does Paul see in her? She treats him like a child.'

'And I suppose *you* never treated him like a child.' Hazel was smirking at me, one eyebrow raised.

Who? *Moi*?

'I didn't. Did I?'

She shrugged her bony shoulders, almost apologetically. 'Well, yes, you did. Some of the time.'

I stirred another packet of sugar into my coffee. Was that true? It had to be, or why would she say it?

'Anyway' – she patted my hand encouragingly – 'I wouldn't worry about it. He's only with her because he can't be with you.'

I stopped stirring.

'That's rubbish.'

''S'obvious.'

'But he practically ignored me earlier.'

'Only because she was there. I'm telling you, he's still carrying a big, flaming torch.'

I didn't quite know what to do with this piece of information.

But I did feel something inside of me soar.

When we were in imminent danger of overdosing on caffeine, we finally left the café. I cajoled Hazel into coming to the cinema with me. She wasn't up

338

to browsing around the shops – too many people for her to cope with just then, she explained. She also apologised for ignoring my phone calls before Christmas. She said she just hadn't been able to cope with talking to anyone – and she still found it tough. Getting through today's lunch unscathed had been a personal triumph for her. Hell – if you could cope with Iseult, you could cope with anything.

But the cinema was the perfect place for her. Because it was mid-afternoon, the Savoy was half-empty. I love going to the cinema in the daytime; it always makes me feel like I'm playing hooky. We chose the least highbrow film there was. Think of the most mindless action movie ever, combine it with the cheesiest chick-flick you've ever seen, and multiply that by ten. It was much worse than that.

We both loved it. Arms cradling massive tubs of popcorn, feet illegally up on the seats in front of us, we hugged ourselves in anticipation. I loved the whole spectacle – the curtains edging back from the screen, the larger-than-life ads, the trailers, even the warning to turn off your mobile phone.... They all heralded the start of two hours of escapism and fantasy. We forgot ourselves, forgot the world around us and lost ourselves in the magic of Hollywood.

Chapter Twenty-six

I left Dublin at half-two the next day. I had planned to stay longer, but there's only so much one daughter can take. And, besides, I couldn't wait to get back to Ballyknock.

Matt had arranged to call around at eight. But I got back at five, and there was no way I was waiting three hours. I decided to call to his surgery instead. As I pulled up outside, I could hardly suppress the excitement that was threatening to burst right through my chest. Lucky I had an airbag. I smiled goofily at myself in the rear-view mirror as I hastily brushed my hair and applied a coat of lipstick. It was a new, cutting-edge, shimmery shade that the woman in the shop had talked me into buying. It was really me, apparently. She must have seen me coming a mile off.

At the sight of the surgery, Terence began to shake and whimper in the back seat. He hadn't relished getting his stitches out.

'It's all right, boy,' I told him. 'It's not your turn this time.'

I stepped out of the car and ran lightly across the gravel and up the steps. The waiting room was empty. There was one other car outside; Matt was hopefully finishing up with his last patient. Even the receptionist had gone home. I sat down in one of the plastic chairs, crossed my legs and admired the fake tan I'd oh-so-professionally applied to my legs that morning. For once, it didn't look as if somebody had poured Bisto haphazardly down my shins. The toenails were looking good, too – new hot-pink shade I'd also been conned into buying. And I was wearing the new underwear I'd furtively bought in Knickerbox the day before. Even though I'd entered the shop wishing I were wearing shades and a fake beard – you'd have thought I was buying a giant dildo, going by the embarrassment I'd caused myself – I had emerged triumphant, head held high, bearing a pretty little bag brimming over with frothy pink lace. I couldn't wait to take my matching bra-and-knickers set for a test drive and see if Matt liked it too. For years, I'd been a slave to white cotton briefs and sensible matching bras; now that seemed like eating vanilla ice-cream all your life, when there were so many other flavours to choose from.

The door to the surgery was slightly ajar, and I could hear the conversation within. It sounded like it was winding up.

'So give him one of these tablets twice a day.'

'Thank you so much, Mr Power.' A woman's voice.

'Oh, please – call me Matt.'

'How much do I owe you – Matt?'

'Tell you what – let's forget about it, since it's your first visit. If the tablets don't work and he needs more treatment, we can talk about payment then.'

'That's very decent of you, Matt. I'm really grateful.'

'Yeah? How grateful?'

My leg froze mid-swing.

A high-pitched giggle. 'Oh, very.'

'Enough to come on a picnic with me next week?'

'Maybe.'

I'd heard enough. I ran out of the waiting room, down the steps, across the gravel and towards my car. I fumbled around with my car keys, which no longer seemed to fit the lock. I dropped the bunch of keys on the ground with a clatter.

'Shit!' I couldn't help exclaiming loudly. Finally, I was in my car. I slammed the door shut and turned the key in the ignition. The engine revved angrily.

The last thing I saw as I swung out of the driveway was Matt's face, a picture of horror,

342

freeze-framed in the surgery window. So I did what every woman worth her salt would do in the circumstances.

I gave him the finger.

Back at the ranch, I waited for the deluge of tears. I waited in vain. I must have been shell-shocked.

So I tried indignation instead. How could he? I'd just wasted the best six weeks of my life on him (mind you, he was the reason they had been the best six weeks of my life). And the very minute my back was turned – the first weekend I went to Dublin – he'd asked another girl out! And maybe she wasn't even the first. There could have been a new girl each week, for all I knew.

'No offence, but your grandson is a right dick-head,' I told Mary Power. She stared back at me impassively.

But, try as I might, I couldn't work up a good head of steam on my anger. I had got a shock, all right; but, behind it all, if I was entirely honest with myself, I wasn't all that surprised. Deep down, I knew the deal. I wasn't in love with Matt any more than he was in love with me. All my life, I'd been taught that you couldn't have good sex without being in love. Well, Matt had blown that particular myth out of the water. Why I'd ever bought into the concept in the first place was beyond me now. It had never proved to be true in my own life.

I had let myself be played, by a player of virtuoso

standard, and I had enjoyed every note. I had used him as much as he'd used me. But 'used' wasn't really the right word. We had *enjoyed* each other – taken pleasure from each other's company, not to mention each other's body. There had been genuine respect and affection. I knew there had been.

As my feelings came into focus, I realised that my overwhelming emotions were disappointment and a sense of loss. I'd so enjoyed our little trysts, and now they were over. Our fling had been flung. Even if Matt wanted to carry on regardless, it wasn't in my nature to share a man with goodness knew how many other women. And it would have been selfish to try to keep him all to myself. A talent like his should be shared. No doubt he felt the same way.

The phone rang. Anticipating this, I had put it on answerphone.

'Lainey, are you there? If you are, will you pick up, please? … Lainey, it's me – Matt. Look … I'm very sorry you had to hear what I think you heard. Give me a ring if you like, and we can discuss it. Bye, then.' He hung up.

I sat in silence for a few minutes, thinking how much I'd miss him. Then I got to my feet and started unpacking my overnight bag. Enough moping. I had things to do and stuff to get ready for work in the morning. I comforted myself with the thought that at last I'd found the one thing at which Matt Power didn't excel: monogamy.

And then I thought of someone who'd never treat me like that in a million years.

At times like this, I found there was only one thing to do: throw myself into my work. It was the one constant that could always be relied upon in an ever-shifting universe. There was always work, and plenty of it.

That Monday was district court day in Ballyknock. Brendan Ryan and I were on opposing sides of a case – a ludicrous traffic accident that had been caused in equal parts by the stupidity of both of our clients. The judge clearly agreed; he made an order for fifty-fifty liability. Couldn't say fairer than that. Having convinced our respective clients that we were mortal enemies, Brendan and I went for lunch together.

'How are you getting on with that dog?' he asked me as we were waiting for our food.

'Great. I called him Terence.'

'Terence? Really? That's unusual.'

'Brendan, remember that day in your office, when you told me that you were going to bring him to the pound and that he'd probably be put down?'

'Yes.'

'Well, did you mean that?'

'Of course not.'

Didn't think so.

Was it just me, or were all men lying bastards?

Talking of lying bastards, I was relaxing at home one evening the following week when there was a knock on the front door. I was understandably irritated, as there were still ten minutes of *EastEnders* left to run. Who could be calling at such an inconvenient hour?

The last person in the world I expected to see, that's who. If Elvis Presley himself had turned up at my front door, sporting a white sparkly jumpsuit and singing 'Heartbreak Hotel', I couldn't have been more surprised.

I didn't recognise him at first. His hair was transformed, for a start: dyed blond, shaved at the sides, gelled into a disorganised peak at the top. He seemed sleeker, less chunky. He was wearing dark-grey flared trousers and a tight-fitting black polo-neck.

He looked like a hairdresser.

'Come in.' What else could I say?

Jack nodded at me and sheepishly entered the house. Hands deep in pockets, he looked around as if seeing the place for the first time. He sat on the couch, his tense body leaning forward. I tried not to think about the last time he'd sat there.

'I'll put the kettle on,' I said. Well, it always worked on *EastEnders*. When in doubt, make a nice cup of tea.

I handed him his mug, taking special care not to touch his hand with my own. Then I sat down next to him, balancing precariously on the edge of the couch.

'How have you been?' I asked.

'Fine. You?'

'Fine.' There was that word again.

There followed about thirty seconds of the most uncomfortable silence I'd ever endured. When I couldn't stand it any more, I said, 'Did you cut your trip short?'

He nodded. 'By about a month. I needed to come home and sort a few things out. I might be going back. I haven't decided yet.'

'How was New York?'

'Brilliant. Loved every second of it. I was only there for a couple of months, though; I spent the rest of the time in San Francisco.'

Oh. I took several sips of reviving tea, which luckily was hot and sweet.

'Lainey … I have something to tell you.'

'Go on.' I looked up at him and our eyes locked. He gazed at me imploringly. He looked as if he was about to speak, several times, but the words always seemed to get jammed in his throat.

'Oh, Jesus. This doesn't get any easier.' He hid his face in his hands.

'Just say it, Jack.'

A pair of turquoise eyes looked searchingly into my own.

'I'm gay.'

I nodded and took another sip of tea. I had already known. I'd just needed him to come out and say it. I could feel his eyes burning into the side

347

of my face, but all I could do was stare at the floor.

'For Christ's sake, Lainey, say something – please.'

'Do your parents know?'

He slumped back into the couch. 'I told them last night. Not long after I got in.'

'How did they take it?'

'Mum was great. I mean, she cried a little at first. But, as she said to me, it's not as if I'm her one shot at having a grandchild.'

'You're her favourite son anyhow. Now you can be the daughter she never had.'

Jack checked to see whether or not I was being bitchy. Then we both started to laugh.

'Another cup?'

'Yes, please.'

I boiled up the kettle again.

'How about your dad?'

'Not so good.'

I gathered from the pained expression on his face that this was an understatement.

'Maybe he just needs some time to get used to the idea.'

'Maybe. But I don't think either of us will live that long.' He sounded utterly miserable.

My own mood, however, was becoming more jubilant by the second. You may find this strange; but, you see, for five months I'd thought that Jack had rejected me because I was physically repulsive. But his rejection had had nothing to do with me at all. He couldn't have fancied me if he'd tried. Not even if I'd had the body of Naomi Campbell. Unless …

'You're not bi, are you?'

'Nope. I'm afraid I'm a one-hundred-per-cent bona-fide poof.'

Hooray! He was gay! That meant I was okay!

He was queer. A shirt-lifter. A woolly woofter. An arse-bandit. A sausage-jockey.

What fantastic news!

'You know, you're taking this very calmly. I thought you'd freak.' Jack was studying me carefully.

'I'm just glad you didn't run off to America because of my disgusting thighs.'

'Is that what you thought? I'm so, so sorry.' He took my hands in both of his. 'I felt so terrible after the way I left things that night. And then just leaving the country without any explanation … what must you have thought of me?'

'I thought you were a right prick.'

'Of course you did. You had every right to. But I never meant to hurt you, Lainey.'

'But you did. I just wish you'd told me the truth. I would have understood, you know.'

'I know, I know. I'm sorry.'

'What did you think you were at, anyway?'

'Oh, I don't know. I was in denial, I suppose. And I was under a lot of family pressure to get a girlfriend.'

'You mean you went out with me to keep your mammy off your back?'

'Something like that. I suppose you think that's terrible.'

'I do, as it happens.'

'I don't blame you. But look at things from my point of view. Do you think it's easy being a gay farmer in Ballyknock?'

No, I didn't suppose it was.

'So can we get over this and be friends?'

'I don't know, Jack…. It all feels very weird.'

'It's bound to. You've only just found out. But in time you might feel differently. I mean, we always got on great, didn't we?'

This was true.

'And if I was straight, I'd definitely choose a girl-friend like you.'

I wasn't sure about this one. 'Is there something masculine about me, then?'

'God, no! Just the opposite. That's another reason I thought you'd be the perfect cover. You've got long blonde hair and – if you don't mind me saying – quite a large chest.'

He should know. He'd seen it in all its glory.

'You reminded me of the women I used to pretend to fancy in the girly magazines that the lads would pass around in school.'

I didn't know how to take that. Did I really look like a Page Three tart? The perfect cover for a gay boyfriend? Maybe I could hire myself out.

'You've gone all quiet again. Say something – please,' said Jack.

350

'I was just wondering....'

'What?'

'When you went to San Francisco – did you wear flowers in your hair?'

'Only on special occasions.'

Jack stayed for a few hours. He didn't seem to be in a big hurry to go home. It was odd, but kind of nice at the same time. He told me about this man he'd met in California. Jack liked him a lot, but he wasn't sure how serious the other guy, Chuck (no, honestly), was about him. It was a typical girly chat, really.

As he was leaving, he asked me, 'Will you come to the pub with me tomorrow night?'

'Which pub?'

'Power's. Where else?'

'I'm not sure if that's a good idea.'

'Ah, come on. I need the moral support.'

'Well, the thing is, I'm kind of trying to avoid Matt.'

'What's wrong with Matt?'

'Nothing. It's just …'

'Oh, no. Don't tell me you and him …'

''Fraid so.'

'How could you? And me barely cold in the grave.' He was smirking at me.

'I needed someone to help me get over you.'

'So you picked my own brother? Shame on you!' Jack was enjoying occupying the moral high ground for the first time that night.

'Actually, he picked me.'

'I don't doubt it. He's like a bitch in heat, that lad. But you needn't worry about bumping into Matt. He's probably forgotten all about you by now and moved on to the next blonde.'

'Thanks a lot.'

'Oh, you know what I mean. He doesn't have a faithful bone in his body. If you were the last woman on earth and he were the last man, he'd still find some way to cheat on you. Granny Mary was right about him. "That Mattie would flirt with a gatepost," she used to say. But I shouldn't be hard on him. He took my news very well – said he'd known all along.'

'I wish he'd told me,' I said.

'I wish he'd told me, too. Would have saved us both a lot of bother. So, anyhow, you needn't worry about him.'

'Well, it's not just Matt. It's your mother too.'

'What's wrong with Mam?'

'Nothing. I'm afraid she'll blame me for turning you.'

Jack laughed raucously. 'Don't be daft, woman.'

'I'm not being daft. I know that's what she thinks.'

'Trust me. She doesn't. Please say you'll come.'

'Oh, all right. Anything to shut you up.'

He turned to me one more time before getting into the jeep.

'And you never know – you might get lucky. My brother Timmy will be there, and he's single.'

352

'Do you really think I'd touch another Power man with a bargepole?'

He bellowed with laughter again. He was sounding more and more like the old Jack I used to love – still loved, really.

'I'll pick you up at nine.'

Chapter Twenty-seven

'Wow! I can see I'm not the only one who's changed. You look gorgeous. I love your hair; it really suits you down.'

'Are you going to keep commenting on my appearance all the time, now that you're a poof?'

'Might do. I'll even give you a makeover if you like.'

'Not just now, thanks.'

I looked him up and down. Tight black T-shirt. Black PVC trousers. Diamond stud in his ear.

'Jack, I hope you're not going to act like a gigantic cliché now that you've come out. I mean, look what you're wearing. I'm not saying that you don't look well – because you do – but, seriously, aren't things going to be hard enough for you tonight? Do you really want to walk into the pub dressed like that?'

'I figured, why not? Give them something to really talk about. I've been hiding my light under a bushel for far too long.'

'Fair enough,' I said. I guessed that it was probably just a phase he was going through, that once he got used to his new identity he'd start dressing normally again. I hoped. I clambered into the passenger seat. 'Just try not to drive like a maniac, please.'

'Just try not to be the passenger from hell, please.'

'Oh, shut up.'

'You shut up.' He grinned, leaned across and kissed me on the cheek. Then he drove off down the hill like a maniac.

I turned and looked at him from time to time, marvelling at how I'd been fooled for so long. It seemed so obvious now. Of course he was gay. He was virtually the perfect man in every way; how could he possibly be heterosexual?

It was like George Michael in the 80s. A generation of girls had fallen head over heels in love. And did any of us so much as suspect he was gay? Not one. We were too busy obsessing about that dazzling smile, that orange tan, those muscular calves, those nifty dance moves, the dashing white shorts, the highlights. There was a time when

George's mug shot graced the wall of every unisex hair salon in the country. And still we didn't cop. Looking back, it seemed surreal.

I was the first to walk into the pub, as Jack was having difficulty finding a parking space. It was Thursday night – music night – and the place was already packed.

Shem was the first to see me. 'Ah, here she comes. Lock up your sons.'

'What's that supposed to mean?' I was in no mood.

'Nothing,' said Shem, alarmed and back-pedalling furiously. 'I didn't mean a thing by it. Just a turn of phrase, that's all. Can I buy you a drink?'

I must have seriously rattled him. Shem never offered to buy anybody a drink.

'I'll have two bottles of Miller, please.'

'Two!'

I nodded. 'I'm very thirsty tonight.'

A woebegone expression on his face, Shem turned to Johnny. 'Two bottles of Miller for the lady.'

Johnny nodded curtly at me and got the drinks with his trademark rapid-fire movements.

I made space for Tom Delaney, who was returning to his barstool from the jacks – at least, I assumed that was where he was coming from; it would explain why his fly was undone. Away from his barstool, he was revealed as a big, shambling wreck of a man. He climbed back onto his throne and regarded me curiously, the stem of his pipe rattling between his few remaining teeth.

The sudden draught on my back told me that somebody had just walked in behind me. The looks on Shem's and Tom's faces told me that person was Jack. He came up and stood beside me.

'Shem! Long time no see. How are you going?'

Jack held out his massive hand for Shem to shake. Shem took it silently and moved his own hand feebly up and down before letting it drop.

'Tom! Good to see you.'

Tom couldn't or wouldn't take Jack's proffered hand. His mouth hung open, revealing the full magnificence of a lifetime lacking in oral hygiene. Jack patted him on the shoulder instead. Whether he actively meant it as an insult, or whether it was a reflex reaction, I couldn't be sure; either way, Tom swiped at his shoulder as if he'd just been injected with a deadly virus. Johnny was watching all this like a hawk.

Furious with the men, I snatched up the two bottles of beer, handed one to Jack and steered him away from the two old farts. 'Come on. Let's find a seat.'

The hurt was evident in Jack's features. He'd known Shem and Tom his whole life.

'Don't worry,' I whispered into his ear, 'he probably thinks you're after his body.' This raised the ghost of a smile.

Our next problem was to find somewhere to park ourselves. The music room itself was jammed.

The strange looks we were getting from all and sundry made the prospect of asking anyone if we could join them at their table seem quite daunting.

'Over here, Jack!' came a familiar voice from the far recesses of the room.

Matt Power and a blonde girl were sitting in a dark corner booth.

Jack gave me a look. 'Would you mind?'

'It doesn't look as if we have much choice.'

So we went over and sat down with Matt and this week's totty.

'How are you, Lainey?' He actually winked at me. The nerve!

'Couldn't be better. You?' I eyed him coldly. Okay, so I hadn't been mortally wounded by his conduct, but that didn't mean he should get off scot-free.

'Great form. This is Anita.'

He clearly had a type, anyway – although this latest model was younger, skinnier and blonder than me. Every woman's worst nightmare – I'd been replaced by a younger blonde! Anita gave me a suspicious look, which I decided to ignore.

Matt turned his attention to his brother. 'Jesus, Jack. What the *fuck* are you wearing?'

'What's wrong with it?'

'You're asking for trouble, mate. Could you not tone it down a little, for your own sake?'

'This is me, Matt. I'm not hiding it any more. I did that for far too long.'

'All right. On your own head be it.'

358

Anita was clearly smitten with Matt. She was glued to his arm, gazing continually into his eyes and giggling at everything he said. She didn't go unrewarded: he paid her plenty of attention. Matt had the knack of making a girl feel as if she were the only person in the room/field/tree. I should know. I admit I felt the odd pang of jealousy, but mostly I felt sorry for her. She was young and even more foolish than I was. I wondered if she had been the one in the surgery the week before. If I got drunk enough, I might ask her.

Jack put on a great show, being entertaining and expansive as usual, making sure Anita felt included. It couldn't have been easy for him, but he made it look like it was.

A mass exodus from the music room, as the musicians took a break, was our cue to move in. We received a mixed reception from the remaining inhabitants. Some nodded; some gaped, wide-eyed, at Jack and then quickly looked away again; some of them greeted Matt warmly. None of them greeted Jack warmly. But we were in. When we were seated, I squeezed Jack's knee in support.

'Careful,' he said. 'Someone might start a rumour that I'm straight.'

The musicians returned, and the session recommenced. I was relieved; it made the fact that none of the locals were talking to Jack less obvious. They played a selection of tunes, the music transforming the plain, box-shaped little room into an aural paradise. As usual, Johnny entered the room mid-way into the session, set down the glasses he was collecting and sat down at the piano, joining in seamlessly. Then the call was made for people to sing.

A woman called Jackie, who was home from England, murdered two Mary Black numbers in quick succession. She was a musical serial killer. She suffered further from comparison when Matt sang 'Raglan Road' directly after her. If Anita hadn't been impressed enough beforehand, she now looked ready to lay down her body and soul for Matt – and she probably would, in a few hours' time.

Next, Dixie, the most ancient of the accordion players, sang 'Don't Forget Your Shovel'. Never mind the shovel, he forgot most of the words. He got through by making up a lot of them and inserting a few well-placed 'la-la-la's. He was still better than Jackie.

'Okay, who's next to give us an oul' tune?' Johnny shouted enthusiastically, fingers poised above the piano keys, raring to go.

'I'll go.'

The room fell prey to the most deafening silence in the history of deafening silences. I wanted the ground to open up and swallow me whole – and I wasn't even the one who had offered to sing. *What is Jack thinking?* I thought. I looked across at Matt. His face had the same expression I could feel on my own.

There was an ominous scraping sound as Johnny pushed back his stool, got up from the piano, picked up the empties and walked back to the bar. Nobody said a word.

'Will one of you accompany me?' There was a desperate, fake cheeriness to Jack's voice.

Silence. Then: 'I will.'

This time it *was* me that had spoken, although I scarcely believed it myself.

'Thanks, Lainey.' Jack squeezed my arm as I stood up and walked shakily across to the piano.

'Don't thank me yet,' I hissed back. 'I'm a tad rusty.'

I sat down on the piano stool and looked down at the alien keys. *What was I thinking?* The musicians and locals alike looked alarmed as Jack rose from his seat and stood in the centre of the room, a giant, PVC-clad figure. This was not the custom in Power's Select Lounge and Bar; people were meant to remain sedately in their seats whilst singing.

I held my breath as Jack began. His voice strong and clear, he sang the opening lines of Gloria Gaynor's 'I Will Survive'. The ultimate gay anthem. You go, girl!

He made it through the first verse unaccompanied. I played a few faltering notes; then a few more. By the time he got to the chorus, we were sucking diesel!

Jack started to clap his hands in time to the music, gesturing to his audience to do the same.

Matt and Anita began to clap enthusiastically. I would have too, if my hands hadn't been otherwise occupied. Behind me, I could discern a few half-hearted clapping noises.

When the song ended, Jack got just enough applause that he announced he was going to sing another song.

'This one is especially for the mammy,' he declared. He bent his head towards me and hissed, '"Dancing Queen".'

'Come on, Jack. Would you ever sit back down? How am I supposed to know how to play "Dancing Queen"? And you never liked Abba before. Don't tell me your taste in music has gone the same way as your taste in clothes.'

'Come on, Lainey. It'll be a laugh. Give it your best shot.'

I gave it my best shot.

Someone must have gone to get Bridie, because she appeared at the door during the second verse, looking proud as punch. And well she might. Not only was her son a fine figure of a man, he was a damn good singer, too – not to mention a pretty decent performer. He confessed to me later on that he'd taken singing lessons in San Francisco.

My relief at the end of 'Dancing Queen' was short-lived: Jack announced his intention of singing 'just one more'. By the time he finished 'I Am What I Am', you couldn't get in the door of the music room. You couldn't see out of it, either; it

362

was too crowded with bodies. The round of applause that followed fairly lifted the roof.

Jack dragged me to my feet and forced me to take a bow with him. I stopped laughing long enough to tell him how proud I was of him.

'I'm proud of you, too,' he said. 'You're the best fag-hag I've ever had.'

'Oh, shut up, you great big raving queen.'

Chapter Twenty-eight

It had been two weeks since that memorable night in the pub. It was mid-May, and the weather was still uncommonly good.

A lot had happened. My parents had returned from Beijing, bursting with the news that Tatiana, Chen and LuLing were coming home to live in Dublin at the end of the year. My mother was now an expert on all things Oriental ('Imagine not knowing that the samurai were an ancient Japanese warrior caste'). Hazel had got that job she'd been telling me about. She'd already started and was loving every minute of it. Her working day began at quarter past nine, she had a twenty-minute coffee break at eleven, an hour and a quarter for lunch and more coffee at four, and she went home at half-five on the dot. And she did this only three days a week. No wonder she loved it. Where did I sign up?

Things had improved considerably for Jack at home, too. Bridie had summoned the whole family – including Johnny – and given them a stern lecture concerning their behaviour towards Jack. Jack said the grand finale of her speech had been when she told the assembled throng, 'He's here, he's queer, get used to it.'

Apparently, she was a huge fan of *The Ellen Show*.

Jack and I laughed solidly for about ten minutes when he told me this. Then we spent the next ten minutes making up alternative slogans: 'He's here, he's queer, so have another beer,' 'He's here, he's queer, he's got a pierced ear' and – Jack's personal favourite – 'He's here, he's queer, and what a great rear.'

But I knew that Jack's laughter was partly a cover-up. It would take more than a good sound telling-off from Bridie, undisputed boss of the household though she was, to sway Johnny and a couple of Jack's elder brothers. The harsh truth had to be faced: it might never happen.

I put these thoughts out of my head. It was far too nice a day. I had absconded from work early – one advantage of being your own boss. And that's what I had become since I'd moved down to Ballyknock.

'My own boss.' I said the words out loud. They did have a lovely ring to them. As long as I got my work done, I could come and go as I pleased. I had settled into a nice little routine of 9.30 to 5.30 – a far cry from crazy Dublin working hours. There were a few disadvantages, sure. The facilities weren't so hot and my office wasn't exactly luxurious; but we got by. Then there was the drawback of being apprehended by clients in the local supermarket and pumped for free legal advice. At least I didn't have to worry about clients approaching me after Mass; I avoided this by not going to Mass. But, all in all, I had few complaints.

I strolled along the now-familiar roads around Ardskeha. Terence scampered a few yards ahead. The only sign of his recent ordeal was a funny patch on his left side where the fur hadn't fully grown back yet after his operation. He turned and looked back at me, as if telling me to step on it. He had a piece of wood in his mouth. It stuck straight out like a single, giant, rotten tooth.

I'd lately come to the realisation that Terence and I had a lot in common. We both needed a pat on the head every now and then, and someone to feed us biscuits.

The sun shone pleasantly on our respective heads, and the birds were in fine voice; it was like having our own private concert. The hedgerows were lush with bluebells, buttercups, cow parsley and clusters of small, white, as yet unidentified flowers, which I intended to look up in my new wildflower book when I got home. But the un-disputed winner of Flower of the Day had to be the hawthorn – masses of white, sweetly scented blooms, hanging overhead like heavy clusters of precious gems. Who needed Aladdin's Cave? Everything was so beautiful, so fertile, so alive. I was reminded of that passage from the Bible – I couldn't recall the exact words: something about lilies in the field not having to toil, yet Solomon in all his glory was never clothed as beautifully. That day, I felt as if I fully understood those words for the first time. Maybe I'd resign and sit around in a hedgerow all day long. Nice work if you could get it.

I was so lost in the joys of nature that I didn't realise I'd walked further down this road than I'd ever walked before. The views were familiar – the river valley still to my left, the fields still rolling uphill to my right – yet different. Terence seemed more excited than ever. He hadn't been here before either. We crossed a small, ancient-looking stone bridge, the river beneath it reduced to a mere trickle by the unusually dry weather.

I rounded a bend, and my eye was caught by a flash of vivid blue. It was in a small raised area at the corner of a crossroads. As I drew closer, I saw that it was a tiny old graveyard carpeted with bluebells. I'd never seen such a stunning mass of wildflowers. It was as if the bluebells were on steroids. Well, I reasoned, they *were* well fertilised. I hoped that, when I died, I would get the opportunity to nourish such beautiful flowers.

The entrance to the graveyard consisted of a small wrought-iron gate set into a high, rough stone wall. I looked around, but there was nobody there. With some difficulty, I managed to draw back the rusty bolt and let myself in.

I called Terence, who bounded in behind me and cocked his leg against the nearest headstone before I could stop him. The stone – like many of the others – was clearly very old; any words that hadn't been eroded over time were concealed by moss. They weren't all like that, though. Some were newer. I carried out a swift survey and found that the most recent date was 1986.

I sat down companionably beside this flat tombstone. Looking back, it seems like a strange thing to have done; but, at the time, the place was so peaceful – magical, even – that I just wanted to stay and absorb the feeling for as long as possible. It was as if the emotional turmoil of the last few months had never existed – or, if it had, it simply didn't matter any more.

I examined the tombstone beside me more carefully. It might have been the most recent, but it hadn't escaped the ravages of time. Trailing ivy obscured most of the wording and the stone was dappled with moss. There appeared to be a verse on it. I tugged at the ivy to reveal the first words:

Gather ye rosebuds while ye may,
Old Time is still a-flying;

I pulled away the remaining ivy to reveal the rest of the verse.

And this same flower that smiles today
Tomorrow will be dying.

It seemed like an odd choice of verse for a tombstone. Who did the grave belong to? I scraped away the moss at the top of the stone.

Mary Power
of Power's Cottage, Ardskeha, Ballyknock
Died 16 May 1986, aged 84
R.I.P.

And her daughter
Ellen Power
Died 10 January 1940, aged 6 weeks
R.I.P.

'Happy anniversary, Mary,' I whispered. It seemed important not to talk too loudly. Somehow, I wasn't rattled; I was just overcome with sympathy. Poor Mary, to lose a child like that. I felt I should say a prayer or something. I blessed myself and said a quick Hail Mary. Then I just sat for a long time.

The sun beating down on my head seemed to be willing me to stay. So did the birds, the trees, the bluebells – the silent inhabitants of the cemetery. I felt as if I was melting into my surroundings. And it was at that precise moment that I admitted to myself the knowledge that had been building up inside me for some time now. I had been feeling it every time I looked at Terence, or Slinky. Or the other day, when I'd been planting flower seeds in the garden of Power's Cottage and had seen that they wouldn't bloom until September, when I'd be long gone. When I caught my first glimpse of the cottage every time I drove up the hill. When I looked across at the rolling hills, the river valley, the mares and foals in the fields. Even when I tasted Patricia's jam or sat in on the sessions in the pub.

I didn't want to go back to the city. I wanted to stay here – to make this place my home.

The thought, once acknowledged, didn't overwhelm me as I would have expected. Rather, it was a relief to get it out in the open.

I must have been sitting very still, thinking these thoughts: a butterfly that had been flitting around the graveyard alighted delicately on my knee. I felt that she was staring at me, but that was ridiculous. I stayed still as a statue for several minutes until she flew away. My eyelids heavy from the unrelenting sun, I lay down on a bed of moss and bluebells and closed my eyes.

I'm not sure how long I slept, but when I awoke, the sun had travelled right across the sky and was beginning to drop. I shivered. The cold must have woken me up. I sat up and rubbed my eyes. Terence was lying beside me, panting lightly, looking at me intently and waiting for my next move.

'Why didn't you wake me?'

He sat up and licked my hand in response, then looked at me again, head cocked to one side. The downward tilt of his eye, the upward tilt of his ear … I could have sworn that he was smiling at me.

'Come on, boy,' I said, struggling to my feet, 'let's go home.'

Slinky was there to greet us when we arrived back at Power's Cottage. She ran along the fence like a gymnast on a beam and made a perfect dismount, before wrapping herself around my legs and meowing hungrily up at me. It was way past her dinner-time.

I'd only intended to be out for half an hour, so I'd left every window in the house wide open – something else I couldn't do in Dublin. I opened the front door and went inside, the two animals hot on my heels. The gust of wind I brought in with me made the wind chimes inside the door jangle. In fact, the whole house felt breezy, as if the inside had become the outside. And it smelt so fresh, so fragrant – although it wasn't just fresh air; there was some sort of flowery scent…. I inhaled deeply. Roses.

Up ahead, Slinky stood motionless in the doorway to the sitting room. Then she arched her back, her fur standing on end, and spat viciously.

371

'What is it, Slinky?'

She flew between my legs and back out the half-open front door.

'Who's there?' I called out.

I advanced slowly and peeked into the sitting room. Terence whimpered and hid behind me, his tail between his legs. There was nobody there, but the scent of roses was more intense. I moved cautiously into the room and glanced above the fireplace for Mary Power's reassuring image. The picture was crooked – as if someone had taken it off the wall and failed to replace it properly.

I went over and adjusted it. Mary Power and I smiled at each other.

'Thank you,' I said – or did I just think it?

Because now I knew exactly what I had to do.

Chapter Twenty-nine

I didn't arrive in Dublin until well after eight that Friday evening. I had called the office, but there was no reply. Tyrone wasn't answering his mobile, either, so I chanced calling around to his house.

Tyrone lived in Ranelagh, in an elegant red-brick building with a well-established, well-manicured front garden. It was a shame he didn't have someone to share it with. I felt an unexpected wave of pity towards my boss. For all I knew, that pity was misplaced. He chose to live this way; maybe he liked it. And, besides, what was I doing wasting my sympathy on a man who lived in a house worth over two million? It was amazing that he and his money hadn't been snapped up by some manipulative minx a long time ago. There was no way he was short of offers. Much to his amusement, his name often cropped up on 'Most Eligible Bachelor' lists.

As luck would have it, he appeared to be in. At least, the light was on in the front room. I rang the doorbell and peered in at the bay window; I could just make out a shadow moving behind the heavy curtains.

Tyrone opened the door a few seconds later. He was still wearing his work shirt and suit trousers; his jacket and tie had been replaced by an enormous, grey, hand-knitted cardigan. He was holding a crystal tumbler containing dark-orange liquid and ice. I was sure he wasn't meant to be drinking scotch, but tonight wasn't the night to bring it up.

'Hi. Nice cardie.'

'Lainey? What are you doing here?' His unkempt silver eyebrows were raised in surprise.

'I thought I'd check up on you. Find out what you *really* get up to on a Friday night.'

'Is something wrong?'

'No.'

'You'd better come in.'

He held the door open wider for me and I entered the long, dark hallway. On the rare occasions when I had visited Tyrone at home, I had always got the same feeling. It wasn't anything I could put my finger on, exactly, but the place needed a woman's touch. Not a woman like me, obviously. I meant one with proper home-making skills. Personally, I wouldn't have had a clue where to start.

Tyrone hurried ahead of me into the living room. I followed him in, just in time to catch him hiding something behind a stack of books. Judging by the aroma in the room, it was probably a dirty ashtray. But I wasn't going to say anything about that either.

'Drink?'

'Got any whiskey?'

'Um … don't know. I'll have to check.'

'I'll have a whiskey and 7-up, if you have it.'

This made him wince, as I had known it would; I knew how much it irked him to dilute his precious firewater. But I couldn't resist. He went off to fix my drink, turning the volume down on the stereo on his way out of the room.

Not for the first time, I was struck by the similarity between my boss and Inspector Morse – although, while Morse had ice-blue eyes, Tyrone's were molten brown; and, while Morse listened to opera, Tyrone existed on a strict musical diet of diddly-eye. You could take the man out of the bog….

He returned. 'There.' He pressed the drink into my hand. 'Enjoy – although I don't know how that's possible. Anyway, cheers.'

We clinked glasses and he sat down opposite me in his armchair, a quizzical look on his face. 'Are you planning on telling me what this is about, or am I going to have to guess?'

'Can't a girl pay her boss a friendly visit once in a while?'

'Come off it. What have you done? Have you sold somebody the wrong house?'

'No!'

'You called the district court judge a grumpy old bastard and he held you in contempt?'

'No.' I was laughing now.

'What, then?'

'Tyrone, I've been thinking.'

'This should be good.' He leaned back in his armchair and took a large gulp of his drink, as if steeling himself.

'Well, you know I've been in Ballyknock for about seven months now –'

'Let me stop you there. I think I know what you're going to say. I understand you must be dying to get back to your life in Dublin; but I swear to you, I only need you there for a couple more months. And I won't forget what you've done.'

'It's not that at all.'

'What, then?'

'Well, the thing is … I really like it down there. I was thinking I might like to stay.'

Tyrone blinked at me a couple of times. I took the opportunity to keep babbling.

'I mean, business has been booming – there's plenty of work for two solicitors. And you wanted to cut back on work; I'd be there to take the pressure off whenever you needed me. You'd be able to take lots of afternoons off to play golf or go fishing.'

He interrupted, 'I was planning on doing that anyway.'

'I know. I mean, obviously, you're the boss and you're entitled to do whatever you want. But me being there would make it easier for you to get out and about. What do you think?'

Tyrone took another gulp of scotch and stared off into space. I sat there, breath bated. I couldn't tell whether or not he was trying to make me sweat.

When I couldn't stand it any more, I said, 'Will you even consider it?'

'No. I won't consider it –'

'Oh, Tyrone, why?'

'Because I don't need to. You're hired.'

'Really! Oh, thank you!' I jumped out of my seat and clapped my hands. 'Can I hug you?'

'Best not. An old fogey like me might get funny ideas.'

'Oh, Tyrone, this is brilliant! I can't thank you enough.'

'There's no need to thank me. A girl like you might come in useful around the office. You can make my coffee and type up my letters when Patricia's off sick.'

'Very funny. Seriously, though, you won't regret this.'

'I know I won't. I only hope that *you* don't.'

'Don't worry about me. I'll be fine.'

377

I had decided to stay with my parents that night, on the basis that I couldn't stomach Iseult. It was near ten when I arrived home. The house was in darkness and the driveway was empty. *Shit*. I'd forgotten my key. I fumbled around in the rockery in the front garden…. Bingo. Mum still kept a spare key under the ornamental Buddha.

I let myself in, turned on all the lights and looked around for clues to my parents' whereabouts. I was filled with childish indignation that they weren't home when it suited me. So what if they didn't know I was coming? Where were they, anyway, at this hour on a Friday night? My parents never went out any more. They were far too old for that sort of thing.

It wasn't until the next morning that the mystery was solved. I stumbled into the kitchen, bleary-eyed and dishevelled, at about half past nine, wearing a white towelling robe that I'd owned since the age of sixteen. My mother was already up and about – showered, dressed, made up and clattering about the kitchen. She was humming a tune I didn't recognise.

'Morning, Elena. Sit down and I'll make you a nice healthy breakfast.'

I didn't like the sound of that. Past experience indicated that this would involve lots of bran. I'd munch on a few spoonfuls to keep her happy, then buy a Danish on the way out.

'Aren't you surprised to see me?' I asked.

'No. Sure, isn't that fancy car of yours parked right outside?'

'So where were you last night? I didn't even hear you come in.'

She beamed at me as she busily opened and closed presses. 'We went ballroom dancing. It's your father's new hobby.'

Dad? Ballroom dancing? Never! 'Was it his idea?'

'No, it was mine. Last night was his first night, but I really think he's taken to it already.'

The image of Dad doing the foxtrot, wearing a monkey suit and a snooty expression, was too bizarre to contemplate. I'd only seen him dance once before – when he'd got pissed at my cousin Eileen's wedding. He'd forced the mother of the bride to jive with him, humiliating her thoroughly before putting his back out. I hoped Mum wouldn't be too disappointed when this particular hobby fizzled out after a couple of weeks.

'Now! Get that down you. Wait till you see all the photos we took in Beijing.'

She all but ran out of the room, but not before handing me a bowl full of something that looked as if it should have been served in a nosebag. She returned seconds later, smiling broadly and carrying no less than five packs of photos.

'Someone was busy.'

'It was your father with his new photographic equipment. You know, we had to pay a fine at Heathrow – two hundred and fifty euros for excess

379

baggage, just because of him and all his gear. I don't know – that man!' Mum shook her head. But I knew her, and she didn't sound the tiniest bit annoyed to me.

And so for the next hour – or so it seemed – we looked at baby photos. I had to admit that my niece was adorable, even though I said so myself. I could claim no connection to the jet-black spiky hair, the cinnamon skin, the massive brown eyes; but the nose…. Was it possible that she had my nose? There were a variety of poses: LuLing sleeping; LuLing crying; LuLing smiling (wind, apparently); LuLing staring at the ceiling; Tatiana and LuLing; Chen and LuLing; Tatiana, Chen and LuLing; proud granny with LuLing; proud grand-dad with LuLing…. Need I continue?

I chose a few photos to take back with me. They weren't bad. Maybe Dad had a latent talent. Then I stood up. Enough was enough.

'Where are you going?' Mum looked disappointed.

'Upstairs, to get dressed. Then I'm going into town to meet the girls for lunch.'

'So soon! I was hoping you could help me put the photos into albums. I bought ten new ones, you know.'

'I'd love to, but I promised to meet them and I can't let them down. I'll help you with the photos later on.'

'You've hardly touched your breakfast.'

'Ah, Mum. You know I don't eat that mush.'

'It's not mush. It's a nutritious, high-energy cereal, packed with fibre.'

I gave her a look.

'Oh, have an apple, then.' She knew she wasn't going to win this particular argument.

To appease her, I grabbed an apple, rubbed it a couple of times against my ragged bathrobe and took a bite.

'Are you regular these days, Elena?'

'Mum, please!'

It was nearing midday when I pulled up outside the end-of-terrace house in Sallynoggin. The only remarkable thing about the grey, pebble-dashed building was its southside address, which lent it a market value of six times its true worth.

It felt weird being here again after all this time; strange, yet familiar. The Child of Prague – head intact – still stood sentry in the downstairs window. The front door was slightly ajar, held open by a thick green wire that led to an extension lead on the front path. I rang the doorbell a couple of times, but there was no reply. After a while, I tentatively pushed open the door.

'Anybody home?'

The only person who appeared to be home was Pope John Paul II, who smiled benignly at me from his ornate gilt frame on the wall. I followed the green wire along the narrow hallway and through

381

the galley kitchen. It disappeared out the back door. As I followed it, an electrical whirring noise grew louder. I pushed open the back door.

Paul was strimming the hedge, his ears encased in bright orange muffs. I couldn't figure out a way of getting his attention without risking him cutting off an arm, so I sat down on the step outside the back door to wait for him. I was prepared to be patient, but, as it turned out, I didn't have to be; a few seconds later, Paul inexplicably turned and looked right at me. After a puzzled stare, he turned off the machine, pulled the earmuffs down around his neck and walked slowly towards me. He was wearing a pair of old combats and a U2 T-shirt that I happened to know he'd owned since he was seventeen.

He didn't stop walking until he literally loomed over me. I had to crane my neck and shade my eyes in order to look at him properly. Not that this helped me any. His expression was illegible.

'What are you doing here?'

I was being asked that question a lot lately. I was going to have to stop popping up unannounced all over the place.

'I was in the area, and I thought I'd call in and see how you were doing.'

'What were you doing in the area?' Still the stony countenance.

I didn't blame him for being suspicious. He of all people knew what a consummate liar I was. But

I wasn't worried: I had my story learnt off pat, as usual.

'I was at the hairdresser's I used to go to – you know, the one above the Spar in the village. I wanted to see if they could fit me in.'

'And could they?'

'No.'

'Maybe I can help you out.' He held the strimmer above his head and revved it theatrically.

I laughed. 'You're okay. It was a wash and blow-dry I was after, not a full decapitation.'

To my immense relief, Paul smiled and sat down on the step beside me.

The truth, for those of you who are interested, was that I'd remembered that his mother routinely got him to come around on Saturday mornings to do various odd jobs ('The devil makes work for idle hands, Paul').

I watched Paul shyly as he made small talk. The veins in his hands and forearms were protruding in the heat. A rivulet of sweat ran down his forehead, his temple, his cheekbone, his jawline, his sinewy neck, before disappearing in a trickle down the frayed neck of his T-shirt.

'Would you like a cool drink?' I said, interrupting whatever it was he had been saying.

'Um … yeah, that'd be nice.'

I went back into the kitchen and rooted around in the fridge and presses. All I could find was Ribena. And it wasn't even Toothkind. I remembered Paul's mother serving it to me in a wineglass, the one and only time I'd been to dinner at the house – as if that was fooling anybody.

I could do better than that. I slipped out of the house and around the corner to the off-licence. What a wonderful thing to have right on your doorstep! Completely wasted on Paul's mum, of course. I purchased a six-pack straight from the fridge and fairly skipped back to the house, delighted by my own ingenuity. I triumphantly handed Paul a beer.

'There you go. What every working man needs after a hard day's graft.'

'What's your excuse, then?'

'I don't need one. Does your mother not object to living around the corner from an offie?'

'You know her. She objects to anything that might possibly lead to somebody somewhere having some fun.'

'Where is she, anyhow?'

Paul took a large gulp of beer and sighed. 'Mass. Where else?'

'Is it a holy day, then?'

He looked at me solemnly. 'Lainey, don't you know that every day is a holy day in the O'Toole household?'

We both giggled, savouring the cool, bitter tang of the beer and the contrasting hot, sweet caress of the sun.

'I could help you, if you like,' I said.

'With what?'

'The gardening.'

'What, *you*?' Paul found this extremely funny.

'Yes, me. What's so funny about that?'

'Nothing. It's just that manual labour has never been your thing.'

'How do you know? You've never seen me doing manual work.' I was quite indignant.

'Exactly.'

'Well, the offer stands.'

'Thanks.'

'You're welcome.'

I wasn't looking at him, but I could tell he was still smiling to himself. Oh, well; let him. Wasn't it better than having him annoyed with me? I really hadn't been sure what kind of reception I'd get. I should have known. Paul could never be mean to anyone for any length of time.

I still didn't fully understand what I was doing there. And I still wasn't sure what I wanted to say to him. All I knew was that I'd had to come.

'When are you expecting your mother back?'

'Any time now. Why? Are you afraid she'll kick you out?'

'She wouldn't – would she?'

'I don't know.' He smiled. 'Maybe if she sees the beer.'

'Tell you what. Why don't I help you finish up here, and then we can go out for lunch? My treat.'

Paul looked doubtfully at me.

'That's if you don't have other plans,' I said. *Involving Iseult*, I thought.

'No,' he said slowly, 'I don't have plans. It's not that. I'm just concerned about your clothes getting wrecked.'

'Is that all? Don't worry about my clothes. That's what God invented washing machines for. Come on – the sooner we get started, the sooner we finish.'

Chapter Thirty

For the next hour, Paul strimmed while I collected branches and dumped them on the compost heap. It was all I was qualified to do, really. Paul was by far the more expert gardener.

Watching him when he wasn't looking, I decided I liked him with his gardening hat on. It suited him better than the stuffy accountant look. He almost reminded me of that gardener bloke off the telly whom I fancied. Come to think of it, I fancied nearly all the gardeners on the telly, even the overtly gay ones. I didn't know what it was. There was just something so *earthy* about what they did for a living. Some occupations were just more attractive than others. Photographers – I liked those, too; but they had to be proper ones, mind, not amateur photographers like my father who wore slacks. Building labourers, especially on hot days when they removed their checked shirts and performed daredevil stunts on scaffolding. Mechanics – all that oil. And cowboys…. What can I say? The ultimate in masculinity.

Accountants didn't feature too high on the list.

By the time we'd finished the garden, my pristine white top wasn't all that pristine any more. I didn't care. I was happy. We decided that we each deserved another tinny after all our hard work. We were just cracking into them when the back door flew open and the Wicked Witch of the Southside stuck her head out. We instinctively hid our cans behind our backs like bold children.

'Elena.' Her greeting was cool.

'Hello, Mrs O'Toole.'

'Paul, what about that fruit tree? It needs pruning.' I'd forgotten what an annoying, high-pitched, nasal Cork accent she had.

'I'll do it later. Me and Lainey are just heading out for a spot of lunch.'

She sniffed. 'But I'm just after buying us a couple of lovely chops.'

'I'll have mine for my tea.'

'Okay, so.' She slammed the door shut, her face like a slapped arse.

'Oops,' I said. I looked searchingly into Paul's face. 'We don't have to go out for lunch, you know.

I could piss off and leave you both here to enjoy your chops.'

'No! Don't mind her. I'm just going to run upstairs and have a quick shower – five minutes at the most, I promise. Will you be okay?'

'Yeah, fine. Go ahead.'

I watched as he hid the remaining cans in the shed and then disappeared into the kitchen. He flashed me an encouraging smile as he left. I could see his mother quizzing him inside. 'What's *she* doing here?'

I tried to see things from her point of view. She was probably lonely. And the one day of the week when she got to see her only son, I – brazen hussy that I was – spirited him away for the afternoon. I could see her moving around in the kitchen. I supposed I should go in and talk to her. I could hardly stand out here when she was only a few feet away, behind the door, and there was no way she was going to make the first move. It was up to me. Time to make nice.

I knocked gently and opened the door into the kitchen. I gave Mrs O'Toole my best conciliatory smile, but all she did was look me up and down disapprovingly. The top I was wearing, which had seemed perfectly acceptable two minutes earlier, suddenly felt obscenely low-cut and tight-fitting. Mrs O'Toole herself could easily have been mistaken for a plain-clothes nun. She was wearing what could only be described as a smock – grey –

and she had a plain gold crucifix around her neck. Her hair was atrocious. It was as if she'd gone to the hairdresser's and said, 'Make me look as un-attractive as possible.' And as for make-up – forget it. She was poles apart from my own mother, who wouldn't be seen dead without her lipstick. (I'm serious. She'd literally given me instructions as to the exact shade and brand of lippy she wanted to wear when she was being laid out. Dad had told me that she'd tried to include this in her will, but that the family solicitor wasn't having any of it. I think he might have been having me on.)

It was a pity about Mrs O'Toole, because you could tell she was pretty, deep down. Her features were regular and her bone structure good. Her waist was still tiny, too – must have been all that fasting and clean living. I mentally sifted through the selection of oul' fellas I knew in Ballymuck, bachelor clients and Power's regulars alike. There had to be somebody I could set her up with.

'Cup of tea, Elena?'

'Yes, please!' I said this as if she'd just offered me a free week in the Algarve. A breakthrough!

I did my best to make desperate small talk, as the red light of the Sacred Heart shone down on my head. Had she been away recently? Oh, yes; she'd just come back from ten days in Lourdes. And had she had a good time? Oh, yes. She'd had a lovely time pushing wheelchairs around and attending candlelight vigils. (I prefer candlelight dinners, myself.) She'd even bought a brand spanking new holy-water font for the hall. She showed it to me. Blue and white plastic. 'Isn't it gorgeous!' I said. Honestly, I made myself sick sometimes. I was going straight to hell, I had no doubt about it.

When I had run out of things to say – after about two minutes – Mrs O'Toole said, 'So how long have you been back on the scene, then?'

I was taken aback. 'What? … Oh, no – Paul and I aren't together. I just called by to say hello. As a friend.'

She shot me an incredulous look and said, 'I was wondering why that skinny girl hadn't been around much lately.'

Skinny girl? It had to be Iseult. Did that make me the fat girl?

I was just about to reiterate that I was no longer her son's girlfriend when said son burst through the door. That had to have been the quickest shower in history. There were clearly advantages to having little or no hair. Paul was most likely terrified of leaving me and his mother alone in the same room for any significant length of time. He'd probably been imagining all manner of carnage while he was upstairs.

'Ready?'

As ready as I'll ever be.

Half an hour later, we were sitting in a hotel in Dalkey. The lunchtime rush was over, so we managed to get a table by the window, overlooking the sea. The waves lapped indolently against the rocks and the horizon disappeared into the haze. I broke the habit of a lifetime and ordered a salad, shocking us both.

It came to light, in the course of the conversation, that Paul had the next two weeks off work.

'Are you going away?'

'No.'

'What are you going to do, then?'

'Don't know, really. Just hang about.'

'That's a bit of a waste of your annual leave, surely?'

He shrugged. 'There are a lot of jobs to be done in my mother's house – painting, tiling, that sort of thing. It'll be good to get them out of the way.'

'Two weeks with your mother? You'll go nuts.'

'Will you just drop it, please?'

I looked at him in surprise. 'Take the head off me, why don't you?'

'Sorry. I didn't mean to snap.'

'But you did.'

'Look, if you must know, I was supposed to be going on holiday with Iseult. Today.' He glanced at his watch. 'I should have been landing in Ibiza about now.'

That shut me up. The great unmentionable had finally been mentioned. I speared a piece of cucumber with my fork and chewed it solemnly, keeping my focus on my plate.

'Well?' said Paul.

'Well what?'

'Don't you want to know why I'm in Dalkey instead of Ibiza?'

'Only if you want to tell me.'

'We broke up last week. It was too late for me to swap my leave with anyone else. So here I am – two weeks on my hands, and nothing to do with them.'

So many questions were buzzing around in my head. What had gone wrong? Who had dumped who? Why hadn't Chris told me? Who had dumped who?

'Did you – I mean, I'm very sorry to hear that.'

'Are you really?'

'Of course.'

'I finished with her, by the way.'

'Did you?' I tried to keep my tone as neutral – and as sincere – as possible. 'Poor Iseult. Was she very upset?'

'Hardly. She's brought her new boyfriend to Ibiza with her.'

'No! You mean they've gone on *your* holiday together?'

'I don't mind. She paid me back my half, so she can do what she likes.'

'Who is he?'

'Some hot new actor. She met him while he was being interviewed for the magazine.'

393

'What's his name?'

'Dylan Mayberry.'

'Never heard of him. He must be crap.'

'He's got a bit part in the new James Bond.'

'Everyone knows you don't have to be able to act to be in a Bond movie. I'm telling you, he's probably crap.'

Paul was laughing. 'You don't have to do this, Lainey. I'm not upset.'

'You sure?'

'Positive.'

He played around with his food for a bit. 'I thought you'd have heard already.'

'How would I hear?'

'From Chris.'

'That one? You know what she's like. It wouldn't even occur to her to let me know. Although, of course,' I added quickly, 'why would she?'

'Yes, of course. Why would she?' he answered equally quickly.

We both ate silently for a while. It occurred to me that Paul must have thought I knew about his single status when I'd turned up at his house that morning. I tried to work out what that told me, and came to the conclusion that it told me absolutely nothing.

I couldn't resist asking the next question.

'Paul, can I ask you something? Just one final thing about Iseult, and then I promise I'll shut up.'

'Shoot.'

'Why on earth did you go out with her in the first place?'

Paul sat back in his chair, folded his arms and laughed. 'So it wasn't my imagination. You really *didn't* like her.'

'Oh, I'm sure she would be lovely if she weren't so horrible. I wasn't exactly her favourite person either, was I?'

'Oh, I don't know. Sometimes I used to think she was jealous of you.'

'Of me? Why?'

'Can't think of a good reason.'

'Thanks.'

He grinned at me. 'No, she was always pumping me for information about you.'

'You still haven't answered my question.'

'Why did I go out with her?'

'Yes. You'd want to have a pretty good explanation.'

'If I tell you why, you have to promise not to tell another soul.'

I moved forward in my seat. This sounded gripping.

'I won't tell anyone. Brownie's honour.'

'Why do you always say that?'

'It's a long story. Now, come on. Spit it out.'

'Okay. The night we got together, I was out with the lads after soccer practice. We went to this poxy new bar that we normally wouldn't be caught dead in. But we couldn't get into O'Brien's, and we had to watch the Arsenal match somewhere.'

'Naturally.'

'So there I was, minding my own business, watching the match, when who walks in but Chris and a bunch of her noisy mates. Iseult was there, and so were all those losers that were at your going-away. At half-time, Iseult comes and sits down next to me. She's sidling up to me and doing those things that girls do when they're interested.'

'Like what?'

'You know – smiling too much, giggling, hair-flicking, touching your hand all the time … that sort of shit.'

'Do I do that?'

'No, you're different.'

'Well, don't say it's the kind of thing "girls" do, then.'

'All right. Point taken.'

'Go on.'

'I will if you'll let me. So the second half starts, and she's still sitting there. And I'm thinking, *What's she playing at? The match is back on. Why doesn't she feck off back to her friends?* But she just sits. And you'll never guess what happens next.'

'What?'

'Do you remember that guy Diarmuid, who was hitting on me that night in the restaurant?'

'The model.'

'That's him. Well, doesn't he come over to join us? Lainey – he starts to come on to me. Right in front of my mates.'

'No!'

'Lainey, he touched my knee.'

'No!'

'I'm not joking. I didn't know where to look. It's not funny, you know.'

'I never said it was.'

'Then why are you laughing?'

'I'm not. Come on, tell the story.'

'So, anyway, all my mates are looking at me. No one's even watching the match any more. I had to do something. So I pretended to be into Iseult. I mean, what else could I do? I was mortified. To cut a long story short, I ended up kissing Iseult, and Diarmuid went off in a huff. Next thing I know, we're a couple and she's organising dinner parties at my flat and inviting all my friends.'

'Poor Diarmuid.'

'Fuck Diarmuid. I didn't even get to see the second half. And that match was crucial.'

I couldn't contain the laughter any more. Poor Paul. Caught between Diarmuid and Iseult. Between a rock and a hard place. Between a pair of rocks and a hard-faced bitch.

Paul watched me laughing, the ghost of a smile on his lips, his dimples coming out to play.

'Did you like my little story, then?'

'Yes, thank you. Highly entertaining.' I was wiping the corners of my eyes with my napkin.

'Will I order coffees?'

'Please.'

397

I attempted to size him up as he played with his cappuccino, chatting amiably on and off, the rest of the time staring unselfconsciously out to sea.

This was my opportunity.

My reason for coming here seemed so clear now. I took a deep breath.

'Paul?'

'Yes?' He tore his eyes away from the ocean and smiled deeply and warmly into mine.

'Since you have all this time off and nothing to do with it, why don't you come and stay with me in Ballyknock? I mean, not for the whole two weeks, obviously; just for a few days, at first, and you can see how you get on – not that you're not welcome to stay for the two weeks if you like. I have a spare room. You could stay there and I could show you around. There's loads to see and do, and people to meet, and you could see where I work, and there'd be no strings – honestly.'

I finally ran out of breath. I sat looking at him looking at me, feeling totally exposed.

At last he spoke.

'I'd love to.'

Chapter Thirty-one

I drove us back down to Ballyknock that Sunday. The journey was a little like that scene at the end of *The Graduate*, when Dustin Hoffman and Katherine Ross – still in her wedding dress – are sitting at the back of the bus. He's just burst in on her wedding to another man, and they've run off together. Then they both comprehend, at the same time, the full enormity of what they've done. And they can't think of anything to say to each other.

It was a bit like that with me and Paul. We had both made what felt like a momentous decision, and neither of us knew what to say next. I turned on the car radio to ease the awkwardness, and began to wonder if I had made a huge mistake.

We had to pick up Terence on the way home – Patricia had graciously agreed to mind him for the weekend. She nearly caused herself an injury at her own front door, craning her neck to make out who was in the car with me. If she did hurt herself, I knew the name of a good solicitor…. I had a feeling she'd be in my office first thing the next morning, searching for phantom files. I decided to save her the bother.

'Patricia, I have somebody here I'd like you to meet.'

She followed me like a novice nun about to have an audience with the Pope.

'Patricia, this is Paul. Paul – Patricia.'

They shook hands through the open car window.

'Paul is my ex-boyfriend. He'll be staying with me for a little while. He's on his holidays.' Best to be upfront right away.

'Hello, Paul. Lovely to meet you. Are you a solicitor too?'

'No, I'm an accountant.'

'Really? Isn't that lovely! And how long do you think you'll be staying with us for?'

'Probably just a few days.'

'Is that all? We'll have to do our best to convince you to stay longer, won't we, Lainey?'

'We will, Patricia.'

'And how long did you say you two were going out for?'

'We didn't. Look, we're pretty tired after our journey; we'd better be off. Thanks again for looking after the dog.'

'Not at all. He was no trouble. See you bright and early tomorrow morning.' What – she was planning on coming in before ten, for a change?

'God, she's nosy. Are they all like that down here?' asked Paul as we pulled away from Patricia's house. I could see her receding figure, waving at us enthusiastically, in the rear-view mirror.

'No, she's the nosiest I've met. But she's very nice. And wait until you taste her jam.'

I found that I wanted him to love everything about Ballyknock and everyone in it.

Slinky – intrepid little explorer; she had been missing for the best part of a week – was waiting for us back at the cottage. Having feared the worst, I scooped her up and hugged her tiny, purring body before letting us both into the house. She licked my hand with her little sandpaper tongue.

'Um … you don't let the cat indoors, do you?' said Paul.

'Of course I do.'

'What about toxoplasmosis?'

'Toxoplas-what?'

'Toxoplasmosis. You get it from handling cat shit.'

'Funnily enough, fondling cat turds has never been a major hobby of mine.'

401

It probably wasn't the best time to mention Slinky's endearing habit of making a little nook for herself on my unmade duvet. The story made us both look bad.

Paul followed me into the house, and I gave him a quick guided tour.

'What do you think?'

'I'm impressed. It's not what I expected. I thought it would be more basic. But it's like something out of an *Ideal Homes* magazine.'

I beamed with pleasure, as if I'd designed and built the cottage myself. Terence, who had joined the tour halfway, wagged his whole body with delight at being home and at the prospect of having an extra playmate. He gazed up at Paul expectantly.

'Um … you keep the dog in the house, too?'

'Yes. Where else would I keep him?'

'I just assumed he'd be chained up outside.'

Chained up outside! How would *he* have liked to be chained up outside? I was a little annoyed, but I decided not to mention for the time being that Terence slept at the foot of my bed.

Talking of bed, we retired soon after that. I showed Paul to his room and exited rapidly, muttering 'Good night' to his feet before closing the door firmly between us.

As luck would have it, it poured with rain all day Monday. The spectacular views that I'd been raving about were virtually non-existent. I sped home from work that evening torn between eagerness to see Paul and anxiety that the first day of his holiday had been a complete washout.

He was waiting for me in the kitchen, wooden spoon in one hand, tea-towel in the other. It was lovely having someone to come home to. I almost asked him then and there to be my wife.

'What did you get up to today?'

'Well,' he began primly, 'I cleaned the kitchen from top to bottom.'

'But I only cleaned it last week.'

Paul gave me a look that said, *Call that cleaning?*

'Are you casting aspersions on my housekeeping skills?'

'What housekeeping skills?'

'I resent that,' I said – although privately I felt it was fair comment.

'I don't know how you haven't contracted salmonella.'

'I don't eat salmon.'

'If you were a hotel, they'd close you down.'

'But this isn't a hotel, Paul.'

'If it were, at least I'd be able to sue you if I got food poisoning.'

'Oh, give it a rest. What's for dinner? I'm starved.'

'Is chicken stir-fry all right for Madam?'

'Yes, thanks. Smells great. Where did you get the wok? Did you bring it with you?'

'No, Lainey. It was in the press under the cooker.'

Really? Fancy that.

I did know where he'd got the ingredients. I usually had plenty of healthy food in my kitchen. This was because only the unhealthy stuff actually got eaten. Maybe with Paul here, I wouldn't have to keep throwing my veggies out all the time.

Dinner was amazing. I contributed by opening a bottle of wine and clearing up afterwards. *Quid pro quo.*

At about eight, I noticed that Slinky hadn't come home for her tea. 'Did you see the cat today?'

Paul pursed up his lips like – well, like Slinky's arse, actually. 'Yes, I did, as it happens. You'll never guess what he did.'

'She.'

'Whatever. I was taking in the washing off the line –' What washing? Oh, yes ... I vaguely remembered hanging out a load sometime last week. 'And I had it all neatly folded and ready to iron, and I turned my back for two minutes – and wasn't the cat fast asleep on top of the pile!'

No! What scandalous feline behaviour.

'So I had to wash it all again.'

'That was a tad extreme.'

'Lainey! You'd never know what you might catch.'

You never knew. Toxoplas-whatdoyoucallit or anything.

Slinky did little to redeem herself the next day by jumping in through the open window with an almost-dead baby rabbit in her mouth. I tried my best to explain to Paul that this was probably intended as a welcome gift to him, but he wasn't having any of it.

It had bucketed down all day long again. Paul hadn't had a very good day. He had broken the fridge whilst attempting to defrost it with a blowtorch ('It was a disgrace, there was a yoghurt in there that was older than me,' yadda yadda yadda). I was beginning to despair. At this rate, he'd be gone by Thursday.

But, on Wednesday, the heavens stopped conspiring against me. The day dawned bright and clear and stayed that way. I drove home at lunchtime to say hello, but there was no sign of Paul or Terence. When I got home that evening, the first thing I saw was a bunch of wild flowers sitting in the middle of the dining-room table.

'Where did they come from?'

Paul emerged from the kitchen, grinning. He looked thoroughly at home in a pair of biodegradable trousers and a lived-in T-shirt. I'd rarely seen him look so relaxed. Or so scruffy.

'Do you like them?'

'They're gorgeous.'

'I picked them while I was out on a walk.'

He described to me where he had been. It was more like a hike than a walk.

'While I was picking them, a guy on a red tractor stopped and asked me why I was weeding along the side of the road.'

'Where did the vase come from?'

'The cupboard under the sink. Lainey, did you open *any* of the presses before I got here?'

I ignored this. 'Did you bring Terence with you?'

'It wasn't so much that I brought him as that he decided to come along. I told him to stay, but he wouldn't. You're not very obedient, are you, Terence?'

Terence sat between us, looking from one face to the other with adoring doggy eyes. He woofed softly at the sound of his name. If Paul really hadn't wanted to bring him, he could have locked him in the house, but I decided not to point this out.

Paul enthused about the countryside for about an hour that night. He didn't say a thing about going home.

On Thursday evening, I came home to an even more elated Paul.

'The local priest called around to welcome us to the community.'

'Us?'

'He assumed I was your husband.'

'Did you put him right?'

'I told him I was just a houseguest. He knew all about you, though – that you were the local solicitor, and that you worked for Tyrone and came from Dublin.'

I was still confused. 'What's so great about a priest calling round? Was he very nice?'

'Far from it. He was a complete bastard. He sat there for half an hour, drinking your tea and eating your biscuits and giving out about solicitors. According to him, it's your lot's fault that all those priests have been done for sexual abuse. He particularly hates Tyrone, by the way.'

Tyrone had handled a few such high-profile cases.

'I hope you stuck up for me.'

'No.'

'Thanks a bunch.'

'But Terence did. While the priest was ranting on, I was watching Terence out in the garden. He got sick and then ate it.'

'Charming.'

'So I let him in, and he went straight over to the priest and licked his hand.'

'Did you, Terence? Good boy!'

'He shed a shitload of fur onto the bottom of your man's trousers, too.'

'Oh, did you? You're such a good boy.'

We petted Terence profusely and promised him extra treats for his supper that night.

'Lainey....'

'Yes?'

'Is it all right if I stay till the end of the week?'

'You can if you like.'

The end of the week came and went, and neither one of us said a word about Paul going home. I took a few days off work and we toured the countryside. I brought him to hot spots that Jack and Matt had shown me. I didn't tell him that, of course. What do you take me for? Have you forgotten that I'm a lawyer and therefore used to being flexible with the truth? We even went out for a drink in Power's with Jack one night. I was a little nervous, but the two men got on great. It seemed that Paul only had a problem with gay men when they tried to chat him up.

We were sitting in the conservatory one evening towards the end of the second week, in total silence, watching the sun sink down into the river valley. A spider spun a silken palace in the corner of the room. We watched the birds having their final feed before bedtime, singing their sweet incantations. Paul had made me a little birdhouse, using pieces of wood and old tools that he'd found in the shed.

We had just had a long conversation about his father. It was the first time Paul had ever really talked to me about him. He sat motionless, glass of wine in hand. Slinky was curled up fast asleep in his lap and Terence lay across his feet. He turned his head slowly towards me.

'You're going to find it hard to leave all this behind.'

'Hmmm?' I was so relaxed that at first I didn't register what he was saying.

'When you come back to Dublin; you're going to miss this place. When are you coming back, again?'

'I'm not.'

Paul sat up, and Slinky poured off his lap like hot oil.

'What do you mean, you're not?'

I forced myself out of my drowsy haze. 'I've decided to stay here.'

'Forever?'

'Well, I don't know about that. For the foreseeable future, anyway. Sorry I didn't say anything before. I've been meaning to tell you.'

Nothing was said for a while.

I finally broke the deadlock. 'Could you ever see yourself living somewhere like this?'

Paul smiled at me gently. 'I suppose so. If the circumstances were right.'

It was Saturday. Already. Paul was due back in the office that Monday. The atmosphere was strained, for the first time since his arrival.

He had insisted on cooking a special meal, to thank me for letting him stay. While the preparations were in full swing, I went out for a walk – partly to get out of the way, and partly to clear my head. So many thoughts were whirling around inside it. The two weeks had gone so well … only not as well as I had hoped.

Paul was still my ex-boyfriend.

The delicious cooking aromas wafted down the hill to greet me on my return.

'Mmm. What *is* that?'

'Thai chicken curry.'

'No, that other smell. Something sweet.'

Paul smiled proudly. 'Peach pie. There were all

these peaches in the fruit bowl, just going to waste, so I thought we could use them up tonight.'

I couldn't help but notice Paul's edginess through-out the meal. Even when we were sitting on the sofa afterwards, he seemed ill at ease.

'Paul, what's wrong?'

He rested his forehead in his hand, covering his eyes. 'I have some things I want to say to you.'

I swallowed. 'Go on.'

It took him a while to get going.

'Well … first of all, I can't thank you enough for letting me stay with you these past two weeks. I've had a brilliant time, and it was just what I needed.'

'I had a great time too.'

'Did you really?' His voice was sharp.

'Yes, really,' I said softly, admiring the curls that were starting to develop at the nape of his neck. I'd never known he had curly hair.

'Because I don't know why you invited me down. Let's face it, I was a crap boyfriend.'

'You weren't –'

'Yes, I was. Let me finish, please, Lainey. I was petty, jealous, insecure, controlling –'

'Paul –'

'Don't try and deny it.'

'Well, okay; it's partly true. But it's not as if I'm without fault, and it didn't stop us from having fun a lot of the time – did it?'

'I suppose not.'

'And we've had fun these last two weeks.'

He nodded.

'There you are, then.'

But Paul wasn't planning to forgive himself that easily. 'I was such an idiot, though – that time in the hotel in Kerry. I can't believe the way I acted. Like with Eric – how could I have been so stupid? I'm so sorry, Lainey. I don't blame you for dumping me. I deserved it.'

'Paul! There's no need to be sorry.'

'There's every need.' He startled me by gripping my hand urgently. It was the closest physical contact we'd had since he'd got there. I swallowed again. Paul's hazel eyes were fairly glowing.

'I'd do anything for another chance, Lainey – a chance to show you how much I've changed. Anything.'

It was all I could do to breathe.

'Hold on. Don't say anything yet.' He stood up abruptly, went into his room and returned carrying a book.

'Is that for me?'

'For both of us, really. If you want.'

He handed me the book.

Tantric Sex. I could feel myself blushing as I flicked through the pages.

'I bought it a few days ago.'

'Did you, now?'

'Yes. I've been reading it while you were in work. There are some things in it I thought we could try … but only if you want to. I'll understand

411

if you're not interested.'

I took a deep breath.

'Well, seeing as how it *is* Saturday night … this position on page fifty-five looks interesting.' I showed him the page. 'If you think your thigh muscles are up to it.'

As I led him by the hand to the bedroom, he said to me, 'Would it be okay if I stayed for another week?'

Epilogue

It was the perfect day for a wedding – Midsummer Day. It was also two years to the day since Paul had decided to hand in his notice and move permanently to Ballyknock.

A marquee had been erected in the garden of Power's Cottage. Festooned with flowers and fairy lights, it ran from the gable end of the house right down to the cherry tree. Beautiful though the marquee undoubtedly was, none of us could bring ourselves to go inside just yet. The glorious evening was too enticing. Instead, we all sat and chatted at wooden picnic tables.

My father and Chen had turned their newly dry-cleaned suit jackets into goalposts and were trying

413

to teach LuLing how to play soccer. Like any woman worth her salt, she couldn't see the point. Every time the ball came near her, she picked it up and ran with it, giggling hysterically as her daddy and granddad gave chase, her chubby little legs going like pistons. Dad and Chen discussed it and came to the conclusion that she might be more suited to Gaelic football.

But everybody else knew that ice-skating was her thing. Mum had insisted that Tatiana bring LuLing skating the moment she could walk – and LuLing, in her custom-made skates, had taken off across the ice as if she was born to it. She now went twice a week, and her mammy and granny had excessively high hopes involving Olympic gold medals.

Annie sat down on the fragrant lawn beside me and called out to her husband, 'Don't come running to me when you've got grass stains all over your jacket.' Chen grinned at her and continued chasing LuLing around the garden.

'How are you feeling?' Annie asked, looking searchingly into my face.

'Like Humpty Dumpty's sister.'

'And the ankles?'

'Up like puddings.'

'You poor thing. I was the same with the twins.'

Annie had given birth to twin girls three months previously, thereby making Chen the proudest father in Ireland. Before that, she had worked part-time as a secretary in Tyrone's Dublin office; upon returning to Ireland, she had discovered that she didn't have the heart to return to secondary-school teaching. Tabitha and Thomasina, she had called the twins. I had pleaded with her to give them plainer names – had she forgotten what it was like to be teased in school? all those years of being called Tatty or Titty-Anna? But she now claimed that this had been a character-building experience. Maybe she was right, but I wasn't taking any chances myself. If I had a little girl, I was going to call her Ellen.

We were joined by Paul, who handed me my seventh sparkling mineral water of the evening. He had added a strawberry and a chunk of lime, in an effort to make this one more exciting. He sat down behind me and tried to put his arms around my waist; finding none, he instead placed his arms as far as they could go around my distended belly.

I often wondered what he thought of me now – this big mound of leaks and rumbles that had once been his girlfriend. Sometimes I felt that he was waiting for me to go into labour like a scientist waited for a volcano to erupt – wanting to be there, but afraid of getting caught in the lava flow. I felt afraid sometimes, too. But there was no escaping my own body.

'You look lovely,' he whispered into my ear, and kissed my jawline.

I appreciated his efforts, I really did. But they didn't stop me from feeling like Demis Roussos in my party dress.

'How do you feel?' It was a question I was being asked a lot of late.

'Great.'

It was true. I did feel great most of the time – like a big, fat, happy Buddha, or a placid, well-tended sacred cow.

The pregnancy had been an accident – a happy accident. It's amazing how the simple process of weeing on a stick can change the course of your whole life. It was almost time to test out my allegedly child-bearing hips. Not to mention Paul's paternal skills.

Paul was a transformed man since he'd moved from the city. It wasn't just his hair, which was now wavy and curled about his shirt collar (he looked like the gardener off the telly), and it wasn't just his new casual style of dressing. He'd given up accountancy and was working as an organic farmer. He spent most of his days happily up to his armpits in muck. When he wasn't working, he was growing lilies in the back garden of our new home, a few miles away, or making organic crab-apple jelly from a recipe Bridie Power had given him. It had been passed down from Granny Power.

Healing the rift between his father and himself had been a real turning point for Paul. His own impending fatherhood had spurred him into making contact. Relations had been awkward at first, and it had been hard for Paul to forgive and forget. But his father's explanation that he had been repeatedly warned off by Paul's mother rang true, somehow. Of course, they were unlikely ever to have the ideal father-son relationship – it was too late for that; but perhaps Mr O'Toole could repair some of the damage by treating his grandchild the way he should have treated his own little boy. He had already visited us for a week that spring, and he was due to fly over again the second his first grandchild was born.

As for Mrs O'Toole, she had so far refused to visit us in our 'house of sin' or to acknowledge our baby, conceived as he or she had been outside holy matrimony. As far as I was concerned, this made life even more perfect. Paul still held out hope that she'd have a change of heart once the child was born. But, even if she didn't, he had his own family now.

Brendan Ryan – local solicitor extraordinaire – emerged from the mouth of the marquee.

'Can we have everyone in for the tango demonstration?' he roared.

He was wearing a new fireman-red cardigan that his wife had knitted for the occasion, together with a white shirt, a scarlet tie, black trousers and shoes, and shocking-pink socks. The effect was striking, to say the least. He gave me a freckly grin before disappearing back inside.

Relations between our firms continued to be good. If a mad client came to Brendan's office looking for advice, he sent him directly over the road to us. We would often return the favour. It balanced out and everyone was happy with this arrangement. We still had good-natured spats in Ballyknock district court, which had become even more enjoyable since the previous judge had been forced to retire on the grounds of ill temper.

Paul hauled me to my feet, and we followed the scatterings of people making their way into the tent. I couldn't wait to see this: my parents, the award-winning dancers Mr and Mrs Joe and Teresa Malone, giving a tango demonstration. Once, years ago, I'd asked my father if he regretted not having a son. He'd told me not to be daft – that, if my mother had given birth to a son, she would probably have christened him Rudolf and packed him off to ballet lessons. Dad had said he wouldn't wish such a fate on any young lad. And look at him now – Twinkle-Toes himself.

We scanned the room for prime seats.

'Over here!' It was Hazel, looking radiant. She was wearing a sky-blue trouser suit, an all-over St Tropez tan and perfectly sculpted eyebrows.

Of course, I knew one of the reasons for this radiance. Rumour had it that she was getting a good seeing-to from Mattie Power on a regular basis. (True, she wasn't blonde, but he didn't seem to mind.) But he couldn't claim all the credit. Hazel was a new woman since she'd taken a year out to travel the world. She'd returned six months ago and set up her own accountancy practice – in Ballyknock village. Her poky (so far) office was upstairs from the new premises of Power, Malone & Co. Solicitors. The entire population of Dublin would be living down here soon.

Unfortunately, she and Chris had never regained that closeness they'd had before Hazel's meltdown. For some reason not even fully understood by Hazel herself, she had taken out the worst of her frustrations on Chris. The wounds she'd inflicted had never fully healed, and both of them accepted that perhaps they never would. Sometimes you can't go back. Other friends had flowed into their lives, filling the void that each of them had left in the other.

Chris had been fired by the film company when her first short film turned out to be a spectacular flop. Undeterred, she'd moved over to Essex for six months to do a diploma in interior design (and to give the Essex girls a run for their money). Shortly after her return, she and Jack Power had set up their own interior design consultancy firm in Dublin.

Of course, Chris claimed to have known all along that Jack was gay. Nice of her to fill me in, as usual. Jack, in turn, claimed that Chris was the ultimate gay icon. I'd always known she'd find her niche sooner or later.

I sat down beside Hazel, who was sharing a table with Jack, his partner Chuck – whom he'd wasted no time in importing from San Francisco – Bridie and, last but not least, Johnny. Jack pulled his seat up beside mine.

'How's it going?' I whispered into his pierced ear. The earring was the only discernible sign of his gayness – other than Chuck, of course. These days, Jack mostly dressed like a boring, straight, old fart.

'Could be worse. No blood spilled yet.'

I glanced over at Chuck, who was chatting to Bridie. Johnny sat on the other side of his wife, sipping a pint and looking distinctly uncomfortable.

Jack had discovered that Ballyknock wasn't quite ready for him. One of the brothers had taken over the running of the farm, and Jack now lived in a stylish apartment off Dublin's South Great George's Street, with Chuck. Both his career and his personal life were going swimmingly. He sang in a gay nightclub every second Saturday night. I sometimes went up to see him – usually on the nights he was in drag, because they were the best. He had confessed to me recently that it was his greatest regret that he was too old to audition for boy bands.

I decided this would be a good time to ask him.

'Jack, I have a favour to ask you.'

'How could I refuse anything to a woman in your delicate condition?'

'That's why I'm asking you now.'

'Sounds scary. What is it?'

I took a deep breath. 'Will you be the baby's godfather?'

His face broke slowly into a grin. 'Don't you mean godmother?'

'I'm afraid Annie's already got that gig.'

'You could have two. I could be its fairy godmother.'

I pretended to consider this for a moment. 'All right, then. Will you do it?'

'I'd be delighted.'

Sorted.

The remainder of the Power clan, including Matt – current holder of the title of Ballyknock Bachelor of the Year – and the various little snot-nosed baby Powers, were distributed around the nearby tables. Amongst them sat Shem and Tom Delaney of the Rusty Teeth. Shem had been widowed about a year before. He'd recently started doing a line with Cissy Walsh from the post office. Patricia and the other matrons of Ballyknock were scandalised by his behaviour – the poor woman barely cold.... I suppose nobody likes to feel that they're dispensable.

As the applause following my parents' tango petered out, the bride and the groom took the floor. Tyrone took his blushing, blooming, blissful, blossoming bride in his arms for their first waltz as a married couple. Barbed Wire – who, we'd learnt today, had been christened Barbara Ann after the song – looked up lovingly into her new husband's face and smiled a smile that made her look ten years his junior rather than his senior. She had moved down to Ballyknock with him to continue as his secretary, and the rest, as they say, was history.

As for me, it had been a while since anyone had accused me of being proper. I'd long since found the thing that had been missing from my relationship with Paul the first time around.

It had been me all along.

I noticed that the champagne reserves were running low. I went into the kitchen of Power's Cottage, where I knew the extra bottles were being kept. I felt another twinge as I got up. I'd been having contractions for almost an hour now. Lucky they hadn't come any earlier; I had only ticked the last item off my 'Baby – to do' list that very morning. The contractions were still weak enough and far enough apart not to be a worry. But I'd have to tell Paul soon. He was having such a good time that I was reluctant to spoil his fun. And, besides, why would I want to sit around in a hospital when I could be here, amongst family and friends?

Feeling surprisingly calm, I uncorked a bottle of champagne and poured myself a glass. It was the first time alcohol had touched my lips in eight months – it could hardly do the baby any harm at this stage. I glanced up at Mary Power, who smiled regally at me from her place of honour above the fireplace.

'Well, Mary,' I said, raising my glass to her, 'things haven't turned out too badly after all. Cheers.'

I clinked my glass against her glassy frame.

Then I stepped back out into the sunshine.

TARA HEAVEY

A Brush with Love

PAN BOOKS

Loving some men should be against the law . . .

Legal secretary Fern can't quite believe her luck when posh barrister James Carver takes a shine to her. With her mahogany-brown hair – 'I blend in with the office furniture' – and green eyes, she doesn't feel in any way special. After all, a typing speed of 60 wpm and a dream of being an artist hardly make her a catch. Flattered and thrilled at the attention, Fern is smitten even when James turns out to have some very strange habits . . .

When will Fern see that he is a total rat? When she gets the sack – for slapping a judge – or when she suspects he's seeing someone else? With her family breaking apart and her love life in disarray, Fern refuses to see the truth about James – or about herself, and why she's running away from a man who really loves her . . .

CLARE NAYLOR & MIMI HARE

The Second Assistant

PAN BOOKS

The Agency: Hollywood's premier talent agency. A place of polished marble floors, brilliant sunlight, Gucci sunglasses (this season's, naturally) and celebrity clients you've never met – though you know who they're sleeping with.

The Second Assistant: one Elizabeth Miller, newly employed by under-educated, in-over-his-head agent extraordinaire Scott Wagner and his sidekick Lara – the woman who hates everyone and everything in Hollywood.

Day One: Lara warns Elizabeth never to date anyone in the business. And Elizabeth thinks it'll be a doddle. But then she finds herself floating in her boss's pool wearing only a g-string and a borrowed diamond necklace.

The End of the Line? Not for Lizzie. She's a survivor, and no Machiavellian assistant or lecherous studio mogul can douse her dreams of climbing up from the bottom of the Hollywood ladder.

Hilarious, sassy and utterly unputdownable, this is life in the Hollywood fast line – with the top down.

MORAG PRUNTY

Superstar Lovers

PAN BOOKS

She's back! The author of the hilarious Poison Arrows *returns with a page-turning, salacious tour through the underbelly of the music industry.*

Employing her customary razor-like humour, Morag Prunty introduces a host of characters whose lives have been chewed up and spat out by this harsh, celebrity-obsessed world.

There's Molly, a lonely twenty-something, who trudges to the newsagents every day for her fix of *VIP, OK!* and *Hello!,* anything to give her life a much-needed injection of glamour . . .

There's Alfie, burned-out boyband member who's kissed the good times goodbye and is now all washed up . . .

There's Corinne, damaged former lover of Mal, Ireland's biggest-ever rock export, and there's Helen, his long-suffering . . .

In her inimitable way, Morag Prunty introduces a range of fascinating characters and gives them a sprinkle of magic dust in this witty dissection of the vagaries of fame and celebrity.

OTHER PAN BOOKS

AVAILABLE FROM PAN MACMILLAN

TARA HEAVEY
A BRUSH WITH LOVE   0 330 41977 3   £6.99

CLARE NAYLOR & MIMI HARE
THE SECOND ASSISTANT   0 330 42007 0   £6.99

MORAG PRUNTY
SUPERSTAR LOVERS   0 330 41910 2   £6.99

SARAH WEBB
THREE TIMES A LADY   0 330 41216 7   £6.99

All Pan Macmillan titles can be ordered from our website,
www.panmacmillan.com, or from your local bookshop
and are also available by post from:

Bookpost, PO Box 29, Douglas, Isle of Man IM99 1BQ
Credit cards accepted. For details:
Telephone: 01624 677237
Fax: 01624 670923
E-mail: bookshop@enterprise.net
www.bookpost.co.uk

Free postage and packing in the United Kingdom

Prices shown above were correct at the time of going to press.
Pan Macmillan reserve the right to show new retail prices on covers
which may differ from those previously advertised in the text
or elsewhere.

and his system of domination, hostility and oppression. Instead, have confidence in the Lord Jesus. If you do, you and all those in your household will experience liberation.'

The man is transformed from a hostile jailer into a generous host. He invites the men into his home. He and his family hear the good news of Jesus and the kingdom of God. The jailer washes the wounds his associates had inflicted, and then Paul and Silas baptise the man and his family. (The mutual washing offers a tender and beautiful image.) Finally, they share a meal together. But the story still isn't over. Paul and Silas stage a kind of sit-in at the jail the next day, requiring the city officials to apologise for their injustice before escorting Paul and Silas out of the jail.

So what happens when God's kingdom of liberation and reconciliation confronts Caesar's empire of fear and hostility? Starting with the most marginalised – women and slaves – the gospel proclaims liberation first to the oppressed and then to the oppressors, since both oppressors and oppressed are dehumanised through injustice. Mid-level functionaries (like the jailer) and top-level magistrates are given the chance to defect from hostility and practise a better way of life. The seeds of gospel transformation are sown, and a community to continue the work of transformation has been established. So Paul and his community organising team move on.

This was what Christian mission originally looked like – without TV or radio, without pianos, organs or rock-and-roll bands, without offerings and invitations to walk down an aisle, without national headquarters and retirement plans, and without fiery preaching that inspires hostility against anybody.[5] And this is what we need today.

Imagine teams of unlikely people – Christians, Jews, Muslims, Hindus, Buddhists, people from the whole range of indigenous religions, together with agnostics and atheists – coming together, not in the name of the Christian (or any other) religion, but seeking to walk in the way of Jesus, learning, proclaiming and demonstrating 'the way of liberation'.

Imagine they begin, as Paul, Silas and company did, in solidarity with the most marginalised and vulnerable – children, women, slaves, the homeless, refugees, the poorest of the poor. Imagine how their work among the most vulnerable would eventually lead them into confrontation with systems of injustice – the fear-based systems that exclude and exploit. Sometimes there would no doubt be sufferings and setbacks, but if, like Paul and Silas, the teams keep faith and refuse to be intimidated, these setbacks will lead to unexpected and even earth-shaking breakthroughs. In the process, others will *want to* join them – without threats or promises, but simply because of the beauty, goodness and truth of their words and actions.

Mission work like this will always involve charity – directly helping those in need: food for the hungry, water for the thirsty, clothing for the naked, shelter for the homeless. But if the hungry, thirsty, naked and homeless need food, water, clothing and shelter, what do the oppressed, excluded and endangered need? Very often, they need new laws and policies to protect them and ongoing reforms to ensure ongoing justice for them. So, charity will also lead to advocacy – speaking and working on behalf of the voiceless and powerless, using the tools of local, national and global citizenship to work for the common good.

But beyond charity and advocacy, people need opportunity. They need opportunities to learn, opportunities to work, opportunities to move and make a new home. Imagine the role people of faith could have in providing opportunity – classroom teachers and alternative educators, business owners and social entrepreneurs, city planners and civil engineers, immigration lawyers and ethical employers, bankers and venture capitalists. Imagine students learning in new ways, workers being hired into new jobs, and new neighbourhoods and social circles welcoming people who have been driven from their previous homes by various forms of hostile, oppositional clannishness.

Sadly, this clannishness has often been reinforced by religion. That's why community organisers working for the common good must often stand in solidarity with people of other faiths to challenge the clannishness of their own faith. They must use their insider status for the protection and benefit of outcasts or outsiders, just as Jesus constantly did.[6]

So we who follow Jesus will discover our true identity not by favouring our fellow religious insiders to the exclusion of others, but rather by going out of our way to serve Muslims, Hindus, Buddhists, Jews and atheists – doing for people of other religions no less than we would wish people of other religions would do for us. And we will deepen this identity not only by serving others, but also by serving alongside them. In the words of Vatican II, we will 'through dialogue and collaboration with the followers of other religions' work for the common good of all, thus advancing the commonwealth of God.

CHAPTER 26

How With-ness Complements Witness

> Without compromising the absolute commitment inherent to faith, Christianity can be considered as a relative reality; not, however, in the sense in which 'relative' is opposed to 'absolute,' but in the sense of 'relational.' The truth to which Christianity witnesses is neither exclusive nor inclusive of all other truth; it is related to all that is true in other religions.
>
> Claude Geffre[1]

It was Good Friday and our worship team had transformed our large gathering space into Stations of the Cross.[2] At each station, participants would engage with an activity to enter into the story of Jesus' final day – kneeling on rocks and gravel, lifting a heavy wooden crossbeam, pounding a spike into wood, pondering a picture or statue. One station commemorated Jesus speaking to the daughters of Jerusalem, urging them not to weep for him, but for themselves and their children (Luke 23:26–31). As I stood at that station, I realised I had never before pondered those words, 'Do not weep for me.' For me, the whole purpose of Good Friday was to weep for Jesus. Why would he say *not* to do so? That soon led to another question: for whom would Jesus have me weep today?

I had recently read an article about the ongoing genocide in Darfur, and as I stood at that station of the cross, I felt that on that Good Friday, Jesus would have me weep for Darfur . . . for families driven from their homes, for children bereft of parents, for girls subjected to brutal rape, for elderly people living in fear. In the following weeks, my concern for Darfur wouldn't go away. A vision took shape. I shared it with friends at Sojourners (http://sojo.net), and together we developed a public demonstration we called Worship in the Spirit of Justice. We chose five significant locations in Washington, DC, and there we staged public worship on consecutive Sundays. One week we gathered in front of the Lincoln Memorial, one week in front of the Capitol, one week near the National Press Club, one week near the White House and one week near the Sudanese Embassy. At each location we sang, prayed, read Scripture, preached and worshipped God as the God of justice, the God who cares for all people – whatever their race, religion, economic status or nationality.

One week we invited a rabbi, David Saperstein, to preach, and everyone agreed he was our best preacher. He preached from Leviticus 16:19, 'Do not stand idly by while your neighbour bleeds', recounting how the Jewish experience of Holocaust moved him not only to speak out against anti-Semitism, but against violence and genocide against anyone anywhere.[3] Each week we had Sudanese people share their moving and unforgettable stories of survival, some of them Christians who had suffered in Southern Sudan, others Muslims who had suffered in Darfur.

Although our speakers included Christians, Jews and Muslims, we didn't describe our gatherings as inter-faith worship. No, it was explicitly Christian worship. But we discovered that explicitly Christian worship can be explicitly hospitable to Jews, Muslims and others.

I'm certainly not against inter-faith worship, and I think there's a vital need for multi-faith worship as well.[4] But I am especially interested in worship in one's tradition that practises hospitality to the other. So as a Christian, I can welcome Hindus or Buddhists to be guests in Christian worship. They can participate or observe, as their consciences will allow, knowing their presence does not imply understanding of or agreement with everything that goes on. Similarly, if I am invited as a Christian to be the guest of Muslims or Jews in worship, I can joyfully accept the invitation, participating or observing as my conscience will allow, knowing that my presence doesn't mean I fully understand or agree with everything that is said or done. (The fact is, we Christians all share this understanding when we attend any explicitly Christian gathering, too. How often do we fully understand and endorse every single word of every single prayer, song or sermon, even within our own congregation?)

In the years before the 2001 terrorist attacks, I wouldn't have considered 'with-ness' to be an important dimension of Christian worship or mission. I believed in *witness*, not *with-ness*. I believed in *speaking to* and *working for* people of other faiths, not conversing and working *with*. But since 2001, I've been convinced that Christian identity involves both *witness* – graciously and confidently sharing our unique, Christ-centred message, and *with-ness* – experiencing solidarity with people of other faiths, worshipping in one another's presence and working together for the common good.

As I've spoken out on behalf of with-ness, some of my critics have responded quite aggressively – one even accusing my friends and me of being sympathisers with Al Qaeda![5] But I've learned that the best way to 'turn the other cheek' as a writer and speaker is simply to dust myself off, get up and write or speak again. Instead of defending myself by responding to the last criticism, I try to move forward to the next project in my mission.

So in that spirit, after a season of protracted and intense criticism from some of my fellow Christians, a few years ago I felt I was being called to go even further in with-ness. I wasn't sure what that would mean, so I prayed for guidance. The answer came when I was speaking at a church in Michigan, where my friend Rob Bell was pastor. After one of the services, an enthusiastic woman named Nadyne came up front, waited patiently in a rather long line and then told me that she had developed a deep friendship with a Muslim woman named Soraya. They formed a group called Peace Moms, and she wondered if I'd like to join her the following summer in participating, as a Christian, in the Muslim fast of Ramadan with her friend.[6] Instantly I felt the Holy Spirit speaking deep inside me: *This is it. Do this.* 'I'm in,' I said.

As the month of Ramadan approached, I called my Muslim friend Eboo Patel, explaining my desire to be in public solidarity with Muslims and asking him if he would be my 'sponsor'. He wasn't comfortable with the word *sponsor* and expressed some valid concerns about the way I was using the word *solidarity*, but gladly offered to be my friend and advisor through the fast – to extend hospitable *with-ness* to me.

In terms of community organising, you might say my fast became, along with a personal spiritual discipline, something of a demonstration or non-violent action in protest of religious clannishness, fear and hostility.[7] I blogged about my experience several times during the month, and most of the responses were deeply moving and encouraging. A number of Christians felt moved to join in the fast, many of them reaching out to local mosques, making their first Muslim friend and experiencing warm hospitality for the after-sundown fast-breaking meal. Some amazing spiritual and social breakthroughs occurred. I received notes from Muslims around the world as well, nearly all positive, saying, 'We have never heard of a Christian having respect for our religion. Thank you,' or 'We only hear about Christians insulting our prophet or disgracing the Quran, never about them respecting us and joining us in our fast. Thank you.'

My journey into with-ness had begun several years earlier. I was attending a conference on religious violence where a Muslim scholar delivered a sparkling and informative lecture. I came up to her later with a long list of questions, which she answered patiently and brilliantly. We exchanged e-mail addresses, and some time later I received a note from her.

After meeting you, I Googled your name and the words *Muslim* and *Islam*. I read about all the times you have stood up for Muslim people. I was moved by the ways you have shown sincere love for us. I also read the horrible things your fellow Christians said and wrote about you for doing so. I want to thank you for your courage. You have risked your reputation as a Christian to protect Muslims from prejudice and violence. You are saving lives.

That was moving enough, but then came her last sentence: 'You are a true Christian.'

I would have been honoured if she had said to me something parallel to what one of my Buddhist friends once said to me: 'I know you aren't a Buddhist in name, but you are one in heart.' I knew this was the highest compliment that friend could give me, and I was touched. But this woman's words struck me even more powerfully because, I think, she wasn't trying to include me in the clan of Islam. Inclusion of this sort can be a form of colonisation, asserting that one's own clan includes all good people, albeit anonymously. Instead, she was affirming me in my otherness. And she was saying something not just about me, but about Christ and the kind of Christianity he would want there to be. She saw that the true way of Christ is to show solidarity with the other – to work, not for the good of one's religious clan alone, but for the common good, the good of all.

A Christian friend of mine, Cindy, discovered the power – and cost – of with-ness. She was born with one arm fully formed and the other partially formed. While doing graduate research in East Africa, she learned that in many places in Africa, children born with physical disabilities like hers are hidden away, considered cursed by God or demons, a shame to the family. If Cindy had been born there, she probably wouldn't have been allowed to go to primary school, much less graduate school.

She immediately felt a calling from God to do something for African children with disabilities. She went home and began raising funds to help pay school fees and get needed support and supplies for these children.[8] Her motivation flowed from her Christian faith, and most if not all of the donors to her new charity were fellow Christians.

Cindy made a decision that her fledgling organisation would serve all children, whatever their religion. They would involve qualified adults as educators and administrators, whatever their religion. If Christians and Muslims could work together for needy children, that would be an asset, not a liability, in her mind. But over time, Cindy experienced pushback for her stance. Some of her Christian donors saw her work as 'less Christian' because she made service and education, not religious conversion, her primary aim. But Cindy couldn't back down. Backing down would be a betrayal of her true identity as a follower of Christ as she understood it.

I think of another friend we'll call Mike who went to a Muslim-majority country specifically to convert Muslims to Christianity. After some time there, he got a sick feeling: he felt he was serving neither God nor the best interests of the people around him, but was instead serving the colonising agenda of the religious clan that sent him. So he changed the direction of his work. He started mobilising Christians and Muslims to work side by side in helping the poor. 'Something happens', he told me, 'when we work together for the poor. We all change. I know that both the Christians and the Muslims feel they are encountering God in one another, and together we are encountering God as we join God in serving the poor.'[9] He discovered that *witness* led him to *with-ness*.

Meanwhile, similar things are happening among people of other religions. I think of a prosperous Hindu engineer named Sailesh who left his lucrative high-tech career because he developed a passion to do something about the global environmental crisis. He is developing important technological breakthroughs to help people in poor countries to improve their lives without adopting the consumptive, environmentally destructive ways of the West. He contacted me and said, 'I am doing this as a Hindu, but I feel I should not move forward unless I have Christians and Muslims and others working alongside me.'[10]

I already mentioned Eboo Patel, my co-faster when I participated in the fast of Ramadan. Eboo formed an organisation – Interfaith Youth Core – designed to bring young people of different faiths together to serve.[11] He knows that talking together is important – but that inter-faith dialogue becomes much deeper in the context of multi-faith collaboration. Words are good, but actions are better – especially actions that bring us together solving problems that affect everybody. And when one of our biggest global problems is hostility between religions, this kind of mission-with is doubly important.

What Soraya and Nadyne, Eboo, Cindy, Sailesh, Mike and so many other people are doing is a lot like what Jesus did: bringing together unlikely people to serve and heal together, to liberate the oppressed and their oppressors together, and to model, in their collaboration, the kind of harmony and human-kindness the world so desperately needs. Their shared commitment – to inter-faith collaboration for the common good – doesn't make them all Christians, but it does make them all a little more Christ-like. I'm sure I'm not alone in wondering what good having the former label is without having the latter quality of character and behaviour.

CHAPTER 27

How Mission Can Reorganise Organised Religion

The eschatological fullness of the Reign of God is the common final achievement of Christianity and the other religions.

Jacques Dupuis[1]

I mentioned earlier that I was in East Africa a few months after inter-tribal violence had rocked Kenya. Shortly after returning home, I was listening to a conversation between a Kenyan and an American. The Kenyan explained the background for the outbreak, the tensions among Luo, Luhya, Kikuyu, Maasai and others of the fifty-odd tribes in the country. The American asked, 'Which tribe are you from?' The man hesitated for a moment and replied. 'I could answer your question because I am not ashamed of my tribe. It is part of who I am, and I know who I am. But at the risk of sounding rude, I would rather not answer, and let me explain why. In reality, in every country, there are only two tribes: the haves and the have-nots. It is enough to say that I am from the haves, and I want to use the advantages that have come to me by accident of birth on behalf of the have-nots, whatever their tribe. So although I am from one tribe, I exist to serve people of all tribes.'[2]

Like that man, I know who I am. I am a Christian. I love my heritage and thank God for it. But my identity as a Christian can never be a barrier, a wall, a reason for apartheid. Rather, my identity as a follower of Christ requires me first to move towards the other in friendship, and then to move *with* the other in service to those in need. In so doing, both the other and I are transformed from counterparts to partners. This is good news for both the haves and the have-nots. The haves suffer dehumanisation – a loss of human-kindness – when they hold themselves aloof from their fellow humans, just as the have-nots suffer when the haves hoard wealth and opportunity at the have-nots' expense. The gospel calls both to discover salvation in encounter with the other, in the love of God.

What might this renewed sense of Christian identity and mission mean for our collectives and institutions known as 'organised religion'? The term, of course, has a lot of detractors. I often ask those who speak critically of organised religion what they're more critical of: being organised or being religious. They most often reply they have problems with both. Then I'll explain that the word *religion* is based on the root *lig*, meaning 'to bind or connect together' (as in *ligament*), so *religion* means reconnecting or re-bonding broken relationships – with God, with neighbour, with stranger and enemy, with non-human life, with all creation. Generally their eyes get a little brighter and they realise that sounds like a good thing. But what about the organised part?

I might then suggest that the problem isn't organisation, but the purpose and effectiveness of the organisation. What if religious communities were well-organised to bond broken relationships – between the haves and have-nots, for example? Suddenly, the idea of organised religion has a completely different feel.

Try imagining what might happen if our religious communities started organising for the common good, for holistic or integral mission – mission that integrates witness and with-ness. Imagine that the leaders of our various faith traditions actually began meeting with one another – not merely for something called 'inter-religious dialogue', but to become friends, to share their personal values and spiritual experiences, to seek mutual understanding, to practise the neighbourliness and hospitality towards the other that their traditions preach. And then, from there, imagine that they started setting an example – say one day a month or two weeks a year – working side by side modelling with-ness, collaboration for the common good, on behalf of those in need. Imagine the Pope and the Dalai Lama, a televangelist and a Muslim imam, a leading rabbi and an Orthodox Patriarch, side by side, serving meals in a refugee camp, distributing mosquito nets, digging wells or assisting dentists in providing dental care to a poor village.

Now imagine that these religious leaders devoted say a month a year to meet together . . . dreaming, praying and working for the well-being of all. (Some might say they couldn't spare that much time, since the internal demands of their organisations wouldn't allow it. But shouldn't the external demands of the future of humanity and the planet have some demand on them, too?) Imagine if they led their various religious communities to sign treaties or agreements of non-aggression and mutual protection – if they decided to boldly move ahead in peace-making when nation-states shrink back. Imagine that they showed up in person when one of the presidents or prime ministers or party leaders supposedly under their care spoke or acted in hostility towards others, bringing the power of their religion to bear on the powerful for a change. And imagine if their top-level example were then to inspire religion-wide acts of friendship and collaboration worldwide, getting the haves to see the have-nots as their sisters and brothers, fathers and mothers, sons and daughters.

Imagine if organised religion organised billions of people and trillions of dollars to tackle the challenges that our economic and political systems are afraid or unwilling to tackle – a planet ravaged by unsustainable human behaviour and an out-of-control consumptive economy, the growing gap between the rich minority and the poor majority, and the proliferation of weapons of all kinds – including weapons of mass destruction.

'Wow,' people frequently say when I propose these possibilities. 'If they did that, I might become religious again.' Some quickly add, 'But I won't hold my breath. It'll never happen.'

It wouldn't be impossible to prove them wrong, since with God all things are possible.

This possible impossibility is, I think, what Jesus meant when he claimed that the kingdom or commonwealth of God was *at hand*. It was not *out of reach* – impossible; nor was it *in hand* – already attained. It was simultaneously in reach and not yet seized, a gift already fully given, and not yet fully received, opened and enjoyed.[3] Jesus embodied this truth to the edges of Judaism and beyond, and the apostles spread it 'to the uttermost parts of the earth': God's commonwealth was a table where the Pharisees and prostitutes were equally welcome, the chief priests and the Samaritans, the Sadducees and the Roman centurions, the poor homeless leper and the rich young leader, Onesimus the slave and Philemon the slave master, Gentile and Jew, male and female, one and all. A new religion called Christianity (that conflicted term, of course, didn't exist yet) wasn't the point; the kingdom or commonwealth of God was the point . . . for Jesus, for Paul and for all the apostles.

What did Jesus mean by the term *kingdom of God*? He himself resisted defining it, preferring to tell what it was *like* rather than what it *was*, enlarging it for imaginative encounter through symbol and story rather than shrinking it for rational encounter in formula or proposition. He surely meant something far bigger than any religion should or could contain. He meant something that his movement (later called, for better or worse, *the Church*) was to seek, to receive, to enter and to participate in . . . not to own, control, commodify or rule. He meant, among many other things, a profound transcendence of dualisms in a larger, unitive harmony, a unitive harmony that Christian mystics – and mystics of every religion – point to again and again as that which cannot be defined or even fully named.

To get a feel for the dimensions of that unitive harmony, we might ask – both playfully and reverently: what could be bigger than God?[4] The commonwealth of God, we might answer, in that it contains all of God and all of creation. And all of creation contains all of humanity, with all our languages and cultures – and religions. So in this way, Jesuit theologian Jacques Dupuis concluded his monumental *Towards a Christian Theology of Religious Pluralism* with the resonant – and profoundly Christian – words with which we began this chapter.

Organised religion is not an end in itself. It organises for a purpose. So 'organised Christianity' must, from this generous and emergent Christian perspective, organise to receive, experience, celebrate and live the commonwealth of God. This gift has already been given and so is already present, but we have yet to awaken to it, receive it, open it and enter it fully. We have, for two thousand years, been exploring its frontiers, as it were, but it beckons us to venture deeper in. The deeper we enter, the more we feel welcomed home, experiencing the profound belonging that Jesus called 'My Father's house', in which there is no hostility, only hospitality. There we experience God's welcoming embrace of us, but not only of us: of all the others, too. So in Revelation, when the seventh angel blows his trumpet, loud voices do not shout, 'Everyone has joined our religion, or been destroyed.' No, they shout, 'The kingdom of the world has become the kingdom of our Lord and of his Messiah!'

When we have that vision of the *telos* towards which we are moving, our attitudes change and our identity changes. We anticipate what Pierre Teilhard de Chardin called a 'marvellous convergence', and our anticipation inspires participation. We work and pray for that marvellous convergence. We sing and dialogue for it. We even organise for it. And in so doing, we see, receive and enter the gift that has already been given to us in, through and with Jesus: yes, the kingdom, kindom, reign or commonwealth of God.

CHAPTER 28

How Evangelism Is Like a Windmill

Do not leave others where they have been. But do not try to bring them to where you are, either, as beautiful as that place might be to you. Rather, invite them to go with you to a place neither you nor they have ever been before.

adapted from Vincent Donovan[1]

It was an idyllic day – a perfect breeze, sunny skies, windmills turning with a rhythm at once natural and humane. I had been to Holland many times, but this was my first visit to the windmills. My host Sam and I climbed up into the belly of one of these engineering marvels.[2] As we watched the wooden gears turning in perfect calibration, Sam started telling me about the inhumanity of the system in which the windmills played so important a part. Peanut oil squeezed from imported Indonesian peanuts provided a painful metaphor for the crush of colonialism on the Indonesian workers who planted, harvested and packed the peanuts for processing in Holland. There was no malicious intent in all this, Sam explained: Dutch shipbuilders, traders and windmill operators were simply making a living using the means of wealth production at hand. But much injustice can occur with little or no conscious malice, so we both felt at once the beauty and agony of the windmills as the huge gears turned and groaned around us.

It's nearly a cliché in many circles to say that the old evangelism – evangelism as we knew it – was, like the windmills, an unwitting accomplice in the story of European colonialism and empire. Protestants from Northern Europe raced against Catholics from Southern Europe to convert and educate 'savages' and 'heathen' around the world. Their conversion usually meant being co-opted and domesticated so they would become docile, cooperative producers of goods and services in the Northern or Southern sectors of the Euro-American economic system. The benefits to the Euro-American colonisers were obvious: profits from cheap raw materials and equally cheap cooperative labour. The 'benefits' to the colonised were far more complex and ambiguous.[3]

This evangelism-plus-domestication was often undertaken on a completely unconscious level. The missionaries of the colonial era – including my own grandfather and grandmother – were sincere and good-hearted to the point of enormous personal sacrifice, motivated by a sincere desire to save souls for heaven. No malice was in play. But neither the naivety nor the sincerity of the colonial-era missionaries could nullify the unintended consequences of their work, some of which were tragic – whether those dimensions were social, economic, cultural, psychological or political.

Some missionaries felt a growing ambivalence about these impacts as they watched them unfold over time, and some became outspoken critics of the economic, social and environmental exploitation inherent in the colonial system.[4] For most, though, civilisation and development were seen as unmitigated blessings from heaven. In many ways they were blessings. Girls began to be educated along with boys, for example, and hospitals saved uncountable lives. But the costs and losses have been immeasurable, too.

Since nearly everyone these days is aware of these costs and losses, I imagine that many readers will assume there is no place for evangelism in this emerging understanding of strong-and-benevolent Christian identity. 'You have your religion and I'll have mine' seems to be a step away from the evangelistic abuses of the past. But while taking a step from harm to harmlessness might be good in some ways, it's not good enough. We must rise to higher ground, from benign to benevolent, from harmlessness to human-kindness. When we do, we will make a surprising discovery. Just as there is a great future for windmills beyond their morally compromised use in the age of colonialism, there is a great future for a new kind of evangelism, although it will be so different that it may well need a new name.[5]

Nobody has conveyed this new/renewed dimension of Christian mission more poignantly than a Catholic missionary named Vincent Donovan. His experience 'on the mission field' forced him to face the dark sides of the colonial-era missionary project, and the words that opened this chapter capture his transformed vision.

This shared journey is not the call to convert from your religion to mine. It is, rather, the invitation for both of us to seek a deeper conversion that begins in our deepest religious identity and transforms all of life. Whatever our religion, this conversion transforms the way we see us-ness and otherness. We still cherish our distinctive religious identity, but we abandon what my friend Samir Selmanovic calls *religious supremacy*. We are converted from hostility, from seeing the other as a threat to be feared, pitied, eliminated or refashioned into our image. We are converted into hosts and guests, practising and receiving hospitality, sharing our treasures as gifts. Karen Armstrong said it well:[6]

> Sometimes it's the very otherness of a stranger, someone who doesn't belong to our ethnic or ideological or religious group, an otherness that can repel us initially, but which can jerk us out of our habitual selfishness, and give us intonations of that sacred otherness, which is God.

The shared escape from 'habitual selfishness' and this shared listening for 'sacred otherness' is not a claim by or for any religious institution or tradition, including one called Christianity. Instead, it makes a proposal to members of each religious tradition, inviting them to turn away from all hostile identities and turn towards God and neighbour, stranger, outcast, outsider and enemy.

In so doing, this proposal celebrates a joyous opportunity for everyone, whatever their religious affiliation: the opportunity to encounter the God who loves everyone and every created thing. But according to Jesus, the genuine encounter with God never ends there. It always leads to a fresh encounter with the other as well. So our proclamation isn't simply a matter of pointing others to God: it is about inviting others on a shared journey to *and through* God to the neighbour, the other, the enemy – and, we might add, to all living creatures and the creation that sustains them.

In this way, the old language of saving souls grows more meaningful than ever: it is our mission to save souls from the dehumanising effects of hostility to God and other; souls, yes, and the bodies on which souls depend. And the human societies on which bodies and souls depend. And the natural ecosystems on which bodies, souls and societies depend. And this precious planet on which everything depends. So more than ever, we are engaged in the sacred mission of salvation – including salvation from the disastrous effects of misguided, distorted, dysfunctional religion, beginning with our own. This saving mission calls every individual – each soul, if you will – to make a saving decision: the choice to live not for our own selfish interests alone, and not for the groupish interests of our clan or caste or civilisation alone, but for the common good, the good of all creation.

That term *common good* and its cousins, *commonweal* and *commonwealth*, are, I am increasingly convinced, excellent synonyms for Jesus' term *kingdom of God*. Similarly, Jesus' word for this radical turn from self-interest towards the common good was *repent*. And here Christians face a special challenge, because Christ's good news calls *us* to repentance before it calls anyone else. It calls us to repent of the many ways our Christianity has become an oppositional clan or hostile caste or supreme civilisation that demands loyalty due only the commonwealth or kingdom of God.

Clans and castes and civilisations are part of our history. They are a given in human society. If we abolished them all today, new ones would emerge tomorrow. And they have a real value: they conserve shared memory, they preserve shared values and virtues, and they serve as the 'identity tents' in which generation after generation of children learn to move beyond *me* to *we*. But when our clans, castes and civilisations teach generation after generation of children to hold oppositional identities, rendering them hostile towards other people who have been raised in their respective little identity tents, then our clans and castes and civilisations must be repented of, including our Christian clans and castes and civilisations.[7]

That is a great gift of a multi-faith world to Christians: in challenging us to repent of our clannishness, caste-liness and cultural exceptionalism or supremacy, our multi-faith context challenges us to become better − meaning more Christ-like − Christians.

Although this new approach to Christian mission is indeed warm, it is not fuzzy or fizzy, the spiritual equivalent of the old Coke commercial about the world singing in perfect harmony. It is frank, pointed and even confrontational about discordant forces among and within us that won't yield to harmony even when enticed by a cool sugary drink. It warns us what to expect if we don't change our ways − not a fiery torture chamber after death, but a death trap in this life: war, hate, violence and fear; famine, disease, floods and drought; hunger, riots, refugee camps and crime. Because it is willing to challenge the status quo of oppositional identity, it requires a lot of guts and resilience, because there are few things more dangerous than approaching with open hands an angry gang with clenched fists.

Surprisingly to some, in deepening our engagement with the love of God, this new era in Christian mission may require us to speak again of the wrath of God. But it is not the wrath many of us encountered in our religious past, the divine mascot of *us* who

243

is ready to bark, bite and devour *them*. If we speak of an angry God at all, we will speak of a God angry at indifference, angry at apathy, angry at racism and violence, angry at inhumanity, angry at waste, angry at destruction, angry at injustice, angry at hostile religious clannishness. That anger is never against *us* (or *them*); it is against *what is against* us (and them). It is not out to destroy us; it is out to destroy what is out to destroy us. If we compare it to a fire, it is not a fire that consumes good things. Only an evil fire could consume good. The holy fire of God can consume only evil things – things that would be better off not existing. And since human beings bear the image of God, their humanity can never be considered an evil thing. The greed, pride, fear, craving and hostility that infect humanity – *they* are the evil thing – and they are what God loves to save us from.

So that is the salvation we must proclaim, including salvation from dysfunctional religion itself. That's why God's good news is neither a call to convert from one religion to another, nor an injunction against the freedom of religion that would restrict people from converting if they so desire.

So if a Muslim or Hindu community is destroying Muslims or Hindus, if it bores them with irrelevance, wastes their time and energy with meaningless and pointless rituals, if it turns them against others and obstructs the common good, I hope a Christian community will open their doors wide and offer sanctuary and healing. How could anyone turn them away? How could anyone refuse them water for baptism? How could anyone refrain from breaking out the bread and wine and welcoming them to the table?

But the same must be said when Christians are being destroyed, bored, wasted or turned hostile by their Christian communities, and other communities (often agnostics or atheists) offer them sanctuary. That's why this saving mission vigorously supports religious freedom, including the freedom to change religions and the freedom to be non-religious, multi-religious or spiritual-but-not-religious.[8]

Contrary to some accusations, we advocates of this emerging missionality do not downplay Jesus. We celebrate Jesus more than ever. But instead of holding Jesus hostage as the private property of the Christian religion, we dare proclaim that God has already offered Christ as a gift to the world ('For God so loved the world that he gave . . .'). Christ does not, then, belong to any single religion, especially our own. No, Christ already belongs to everyone everywhere. As the Christmas carol puts it, 'Let every heart prepare him room and heaven and nature sing'. And so we challenge every religion – including all forms of Christianity – to prepare him room and sing.

We are not saying, 'Take Jesus and custom-design him to fit into your existing culture or religion,' even though that's exactly what we Christians have done repeatedly throughout our history. Instead we say, 'Welcome Jesus into your community and watch as he turns your water into wine, trades your temples of stone for temples of humanity, turns over the tables of your religious-industrial complex, and invites you to be born again, not as a one-time experience but as an ongoing transformation. Welcome Jesus and watch everything change.'

So this emerging missionality is neither universalistic, exclusivistic nor inclusivistic in the traditional sense. Those old terms are framed within assumptions (about original sin and hell, about God and vengeance, etc.) that we have come to acknowledge are part of the problem. We aren't taking new positions framed within old approaches: we're seeking a new approach altogether.

But at the same time, our saving message is indeed exclusive in the sense that it excludes hostility, injustice, apathy and violence And it is inclusive in the sense that everyone is welcome to participate, regardless of religious label. And it is universalist in the sense that it will not rest until everyone who wants to can and does experience the abundant life of shalom, humility, kindness and justice that God desires for all. We want to share the treasures of Christ universally, with everyone, everywhere, in every religion.

But sharing is never a one-way street. It is always about receiving as well as giving. In generosity, we freely share our treasures with people of other faiths, *without requiring them to convert.* And in that same spirit, we gratefully receive the treasures generously offered to us by other faiths – *without needing to convert.* So we Christians generously share our treasures with others, and we receive the gifts generously offered to us by Jews, Muslims, Buddhists, Hindus, agnostics, atheists and others. We don't force everything we have on them: giving is not imposing. Nor must we receive everything they may offer. The freedom to say 'No, thank you' or 'Not right now' is essential to human dignity and generosity.

We never forget that there is a difference between a guest and a thief, just as there is a difference between quotation and plagiarism. The former respects the right to privacy and property and the latter doesn't. So the new evangelism encourages generous sharing of spiritual treasures but doesn't condone their theft, pirating or misappropriation. It sees the importance of each faith maintaining its own identity – and believes that can be done without hostility and with generosity.

Meanwhile, in this emergent missionality, we respect the freedom of people of any religion including our own to be hostile. We understand that hostility is often an unchosen reflex or unconscious habit, not a chosen response, so we don't insult, shame or condemn people for practising the kinds of religious hostility we are seeking to provide an alternative to. The very act of insulting, shaming or condemning others for hostility would be hostile and therefore inappropriate, not to mention absurd. And besides, we have learned from our own mistakes that religious people engage in hostility not because they are inherently hostile, but because they perceive things they love are under threat. Their aggression often boils over from a loving defensiveness.

So our new approach demands a great deal of us: graciousness, understanding, empathy, non-retaliation, non-defensiveness and patience when wronged. In fact, it requires us to rejoice when unfairly persecuted, rejected and slandered, because we know that it is only from the position of vulnerability, when we stand at risk of being misunderstood, excluded and misrepresented, that we can embody and speak the good news. (Mustn't our good news come in risk, not power; in weakness, not strength; as apparent foolishness, not with worldly coercion; with rough edges, not slickness? If we employ power, domination, persuasion and slickness, wouldn't we be conquering, colonising and selling, not evangelising?)

Finally, our saving mission respects privacy and avoids pressure. We know that people need time to reflect, privacy to come to themselves, and space to consider turning around and choosing a new path. Yet we also know that choices must be made, convictions confessed, regrets acknowledged, costs counted. So we urge people, as soon as they are ready, to speak out and confess where they stand, who they are becoming, where they are going, how they believe, and why. With both patience and urgency we invite people to 'fess up, sign on, join in and come out of the closet. This requires courage and grace – the courage to differ, and the grace to do so both gently and firmly.

So we constantly issue what we might call an *alter call* instead of an *altar call*. We do not invite people to another religious altar where another hostile deity can be appeased by another list of protocols, thus engendering another set of hostilities. No, we invite people to alter their understanding of God entirely, to come to know God as revealed in the human-kindness of Christ . . . to discover a God who needs no appeasement but who seeks to bring all things into joyous reconciliation. In light of this altered experience of God, we invite people to alter their self-understanding as well, discovering a new identity that alters everything – leading to a conversion so deep it fills with new meaning old, spent, clichéd terms like *born again*, *saved*, *converted*, *confirmed*, *baptised* or *catechised*.

Because the cost of embracing a strong and benevolent Christian identity is so high, we must provide lots of support for those who respond . . . support through fellowship, support through teaching (knowledge) and training (know-how), support through ritual and symbol, support through guided practice and mentoring. But since we are still young and inexperienced in this new identity, we have a long way to go in learning how to provide this support, and each of us must take whatever little we have learned and pass it on to others, even as we look for others who can pass more on to us.

This book represents my sincere and highly improvable contribution to that process. I conclude with my *alter call* to you, inviting you to become, even now, not only a believer, but an evangelist in this way of holding Christian identity in a multi-faith world.

Yes, sailing ships were used to transport slaves, and yes, windmills were part of the colonial economy. But the wind can't be held responsible for the uses towards which it was put.

So I invite you to feel and enjoy the wind of the Spirit that flows around and within you at this very moment. I urge you to unfurl your sails and welcome the Spirit's power in your life. I bid you rejoice that the wind of the Spirit blows everywhere and can't be contained in anyone's box, no matter how big or small, old or new. And I point you to Jesus, this strong and kind Galilean man who was filled with the Spirit, who walked the way of peace and bids us to follow. Let us who identify ourselves as Christians boldly follow Jesus into new territory to explore new possibilities we have never even dreamed of before. Let us, with him, cross the road in order to encounter the other and, in so doing, encounter the Other.

CHAPTER 29

How a Hindu Can Help Christians Discover Their True Identity in a Multi-faith World

The tremendous question presses itself upon us: Will the present Christian Church be big enough, responsive enough, Christlike enough to be the organ through which Christ will come to our multifaith world? For mind you, the Spirit of Christ is breaking out beyond the borders of the Christian Church. Will the Christian Church be Christlike enough to be the moral and spiritual center of this overflowing movement of the Spirit? Or will many of the finest people in our multifaith world accept Christ as Lord and master of their lives but be forced to live their spiritual lives apart from the historic Christian Church?

adapted from E. Stanley Jones[1]

My friend Rob Bell stirred things up a while back with a book called *Love Wins*. You wouldn't think that would be such a controversial proposition for Christians, but Rob suggested something daring: *if love has the final word, hell and damnation can't*. The book raised questions similar to the ones we raised in

Part Two of this book, questions about some of our long-held theological assumptions that may have outlived both their practical usefulness and their biblical credibility. You could almost hear the theological gears clicking in some readers' minds: *If Christianity isn't a plan for avoiding hell, why be a Christian?* and *If we lose hell, our religion loses its reason for existence.* The idea that there could be even better, stronger, more compelling reasons for Christian faith than hell-avoidance didn't seem to cross many minds, and even fewer seemed to 'get' the alternate vision of Christian faith that Rob was proposing. Many couldn't get past the first page, where Rob challenged an assumption that many Christians share: *because Mahatma Gandhi died a Hindu, not a Christian, he is in hell at this moment.*

Gandhi's eternal destiny, it turns out, troubles Christians on both sides of the hell debate – upsetting some that he might not be granted access to heaven and upsetting others that he might. As different camps of Christians continue to debate and speculate about Gandhi's fate, it seems appropriate to let Gandhi get a word in edgewise . . . through a conversation he had with a Christian missionary named E. Stanley Jones.

Jones (1884–1973) was a professor at Asbury Seminary before becoming a Methodist missionary to India. In India he became friends with Gandhi and, years later, he wrote a biography of Gandhi that inspired Dr Martin Luther King Jr to commit himself to non-violence in the civil rights movement. Jones wrote many other books as well, and his most famous, *Christ of the Indian Road* (1925), sold over a million copies.[2]

The life and work of E. Stanley Jones serve as a beautiful example of the strong and benevolent Christian identity we have been advocating in these pages. Like other great Christian missionaries in India,[3] Jones neither watered down his deep commitment to Christ, nor did he set out to knock down the world's third-largest religion so he could replace it with Christianity. He looked for a way that Christ could enter, incarnate himself within and bless Hinduism just as he had done in sectors of Judaic culture, Greco-Roman culture, Celtic culture, Anglo-Saxon culture and many other cultures through history.[4] He envisioned a time when a new movement of Indian followers of Christ would model a new, non-Western kind of Christian faith, one that respected the Hindu roots in which it grew and one that brought blessing to its Hindu and Muslim neighbours.

Gandhi's relationship with Christian faith was long and complex. Although he never joined the Christian religion, he loved Christ and wanted Indian culture to welcome what Christ had to offer, as his famous interchange with E. Stanley Jones made clear. Jones asked, 'I am very anxious to see Christianity naturalized in India, so that it shall no longer be a foreign thing identified with a foreign people and a foreign government, but a part of the national life of India and contributing its power to India's uplift and redemption. What would you suggest we do to make that possible?'

Gandhi replied, 'I would suggest, first of all, that all of you Christians, missionaries and all, begin to live more like Jesus Christ.' Reflecting on Gandhi's statement, Jones commented, 'He needn't have said anything more – that was quite enough. I knew that looking through his eyes were the three hundred millions of India, and speaking through his voice were the . . . millions of the East saying to me . . . "If you will come to us in the spirit of your Master, we cannot resist you."'

Gandhi continued, 'Second, I would suggest that you must practise your religion without adulterating or toning it down.' And again, Jones commented, 'The greatest living non-Christian asks us not to adulterate or tone it down, not to meet them with an emasculated gospel, but to take it in its rugged simplicity and high demand. But what are we doing? As someone has suggested, we are inoculating the world with a mild form of Christianity, so that it is now practically immune against the real thing.'

Gandhi then said, 'Third, I would suggest that you must put your emphasis upon love, for love is the centre and soul of Christianity.' Once more, Jones observed, 'He did not mean love as a sentiment, but love as a working force, the one real power in a moral universe, and he wanted it applied between individuals and groups and races and nations, the one cement and salvation of the world.'

Gandhi concluded: 'Fourth, I would suggest that you study the non-Christian religions and culture more sympathetically in order to find the good that is in them, so that you might have a more sympathetic approach to the people.'

On these four points, the Hindu leader and the Christian missionary were in full agreement. We might call them four cornerstones or four foundations for Christian identity in a multi-faith world. But I think it would be better to imagine movement rather than stasis, so we can think of them as four pistons in an engine or four wheels on a car. They can help us take what we've learned in this book, translate it into action and live it on the global multi-faith road as Jones sought to live it on the Indian road.

As Gandhi said, Christian identity in a multi-faith world must be marked first and foremost by *Christ-likeness* – so that we experience spiritual formation in Christ-like character, Christ-like vision and Christ-like virtues and values.[5] Second, Christian identity must focus on unadulterated, undiluted Christian *practice* – full-bodied, caffeinated, high-proof devotion in action.[6] The third mark of Christian identity hardly needs to be said in light of the first two: to emphasise *love* as 'centre and soul' of our faith, love for God with all our heart, soul, mind and strength, and love for neighbour, stranger, outcast, outsider and enemy. And fourth, we must approach other religions and cultures – and the people who inhabit them – with what Gandhi called 'sympathy', but we might better call understanding, respect, human-kindness or *benevolence*.[7]

If you are a Christian, you already know that some Christian communities will not help you practise this kind of Christian identity animated by these four driving forces. Some will pile on strictures and baggage and qualifiers and burdens and arguments that will tie you down, hold you back and do you in. Others will require you to imitate their hostility as a proof of your orthodoxy. These kinds of communities will frustrate you, and you will frustrate them.

That's OK. We shouldn't be surprised. This is to be expected. This is exactly why the good news of Jesus Christ is so needed – good news of reconciliation, proclaimed in word and deed. Because thankfully, while some groups constrict and others fight and still others wrinkle, shrink and wither, many communities of faith are coming alive in a fresh, new way. They are becoming more and more committed to developing more and more Christians with this kind of joyful, peaceful, contagious strong-benevolent identity. And more good news: if you can't find this kind of faith community, you can form one. You really can. It might be as simple as inviting a few friends over for dinner (or gathering online) to read and discuss this book and books like it together.[8]

Everyone is crossing roads. Many, like the religious leaders in Jesus' paradigmatic story (Luke 10:25–37), cross the road in fear and prejudice to avoid contact with the other. But some, like the good Samaritan, cross the road in compassion and solidarity, moving towards the other to touch, to heal, to affirm human-kindness. In that spirit, we have begun crossing the road, and on the other side we are discovering the other as neighbour, and God as loving Creator of all.[9] This crossing forever changes our identity. Each page that we have turned has been a small step in embracing that new identity, in making room for it to be born within us.

For all our progress, we still have a long way to go. We have only begun to face and trace the darker threads of our history and to own them and integrate them with the brighter hues in our tapestry of faith (the historical challenge). We are just begin-ning to reformulate and celebrate our doctrine as a healing teaching rather than an exclusive litmus test (the doctrinal chal-lenge). We are neophytes when it comes to reinvigorating our liturgy for strong-and-kind spiritual formation (the liturgical challenge). And we have a long journey ahead in reframing and practising our mission in a politically conflicted, ecologically precarious, economically unjust and spiritually diverse world (the missional challenge). But to be crossing the road at all is great progress in comparison to being huddled defensively on our opposite corners, glaring from a distance in fear, pride, isolation and ignorance. So, just as Jesus introduced an outsider – a despised Samaritan – to teach his companions about the greatest commandment, a Hindu has given us a final word in these final pages.

Let's also hear the voice of a Muslim, born under apartheid in South Africa. While many of his peers veered into Islamic radicalism – some of them later joining the Taliban – Farid Esack pioneered Islamic liberation theology, working non-violently with Christians, Hindus and others to overcome apartheid and gender inequality, and to pursue justice, peace and the common good. Here is how he concluded his book on the rediscovery of a strong-benevolent Muslim identity:

> These are but some of the many issues that we know little about and need to address. It is not going to be easy. What we do know is that our world has become small and the dangers threatening it, multifarious . . . Humankind, especially the marginalized and oppressed, need each other to confront these dangers and the challenges of liberation. Let us hope that, because of, and not despite, our different creeds and worldviews, we are going to walk this road side by side. Let us hope that we will be able to sort out some of the theological issues whilst we walk the road.[10]

Our varied histories have brought us to a crossroads. We can stand our ground here on our opposite corners and defend the frigid distance between us. Or we can cross the road. With outstretched hands, smiling faces and open hearts, we can move towards one another, meet in the middle and walk side by side beyond the limits of our old suspicious, segregated spaces. We can reject the mutual hostility by which we have defined ourselves, respect the different gifts we bring one another and inject fresh hope into the global human equation through the unexpected factor of human-kindness. Walking together, we can face our common threats and seek the common good, forging a future that would have been impossible any other way. In so doing, as Farid Esack said, we will all feel like beginners, for we will all have to acknowledge how little we know.

Becoming like little children is not such a bad thing. If we are humbled to the point of beginning anew and seeing afresh, maybe, just maybe, our identities will be transformed by grace so that we will reflect more fully the One in whose image we are created. Perhaps this encounter with the other is the crossroads to which God has been leading us all along. Perhaps this choice now – to move forward or to hold back, to open arms or to clench fists, to identify ourselves by opposition and hostility or to identify ourselves by hospitality and solidarity – perhaps this is our defining moment.

So imagine, then, Jesus, Moses, the Buddha and Mohammed crossing the road to encounter one another. Imagine us following them. What will we discover together in that crossing?

Surely, it will be holy and humbling in that sacred space. Surely there will be joy, grace and peace. Surely justice, truth and love. We will find hospitality there, not hostility, and friendship, not fear, and it will be good – good for our own well-being, good for the poor and forgotten, good for our grandchildren's grandchildren and good even for the birds of the air and the flowers in the meadow and the fish out at sea. God will say, 'This is very good.' And we will say, 'Amen.'

Acknowledgements

First, thanks to those who read this book and made important suggestions, especially Sailesh Rao, Paul Rauschenbusch, Jeff Burns, Michael Hardin, Paul Neuchterlein and Rabbi Or Rose. Where I followed their advice, the book is better; where I didn't, it's not their fault. Thanks to Joy Madeiros of Oasis Trust (http:// oasisuk.org) for a stimulating conversation eight or nine years ago that planted a seed for this book. Thanks to all who guided me to important scholarship, especially Sheila Bravo, Amanda Henderson and Samuel Ewell. Thanks to Michael Hardin, Tony Bartlett, James Alison, Suzanne Ross and others who have helped me more deeply appreciate René Girard. Thanks to Carl Medearis, Rod Cardoza, Bart Campolo and Jeff Burns, for their friendship, conversations and connections related to this book. Thanks to Ted Durr and Imam Shamshad Nasir and other friends in the DC area who rose to the occasion after 11 September 2001. Thanks to Jeff and Janet Wright for introducing me to Israel/ Palestine, and to Bowie Snodgrass and Samir Selmanovic for pioneering multi-faith community. Thanks to Rabbi Shawn Landres, Mark Braverman, Marc Ellis, Michael Lerner, Eboo Patel, Soraya Deen and Nadyne Heinert for all you've taught me.

Thanks to all my colleagues on the speaking circuit, especially Jay Bakker, Nadia Bolz-Weber, Tony Jones, Doug Pagitt, Phyllis Tickle, Gareth Higgins, Frank Schaeffer, Diana Butler Bass, Marcus Borg, Dom Crossan, Jim Wallis, Pete Rollins, Bart Campolo and Tony Campolo. In your diverse ways, you are itinerant evangelists of a new Christian identity.

Thanks to booksellers and all in the publishing industry who are steering a course through choppy waters. Thanks to bloggers who use the new media to alert people to good things in the old. Thanks to Wendy Grisham, Katherine Venn and everyone at Jericho, Hodder and Hachette: you are a pleasure to work with, and I am so grateful to be on your team. (And special thanks to Joanna Davey for the brilliant title brainstorming!) Especially enthusiastic, heartfelt thanks to Kathryn Helmers and everyone at Creative Trust, whose guidance and support mean more to me than I can say, and to Luci Neuman, Joe and Suzanne Stabile, and all my colleagues at Life in the Trinity Ministry, for giving me a professional home. Thanks to Kyle Bennett and the people of St Mark's for great pastoral care.

Thanks to Grace, whose companionship makes everything in life better, and thanks to my parents for raising me in the first half of life, and to my kids for raising me in the second.

Thanks to all of you who will read this book and translate it into kind, generous, road-crossing action, each in your own creative way. Thanks to all of you who will recommend this book to friends, both those you know will love it and those you suspect might not, but still should read it anyway.

And finally, thanks be to God. Each book I've written has stretched me and matured me in the writing of it, and that's especially true for this one, which gives me reason to hope that the same will be true for all who read.

For more information and additional resources, including a downloadable group study guide, please check out http://www.brianmclaren.net.

Notes

Chapter 1

1. Samir Selmanovic, *It's Really All About God: How Islam, Atheism, and Judaism Made Me a Better Christian* (San Francisco: Jossey-Bass, 2009), pp. 267–268. Samir is echoing G. K. Chesterton, who said, 'It is the test of a good religion whether you can joke about it.'

2. Bruce Main asks a similar question in his book *Why Jesus Crossed the Road* (Carol Stream, Ill.: SaltRiver, 2010). His subtitle suggests the energetic direction of his answer: *Learning to Follow the Unconventional Travel Itinerary of a First-Century Carpenter and His Ragtag Group of Friends as They Hop Fences, Cross Borders, and Generally Go Where Most People Don't.*

3. Like this one, in *Potter's American Monthly*: *Q: Why should a chicken not cross a road? A: It would be a fowl proceeding.*

4. We see a great fusion of anti-humour and humour at work in this example: *A pastor, an imam, a rabbi and a Buddhist monk walk into a bar. The bartender asks, 'Is this some kind of joke?'*

5. Jesus was criticised by his more puritan critics for being too friendly with 'the wrong sort' of people. See Luke 7:34.

6. For a good introduction to some of these religious leaders, I'd recommend for Mohammed, *No God but God* by Reza Aslan (New York: Random House, Updated edition, 2011); for Moses, *A History of God* by Karen Armstrong (New York: Ballantine, 1994); for the Buddha, *One Dharma* by Joseph Goldstein (New York: HarperOne, 2003); for Wovoka (or Jack Wilson), *Neither Wolf nor Dog* by Kent Nerburn (Middle Island, NY: New World, 2002). One of the best Christian resources introducing world religions is Adam Hamilton's *Christianity and World Religions* (Nashville, TN: Abingdon, 2005).

7. One answer might be to escape from a mob of their angry, hypercritical and hypocritical followers.

8. It is indeed ironic that some would be furious about their religious leaders being seen walking into a bar together, but are not so scandalised by the fear, prejudice, hatred and violence promoted and defended in the names of their religions.

9. Buddhists are required to follow ten precepts that are sometimes compared to the ten commandments of Judaism. (Monks of the Theravada tradition agree to follow over two hundred precepts.) In addition to abstaining from 'intoxicating drinks and drugs causing heedlessness' (the Fifth Precept), Buddhists are to abstain from 'harming living beings (1); taking things not freely given (2); sexual misconduct (3); false speech (4); taking untimely meals (6); dancing, singing, music and watching grotesque mime (7); use of garlands, perfumes, and personal adornment (8); use of high seats (9); and accepting gold or silver (10).' (See http://www.thebigview.com/buddhism/precepts. html.)

10. The narthex, the lobby or porch area of a church, is itself a fascinating theo-architectural concept. Historically, it was built so outsiders

– the unbaptised or excluded – could 'eavesdrop' on the service, thus serving as a liminal space between exclusion and inclusion.

11. This quote is widely attributed to Blake, but the precise source is unknown. It may be a conclusion drawn from the poem that follows in the text, 'The Little Vagabond'.

12. And, we might add, in a crucified man and among a ragtag band of his followers.

13. The best single book I'm aware of on the subject of Christian identity is Kwame Bediako's masterpiece, *Theology and Identity* (Oxford: Regnum, 1992). In addition, Diana Butler Bass helpfully summarises and applies the work of Anthony Wallace and William McLoughlan in the first chapter of *Christianity After Religion* (New York: HarperOne, 2012). But much more scholarly work is needed on the subjects of Christian identity – its desired characteristics, its formation, its decline, its health, its dysfunctions, its relation to solidarity and so on. On the subject of religious pluralism from a Christian perspective, Catholic (and formerly Catholic) writers have been most helpful to me – among them Peter Phan, Paul Knitter, Raimon Pannikkar, Anthony de Mello, Leonardo Boff and Jacques Dupuis. Samir Selmanovic, quoted in this chapter's epigram, has been a leader and example for many of us in the emergent conversation, as have Native American Christians like Richard Twiss, Randy Woodley, Ray Aldred and Terry LeBlanc.

14. This kind of pseudofriendship expresses the 'love the sinner, hate the sin' mind-set: love the Hindu but hate his Hinduism. We Christians can understand how this would make a Hindu feel if we imagine him saying, 'I love you as a person, I really do, but I hate Christianity.' To accept friendship of this sort would feel like a betrayal of our faith, as if to say, 'That's OK. My religion isn't that important to my identity anyway. No big deal if you hate it, as long as you like me.' My friend and mentor Tony Campolo frequently points out that 'Love the sinner,

hate the sin' is not what Jesus taught. In Matt. 7:1–5, Tony explains, Jesus taught, 'Love the sinner, and hate your own sin.' In *New Seeds of Contemplation* (New York: New Directions, 2007), Thomas Merton made the same point: 'So instead of loving what you think is peace, love other [people] and love God above all. And instead of hating the people you think are war-makers, hate the appetites and the disorder in your own soul, which are the causes of war. If you love peace, then hate injustice, hate tyranny, hate greed – but hate these things in yourself, not in another.'

15. In contrast, by *weak* I mean a faith that is nominal and of little practical significance to one's way of life. Weak or nominal faith tends to grow weaker, less fertile, more brittle and more disposable from one generation to the next, while robust faith inspires future generations to keep it alive so that it can continue to grow, adapt and produce more and better fruit in the future.

16. In contrast, by *hostile* I mean a faith identity that does not bear good will towards other religions, ultimately wishing that other religions would decline and disappear, or at least be marginalised and minimised.

17. Also, as in all my books, I've changed names and details in many of the stories to protect personal and organisational anonymity.

18. It will also be clear that there are important scholars I haven't yet discovered, an inevitability in a field this important, wide-ranging and fast-growing.

19. This urgent choice suggests another possible answer to the title's question: *Why did Jesus, Moses, the Buddha and Mohammed cross the road? In the hope that we would follow them.*

Chapter 2

1. From James Alison, *Broken Hearts and New Creations* (London: Continuum, 2010), p. 165, quoted online in Suzanne Ross, 'Left Behind:

Now What?' *Copy That!* (blog), http://www.ravenfoundation. org/blogs/copy-that/left-behind-now-what/. HarperOne Executive Editor Mickey Maudlin made a similar point in an article about Rob Bell's book, *Love Wins*: 'As a young evangelical, I was socialized to see the biggest threat to the church as theological liberalism. But now I think the biggest threat is Christian tribalism, where God's interests are reduced to and measured by those sharing your history, tradition, and beliefs, and where one needs an "enemy" in order for you to feel "right with God"' (http://www.newsandpews.com/2011/07/ rob-bells-hell-by-mickey-maudlin-harperone-senior-v-p-executive-editor/).

2. Christians, it should be noted, have always lived in a multi-faith world. But for many, living in a mono-religious neighbourhood or nation (whether in Europe, the US or elsewhere) became so familiar that having Hindu or Muslim neighbours move in next door now comes as a shock, even more so when they challenge the notions of Christian privilege to which many Christians have become accustomed.

3. Graduate students have a saying that explains how dissertation topics are chosen: *All research is me-search*. 'All' may be an overstatement. But the saying reminds us that beneath the shades-of-grey paint of scholarly objectivity, intensely colourful, personal motivations inspire most if not all of our important work.

4. Matt. 5:9; 2 Cor. 5:16–21, Jas 3:13–18.

5. I've explored this tension between something real and something wrong in several of my books, most notably *A New Kind of Christian* (San Francisco: Jossey-Bass, 2001) and *A New Kind of Christianity* (New York: HarperOne, 2010).

6. You can read 'My Take: Why I Support Anne Rice But Am Still a Christian' on my blog at http://www.brianmclaren.net/archives/blog/ my-take-why-i-support-anne-rice.html.

7. Simon Barnes uses *bad* in just this sense in *How to Be a (Bad) Birdwatcher* (New York: Pantheon, 2005), and Dave Tomlinson similarly employs *bad* in *How to Be a Bad Christian* (London: Hodder & Stoughton, 2012).

8. 'I'm a Christian, but . . .' is another symptom of CRIS, as explained by Bill Dahl: 'I became tired of answering their questions with, "I'm a Christian, *but* . . ." . . . They had crammed me in a readily available mental box right along with *everybody else*. I instantaneously become "one of those". I placed myself at an immediate and distinct disadvantage by using the *Christian* label.' (From *The Questians*, an e-book available here: http://www.theporpoisedivinglife.com/porpoise-diving-life.asp?pageID=622.)

9. Or when the son of a beloved iconic evangelist insults Mohammed and Muslims? Or when self-identifying Evangelical Christians in the USA rank statistically highest in support of the use of torture, and lowest in support for foreign aid? Or when Bible-quoting Christian Zionists defend Israeli colonists in their expanding violations of Palestinian human rights? Or when their equal-and-opposite counterparts defend Palestinians without speaking against violence used against innocent Israeli citizens? Or when American Christian radio personalities accuse the environmental movement of being a Satanic conspiracy they call 'the Green Dragon'? Or when prosperity-gospel preachers create a kind of religious mafia through which they ensnare and exploit sincere and gullible member/donors? And so on.

10. If you're Mark Braverman or Marc Ellis or Michael Lerner, you write courageous books like *Fatal Embrace* (New York: Beaufort, 2012), or *Judaism Does Not Equal Israel* (New York: New Press, 2009), or *Embracing Israel/Palestine* (Berkeley: Tikkun Books and North Atlantic Books, 2012).

11. By 'the other', I mean anyone who is considered to be an outsider, not 'one of us', belonging to a differing group, gender, orientation, party, community, religion, race, culture or creed. This definition suggestions one of the best punch lines for the title's question: *Why did Jesus, Moses, the Buddha and Mohammed cross the road? To get to the other.*

12. For more on 'the other', see Kester Brewin, *Other* (London: Hodder and Stoughton, 2010). John Franke, in his important book *Manifold Witness: The Plurality of Truth* (Nashville: Abingdon, 2009), writes of 'the Other in its eschatological sense': 'It is the Other that bursts through and shatters all the pretensions of our God talk and leaves our words and ourselves undone. As theologian William Stacy Johnson maintains, the Other . . . enters into our lives and shatters the protective totalities that we construct around ourselves for our security and protection. It is an infinity that claims us and will not let go in its call to move us beyond the constraints of our selfhood, beyond the limitations of our versions of reality and truth and towards the Other, the God in whom we live and move and have our being' (p. 112).

13. The word *host* comes from the Middle English of the thirteenth century. The *host* welcomed the *hostis* – which meant 'stranger'. One can see how the stranger, if trusted, would become the welcome guest but, if feared, would become the enemy – engendering hostility. For more on the relationship between stranger and guest, see Miroslav Volf's *Exclusion and Embrace: A Theological Exploration of Identity, Otherness, and Reconciliation* (Nashville: Abingdon, 1996). See also Volf's *Allah: A Christian Response* (New York: HarperOne, 2011). Both are extremely important contributions to the subject of Christian identity in a multi-faith world.

14. The allusion to John 1:5 is intentional.

15. *A New Kind of Christianity* (New York: HarperCollins, 2010), pp. 293–294 (note 10).

16. For perspectives on this shift, see David Korten, *The Great Turning* (Bloomfield, Conn: Kumarian; San Francisco: Berrett-Koehler, 2006), and Diana Butler Bass, *Christianity after Religion* (New York: HarperOne, 2012), along with the many equally valuable contributions by Phyllis Tickle, Tony Jones, Doug Pagitt, Dominic Crossan, Marcus Borg, Michael Hardin, Tony Barnett, James Alison, Philip Clayton, John Franke and others.

17. Evangelicals and Pentecostals, specialists in evangelism, face a special challenge and opportunity in this light. Strong-hostile identity is common among them. (Citizen-journalists Rachel Tabachnick and Greg Metzger have undertaken the difficult task of monitoring hostile rhetoric and behaviour in these circles. See http://www.talk2action. org/user/Rachel%20Tabachnick and http://debatingobama.blogspot. com/.) Yet anyone involved with evangelism among postmodern people soon realises that to them, a gospel characterised by hostility towards the other (religiously other, sexually other, etc.) is no gospel at all. It may be, then, that some courageous Evangelicals and Pentecostals will make a break from hostility while retaining their evangelistic passion. If so, they could well be among the pioneers and promoters of the strong-benevolent Christian identity advocated in this book.

Part One: The Crisis of Christian Identity

1. Sarah Sentilles, '*Breaking Up with God*: I Didn't Lose My Faith, I Left It,' *Religion Dispatches*, 2 June 2011, http://www.religiondispatches. org/books/rd10q/4650/breaking_up_with_god%3A_i_didn't_lose_ my_faith,_i_left_it.

Chapter 3

1. Paul Knitter, 'My God Is Bigger Than Your God! Time for Another Axial Shift in the History of Religions', *Studies in Interreligious Dialogue* 17, no. 1 (2007): 100–118.

2. A version of this story also appears in *My Neighbor's Faith: Stories of Interreligious Encounter, Growth, and Transformation*, ed. Jennifer Howe Peace, Rabbi Or Rose and Gregory Mobley (Maryknoll, NY: Orbis, 2012).

Chapter 4

1. Diana Butler Bass, *Christianity after Religion* (New York: HarperOne, 2012), p. 121. Diana is quoting a Facebook correspondent.

2. Dean Kelley, *Why Conservative Churches are Growing*, Rose edition (Macon, Ga.: Mercer University Press, 1986), xxiv–xxv. Hereinafter, page references will be given in the text.

3. The term *mainline* derives from a train line in Philadelphia that led to the affluent suburban neighbourhoods where upwardly mobile European immigrants and their descendants lived. These established immigrants – many of them Presbyterians, Lutherans, Episcopalians and Methodists – brought their Protestant affiliations with them from Northern Europe (in contrast to more recent Southern European and Irish immigrants, most of whom were Roman Catholic and, at that time, less affluent).

4. The reasons that old-line and new-line churches developed these differing characteristics are many and complex. Among them – many mainline churches derived their identity from state churches in Europe. State churches had to hold diverse groups together and couldn't so easily divide when differences arose. In contrast, the more 'sectarian' churches came into being by dividing from other groups; their minority identity from the start was a choice (*choice*, by the way, is at the

root of the word *heresy*) of resistance. The former had to learn the skills of containing, managing and resolving diversity and conflict, while the latter mastered the skills of fomenting, mobilising and maintaining difference and separateness.

5. In a critical response to Kelley, Laurence Iannacone argued that rational choice theory offers a better explanation for contrasting growth rates in different kinds of churches: it is not strictness per se, but rather the exclusion of undependable, uncommitted fellow members ('free riders') that makes membership in some churches more rewarding than others. High-demand groups produce high-commitment members who provide greater benefits to fellow members. I don't see their explanations as mutually exclusive; I propose that we add to both explanations the identity-building dimension of hostility.

6. In a follow-up article, Kelley sought for a way to describe the stricter, more demanding churches. He offered this: 'Perhaps the least pejorative label would be *non-ecumenical*.' What Kelley labels 'non-ecumenical' will, in these pages, be described as inhospitable or hostile to the other. See http://www.jstor.org/pss/1386160.

7. If the Christian third of the world's population – in its Catholic, Pentecostal, Evangelical, Orthodox, Anglican, Mainline Protestant and indigenous forms – can't or won't acknowledge and address its own hostility towards people of other faiths, the whole world will suffer. Conversely, if a third of the world's population becomes more robustly benevolent towards the other two-thirds, the whole world will benefit. Together, Christianity and Islam account for about 57 per cent of the world's population, and that percentage is expected to climb to two-thirds by the century's end. Christians and Muslims possess the vast majority of the world's financial and energy wealth, and the lion's share of the world's weapons, including nuclear

weapons. Clearly, the development of more benevolent faith-identities among Christians and Muslims in particular has become an urgent matter of planetary survival.

8. Many new-line Christians in the US still think that they are growing while 'the liberals' are declining. But in the new century, new-line trend lines have begun to mirror those of the old-line, just thirty or forty years later. Diana Butler Bass describes this new reality as the 'religious bear market' in chapter 3 of *Christianity after Religion*.

Chapter 5

1. The quote is usually translated from the French as 'men' instead of 'human beings', and 'religious motivation' is sometimes rendered 'conscience'.

2. Again, by *hostility* I mean animosity, ill will, antagonism and opposition that can be removed only when the other stops being one of 'them' and becomes one of 'us'. By *benignity*, I mean tolerance, harmlessness, a willingness to coexist. And by *benevolence*, I mean affection, good will, neighbourliness, solidarity and support . . . conviviality that doesn't require conversion or assimilation but that appreciates otherness. While those characterised by *hostility* would prefer other religions to remain in error until they are eliminated, and while those characterised by *benignity* would be more or less indifferent to the growth or regression of other religions, those characterised by *benevolence* would hope for other religions to grow into greater wholeness and truth, just as they would hope for their own religion. *Benevolence*, then, is a facet of loving one's neighbour as oneself.

3. From David Gibson, 'Does Religion Cause Terrorism? It's Complicated', *The Christian Century*, 1 September 2011, http://www.christiancentury.org/article/2011-09/does-religion-cause-terrorism-its-complicated/. The article surveys many of the key researchers

studying religious violence today: Charles Kurzman, Mark Juergensmeyer, William Cavanaugh, James Jones, David Schanzer, Jessica Stern, Charles Kimball and Ariel Glucklich. Gibson concludes, 'In general, scholars have concluded that religion – be it Islam or any other faith – is neither the chicken nor the egg when it comes to creating terrorists. Rather, religion is one of many factors in the explosive brew of politics, culture and psychology that leads fanatics to target innocents – and take their own lives in the process.' Glucklich is the author of *Dying for Heaven: Holy Pleasure and Suicide Bombers – Why the Best Qualities of Religion Are Also Its Most Dangerous* (New York: HarperOne, 2009). The book points out the powerful roles of joy and love in motivating religious violence.

Chapter 6

1. From a presentation made at the United Nations' '2007 High-Level Dialogue of the General Assembly on Interreligious and Intercultural Understanding and Cooperation for Peace', Informal Interactive Hearing with Civil Society (4–5 October 2007), p. 1; http://www.un.org/ga/president/62/issues/interreligiousintercultural/remarks.pdf.

2. The original saying, 'We have met the enemy and he is us,' came from the comic-strip character Pogo of the Okefenokee Swamp, created by Walt Kelly. It originally appeared in a 1970 poster and a 1971 comic strip.

3. What my Jewish friend meant by Jews needing Jesus will, I hope, become more clear in Part Three, where I will argue that Christians also need Jesus – a fresh vision of him – to become better Christians.

Chapter 7

1. Richard Kearney, *Anatheism: Returning to God after God* (New York: Columbia University Press, 2011), pp. 138, 147.

2. Sam Harris, 'Killing the Buddha,' http://www.samharris.org/site/full_text/killing-the-buddha/.

3. According to R. Scott Appleby in *Ambivalence of the Sacred* (New York: Rowman and Littlefield, 2000, p. 17), 'about two thirds of contemporary wars turn on issues of religious, ethnic, or national identity. Less than 10 percent begin as interstate conflicts.' Appleby acknowledges that religion is simultaneously a source of 'intolerance, human rights violations, and extremist violence' and a resource for 'non-violent conflict transformation, the defense of human rights, integrity in government, and reconciliation and stability in divided societies'. Quoted in Saira Yamin, 'Understanding Religious Identity and the Causes of Religious Violence', *Peace Prints: South Asian Journal of Peacebuilding* 1, no. 1 (Spring 2008): pp. 1, 5; available at http://www.wiscomp.org/pp-v1/Saira_Yamin.pdf.

4. Jack Nelson-Pallmeyer (*Is Religion Killing Us? Violence in the Bible and the Quran* [Harrisburg, Pa.: Trinity Press International, 2003], p. xi) qualifies Sam Harris's blame of religion as the 'explicit cause of literally millions of deaths' when he says, 'People rarely kill each other for reasons of religious difference alone. They do frequently use God and religion, however, to justify killing when conflicts escalate between individuals, groups, or nations. In the midst of problems rooted in land, oppression, discrimination, or any number of other historical grievances, religion is often called on to justify human violence with subtle or not so subtle references to "sacred" texts, divine mission, or moral purpose.'

5. Miroslav Volf explained the danger in these terms: 'If you are someone who has determined to resort to animosity and violence, then I think it's very hard not to exaggerate differences in our fundamental values. In a sense, hatred needs to emphasize difference so it can appropriately latch itself onto the object of our hatred. Violence

needs difference so it can unleash itself. That's why Jews were called vermin in the Holocaust. That's why Tutsis were called cockroaches in Rwanda. Emphasizing difference precedes violence. We need to see each other as alien in order to unleash our hatred in violence' (http://www.readthespirit.com/explore/2011/2/16/meet-miroslav-volf-whose-allah-is-a-path-to-peace.html). This danger deriving from difference helps explain why many people say, 'All religions are the same,' not realising that the blurring or erasure of differences can create other dangers as well.

6. The atheism of the former Soviet Union, for example, demonstrated that a strong economic and political identity could create no less hostility than a religious identity, as did the Maoist revolution in China and the Khmer Rouge regime in Cambodia. It turns out that the famous dictum, associated with Dostoevsky's Ivan Karamazov, can run both ways: yes, without God everything is theoretically permissible . . . but believers can find ways to use God to justify just about anything as well.

7. Imagine if a movement of sceptics decided that religious people were such a threat worldwide that they must be 'cleansed', leaving only the 'pure' – namely, members of their movement of pure rationalists or sceptics – to inherit the earth.

8. René Girard calls these mirror-imaging hostile pairs 'doubles', and he describes their mutually reinforcing imitation with the term *mimesis* (See *Things Hidden Since the Foundation of the World* [New York: Continuum Books, 2003]). Psychoanalyst Vamik Volkan sees this 'similarity between enemies' as a facet of regression and observes, 'I do not think that humans (as large groups) have ever developed the idea or ability to refrain from being like their enemies once they feel threatened or hurt' ('Large Group Identity, Large Group Regression and Massive Violence', p. 22, available online here: http://www.

austenriggs.org/education-research-the-erikson-institute/erikson-scholar-applications/senior-erikson-scholar/dr-volkans-sample-papers/). Skye Jethani offers a similar diagnosis – saying that all religions have a danger-avoidance component that renders them, ironically, dangerous to one another. See 'Do All Paths Lead to God?' at: http://us2.campaign-archive2.com/?u=87188c8737bc50c1a2fb8e2c9&id=fe94144554.

9. *Is Religion Killing Us?* p. xv.

10. Skin colour and race deserve special attention. In an important *Christian Century* article, Jonathan Tran quotes James Cone: 'American theology is racist . . . It identifies theology as dispassionate analysis of "the tradition," unrelated to the suffering of the oppressed.' See Jonathan Tran, 'The New Black Theology', *Christian Century*, http://christiancentury.org/article/2012-01/new-black-theology/. Tran explains how the racial construction of whiteness in theology plays a critical role, not only in ignoring the suffering of the oppressed, but also in increasing it:

> In European Christianity, the general question about difference settled on the specific question of Jewish difference – what came to be called *der Judenfrage* (the Jewish question). Attempting to espouse a universal conception of humanness independent of and over against the Jewish covenant of promise, European Christians crafted a rival discourse to help explain the Jews (and the non-European others whom the Jews exemplified): race. Speech about 'race' helped construe the Jews as a people inordinately attached to their peculiar practices and outdated laws. The Jews become 'the other' by which European Christianity defined itself. European Christians, in this view, are the universal race because they, unlike the Jews, are able to shed their religious particularity just the way

Jesus superseded the particularity of Jewish law. Or so the story went . . . 'Whiteness' is not so much something as nothing – a mythic conception of non-particularity, the achievement of genuine transcendence, true reason. It is purity, existence free of the blemishes that colored all other races. Thus race became the way Westerners came to understand people's differences and where people belong in the hierarchy of existence.

11. From http://campaignstops.blogs.nytimes.com/2012/03/17/forget-the-money-follow-the-sacredness/. Haidt explores these ideas in more depth in *The Righteous Mind: Why Good People are Divided by Politics and Religion* (New York: Pantheon Books, 2012).

12. From Vamik Volkan, *Killing in the Name of Identity* (Charlottesville, Va.: Pitchstone Publishing, 2006), p. 14, quoted in Yamin, p. 8.

13. See Volkan, 'Large Group Identity, Large Group Regression and Massive Violence'.

14. For example, their group may have been shamed or traumatised in some way that complicates their individual lives. Or they may fall in love with someone their group forbids. Or they may feel the ongoing development of their individual identity is limited or harmed by the restrictions of the large-group identity. Or they may be attracted to affiliate with a rival group, which will require them to leave the shelter of their ancestral tent. By the way, Volkan's use of the term 'big tent' should not be confused with Philip Clayton and Tripp Fuller's more hospitable use of the term, as in *Transforming Christian Theology* (Minneapolis: Fortress Press, 2010).

15. Vamik Volkan, 'Religious Fundamentalism and Violence', p. 21, available online here: http://www.austenriggs.org/education-research-the-erikson-institute/erikson-scholar-applications/senior-erikson-scholar/dr-volkans-sample-papers/.

16. Alison continues, 'Having an enemy is not about the truth; it's about knowing we are good.' See the Raven Foundation website (especially Suzanne Ross, 'Left Behind: Now What?' *Copy That!* [blog], at http://www.ravenfoundation.org/blogs/copy-that/left-behind-now-what) for more information on the development of hostility. Also, see Ted Schwartz's powerful play, *I'd Like to Buy An Enemy*, here: http://tedandcompany.com/id-like-to-buy-an-enemy/.

Chapter 8

1. It would be interesting to analyse a typical 'secular' day in terms of the religious rituals of consumerism. For example, people willingly watch hours of corporate propaganda daily in the form of advertisements. They submit themselves to daily indoctrination by the corporate media. They sing the songs of their religion in the form of corporate jingles or popular songs that praise the ecstasy of commodified romantic love. I explore this theme under Thomas M. Beaudoin's term *theocapitalism* in *Everything Must Change* (Nashville: Thomas Nelson, 2007).

2. I explored some of these consequences in *Everything Must Change* (Nashville: Thomas Nelson, 2007). For example, consumerism promotes greed that creates hostility between nations and classes; it rewards rapid resource extraction that impoverishes and degrades the environment for future generations; it seeks the quickest return on investment without taking into account long-range social consequences; it empowers corporations that privatise profits for shareholders and externalise costs especially upon the poor and powerless; it turns governments into puppets that serve the interests of those corporations without regard for justice and the common good; and it even co-opts and corrupts authentic spirituality by commodifying it for a religious-industrial complex.

3. In this scenario, where most of us abandon strong-hostile Christian identity for a weaker one, what might happen back in the dwindling Christian community where hostility is accepted as a necessary accompaniment to strength? The continuing departure of Christians with an aversion to hostility intensifies the corporate ethos of those who remain. As the Christian community's hostility quotient rises, members of other groups accurately assess Christianity as more and more of a threat to them. From there, any number of unpleasant scenarios might play out, all of them arguing for the pursuit of a strong and benevolent Christian identity.

4. Actually, Jesus suggested that repossession is seven times worse than the original possession (Matt. 12:43ff.). Time will tell if that formula holds in our case. The relationship between possession by demons and possession by identities deserves further consideration. Walter Wink's work is an ideal starting point, including *The Powers That Be* (New York: Three Rivers Press, 1999).

5. I rely on the word *solidarity* heavily in this book, and it deserves further definition. David Hollinger, in 'From Identity to Solidarity', defines it as 'an experience of willed affiliation' (*Daedalus*, Fall 2006, pp. 23–31). He contrasts it with 'mere membership' in a 'community of fate', explaining that '[f]eminism is a solidarity, but womanhood is not. Judaism is a solidarity, but having a Jewish ancestor . . . is not' (pp. 24–25). Solidarity, he says, 'implies a special claim, even if modest in dimensions, that individuals have on each other's energies, compassion, and resources' (p. 24). He explains that 'we all have multiple identities (national, ethnoracial, religious, sexual, geographical, ideological, professional, generational, etc.) and are capable of several solidarities', and we struggle to negotiate the competing claims and entitlements they entail (p. 27). All this is complicated when identities and solidarities are contested, under threat and in

flux, and especially when they are internally torn between 'the impulse for concentration (hold your familiar ground; stick with your own kind; consolidate the richness of your heritage) and the impulse for incorporation (expand your horizons; take on as much of the world as you can; try to locate the source of your dilemmas, however remote)' (p. 27). What I call 'Conflicted Religious Identity Syndrome' is a matter of solidarity that grapples with these three questions: 1. By choosing to affiliate with a group, am I obligated to endorse the hostilities it holds against other groups? 2. Is it possible for me to will affiliation with all people and all creation – especially if I understand Jesus and his gospel as a call to universal solidarity? 3. What do I do when my answer to the second question is in conflict with my answer to the first? As upcoming chapters will make clear, in core Christian doctrines and practices like the incarnation and the Eucharist, Christians affirm that God shows solidarity with all humanity and with all creation. And in Jesus' life and teaching, we see him demonstrating extraordinary, boundary-crossing solidarity with the poor, the oppressed, the outcast, the outsider, the other, even the enemy. It's no wonder that many of us believe *solidarity* will become a critical category for Christian theology and practice in this century and beyond.

6. Or: *If we boldly step out and preach against Christian nominality or lukewarmness, people will assume we are hostile extremists and troublemakers. Religious gatekeepers on websites and in magazines will single us out as conservative and hostile.*

7. In all likelihood, those who seek to 'save their lives' by siding with hostility will, in the long run, be losers, too, because eventually people will be no more willing to stay in religious institutions that support inter-faith hostility than they were willing in the past to stay in religious institutions that supported slavery and racism.

8. *Buycotts* are the opposite of boycotts: instead of mobilising people to avoid businesses and organisations that do harm, they mobilise people to patronise those that do good. The mobilised patrons who intentionally patronise socially beneficial organisations are called *carrot-mobs*. See www.carrotmob.org/.

Chapter 9

1. From a brilliant TED talk called, 'Chimamanda Adichie: The Danger of a Single Story', available as a video here: http://www.ted.com/talks/chimamanda_adichie_the_danger_of_a_single_story.html.

2. Thom Hartmann, *The Last Hours of Ancient Sunlight* (New York: Broadway Books, 2004), pp. 50ff.

3. The semantic and theological functions of 'the name of the Holy Trinity' in that sentence deserve reflection.

4. Thom Hartmann, *The Last Hours of Ancient Sunlight* (New York: Broadway Books, 2004), p. 57.

5. Consider these words from John Winthrop, governor of the Massachusetts Bay Colony, in 1634: 'But for the natives in these parts, God hath so pursued them, as for 300 miles space the greatest part of them are swept away by the smallpox which still continues among them. So . . . God hath thereby cleared our title to this place' (in Hartmann, p. 219). Puritan preacher Increase Mather shared Winthrop's theology of displacement: 'God ended the controversy by sending the smallpox among the Indians. Whole towns of them were swept away, in some of them not so much as one Soul escaping the Destruction.'

6. For a withering critique of Disney's Pocahontas story, see *Islam, Postmodernism and Other Futures: A Ziauddin Sardar Reader*, ed. Sohail Inayatullah and Gail Boxwell (London: Pluto Press, 2003).

7. Thankfully, I think kids in the United States today learn a slightly more balanced and honest view of American history. Meanwhile, some from my generation regularly complain of a 'liberal' bias in textbooks and seek to have them rewritten to reflect the sensibilities of their own childhood education. They apparently believe that their 'conservative' secondary education from the 1970s and before was objective, thorough, balanced and accurate. Whether this is innocent naivety or wilful ignorance, I cannot say. (Readers in Canada, the UK, Germany, France, the Netherlands and elsewhere can, no doubt, find parallel tensions in their standard accounts of national-colonial history.)

8. For more on American exceptionalism, see my *Sojourners* article, 'America the Exceptional' and Randy Woodley's blog on the subject, both available here: http://brianmclaren.net/archives/blog/american-exceptionalism-continue.html.

9. For North Americans seeking to begin such a liberal arts education, I would recommend Dee Brown, *Bury My Heart at Wounded Knee* (New York: Henry Holt, 2007); Jared Diamond, *Guns, Germs, and Steel* (New York: Norton, 2005); Kent Nerburn, *Neither Wolf Nor Dog* (New York: New World Library, 2002); etc. For theological reflection, I would especially recommend Randy Woodley's *Shalom and the Community of Creation* (Grand Rapids: Eerdman's, 2012).

Chapter 10

1. Namsoon Kang, 'Towards a Cosmopolitan Theology: Constructing Public Theology From the Future', in *Planetary Loves: Spivak, Postcoloniality, and Theology*, ed. Stephen D. Moore and Mayra Riviera (New York: Fordham University Press, 2011), p. 280. The section begins, 'Empire-building is all about power-building by creating a devalued other . . .'

2. Here is an excerpt from Eusebius's original telling of the story:

[Constantine] said that about noon, when the day was already beginning to decline, he saw with his own eyes the trophy of a cross of light in the heavens, above the sun, and bearing the inscription, CONQUER BY THIS. At this sight he himself was struck with amazement, and his whole army also, which followed him on this expedition, and witnessed the miracle ... [That night] in his sleep the Christ of God appeared to him with the same sign which he had seen in the heavens, and commanded him to make a likeness of that sign which he had seen in the heavens, and to use it as a safeguard in all engagements with his enemies.

At dawn of day he arose, and communicated the marvel to his friends: and then, calling together the workers in gold and precious stones, he sat in the midst of them, and described to them the figure of the sign he had seen, bidding them represent it in gold and precious stones. And this representation I myself have had an opportunity of seeing.

Now it was made in the following manner. A long spear, over-laid with gold, formed the figure of the cross by means of a transverse bar laid over it. On the top of the whole was fixed a wreath of gold and precious stones; and within this, the symbol of the Saviour's name ...

This spear-cross was further adorned with an embroidered banner that featured the emperor and his family. The finished product, Eusebius said, 'presented an indescribable degree of beauty to the beholder'. He added, 'The emperor constantly made use of this sign of salvation as a safeguard against every adverse and hostile power, and commanded that others similar to it should be carried at the head of all his armies.'

Eusebius, it should be noted, would be considered more of a propagandist than a historian in the modern sense. For more on Constantine's life and work, see James Carroll, *Constantine's Sword: The Church and the Jews – A History* (New York: Mariner Books, 2001).

3. Or imagine, as James Carroll suggests, that Constantine converted to Judaism rather than Christianity. How different history would have been.

4. In this sense, we could refer to Roman Catholic and Roman Protestant Christianity – two wings of a project shaped in part by Jesus and the apostles and in part by Rome and its emperors.

5. In *An Introduction to Political Geography* by Martin Jones, Rhys Jones and Michael Voods (Vancouver, BC: Routledge, 2004, p. 40) *imperialism* is defined as 'the creation and/or maintenance of an unequal economic, cultural, and territorial relationship, usually between states and often in the form of an empire, based on domination and subordination'. Modern imperialism took two forms over the last three hundred years: capitalism and communism. Megacorporations may now be forming a more covert form of imperialism in which nation-states are subtly dominated and subordinated to protect and serve corporate hegemony. For more on imperialism, see Brian D. McLaren, *Everything Must Change* (Nashville: Thomas Nelson, 2007), and relevant works by Namsoon Kang, Joerg Rieger, Richard Horsley, Marcus Borg and John Dominic Crossan.

6. Southern novelist Walker Percy used this term in relation to Christianity's failures regarding race in the United States.

Chapter 11

1. From an address given in Damascus, Syria, on 6 May 2001, about four months before the 9/11 terrorist attacks and the resulting War on Terror. For more information, see Richard Boudreaux, 'John Paul

First Pope to Visit Mosque', *Los Angeles Times*, 7 May 2001, http://articles.latimes.com/2001/may/07/news/mn-60362.

2. It is interesting how seldom if ever anyone suggests that Constantine's vision was demonic in character.

3. In *The Qur'an in the Light of Christ*, ed. Ron George (WIN Press, 2000), Fr Giulio Basetti-Sani, a Franciscan missionary and scholar, describes his initial understandings of Islam in almost identical terms (pp. 20–26). He concludes, 'These were the results I arrived at in 1941, when my sole purpose in studying Islam was to disprove it, to destroy an enemy. It was an enemy because I could not understand it and, hence, was unable to love it . . . This incapacity to comprehend Islam is a heritage of most Christians. It goes back, in part, to their child-hood study of history. It is not easy to free ourselves from the tangle of prejudices which envelops our minds and of which we are not even conscious' (pp. 24–25). Later, one of his mentors disturbed his assumptions (as I described my mentor doing for me in Chapter 5) by offering two quotes. One was from Augustine: *Amor dat novos oculos* (Love sees with new eyes). The other was from St John of the Cross: *Where there is no love put love, and you will find Love Himself.* Thanks to Jeff Burns for giving me this remarkable book.

4. This is the claim Pope Benedict seemed to be making in his famous Regensburg speech, recounted by Miroslav Volf in *Allah: A Christian Response* (New York: HarperOne, 2011), pp. 24–25. Both sides of the equation would be disputed by scholars in each religion, no doubt.

5. Thomas Cahill, in *How the Irish Saved Civilization* (New York: Knopf, 1996), recounts a different response to the Roman Empire: a life-and-death drive to immigrate into it, since the food provided to slaves in the empire was better than starvation outside its borders.

6. Just as Christian texts and the narratives they teach are disputed by critical scholars, there are a number of critical theories within the

Islamic world that challenge this standard version of the origins of Islam. See Ibn Warraq, *What the Koran Really Says* (Amherst, NY: Prometheus Books, 2002).

7. For example, Mohammed's message included deep love and respect for Jesus as a great prophet. But after centuries of Christian anti-Semitism and in the aftermath of Constantine, his Jewish neighbours couldn't be expected to warm to that proposal.

8. Ron George suggests that 30 per cent of the Quran comes from Syrian Christian hymnody and therefore gives evidence to pre-Islamic origins (in his prologue to *The Qu'ran in the Light of Christ*, p. 8).

9. By the way, Christians who seek to vilify Mohammed by pointing out his 'polygamous lifestyle' should remember that biblical heroes from Abraham to David were polygamous, too, and even in the Christian Roman Empire polygamy was widely practised for many centuries. And those who criticise Mohammed by pointing to his military exploits, including conversion by the sword, must be ignorant of the similar exploits of the so-called Christian kings and emperors of Europe, a few episodes of which this chapter will briefly recount. And those who criticise Mohammed's denial of the Trinity should remember the role of the doctrine in solidifying imperial control over minds as well as bodies. They should also remember that the understanding of the Trinity rejected by Mohammed was a misunderstanding, one that should be rejected by true Christians as well. So, we might say that Christians misunderstand the Muslim rejection of a misunderstood version of the doctrine of the Trinity. For more on the latter, see Volf, *Allah: A Christian Response*, especially Chapter 2. There Volf summarises an important line of argument from Nicholas of Cusa (1401–64) like this (p. 54): 'Nicholas argued that the Qur'an is not denying the authentic Christian doctrine of the Trinity, but is rightly rejecting a bastardized version of this doctrine. He stated tersely and

categorically: "In the manner in which Arabs and Jews deny the Trinity, assuredly it ought to be denied by all."'

10. We should not minimise the brutality of the Goths, Visogoths and Huns, and then, some centuries later, the Vikings. Nor should we assume a posture of moral superiority over the medieval Christian kings for doing what they believed was necessary to defend themselves. Nor should we discount the tragic losses that came with the fall of the Roman Empire. The Pax Romana may have been brutal, but few if any would claim the Huns or Vikings brought something better for those they conquered. The point that must be made, though, is that during these difficult times, the Christian faith became deeply complicit with behaviours that seem irreconcilable with the teachings of Jesus. One thinks of Churchill's words about World War I: 'When all was over, torture and cannibalism were the only two expedients that the civilised, scientific, Christian States had been able to deny themselves: and these were of doubtful utility.'

11. See Bonar Ludwig Hernandez, 'The Las Casas–Sepulveda Controversy', http://userwww.sfsu.edu/~epf/journal_archive/volume_X,_2001/hernandez_b.pdf. The article continues, 'These phrases, spoken in 1511 by Antonio de Montesinos, one of the first Dominicans to arrive in the island of Hispaniola, reflect that the Spaniards were not a monolithic band of greedy *conquistadores* who merely sought to exploit and kill the American Indians. On the contrary, the Spanish discovery and subsequent conquest of the New World inspired a serious, if not heated, intellectual controversy regarding the rationality and Christianization of the Indians.'

12. See my article 'America the Exceptional', *Sojourners*, January 2012, available at http://brianmclaren.net/archives/blog/american-exceptionalism-continue.html, and Randy Woodley, 'Jesus and American Exceptionalism', *Emergent Village Voice*, http://www.patheos.com/

blogs/emergentvillage/2012/02/jesus-and-american-exceptionalism-by-randy-woodley/.

13. See Richard Hughes, *Myths America Lives By* (Champaign: University of Illinois Press, 2004) and *Christian America and the Kingdom of God* (Champaign: University of Illinois Press, 2009).

14. Kwame Bediako strikes an important balance: 'The revival of religion [in Europe] towards the end of the eighteenth century which produced the profound sense of missionary obligation, seems also to have intensified this European self-confidence. More radical spirits, it is true, were not unaware of the religious blemishes of the Christian nations of Europe. William Carey, foremost protagonist of the missionary enterprise, was one who held no belief in the religious superiority of Europeans or of "those who bear the Christian name." But this in no way undermined the general conviction that the civilised culture and institutions of Europe owed their enlightened status to Christianity, itself the most "civilised" of all religions' (*Theology and Identity* [Oxford: Regnum Books, 1992], p. 229).

Part Two: The Doctrinal Challenge

1. Diana Butler Bass, *Christianity after Religion* (New York: HarperOne, 2012), pp. 134–135.

Chapter 12

1. From a beautiful picture book for children of all ages, called *Old Turtle and the Broken Truth*, a sequel to the equally beautiful *Old Turtle* (New York: Scholastic Press, 2003, 1992).

2. The term *Christendom* could be a rough synonym for Roman-Imperial Christianity in its Catholic and Protestant forms. Eastern Orthodoxy certainly has areas of overlap with Western Christendom, along with many differences.

3. Arguments like this were made in response to my book *A New Kind of Christianity* (New York: HarperOne, 2010).

4. Some of the new atheists make this argument.

5. *Christianity after Religion*, p. 134.

6. In Africa, this process has been led in recent years by Bolaji Idowu of Nigeria, John Mbiti of Kenya, Mulago gwa Cikala Musharhamina and Mabiala Kenzo of Congo, Alan Boesak of South Africa, Emmanuel Katangole of Uganda, Kwame Bediako of Ghana, Lamin Sanneh of Gambia, Claude Nikondeha of Burundi and many others. In Latin America, the process has been led by René Padilla, Ruth Padilla DeBorst, Elisa Padilla, Samuel Escobar, Justo Gonzalez, Gustavo Gutierrez, Jon Sobrino, Leonardo Boff *and many others*. Also essential have been minority voices in the US and elsewhere, including African-Americans like Dr Martin Luther King Jr and James Cone; Native Americans like Randy Woodley, Ray Aldred, Terry LeBlanc and Richard Twiss; Asian-Americans like Rita Takashimi Brock, Namsoon Kang and Soong-Chan Rah; and Latinos like Gabriel Salguero; *and many others*. Asian leaders (like Fr Jojo Fung in Malaysia) and Middle Eastern leaders (like Jean Zaru, Naim Ateek and Salim Munayer in Israel-Palestine) are also making major contributions. And the process has only begun.

7. The Mesopotamian source myths, grounded in conflict and violence, are creatively adapted in the Hebrew Scriptures, although their chaotic presence can be discerned in many places, just beneath the surface.

8. Wood's actual words for the first fragment are 'You are loved', and for the second, 'and so are they'. The Lord's Prayer, it seems to me, creates this same healing of fractured truth when it asks for forgiveness for 'our sins' and simultaneously forgives the sins of our oppressors, as does the Sermon on the Mount when it calls us to love our enemies,

mirroring the compassionate perfection of God that loves both 'the just and the unjust'. In this world of ecological crisis and alienation from 'nature', we must add that 'and so are they' refers to non-human creatures and even to non-living creations.

9. On the subject of evolution *and* faith (rather than *versus*), see the work of Michael Dowd (http://www.thankgodforevolution.com), especially *Thank God for Evolution* (New York: Plume, 2009). For a theology of evolution, see John Haught (http://web.mac.com/haughtj1/Site/Welcome.html), especially *God after Darwin* (Boulder: Westview Press, 2007).

Chapter 13

1. From 'Being Saved and Being Wrong', http://www.jamesalison.co.uk/texts/eng18.html.

2. Girardians use the term *sacred* to describe to this supernatural, magical power of scapegoating.

3. For more on Girardian readings of Scripture, arranged according to the Common Lectionary, see Paul Nuechterlein's monumental contribution at http://girardianlectionary.net/.

4. Because this is a brief overview, I can't pause to address all the moral ambivalence in the text – surrounding, for example, the flood narrative. I addressed some dimensions of this ambivalence in *A New Kind of Christianity* (New York: HarperOne, 2010), and we will return to the question of hostility and violence in the Bible in Chapter 22. For all its brevity and simplicity, I hope this overview of Genesis models a way of taking the text seriously without taking it literally.

5. Joseph realises in the end that although human intentions are evil, God's intentions are good (Gen. 50:20), and so he imitates God's goodness, grace and generosity.

6. Thanks to Lutheran preacher Nadia Bolz-Weber for this insight from Dietrich Bonhoeffer; see 'Joyless Christians and the Lord of the Rings' at: http://blog.sojo.net/2011/07/13/joyless-christians-and-the-lord-of-the-rings/.

Chapter 14

1. From the *Miscellanies* (1711–1726).

2. For more on this network of emerging African Christian leaders, see http://www.amahoro-africa.org.

3. I have adapted and summarised this material in a short chapter called 'Finding the Seventh Story', in *2010Boston: The Changing Contours of World Mission and Christianity* (Eugene, Ore.: Wipf and Stock, 2012).

4. In the Bible, the Israelites experienced domination by the Egyptians, the Babylonians, the Assyrians, the Medo-Persians and the Romans.

5. In the Gospels, the Zealots represented a group living by the Revolution Narrative, seeking a violent overthrow and expulsion of the Romans. The Pharisees were their close allies.

6. In the book of Daniel, when the Babylonians required Shadrach, Meshach and Abednego to eat a Babylonian diet, or when they required the Jewish deportees to worship Babylonian gods, they were attempting assimilation.

7. The book of Ezra ends with a purification narrative, as Hebrew men are told to divorce their 'foreign wives'. The Pharisees exemplify this narrative as well in their condemnation of Jesus for eating with 'the unclean'. 'Tax collectors and sinners' were their scapegoats. (It's worth noting how the Pharisees themselves – a complex group with an oft-misunderstood history – are frequently scapegoated by Christians due to their consistently negative portrayal in the Gospels. This negative stereotyping has then been used across Christian history to vilify all Jewish people and Judaism in general. It remains for

Christian scholars and communicators to revisit the Pharisees and recount their history in a more balanced and fair way.)

8. As we've already seen, sibling rivalry is a key theme in Genesis. More broadly speaking, the book of Acts (ch. 6) tells the story of foreign widows being marginalised in favour of 'native' widows in the early church. And James preached against another expression of competition (Jas 2, 5) – condemning favouritism for the rich and the marginalisation of the poor, using language that would probably earn him the label *Socialist* or *Communist* today.

9. Many of Jesus' countrymen saw themselves as victims, especially in Galilee, where they were victimised by both the Romans and the Judean elite who collaborated with the Romans. See Richard Horsley, *Jesus and Empire* (Minneapolis: Fortress Press, 2002).

10. Cultural separateness was maintained among the ancient Israelites through purity codes and strict adherence to the Torah, buttressed by their understanding of themselves as 'clean' and of Gentiles as 'unclean'. Baptism originated (as we will see later) as a ritual of maintaining this isolation. Various separatist communities (like the Essenes, with whom John the Baptist shared certain similarities) pursued physical isolation by relocating to the wilderness region near the Dead Sea.

11. The term *Zionism* is fraught with complexity. Here I am only critiquing the popular, superficial form of it that is common in American religious broadcasting and politics.

12. God pronounces a blessing on Hagar and Ishmael (Gen. 16:11ff.) that has become highly problematic in Jewish-Christian-Muslim relations. Not surprisingly, it is also notoriously problematic to translate. The blessing ostensibly calls Ishmael a 'wild ass', although some say the translation should be 'fruitful man' (which is more in keeping with v. 10). It continues (in the NRSV), 'with his hand

against everyone, and everyone's hand against him; and he shall live at odds with all his kin'. But a reputable Jewish translation is far less dismissive: 'And he will be a wild donkey of a man; his hand will be upon all, and everyone's hand upon him, and before all his brothers he will dwell' [http://www.chabad.org/library/bible.asp?aid=8211&showrashi=true]. Some interpreters go even further, saying the Hebrew preposition translated by some as 'against' and others as 'upon' should actually be translated as 'with'. The contested interpretations mirror the competing attitudes towards 'the other' with which the text struggles.

13. Jonathan Tran, reviewing important works by J. Kameron Carter and Willie J. Jennings, writes: 'Jewish flesh is most authentically itself when it welcomes the gentile. This hospitality enacts what Carter calls "the theodramatic constitution of existence." In the same way that God elects and receives Israel, elected Israel receives the gentiles as an extension of God's reception history. "Israel's meaning and significance," writes Carter, "arise out of its being related to the nations before whom the drama of the Jews' election unfolds. The drama of Israel thus is not insular, for it unfolds in such a way as to enfold the nations into its drama"' ('The New Black Theology', *Christian Century*, 26 January 2012, http://christiancentury.org/article/2012-01/new-black-theology).

14. In 2 Cor. 5 and 6, Paul depicts this unique identity in the image of peace ambassadors. We who are 'in Christ' have a special identity – but that identity is not as a new 'us' in rivalry with 'them'. We are sent as peace ambassadors seeking to bring everyone into reconciliation with God and one another. Our whole mission can thus be summed up as 'the ministry of reconciliation'.

Chapter 15

1. Richard Kearney, *Anatheism* (New York: Columbia University Press, 2010), p. 179.

2. Again, for more on this dark side of Christian history, see James Carroll, *Constantine's Sword: The Church and the Jews – A History* (New York: Mariner Books, 2001).

3. The corollary professional bargain might be expressed like this: 'If you want to have a job in a Christian institution, here's something you have to say you believe.'

4. James Alison, *The Joy of Being Wrong* (New York: Crossroad, 1998), p. 237.

5. Jonathan Tran quotes J. Kameron Carter: 'Difference theologically understood arises from the positivity of the hypostatic distinctions [in the Trinity] within which the possibility and, according to the will of God, the actuality or concreteness of creation is located. It is precisely this understanding of difference – difference as witness to and participation within the Trinitarian hypostatic distinctions – that modern logics of race foreclose.' In other words, the politics of whiteness (or sameness, imperialism or colour-blindness) betray the doctrine of the Trinity by asserting that, for example, son-ness and spirit-ness should be abolished or marginalised because of the supremacy of father-ness. See 'The New Black Theology', *Christian Century*, 26 January 2012, http://christiancentury.org/article/2012-01/new-black-theology/.

6. Miroslav Volf, in *Allah: A Christian Response* (New York: HarperOne, 2011), helpfully quotes Augustine of Hippo – 'the total transcendence of the godhead quite surpasses the capacity of ordinary speech' (pp. 139–140) – and offers Nicholas of Cusa as an example of a Christian who offered the Trinity as this kind of gift rather than wielding it like a weapon.

Chapter 16

1. René Girard, *Things Hidden Since the Foundation of the World* (New York: Continuum Books, 2003), p. 277. When Girard speaks of 'only Christ's perfect love', it's safe to say he doesn't intend the word *only* as an exclusive claim for the Christian religion that implies an insult to other religions. Rather, he is contrasting the transcendent, divine, non-violent love revealed in Christ with our typical human energies that are polluted by rivalry and sabotaged by violence.

2. Among other things, my Muslim friend had heard that we Christians believe that God is anatomically a male, and that God had physical sex with Mary. When we say Jesus is the Son of God, he assumed we meant that Jesus was the love-child of this impossible sexual union. When he heard me speak about Jesus, he didn't hear this kind of obscenity. Rather, he heard sincerity and devotion and reverence, which made possible a new level of communication between us.

3. I've written a short fictional tale in e-book form that explores a story like this. You can find more information about *The Girl with the Dove Tattoo* at my website, http://www.brianmclaren.net.

4. Even those who question the Pauline authorship of these texts acknowledge their importance as windows into the early Christian community.

5. See Brian Walsh and Sylvia Keesmaat's *Colossians Remixed* (Downers Grove, Ill.: InterVarsity Press, 2004) for a stunning reading of this text. See also Dominic Crossan, Richard Horsley, Marcus Borg, Joerg Rieger and N. T. Wright for additional insights into counter-imperial themes in the New Testament.

6. Thanks to Dr William Stacy Johnson, personal communication, for many of the insights on Phil. 2 conveyed here and later in the chapter.

7. See Mabiala Kenzo, 'Evangelical Faith and (Postmodern) Others', in *A New Kind of Conversation*, ed. Myron Bradley Penner and Hunter Barnes (Colorado Springs, Colo.: Paternoster, 2007).

8. I wish that space would allow us to examine many other Christological doctrines in this context. For example, the doctrine of the incarnation of Christ is rich with incentives to encounter the other, as evidenced in the Christmas narratives in which Jesus is honoured by 'the other' (the Magi) while being persecuted by 'one of us' (Herod). The doctrine of Christ's humanity affirms to us that Jesus learned and grew in understanding, and provides examples of him doing so, even from 'the other', such as in the story of the Syrophonecian/Canaanite woman (which I explore in *Everything Must Change* [Nashville, Thomas Nelson, 2007]).

9. I first heard this approach articulated by students of Elton Trueblood.

10. Girard, *Things Hidden*, p. 270.

11. The word *grasping* should evoke the taking of the fruit by the first couple, and should contrast with Jesus who 'did not think equality with God a thing to be grasped'. In this light, Phil. 2 might be more a hymn about the humanity of Christ than the deity of Christ, presenting him not as 'existing in the form (or nature) of God', as most translations suggest, but rather as 'existing in the image of God' – as the true human, content in being human, not seeking to grasp for more. In his refusal to grasp at deity, he passes the test Adam and Eve failed. When Christians present Jesus as one who demands that others acknowledge his deity (crudely put, 'Bow down and say I am God or I will send you to hell!'), they contradict the whole spirit of Phil. 2. To add to the irony: if Jesus truly is the image of God (or 'in nature God' or 'in the form of God'), then he reveals that God's true nature is not to grasp at deity! That suggests that God is willing to go 'incognito' – which might further suggest that God is willing to show up in

unexpected places. In other words, if God is humbly manifest in the most unexpected form of a servant hanging on a cross, then perhaps we should expect God to be humbly manifest in unexpected ways in the contexts of other religions, too.

12. Paul makes this very contrast in Gal. 3:28.

13. A defender of the Greek logos would say that hostility is not inevitable – if only the subdominant would accept their inferior position. Conflict arises from their refusal to conform to the logos and stay in their place.

14. Girard, *Things Hidden*, pp. 275–276.

15. Girard acknowledges that the Christian religion has betrayed this essential substitution and has reinstated a God who inflicts violence. He calls this betrayal 'sacrificial Christianity' – a theme to which we will return in a later chapter.

Chapter 17

1. Paul Knitter, *Without Buddha I Could Not Be a Christian* (Oxford: Oneworld, 2009), p. 21.

2. How many Christian churches, I wondered, would have been that flexible with a long-held tradition?

3. As in all stories I tell, a few details of this story have been intentionally changed for privacy purposes, and others may have been unintentionally changed due to my imperfect memory.

4. Sadly, the two rabbis, whose sensibilities had already been assaulted by one Christian, now experienced another assault that they could understand all too well.

5. It's hard to argue against the proposition that Pentecostalism has been the most significant Christian movement since the Reformation. In just over a century, the movement has grown from a single gathering in Azusa, California, to a worldwide phenomenon that includes a

staggering percentage (estimates range from 10 to 30 per cent, with 20 being a good average) of the world's Christians. Today, one in fifteen human beings on the planet identifies as a Pentecostal (or Charismatic) Christian – a category that virtually nobody had ever heard of a century ago.

6. Amos Yong and John Sober Sylvest are exploring these fascinating subjects. See http://www.regent.edu/acad/schdiv/faculty_staff/yong. shtml and http://poj.peeters-leuven.be/content.php?url=article&id= 2058666&journal_code=SID/.

7. This proposal is neither new nor hard to understand. Wouldn't the Spirit as experienced by the Inuit of the Arctic have a different 'feel' than the Spirit as experienced by the desert nomads of Arabia? Wouldn't a desert nomad associate God's grace in a special way with shade and shelter from the unrelenting sun, while an Inuit during the unrelenting dark of winter would associate the Spirit's presence with longed-for sunlight? If different climates would affect their ways of understanding and describing God – one as shade, one as sunlight, wouldn't their different histories do this same? And couldn't these diverse associations with the Spirit be seen as both locally rooted and of universal interest? Couldn't these locally rooted articulations, understood both respectfully and critically as unique phenomena, yield insights to people who have encountered God in different settings? And couldn't those insights be both about the Spirit and about how one's experience of Spirit is connected to one's local environment and local history? For more on these questions, see M. Thomas Thangaraj, *Relating to People of Other Religions: What Every Christian Needs to Know* (Nashville: Abingdon Press, 1997), pp. 15ff.

8. Yes, differences can be contradictions, but they can also be expansions, corroborations, elucidations, connections, corrections,

additions or translations, all contributing to rich and needed conversations.

9. I am affirming what has often been called 'the scandal of particularity', but I am also suggesting that this particularity is scandalously widespread in its dissemination.

10. I wonder to what degree, recalling the conversation in Chapter 6 about our fear of 'us', my friend included the 'in-out' language more to prove his legitimacy to the members of his church who were present, for whom just showing up at the mosque was a huge step out of their comfort zone. The 'I love you' message was what the Spirit was speaking most powerfully within and through his own soul to 'the other', and that's what they heard.

Chapter 18

1. Randy Woodley, *Shalom and the Community of Creation: An Indigenous Vision* (Grand Rapids: Eerdmans, 2012), p. 73.

2. This scenario recalls the journey of Abraham, who left an empire with all the hostilities it entails, not knowing where he would be led. In this light, the journey away from a hostile orthodoxy is a truly orthodox pursuit.

3. For a short and pithy introduction to the subject of atonement, see Tony Jones' e-book, *A Better Atonement*, which is available here: http://tonyj.net/books/.

4. Few areas of doctrine have been more demonic in their application than these – since demonisation of the other leads so efficiently to violence against the other. See Elaine Pagels, *The Origin of Satan: How Christians Demonized Jews, Pagans, and Heretics* (New York: Vintage, 1996). The brilliant and courageous work of Walter Wink has done much to 'exorcise' and disarm these doctrines, turning them from destructive swords into creative ploughshares.

See especially *The Powers That Be* (New York: Three Rivers Press, 1999).

5. In systems theory, this response would be described in terms of the system seeking to maintain equilibrium. In these terms, we might ask what orthodoxy is. Is it the maintenance of a changeless equilibrium established at some point in the past, or is it the ongoing process of adjusting to constant disturbances to achieve an ever new, ever-sustainable and ever-regenerative equilibrium?

6. There is no guarantee that the balanced approach recommended here will succeed, so while we must hope and work for the best option, we must also imagine how to cope with the other options, too – of co-optation, counter-reformulation and collapse.

7. I explored these threats in *Everything Must Change* (Nashville: Thomas Nelson, 2007).

8. Vaclav Havel's wise words come to mind in this regard: 'Keep the company of those who seek the truth – run from those who have found it.'

Part Three: The Liturgical Challenge

1. Paul Knitter, *Without Buddha I Could Not Be a Christian* (Oxford: Oneworld, 2009), pp. 214–215.

Chapter 19

1. Samir Selmanovic, *It's Really All About God: How Islam, Atheism, and Judaism Made Me a Better Christian* (San Francisco: Jossey-Bass, 2009), p. 250.

2. See my books *Finding Our Way Again* (Nashville: Thomas Nelson, 2008) and *Naked Spirituality* (New York: HarperOne, 2011).

3. Or perhaps, as we will suggest in a later chapter, we should focus for one week of Advent on Jesus as friend – friend of all.

4. We should also, as Joy Carroll Wallis wisely says, keep Herod in Christmas, remembering the violence of the slaughter of the innocents and all it has to tell us about the destructive power of fear and hostility.

5. Perhaps in this light, we would be more prone to give the more precious gifts of service and presence rather than cheap presents of plastic, cloth and paper.

6. I plan to explore possibilities in this regard in upcoming books called *Catechesis* and *Subversive Liturgy*. For example, imagine the twelve days unfolding in days of feasting and fasting, with short daily readings and prayers to be shared around a meal; or, instead of a meal:

   1. Feast of Christ the King (Christmas Day) – celebrating God's kingdom as a new way of life characterised by good will (benevolence) towards all people.

   2. Feast of the Shepherds – celebrating in some creative, communal way God's special solidarity with the poor.

   3. Fast of the Holy Innocents – acknowledging the evil of abusive human power that causes children to suffer, and celebrating God's love for children in need around the world.

   4. Feast of the Genealogies – celebrating God's work through history, and in each of our own families, bringing us from violence to peace.

   5. Feast of the Magi – celebrating God's revelation of messianic compassion in all cultures and among all religions.

   6. Feast of John the Baptist – celebrating John's identity as Jesus' forerunner, working on the margins of society, calling all to radical repentance.

   7. Feast of the New Year – celebrating all things made new in Christ: New Testament, New Commandment, New Identity.

8. Feast of the Circumcision – celebrating Jesus' identity within the Jewish people, together with his love for all people, reflected in the words of Simeon and Anna (Luke 2:25ff.).

9. Fast of the Flight to Egypt – recalling the holy family's experience as refugees by fasting for one meal, and then celebrating God's concern for refugees by eating a simple meal of similar caloric intake as the world's poorest share.

10. Feast of Jesus' Childhood – celebrating Jesus' experience in his Father's House as a boy, and his later proclamation that God's House will outlast the Temple and is meant as a place of welcome for all people.

11. Feast of Jesus' Baptism – celebrating the Spirit descending as a dove upon Jesus, and baptism as turning from old identities of hostility to a new identity as God's agents of peace.

12. Feast of the Epiphany – celebrating God's manifestation in Jesus, in his proclamation of Good News for the poor and outsiders in Luke 4:14–30.

7. This reference to Matt. 7:13–14 reflects my conviction that Jesus is not talking about a broad-minded road that leads many to hell and a narrow-minded one that leads a few to heaven, as many seem to assume. Rather, he advocates a difficult way of peace-making and non-violence (5:3–10, 21–26, 38–48; 6:12–13; 7:1–2) that leads to survival and life, and warns of a broad and easy road of violence and hate that leads to the destruction of war, exactly the kind of war that destroyed Jerusalem about a generation later in AD 67–70. This understanding suggests another answer to the question posed in our title: *Why did Jesus, Moses, the Buddha and Mohammed cross the road? To exit from the superhighway of violence and forge new paths of peace.*

8. See Peter Rollins, *Insurrection* (New York: Howard Books, 2011).

9. This is also the season for celebrating the Transfiguration – the day God elevated Jesus over Moses and Elijah, icons of the law and prophets, both of whom – unlike Jesus – participated in religious violence.

Chapter 20

1. Walker Percy, 'Notes for a Novel about the End of the World', in *The Message in the Bottle* (New York: Farrar, Straus and Giroux, 1980), p. 118.

2. Ibid.

3. Luke's story of John's birth sets up this father-son tension in a fascinating way.

4. Jesus addresses the Pharisees with the term twice in Matthew's Gospel, at 12:34 and 23:33. In the second instance, the term is clearly associated with violence and bloodshed.

5. If John is indeed echoing Jer. 46:22, then it is not God who is holding the axe at the root of the tree – it is another nation. The fire, wrath and cutting that are coming will indeed be judgement, but judgement inflicted by the Romans, as happened in AD 70.

6. Peter Rollins, *Insurrection* (New York: Howard Books, 2011), p. 165.

7. Ibid., pp. 167–169.

Chapter 21

1. This hymn was dropped from the Presbyterian hymnal in 1990, and Methodists tried to drop it in 1986, but popular support preserved it in spite of the fact that it reinforces a military model for Christian identity, celebrates 'the cross of Jesus' in the conquering ways of Constantine, and renders 'the other' as 'the foe'. M. Thomas Thangaraj offers several examples of similarly un-otherly hymns in *Relating to People of Other Religions: What Every Christian Needs to Know* (Nashville: Abingdon Press, 1997).

2. The hymn was composed in 1848 and is a good example of a Victorian parlour hymn.

3. Peter Rollins, *Insurrection* (New York: Howard Books, 2011), p. 107.

4. For more on the hymn, see http://www.telegraph.co.uk/culture/music/3668059/The-story-behind-the-hymn.html.

5. In a beautiful reversal, Jesus gives the poor man a name but leaves the rich man nameless. Luke 16:19–31.

6. I, of course, must be open to the ways I do it in my writing. In a previous book, for example, I used the word *tribal* to describe hostile clannishness. An African reader (white, from South Africa) pointed out that in so doing, I was inadvertently putting indigenous peoples in a negative light, as if inter-tribal conflict were more egregious than European 'civilised' conflict. Even my use of the term *clannishness* deserves critical scrutiny. Perhaps I should call it *religious nationalism*?

7. The name of this book's US publisher, Jericho, represents a similar tension. The Jericho story concerns what we would call a war crime, complete with the extermination of women and children. The image of bringing down walls that divide, however, can be employed for reconciling rather than violent purposes, thus subverting the original violent meaning.

8. To learn more, check out http://www.nbsint.org/.

9. Even Joshua, arguably the most violent book in the Bible, offers resources for the deconstruction of us-them thinking. Rahab (ch. 2), an outsider (and a prostitute) is a hero of the story, and Achan (ch. 7), an insider, is a villain. The Gibeonites are outsiders who cleverly gain insider status (ch. 9). And the narrowly averted Gilead massacre (22:10ff.) explores the danger of hastily prejudging insiders and treating them as outsiders.

Chapter 22

1. 'Religions', in *Encyclopédie de la foi*, ed. H. Fries (Paris: Éditions du Cerf, 1967), 4:59–68. Quoted in Jacques Dupuis, SJ, *Towards a Christian Theology of Religious Pluralism* (Maryknoll, NY: Orbis Books, 1997), p. 52.

2. 'The 25 Most Influential Evangelicals in America', *Time*, 7 February 2005, http://www.time.com/time/specials/packages/article/0,28804,19 93235_1993243_1993300,00.html.

3. Later, in settings that seemed more appropriate, I became more outspoken about my own views, although I still endeavour to show respect and sensitivity to my hosts.

4. I am not using the word *fundamentalist* as an epithet here. The person in question has told me on several occasions that 'fundamentalist' is what he is.

5. Richard Kearney, *Anatheism* (New York: Columbia University Press, 2010), p. 160. Additional page references to this book will be included in the text hereinafter.

6. Kearney states, 'The great stories of Israel are, I am suggesting, testaments to the paradoxical origins of religion in both violent conflict and peaceful embrace. This, in effect, makes every dramatic encounter between the human and the divine into a radical hermeneutic wager: compassion or murder. You either welcome or refuse the stranger. Monotheism is the history of this wager' (p. 22).

7. My quotations here come from an unpublished version of his article 'The Way of Peace and Grace', which appeared in published form in *Sojourners* 41, no. 1 (January 2012). (http://www.sojo.net/magazine/2012/01/way-peace-and-grace). Flood also explains his approach in 'Does Defending the Bible Mean Advocating Violence?' *Huffington Post*, 21 November 2011, http://www.huffingtonpost.com/derek-flood/defending-violence-in-the-bible_b_1088517.html. For more on this

important subject, see also James Cone's *The Cross and the Lynching Tree* (Maryknoll, NY: Orbis, 2011) and Philip Jenkin's *Laying Down the Sword: Why We Can't Ignore the Bible's Violent Verses* (New York: HarperOne, 2011). See also the introduction to both books available here: http://www.readthespirit.com/explore/2011/12/19/in-season-of-peace-recalling-christianitys-violence.html/.

8. For more on this subject, see Tom Krattenmaker's helpful *USA Today* article available here: http://www.usatoday.com/news/opinion/forum/story/2011-10-09/islam-muslim-christian-violence/50711860/1. He recounts how 'an adviser to Israeli Prime Minister Benjamin Netanyahu once gave a journalist this chilling explanation for the prime minister's hard-line attitude towards Iran: "Think Amalek."' By mentioning Amalek, the advisor evoked 1 Sam. 15:2–3, where God commands Saul to kill all the Amalekites, '*both man and woman, and infant, ox and sheep, camel and donkey*'. The ancient historian Flavius Josephus described Saul's action as follows: 'He betook himself to slay the women and the children, and thought he did not act therein either barbarously or inhumanly; first, because they were enemies whom he thus treated, and, in the next place, because it was done by the command of God, whom it was dangerous not to obey' (*Antiquites Judicae*, Book VI, Chapter 7).

9. Some might point to Rom. 1 as an example of a passage where Paul emphasises divine retribution. But interestingly, in that passage, the retribution is simply to be 'given up' so that 'ungodly' people reap the natural consequences of their bad behaviour. And then in chapter 2, Paul masterfully overturns the reader's glee over punishment of 'the other', showing that 'we' are no better than 'they'.

10. For more on this subject, see Peter Rollins, *Insurrection* (New York: Howard Books, 2011), and my book *More Ready Than You Realize* (Grand Rapids, Mich.: Zondervan, 2002).

11. Reconciliation differs from inclusion. Inclusion says we can absorb the other into *us*, while reconciliation means we want to be at peace with the other as the other.

12. I've been tempted to point out to my critics who accuse me of picking and choosing that they do the same thing, the only difference being that they pick the violent and hostile passages for prioritisation and choose the inclusive and reconciling ones for marginalisation. But I doubt making that point would further the conversation.

13. Brian McLaren, *A New Kind of Christianity* (New York: HarperOne, 2010). Too many biblical interpreters today still cling to a form of absolutism regarding the Bible. Either the Bible is valid the way they understand a constitution to be valid, or it is not valid at all. (It should be noted that most constitutional lawyers would reject the simplistic assumptions about constitutions that lie beneath these arguments.) Ultraliberal interpreters, of course, use this logic to critique the Bible and downplay its value. Ultraconservative interpreters defend the constitutional approach as if it were the only alternative, fearing that any loosening of absolutist claims will start a long slide down a slippery slope into the fiery abyss of relativism. The former approach generally produces a benign religion of weak identity, and the latter a strong religion of hostile identity. We need an approach that goes beyond the facile binary of absolutism and relativism. Richard Kearney describes the situation well in *Anatheism*:

> So much depends, of course, on what we mean by God. If transcendence is indeed a *surplus* of meaning, it requires a process of endless interpretation ... The absolute requires pluralism to avoid absolutism. (p. xiv)
>
> If the Word was in the beginning, so was hermeneutics. There is no God's-eye view of things available to us. For we are not

Gods, and history tells us that attempts to become so lead to intellectual and political catastrophe. Hermeneutics is a lesson in humility (we all speak from finite situations) as well as imagination (we fill the gaps between available and ulterior meanings). Hermeneutics reminds us that the holiest of books are works of interpretation – for authors no less than readers. (p. xv)

The acknowledgment of our finite hermeneutic situation saves us, I believe, from both relativism and absolutism. (p. xviii)

The absolute can never be understood *absolutely* by any single person or religion. (p. 16)

For faith means knowing you don't know anything absolutely about absolutes. (p. 170)

14. It's highly instructive in this regard to ponder all the passages where Jesus challenges Sabbath conventions. In Matt. 12:8, he shows how he, like David, has compassion on his hungry companions, which reflects both true humanity (as Son of Man or the Human One) and true divinity (because God loves compassion, not sacrifice). In Mark 3:1–6, Jesus heals a withered hand and is angry at the lack of compassion demonstrated by his critics. In Luke 4:33ff., Jesus heals a demonised man and Peter's mother on the Sabbath. In John 5:5–18, he heals a man who couldn't walk for thirty-eight years, and in John 9, he heals a man blind from birth, both on the Sabbath. In Luke 13:10–17, he heals a woman bent over for eighteen years, and when criticised he references the compassion any decent person would have on a thirsty donkey or ox so as to water them on the Sabbath.

15. The 'eye for an eye' construction is found in Exod. 21:24, Lev. 24:20 and Deut 19:19–21. It echoes language found in section 230 of the Code of Hammurabi.

16. When Jesus speaks of binding and loosing, he is not abolishing the law and prophets. Rather, we might say that he is unleashing and fulfilling their true and best intent (Matt. 5:17–19) or spirit (see 2 Cor. 2:6). He thus makes a double declaration of independence – from absolute textual totalitarianism on the one hand, and from absolute moral relativism on the other. He rejects the technical-textual righteousness of the scribes and Pharisees (Matt. 5:20) and argues instead for a kind and compassionate righteousness that refuses to create us and them, insider and outsider, neighbour and enemy (Matt. 5:43–48; Luke 6:27–36).

17. Our doctrine of the Bible, of course, is a subset of a larger doctrine – of revelation. How might that larger doctrine be reformulated in the strong-benevolent Christian identity we are exploring in these pages? How can we cherish the particularly beautiful ways God is revealed within our faith without losing a generosity towards other faiths, and how can we remain generously open to the beauties revealed in other faiths without losing the particular beauties of our own? Even framing the question this way sets us on a constructive path towards answering it.

Chapter 23

1. Richard Kearney, *Anatheism* (New York: Columbia University Press, 2010), p. 77.

2. Among many helpful books on the Lord's Supper, I recommend Nora Gallagher, *The Sacred Meal* (Nashville: Thomas Nelson, 2009), and Dan Schmidt, *Taken by Communion* (Grand Rapids, Mich.: Baker Books, 2004).

3. I explore this understanding of ritual in *Finding Our Way Again* (Nashville: Thomas Nelson, 2008).

4. See the beautiful hymn by Robert Stamps, 'God and Man at Table Are Sat Down', which articulates this view of the Eucharist.

5. I understand that many people use the term *altar* simply as a name for a piece of furniture, to which I have no objection. My concern here focuses only on the idea of pacifying a hostile God with human pain and sacrifice.

6. The doctrine is commonly attributed to St Anselm. Scholars (such as Gustav Aulen, *Christus Victor*, Wipf and Stock, 2003) debate whether Martin Luther was more committed to penal substitution or an earlier understanding called 'Christus Victor'. Hymn lyrics by Phillip Bliss, Isaac Watts and Augustus Toplady have given penal substitutionary atonement a central place in worship for many Evangelicals, and parts of Mainline Protestant and Catholic eucharistic liturgies keep the doctrine alive, albeit subconsciously, in many hearts. Today, some Evangelical authors like D. A. Carson and Albert Mohler tend to identify this theory of atonement with the Christian gospel. Others like Scot McKnight have sought to retain a carefully defined version of it but not as equivalent to the gospel. Others would prefer to purge it from the Christian faith entirely, and still others (I am in this group) urge us to retain the theory as an artefact of theological history but decommission it from contemporary spiritual practice. For two excellent studies on the subject, see Joel Green and Mark Baker, *Recovering the Scandal of the Cross* (Downers Grove, Ill.: InterVarsity Press, 2000) and Mark Green, ed., *Proclaiming the Scandal of the Cross* (Grand Rapids, Mich.: Baker Academic, 2006).

7. According to the theory, this substitute must have been human so that human sin could be imputed to him, yet he must have been divine so that he could neutralise infinite wrath with infinite merit or grace.

8. Should we see God as incapable of being reconciled to us without violence? Should we understand God as inherently hostile to frail and fallible human beings? Should we conceive of God's retribution as the biggest threat to our well-being? Should sin be defined primarily as an

individual legal problem requiring a transaction of forgiveness? Should the deeper and wider existential, social, systemic, historical, ecological and economic dimensions of sin thus be minimised? Should Jesus' life, teaching, signs and wonders, resurrection and ascension be marginalised, as if the only thing about him that really matters is his substitutionary death? Should other meanings of Jesus' death also be minimised in favour of this doctrine? Should God be primarily identified with the political and religious leaders inflicting torture and death on Good Friday, rather than with the innocent man being tortured and killed? Should we be sent into the world primarily with an evacuation plan for heaven and an escape plan from damnation, rather than with an incarnation, reconciliation and transformation plan for our conflicted world? If violence and hostility characterise God's identity, is it realistic to aspire to be better than God by being non-violent and non-hostile?

9. In *The Prophetic Imagination*, 2nd ed. (Minneapolis: Augsburg Fortress, 2001), p. xx, Walter Brueggemann provides two examples of the impact of this shift in identity. The Eucharist, he says (quoting William T. Cavanaugh), helps us identify with a tortured man. In that space, communicants 'resist the state's ability to define what is real through the mechanism of torture'. The Eucharist also helps us resist the numbing effects of consumerism by helping communicants foster a 'lively communal imagination that resists a mindless humanity of despairing conformity'. This dual resistance – to torture and to numbness – helps us remain more truly human, because 'numbness does not hurt like torture, but in a quite parallel way, numbness robs us of our capability for humanity'.

10. I should emphasise that I don't think all Christians who hold penal substitutionary atonement share this kind of Christian exceptionalism with its corresponding us-them thinking and repugnance towards

'the unsaved'. But I do believe the doctrine creates conditions for this exceptionalism to take root in certain circumstances and among people of a certain temperament. Sincere adherents to the doctrine have a responsibility to vigilantly guard against the dangerous though unintended consequences of this Christian exceptionalism.

11. When people begin rethinking atonement, salvation and the Eucharist along these lines, they often wonder, 'What then does it mean to say that Jesus died for our sins?' They assume the *for* in that statement means 'as a penal substitutionary sacrifice for'. It is far more natural, I think, to interpret the *for* more simply. Consider, for example, these two sentences: 'I took medicine for my disease,' and 'I got a ticket for speeding.' In the former sentence, the word for does not mean 'as a sacrifice to appease my disease'. *For* means 'to help cure my disease'. So we understand that Jesus' death intervenes in human history to have a curative impact on our hostility and violence, to turn us towards the ways of peace. And in the latter sentence, *for* doesn't mean 'to pay for'. It means 'because of'. Because I was speeding, I got a ticket, and similarly, because we are hostile and violent, Christ died. God didn't torture and kill Christ; *we* did. And that tells us something essential about both God and ourselves. For more on this word *for*, see Marcus Borg, *Speaking Christian* (New York: HarperOne, 2011).

12. The meanings, mechanisms and functions of sacrifice are more complex (and ambiguous) than most Christians realise. In the pre-Christian Jewish Levitical system, there were a variety of sacrificial offerings (burnt, grain or meal, peace, sin, trespass) offered at different times (daily, monthly, annually and when needed). Although specific instructions for each sacrifice were articulated in the Bible, specific meanings were not. Even the word *sacrifice* – 'sacred gift' – can be interpreted in many ways. Who is doing the giving? Who is receiving? What is the purpose of the gift? What makes it sacred?

For example, when humans give a sacred gift to God, their gift may express repentance and a desire to reconcile and re-bond, as when a husband gives his wife flowers after a spat, a remorseful child brings his mother a picture he has drawn after being disobedient, or a brother offers his alienated brother a 'peace offering' in an effort to 'bury the hatchet'. (The story of Jacob and Esau in Gen. 33 exemplifies this kind of gift.) It may express a vow of love and commitment, as in the sacred gift of a wedding ring. It may express honour and thanks for past achievements, as in a retirement gift or a Nobel Prize. Or it may anticipate and honour the expected generosity of another, as in a hospitality gift.

But there's another dimension to sacrifice, as René Girard and others have suggested. Some sacrificial rituals recall the primal practice of scapegoating and killing innocent victims to restore social order or curry the favour of bloodthirsty gods. Over time, through the ministrations of a priestly class, brutal human sacrifice was gradually domesticated and ritualised into animal sacrifice and further abstracted into various kinds of liturgical drama. Sadly, in many strains of Western Christianity, this meaning has been resurrected to frame the Eucharist, keeping alive the image of a God who can be appeased only through blood, and (cynics might say) guaranteeing job security for a priestly class who have a monopoly on maintaining favour with this easy-to-anger deity.

James Alison suggests that the Jewish sacrificial system intended to dramatise not humans appeasing God, but God giving life (symbolised by blood) to the world through self-giving (in his lecture series, *The Shape of God's Affection*, available here: http://www.jamesalison.co.uk/. See also http://www.jamesalison.co.uk/texts/eng11.html). The climactic moment of the priestly office was not the priest bringing blood into the Holy of Holies to appease God, but rather the priest bringing blood out of the Holy of Holies to be sprinkled on the assembly, symbolising God's life-giving vitality being shed abroad in the world. He sees in Temple sacrifice the inversion of traditional God-appeasement (what Alison calls the Aztec approach), and he sees Jesus embodying that inversion through the cross and resurrection.

13. See John 3:16. The cross, in this context, demonstrates not God's hostility against sinners, but rather sinful humanity's hostility against God: when God self-reveals in Christ, look how we behave! Simultaneously, on the cross Christ demonstrates God's willingness to forgive us sinners, even at our worst: 'Father, forgive them, for they know not what they do.' And the resurrection further celebrates the point. Jesus doesn't return to say, 'Now, go into the world and inflict vengeance on those who murdered me!' Instead, he says, 'Go into all the world to preach the good news of God's reconciling love to every creature.'

14. See Rom. 11:32–12:2; Heb. 13:15.

15. For more on this change in identity, see Cassidy Dale's brilliant (and free) e-book, *The Knight and the Gardener*, available here: http://knightandgardener.com/

16. Advocates of penal substitutionary atonement would minimise the larger narrative of liberation from violence and oppression, and would focus on the blood placed on the doorposts of the houses of Jewish families, seeing in this blood an anticipatory symbol of penal substitutionary atonement. In this understanding, the Passover is less about deliverance from human oppression (by the Egyptians) and more about exemption from divine extermination (by the Lord's Angel of Death). Such a reading of the story is certainly possible – and in some settings popular, but it is not the only possible reading, and I find it far more problematic than the interpretation offered here.

17. See Luke 22:15–18. It's interesting to note that the risen Jesus takes the bread with two disciples en route to Emmaus just two chapters later (24:28–35). Luke does not tell us whether he also drank wine with them. Although this isn't the place for a thorough exploration of the Eucharist in all its rich dimensions, it's worth noting that John's Gospel doesn't present the Eucharist at all. Where Matthew, Mark and Luke have Jesus sharing in the Supper with his disciples on the eve of his betrayal, in John's Gospel, Jesus washes the disciples' feet (John 13), providing a model of love and humble service and pronouncing (Moses-like) a new commandment to love (13:15, 34). John does, however, have Jesus present himself as 'the bread that gives life to the world' earlier in his Gospel (ch. 6). This self-giving of Jesus isn't associated with the Passover at all, but rather with the manna in the wilderness. For John, Jesus isn't a human substitute to satisfy God's wrath, but rather is 'food indeed' given to satisfy the hunger of all humanity (6:35, recalling 4:14). 'Those who eat my flesh and drink my blood abide in me,' Jesus says, the word *abide* resonating with the pivotal passage in John 15, where Jesus images the disciples as branches drawing their vitality by *abiding* in him. The eating/drinking imagery is shocking – seemingly cannibalistic, but there is no hint at all that God needs Jesus' body and blood on which to vent fury: no, it is humanity that needs the self-giving of Jesus, drawing nourishment from him for 'life abundant' and 'bearing much fruit'.

18. In 1 Cor. 10:1–5, he suggests that as the children of Israel were united in Moses through food and drink (manna from heaven and the water that flowed from the rock), so we are united in Christ through food and drink.

19. This is the message of the epistle to the Hebrews, as I understand it. Hebrews is not seeking to explain Jesus inside the framework of blood sacrifice, thus validating that framework (as the epistle is commonly

read). Instead, Hebrews argues that in Jesus, the whole idea of sacrifice is put behind us 'once and for all' (9:28), because blood sacrifice was never what God really wanted or needed (10:8). God wants far more for us than forgiveness alone (10:18): God wants to change our hearts (10:16) so that we do God's will (13:21) – which is a life of love and good works (10:24). In this, we follow Jesus' example (12:2), who endured hostility – without responding in kind (12:3). In so doing, we 'pursue peace with everyone' (12:14) so that 'filial love' will continue and we will show 'hospitality to strangers' (13:1), always empathising with those who are imprisoned and tortured (13:3). The old altar mind-set is the mind-set of insiders (13:10), but Jesus has identified himself with outsiders (13:12). So the old sacrificial system is left behind for ever, and now, sacrifice (in the sense of sacred gift) remains in two senses only: first, 'the sacrifice of praise . . . the fruit of lips that confess his name' (recalling Ps. 50, which is itself a fascinating reflection on sacrifice), and second, doing good and sharing with others, 'for such sacrifices are pleasing to God' (13:15–16).

20. In these chapters on liturgy, I have not addressed the question of including liturgical elements – prayers, readings and so on – from other faith traditions. Should Christians, in an effort to build hospitality and overcome hostility, use Hindu prayers, Buddhist meditations, Sufi poetry, Native American or Jewish rituals, and so on? Not, I would say, before developing a strong and benevolent identity rooted deeply in the Christian story itself, and not before thoroughly considering the unintended negative consequences of mixing faith traditions.

Careless cafeteria-style mixing of different traditions can weaken the integrity of each tradition. It can lead to the kind of weak-benign identity we are seeking to move beyond. And it can promote a kind of consumerist commodification and Borg-like colonisation (recalling the *Star Trek* TV series). But once a strong-benevolent identity is in place, and once these dangers are faced, gifts from other faiths can, I believe, be warmly welcomed and appreciated, just as Paul did (in an admittedly non-liturgical situation) in Acts 17:28. This subject and the related subjects of inter-spirituality and multi-religious identity are beyond the scope of this book. But these subjects are important and worthy of further discussion, and several Christian communities are experimenting wisely and fruitfully with them (and, no doubt, others are doing so less wisely and fruitfully). For those especially interested in this subject, I would recommend the works of Paul Knitter and Thomas Merton (engaging with Buddhism); Bede Griffiths, Raimon Pannikar and Anthony de Mello (engaging with Hinduism); Richard Twiss and Randy Woodley (engaging with Native American spirituality); and Mabiala Kenzo and Kwame Bediako (engaging with African spirituality). But again, I think much work must be done first on the development of deeply benevolent, deeply Christian identity. In order to provide genuine hospitality to the other, it helps to have a strong, stable and healthy home into which the other can be welcomed. And in order to be a good guest as opposed to a freeloader or squatter, it helps to have a strong, stable healthy home to return to as well.

Part Four: The Missional Challenge

1. Alexander Solzhenitsyn, *The Gulag Archipelago* (New York: Harper, 2007), part 4, chapter 1.

Chapter 24

1. Diana Butler Bass, *Christianity after Religion* (New York: HarperOne, 2012), p. 241.
2. Luke 7:34; John 15:15; 3 John 15.

3. Tony Jones, *The Church Is Flat* (Minneapolis: The JoPa Group), 2011), p. 169, quoting Jürgen Moltmann, *The Church in the Power of the Spirit* (Minneapolis: Fortress Press, 1993), p. 119.

4. *The Church in the Power of the Spirit*, p. 115.

5. Ibid., pp. 119, 117.

6. Here is an example of one such adventure in friendship: Richard McCallum, 'A Rabbi, a Priest, and an Imam . . .', Yale Center for Faith & Culture, http://www.yale.edu/faith/rp/rp_hope.htm#mccallum. Here is another: the Peace Catalyst International website at http://www.peace-catalyst.net/.

7. See Gal. 2:11–14.

8. Ivan Illich explores this powerful word in *Tools for Conviviality* (New York: Marion Boyars, 2001).

9. See PeaceMoms, http://www.peacemoms.com.

10. See Faith House Manhattan, http://www.faithhousemanhattan.org.

11. See Mark Siljander's website: http://www.marksiljander.com.

12. See Jeff Burns, 'Walking with Muslims', Interfaith Youth Core, http://www.ifyc.org/content/walking-muslims.

Chapter 25

1. *Nostra Aetate*, Declaration on the Relation of the Church to Non-Christian Religions, proclaimed by Pope Paul VI, 28 October 1965, available here: http://www.vatican.va/archive/hist_councils/ii_vatican_council/documents/vat-ii_decl_19651028_nostra-aetate_en.html. The official Vatican translation uses 'sons' instead of 'children' and 'these men' instead of 'them'.

2. See Luke 8:1–3.

3. This translation of Acts 16:17 from *The Voice New Testament* (Nashville: Thomas Nelson, 2008) reflects my conviction that the word *liberation* (recalling the Exodus) is the best one-word synonym for *salvation*.

4. Paul and friends were known to them not as Christians, but as members of a Jewish sect, and Jewish identity was centred in the Exodus – where God was revealed as a slaveholder-confronting and slave-liberating God.

5. . . . although it evokes hostility from some people.

6. See, for example, how he saved the life of a woman about to be executed for religious reasons in John 8.

Chapter 26

1. From Claude Geffre, 'La singularite du Christianisme a l'age du pluralisme religieux', in *Penser la foi: Recherches en theologie aujourd'hui*, ed. J. Dore and C. Theobald (Paris: Cerf-Assas, 1992), pp. 351–369. Quoted in Jacques Dupuis, SJ, *Towards a Christian Theology of Religious Pluralism* (Maryknoll, NY: Orbis Books, 1997), p. 388.

2. For more on this kind of worship experience, see the Cedar Ridge Community Church website at http://www.crcc.org (with thanks to Bryan Anderson, Betsy Mitchell-Henning, Patsy Fratanduono and others). For more on worship curation of this sort, see 'Meet Mark Pierson, Worship Curator', sparkhouse, http://sparkhouseblogs.org/blog/clayfire/meet-mark-pierson-worship-curator/, and read Mark Pierson, *The Art of Curating Worship* (Minneapolis: sparkhouse press, 2010).

3. Lev. 16:19 is rendered variously in different translations, but this was the rendering from which the rabbi preached.

4. By 'inter-faith worship', I mean a setting where all participants assume they are worshipping the same God, using different language and ritual systems to reach out towards the One who surpasses them all. So Christians might chant Hindu prayers, or Muslims might sing Christian songs – not affirming the literal content of the words, but

seeking the deeper realities to which the words point. By multi-faith worship, I mean a setting where each participant worships according to his own tradition, in the company of others who worship according to their traditions. In this context, Christians participate in the Christian parts of the service and respectfully observe during other parts.

5. Frank Pastore, 'Why Al Qaeda Supports the Emergent Church', Townhall.com, 22 July 2007, http://townhall.com/columnists/frank-pastore/2007/07/22/why_al_qaeda_supports_the_emergent_church/page/full/.

6. See the PeaceMoms website at http://www.peacemoms.org.

7. I walked a fine line between wanting to be public about the fast for the sake of demonstrating with-ness in relation to my Muslim friends, yet not wanting to fall prey to the hypocrisy Jesus warned about – fasting 'to be seen by people'. You can read my blog posts about the experience by going to http://www.brianmclaren.net and searching 'ramadan 2009'.

8. You can learn about Cindy's work – and find out how you can support it – at http://www.kupenda.org/.

9. For reasons of privacy, I am leaving out a lot of interesting details. I should add that I know of several separate stories like this one, unfolding independently in several Muslim-majority countries.

10. For more on Sailesh Rao's work, and for information about his excellent book *Carbon Dharma*, for which I wrote a foreword, see the Climate Healers website at http://www.climatehealers.org.

11. See their website at http://www.ifyc.org.

Chapter 27

1. Jacques Dupuis, *Towards a Christian Theology of Religious Pluralism* (Maryknoll, NY: Orbis Books, 1997), p. 390.

2. His words echo those of Paulo Freire: 'Washing one's hands of the conflict between the powerful and the powerless means to side with the powerful, not to be neutral.'

3. I have written two books on the subject of the kingdom of God: *The Secret Message of Jesus* (Nashville: Thomas Nelson, 2006), and *Everything Must Change* (Nashville: Thomas Nelson, 2007). Yet the subject continues to open up new dimensions to me. It is only in the sense mentioned here – a gift already fully given but not yet widely opened and enjoyed – that I subscribe to the *already/not yet* formula so common in some theological circles. The typical use of the formula does not, in my view, take into account the already-present-ness and already-given-ness of the kingdom inherent in Jesus' declarations that the kingdom is *at hand* and *among* (or within), and especially in his earth-shaking words of Luke 4:21: 'Today, this Scripture *has been fulfilled* in your hearing.' I see the kingdom as fully present and available, even when we fail or refuse to adjust our lives to it.

4. Thanks to Samir Selmanovic for this way of framing the question.

Chapter 28

1. Adapted from Vincent Donovan, *Christianity Rediscovered* (Maryknoll, NY: Orbis Books, 2003). My Muslim friend Eboo Patel expresses the same sentiment in *Acts of Faith* (Boston: Beacon Press, 2007): 'We need a language that allows us to emphasize our unique inspirations and affirm our universal values. We need spaces where we can each state that we are proud of where we came from and all point to the place we are going to . . . We have to save each other. It's the only way to save ourselves' (pp. 182, 180).

2. Sam is a gifted leader, author and blogger. You can learn more about his work at http://www.samlee.org.

3. I explore some of these ambiguities in *Everything Must Change* (Nashville: Thomas Nelson, 2007).

4. Predictably, Protestants often saw the ugliness of Catholic missionary colonialism, and Catholics often saw the ugliness of Protestant missionary colonialism.

5. For more on the subject of evangelism, see Doug Pagitt's winsome and insightful *Evangelism in the Inventive Age* (Minneapolis: sparkhouse press, 2012).

6. From an interview with Bill Moyers, available here: http://www.pbs. org/now/printable/transcript_armstrong_print.html.

7. Speaking as an American, it's interesting to reflect on the ways that denominationalism relates to clannishness and caste. For example, consider these terms: Scottish Presbyterians, British Evangelicals, Dutch Calvinists, Italian Catholics.

8. The subject of multi-religious identity is a fascinating and important one, but beyond the scope of this project. For a good introduction, see Paul Knitter, *Without Buddha I Could Not Be a Christian* (Oxford: Oneworld, 2009).

Chapter 29

1. E. Stanley Jones, *The Christ of the Indian Road* (New York: The Abingdon Press, 1925), p. 63. Here are his actual words, with the phrases I altered in italics: 'The tremendous question presses itself upon us: Will the present Christian Church be big enough, responsive enough, Christlike enough to be the medium and organ through which Christ will come to *India*? For mind you, *Christianity* is breaking out beyond the borders of the Christian Church. Will the Christian Church be Christlike enough to be the moral and spiritual centre of this overflowing *Christianity*? Or will many of the *finest spirits and minds of India* accept Christ as Lord and Master of their lives but live

their *Christian* lives apart from the Christian Church?' The complete textisavailablehere:http://www.scribd.com/doc/46133550/The-Christ-of-the-Indian-Road/.

2. The complete text is available here: http://www.scribd.com/doc/46133550/The-Christ-of-the-Indian-Road/. Johnny Baker blogs about the book in a series beginning here: http://jonnybaker.blogs.com/jonnybaker/2005/10/christ_of_the_i.html.

3. Examples would include Lesslie Newbigin and Bede Griffiths. Important Indian Christian leaders like Raimon Panikkar (whose father was Indian, but who was born in Spain) and Anthony DeMello should also be noted.

4. For example, Jones noted what he called 'five living seeds' in Hinduism: (1) spirit is the ultimate reality, (2) there is a sense of unity running through all things, (3) there is justice at the heart of the universe, (4) freedom should be passionately pursued, and (5) there is a tremendous cost in living a truly religious life (*Christ of the Indian Road*, p. 173).

5. On Christ-likeness, Jones said, 'Here is a new and amazing challenge, for this [movement of people following Christ] outside Christianity is going straight to the heart of things and saying that to be a Christian is to be Christlike. This means nothing less than that ancient rituals and orders and power at court and correctly stated doctrine avail little if Christlikeness is not the outstanding characteristic of the people of the churches. If Christianity centers in the Christian Church in the future it will be because that church is the center of the Christ-spirit' (*Christ of the Indian Road*, pp. 63–64).

6. I know that for many, Christian faith is still seen primarily as a doctrinal system rather than a way of life, elevating assent to certain doctrinal statements above the practices, character and virtues of Christlike living. But that assumption is being questioned and modified on

many fronts, thanks to the work of people like Ruth Haley Barton, Richard Foster, Dallas Willard, Cynthia Bourgeault, Shane Claiborne, Diana Butler Bass, Mindy Calliguire and many others. In a practice-oriented faith, doctrine still matters – but it is subsumed within a practice: doctrine is defined as the never-ending practice of seeking to understand and articulate the mysteries of faith, in conversation with others, and mindful of the past, the present and the future.

7. It is in this context that deep resonances among religions can be seen and appreciated – the non-grasping, for example, of Philippians (2:4–7) and the Buddhist idea of detachment; the 'single eye' and non-judgementalism of Matthew (6:22–23 and 7:1) and the non-dual seeing of Hinduism and Buddhism; the conjugal imagery of the New Testament (Eph. 5:32 and Rev. 21) with the similar imagery in much Sufi and Hindu poetry; the dynamic tension between unity and diversity in both Trinitarian and Hindu conceptions of the Godhead, and so on. These resonances do not argue for throwing all the religions into a blender, pressing 'puree' and then making the simplistic assumption that 'they're all the same' or that their differences 'don't matter'. But, recalling our considerations of the doctrine of the Holy Spirit, these resonances suggest that within God's creation, upon which God's Spirit hovers (to use Gen. 1:2 language), glimpses and experiences of the mysteries of God are ubiquitous. And they suggest that sincere people of differing religions can approach one another with what Gandhi called 'sympathy' (or human-kindness, or benevolence), not suspicion, and in a spirit of generosity, not hostility.

8. I hope to recommend and provide additional resources to help both existing and newly forming faith communities of this kind in the future. Check for links at http://www.brianmclaren.net on the page for this book.

9. Here is another answer to the question, *Why did Jesus, Moses, the Buddha and Mohammed cross the road? To discover the other as neighbour, and to show solidarity with those on the other side.*

10. Farid Esack, *Qur'an, Liberation and Pluralism: An Islamic Perspective of Interreligious Solidarity against Oppression* (Oxford: Oneworld, 1997), p. 261. The quote continues, 'All of us . . . participate in the shaping of the cultural and religious images and assumptions that oppress or liberate the Other, and thus ourselves.' Esack's words suggest a final answer to the question asked by the title of this book: *Why did Jesus, Moses, the Buddha and Mohammed cross the road? To walk side by side and together sort out the theological issues that too often turn their followers into enemies rather than friends.*

Notes

Do you wish this wasn't the end?
Are you hungry for more great teaching, inspiring
testimonies, ideas to challenge your faith?

Join us at www.hodderfaith.com, follow us on Twitter
or find us on Facebook to make sure you get the latest from
your favourite authors.

Including interviews, videos, articles, competitions
and opportunities to tell us just what you thought about
our latest releases.

www.hodderfaith.com

 HodderFaith

 @HodderFaith

 HodderFaithVideo

HODDER
WHERE FAITH IS INSPIRED